Jack Wong Sue DCM, JP
AKR 13

Blood on Borneo

BLOOD ON BORNEO is dedicated to;

The men of AGAS 1

Major Gort Chester OBE DSO
Captain Derek (Jock) Sutcliffe
Lieutenant Fred Olsen BEM
Staff Sergeant Graham Greenwood
Sergeant Skeet Hywood DCM
Lieutenant Don Harlem MID

The POW who died in Sandakan and on the Death Marches to Ranau, or at Kuching and elsewhere in British North Borneo.

The 6 survivors (out of at least 2400 POW) who escaped the Borneo Death Marches.

The 33 POW's who with great courage, survived the March from Sandakan to Ranau only to be slaughtered by the Japanese Nation that had officially surrendered to the Allied Forces 2 days earlier.

The 13 indigenes of the 'Sandakan Underground' some of whom now rest in the 'Heroes Grave' Kuching.

It also serves to perpetuate the fond memory of

Z Men of 'Agas'

AK232 Colonel F.G.L. 'Gort' Chester OBE DSO (British Army)

AK 42 Lieutenant Don A.L. Harlem MID (Australian Imperial Forces)

AK 0471 Sergeant Ma'Aruff Bin Said (Australian Military Forces)

- LEST WE FORGET -

ISBN 0-646 41656-1

www.jackwongsue.com

Published by
© **L.Smith (WA) Pty Ltd T/A Jack Sue WA Skindivers Publication**
Copyright © 2001 Jack Sue

Cover Photograph Jack Wong Sue

Printed and Bound by **Success Print**
61-8-9279 3214
7a Goongarrie Street
Bayswater
Western Australia 6053

Typesetting by **Color Logic**
61-8-9299 6931
2 View Terrace
Darlington
Western Australia 6070

Blood on Borneo

Jack Wong Sue DCM, JP
AKR 13

Launched Special Air Service Regiment HQ,
Campbell Barracks Swanbourne
Western Australia
17th August 2001

This was the date in 1945 when the remaining
33 Australian and British POWs of the
Borneo Death Marches were slaughtered
by the Japanese Nation that had officially
surrendered 2 days earlier.

Second Print 27th August 2001

Third Print 28th March 2002

Revised edition 28th March 2002

CONTENTS

CONTENTS

At 16, Jack received a 'white feather' (sign of cowardice), left his job, enlisted on an overseas Norwegian tanker and remained there; returned to Australia before his 18th birthday. He then applied to join the Royal Australian Navy who rejected him because his father was born in China, so he immediately joined the Royal Australian Air Force's Air Sea Rescue and served on crash boats for four months.

Because of his Oriental appearance and fluency in Chinese and Malay, when asked to volunteer for service behind Japanese lines with Services Reconnaissance Department – later 'Z' Special Unit, he readily accepted.

Post-war, was involved in journalism, television and music until his pre-war and wartime diving captured his fancy and opened WA's first professional dive store, now in its 51st year. Actively diving until a stroke in 1997 paralysed his right side, he was forced into retirement.
Jack Wong Sue now devotes his time to writing.

FOREWORD

Major General Michael Jeffery AC CVO MC KStJ Cit WA

Combat operations in the jungle is a tough, dirty, close range and nerve wracking experience; ask any infantryman!

He will tell you of the huge weights carried on the back, of being perpetually wet, of the constant battle with tropical disease and infection and above all, of the nerves always on razor edge, because the unseen enemy opens fire from only feet away.

However, notwithstanding these difficulties an infantryman has the reassurance and security of being with his platoon, his company and his battalion. There is relative safety in numbers, mutual protection, heavy weapons to call on in a fire-fight and readily available medical assistance if wounded or sick.

The men of the Services Reconnaissance Department and its famous offspring, Z Special Force, had no such security or immediate support.

These were the volunteers for hazardous operations who, in groups of sometimes only four or five and mostly never more than twenty five, were clandestinely inserted onto a Japanese held coast from New Guinea to Borneo, through Malaya to China, by submarine, flying boat, parachute or small boat. They lived in mosquito infested mud flats, in the steaming heat of the jungle and, by deliberate choice, in close proximity to a cunning and ruthless enemy.

In the course of their reconnaissance duties they reported through tenuous communication links on Japanese troop movements, headquarters and allied POW camp locations. They trained over 6000 locals as guerrillas and in their raiding role killed over 1700 of the enemy for the loss of 112 of their own. Of the latter, a number died as a result of torture under brutal interrogation or were executed by beheading. Indigenous and Chinese supporters of the Z Specials suffered even more severely.

It is in the context of this unique, dangerous and demanding environment that Jack Sue DCM JP, a former RAAF crash rescue boat sergeant who volunteered for Z Special, has written an enthralling series of stories in this most interesting and readable book, "Blood on Borneo".

Taken from notes hastily compiled from a wartime diary and aided by a phenomenal memory, the book does not follow a sequential pattern. Rather it is a random collection of Jack's experiences, impressions and observations during nine months spent on active operations behind Japanese lines.

There are many thrilling anecdotes.

Jack tells how he and mate, Don Harlem, with their Malay guerrillas wiped out a ten man Japanese garrison in the town of Trusan. They located and opened a safe containing Japanese occupation currency which they gave to the Malay villagers who, recognising its "intrinsic" worth, used it as high quality toilet paper.

Another story involving Don tells of his deep distress and terrible anger at finding the crucified and partly cannibalised body of an Australian soldier on the Sandakan to Ranau track. Only six of an estimated 2400 allied POW survived this infamous death march.

Submarine insertion was normal for Z Specials and Jack gives us a first-hand feel for life on board the splendidly gallant but cramped and foul diesel smelling USS Tuna. Under heavy airborne depth charge attack, the little submarine calmly and professionally goes through her evasion drills, as she twists, turns and then lies silent, and in the end survives.

But for sheer audacity and courage, Jack's solo effort in entering the Japanese held railway station at Bongawan dressed as a coolie stands supreme. Approaching the Chinese stationmaster Ah Lee and speaking in local dialect in the close presence of Jap officers, Jack "persuades" Ah Lee to give vital information on enemy troop train movements. This data was then used to great effect by the US Air Force on bombing and strafing missions in preparation for the planned allied invasion of British North Borneo.

And so the stories unfold; some on the operational aspects of life behind the lines, others on the mostly kind and attractive village people who supported Z Special, whilst interleaved through it all is Jack's fascination with the beautiful flora, fauna and undersea life of Borneo.

Of particular moment is Jack's deep affection for his Z Special mates and in particular his guide, mentor and father figure leader, Gort Chester.

All these things come together in wonderful cameo type stories packed with incident, keen observation and wise reflection.

As Jack himself says in his introduction, this is not intended as a great literary work. Rather it is a collection of stories of supremely brave men; living, fighting and dying in that most traumatic of war situations – behind the Japanese lines in a jungle environment – where the risk of capture, torture and execution was always high. Yet Jack and his compatriots of Z Special took that risk willingly and bravely and in so doing, made a noble contribution to the defeat of a tough, cruel, but courageous enemy.

It is a book that should be read by all Australians.

Canberra 2001.

Sandakan in 1952 after rebuilding the first time. The town was burnt down in a giant fire and rebuilt a second time.

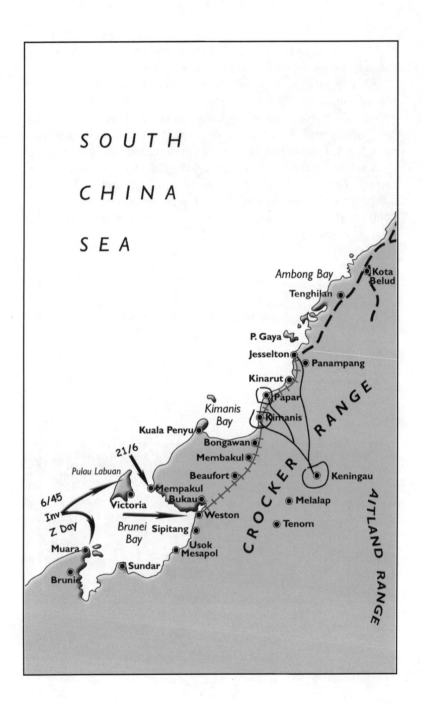

SOUTH

CHINA

SEA

Ambong Bay ● Kota Belud

Tenghilan ●

P. Gaya

Jesselton ● ● Panampang

Kinarut ●

Papar ●

Kimanis Bay ● Kimanis

Kuala Penyu ●

Bongawan ●

21/6

Membakul ●

Pulau Labuan

Beaufort ● ● Keningau

Mempakul ● ● Melalap

Victoria Bukau

6/45 Weston ● ● Tenom

Inv

Z Day Brunei Bay Sipitang ●

Muara ● Usok

Mesapol

Sundar ●

Brunei

CROCKER RANGE

AITLAND RANGE

VIII

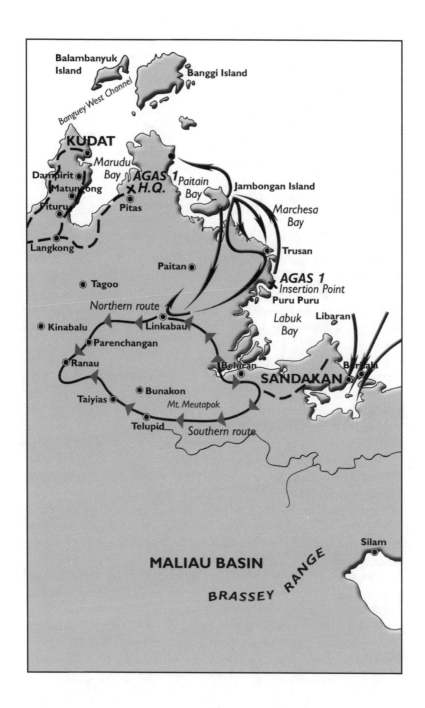

Balambanyuk Island

Banggi Island

Banguey West Channel

KUDAT

Marudu Bay

Dampirit

AGAS 1 H.Q.

Paitain Bay

Jambongan Island

Matungong

Pituru

Pitas

Marchesa Bay

Langkong

Paitan

Trusan

Tagoo

AGAS 1 Insertion Point

Puru Puru

Northern route

Labuk Bay

Libaran

Kinabalu

Linkabau

Parenchangan

Ranau

Beluran

Berhala

SANDAKAN

Bunakon

Mt. Meutapok

Taiyias

Telupid

Southern route

Silam

MALIAU BASIN

BRASSEY RANGE

AUTHOR'S NOTES

During 1948/49 when I first thought of writing 'The Borneo Death Marches 1945', I submitted a short article 'Insertion Point Borneo' to the editor 'Life and Letters' Mr. Ivor Birtwistle for publication in the Saturday 'West Australian'. The short article contained nothing that contravened the security requirements of the day. It was accepted and published.

Within a week, I received a letter from the then Minister for the Army. From memory, I think it was a Mr. Cramer or Mr Ford who advised me that certain wartime matters including clandestine operations in Borneo and matters pertaining to the Australian and British POW at Sandakan were under strict security regulations. I took the advice on board as a gentle warning.

Hoards of displaced people were flocking into Australia with interesting stories to relate from all the war-torn countries of WW2 including Asia. Fluent in Chinese, Malay – and a bit of English - I was offered a position in 1949 to join the editorial staff of the Perth Sunday Times. I distinctly re-call the editor the late Frank Davidson and the editor of the Perth Mirror Ron Clarke, telling me that I should write a book on my experiences behind Japanese lines in Borneo if and when security regulations were eventually lifted. Little did we realise that many, many years were to pass before that would eventuate; anything concerning the Borneo Death Marches was taboo.

Almost 20 years after the cessation of WW2 when regulations were easing, my wartime compatriot the late Lieut. Don Harlem of Sandy Bay Hobart, and I, decided to jointly write the book supported by the Australian War Memorial Research Grant Scheme. Following Don's sudden death in the mid 1980s, his wife Betty and family were unable to locate his script and research papers and that posed a problem. Don was writing the end of the Death Marches in the Ranau area where he spent most of his time. For my part, I was writing the story of the commencement of the marches from Sandakan. The story was shelved.

Since the 1980s, several books have been written on the subject by various authors. Of those, I consider Max Hall's 'Kinabalu Guerrillas' Lynette Ramsay Silver's 'Sandakan – A Conspiracy of Silence', Athol Moffit's 'Project Kingfisher' and 'Borneo Australia's Proud but Tragic Heritage' by Kevin Smith to be the most accurate and recommend them to interested readers.

This is the first written eye witness account to be published. To my knowledge, of the seven original members of Operation 'Agas 1' led by Captain Gort Chester inserted close to Sandakan by the U.S. submarine Tuna, only two members are still alive in Australia – signaler Skeet Hywood DCM of Adelaide and myself. Fellow signaler Graham Greenwood Royal New Zealand Army (RNZA) presently resident New Zealand, wrote a limited edition of his experiences – only 10 copies were produced.

I believe there is little more that can be written on the marches, although much of the Sandakan Saga still remains a mystery and will remain so for many years. I believe also that the Australian Government is currently holding undisclosed information re the Borneo Death Marches, the strange disappearance of HMAS Sydney and many other mysteries of WW2 that will remain conveniently forgotten while the immediate next-of-kin are alive.

Some years ago, prominent Sydney authoress Lynette Ramsay Silver and Major Tom Hall (retired) former Commanding Officer 1st Australian Commando Regiment, remarkably traced the bodies of two Operation 'Rimau' men buried as 'unknown' in Kranji War Cemetery Singapore. Later, they flew to Indonesia to accompany a British expedition to recover the remains of another. The 23 members of ill-fated Operation 'Rimau' lost their lives after they attacked Singapore Harbour. Twelve months earlier, the audacious and successful Operation 'Jaywick' sunk 7 ships; a total of 40,000 tons in the harbour during September/October 1943.

The unscathed 78 foot captured Japanese fishing boat 'Krait' returned intact with all 14 'Z' men to Australia after 33 days cruising in enemy waters at 6.5 knots flying the 'poached egg' Japanese flag.

Assisted by the priceless records she possesses, Lynette Silver has in the last three years, located and identified the graves of 36 men who lost their lives in Borneo. 35 were POW sent to Sandakan, British North Borneo. The other was that of 'Z' Sergeant Jim O'Dwyer AMF of Operation 'Platypus 7' who lost his life while on a secret mission in Dutch Borneo.

Of the party of 4 'Z' men, the leader of 'Platypus 7', Flight Lieutenant Alan Martin RAAF, parachuted into a tree outside the Japanese barracks and inadvertently became a witness to the plight of his three companions who landed inside the barracks. According to captured Japanese documents, the three valiantly fought their way out at heavy cost to the enemy. A few days later however, all three were ambushed.

Post-war, the bodies of Signaller Pte.Ernest Myers RNZEF and Malay born Sgt. Ma'aruff bin Said AMF were recovered from the barracks site and identified. Jim O'Dwyer remained 'missing, believed dead' despite attempts to locate his remains by his son Mike, a well known Queensland business-man and inventor who had established in 1989 that a third man had definitely been killed.

Mike was only an infant when his father disappeared in the jungles of Dutch Borneo, now East Kalimantan.

It was not until 2000 that Lynette Silver located and identified the grave of his father, whose body had been recovered at the end of 1945 but had been reburied as an 'unknown' soldier.

Snagged in the tree, sole survivor party leader Alan Martin cut himself free of his parachute harness and fell to the ground 80 feet below, severely injuring himself. Days later, he was found by friendly natives who attended his injuries and assisted his return to Allied lines.

Alan and Ma'aruff were well known to me. Alan Martin was a highly respected weatherman with experience ranging the length and breadth of Western Australia as well as the Antarctic, and was a prominent blue water sailor. Ma'ruff pre-war, was a pearl diver indentured from Koepang to Broome in the north of Western Australia and trained with me at Frazer Island Queensland. He parachuted into our territory as a member of Captain Nick Combe's 'Agas 2' where he served for a number of weeks before extraction and transfer to 'Platypus 7'.

There are still hundreds of POW bodies resting in the Commonwealth War Cemetery at Labuan Island posted 'known only to God', some of whom may eventually be identified. Other remains still await recovery along the Sandakan to Ranau Death March routes at unknown locations where they collapsed from exhaustion unable to continue or succumbed to illness due to lack of food and medical attention. These unfortunates were shot or butchered and left where they lay; others who escaped from the rentis and their marching companions perished in the jungle, never to be found.

In the 1980s, my friend of many years Sir Reginald Barnewall of Tamborine Mountain Queensland was one of 16 members in one of my 'Back to Borneo' safaris. I feel sure he will vouch for the authenticity of the following incident that was connected with the former POW Camp Sandakan.

Only hours before our return to Australia, an old Chinese lady who lived alone near the Sandakan POW camp site, rang me at the Tsiang Gardens Hotel Sandakan. Through receptionist Cecilia Ha who spoke the old lady's Chinese dialect, the poor dear offered to lead me to a 'lubang' (Malay for hole) in the ground that I interpreted as being a cave. She claimed the head height 'lubang' discovered by her husband and herself, contained Japanese uniforms, swords and a box of Australian Metal Identification Discs (meat tags) but insisted I was to go to her home, alone.

Under what can only be described as extremely mystifying circumstances, I was prevented from meeting up with the old lady. Twelve months later during my next tour there, I learned that the old lady had passed away.

Determined to return to locate the 'lubang'', I was not to know then that lady luck had booked me for open-heart surgery 1997 (5 bypasses and re-placement of aortic valve) that would hospitalise me for 11 months and confine me to a wheelchair. As well, it would temporarily curtail my activities in Borneo, almost wipe out my one man retiree's diving business - W.A. Skin Divers (Est.1951) Midland – now managed by my son Barry.

Hours after successful surgery I suffered a stroke while in an intensive care unit. I lost the use of the right side of my body completely, including my voice, which luckily was restored two days later following two sessions in the hyperbaric chamber. Being a diver, I jokingly referred to it as the 'barbaric chamber', much to the amusement of my friend the 'commanding officer' (CO) of the chamber, Doctor Harry Oxer, Royal Fremantle Hospital.

Unable to write – being right handed – when I was able to get around in an electric wheelchair, tired of the bed and inactivity, I learned the barest essentials about computers at the education centre of the Shenton Park Annexe of Royal Perth Hospital. I immediately commenced writing this book with one finger left hand, a far cry from my pre-stroke days when I was an accurate 50 words per minute touch typist.

Four months after my discharge from RPH in 1998, with my son Barry, daughter Aneeta and the Film Documentary Company Miller/Carlyon of Melbourne, Terry Carlyon, Keith Platt and the Sue tribe members, we flew to Borneo for the filming of the SBS documentary 'Jack Sue - A Matter of Honour'. Our arrival in Borneo brought forth shades of the old lady episode from a totally unexpected source. God willing, we plan to return in the not too distant future to solve the strange mystery.

Told in 1997 that I would never walk again, I am now back on my feet with the aid of a quad stick over short distances in my home and managing the stairs. My right arm and fingers are slowly responding to treatment from my wonderful team of voluntary alternative medicine and other specialists, who attend me weekly. To them I remain eternally grateful. The dense stroke also curtailed my pastimes of underwater photography, wreck diving etc, and my beloved piano. However, with positive thinking and God willing, I will resume these activities.

In reading this book, a few points need to be borne in mind. It is not chronologically written. In anybody's language, 55 years is too long to recall specific dates and times. Where dates have been quoted, these have only been possible by the return of a wartime diary written in 1946 after my return to Australia, subsequently lost and returned to me in 1997.

The late well known Perth and Sydney journalist Terry Zanetti when cleaning up his affairs prior to his death in 1997, located my wartime diary and returned it to me in RPH (Shenton Park Annexe) where I was recovering. I had forgotten that I loaned it to him 30 years earlier when he was with the Perth Daily News.

The original format of this book has been altered from the history of the Death Marches to one of personal experiences during the nine months I spent behind Japanese lines. References to the Death Marches and associated atrocities are included only where considered appropriate or necessary. The book's chapters represent accounts of some of the prominent incidents that happened to us behind Japanese lines in BNB (British North Borneo) and associated 'Z' training in Australia. A digest perhaps?

No claims are made as to the accuracy of the intelligence gathered. If anything, it is readily admitted that certain information is incorrect. However, in support of my 'Z' members of operations 'Python' 1 and 2, 'Agas' 1 to 5 and ' Stallion' 4, who I believe have been seriously maligned by certain writers and historians, there are a number of points to be considered by the reader before casting judgment.

First and foremost, one needs to recognise the fact that in 1945 when we first landed behind Japanese lines, the large island of Borneo was better known as the country of 'the wild man from Borneo', one of the few remaining fascinating frontiers of an otherwise civilised world.

Little was known about the Straits Settlement Colony of British North Borneo (BNB) - now renamed Sabah – yet every snotty nosed kid at school knew of the 'Wild Man From Borneo'.

The practice of head hunting by the Dyak, Iban and other blow-pipe armed primitive pygmy warrior tribes had barely been discontinued when it was renewed afresh after the Japanese bloodless occupation in 1942, their introduction of the Samurai sword and the resultant atrocities. Likewise the sea pirates – the Sulus, Bajaus, Philippinos and certain Chinese groups among others - were as blood thirsty as their land cousins.

The capital city Sandakan was the equivalent in size to average country towns in the back blocks of Australia. The few scattered ports dotted around the tiny nation's coastline represented the commercial and export centres for inland agricultural, light industrial and timber products shipped down the many rivers of BNB. Again, these ports unlike those in Europe, were isolated and lacked interconnecting roads, transport services and possessed only primitive and limited communication systems etc.

From east to west, jungle rentises (bridle or pony trails barely 6 feet wide and frequently less), traversed gradients of 3:1 ratio from sea level to 7,000 feet. The totally isolated capital city of Sandakan on the east coast depended on these rentises for communication with other ports on the more populated west coast through hinterland kampongs (villages) and logging centres.

With the exception of its ports, most of the hinterland depended on pony courier services in the 'dry season'. Otherwise, communications were via native canoes and small boats on the river systems that BNB certainly did not lack. Coastal steamers and native inter-island vessels maintained communications, freight and passenger services.

Until the coming of the Japanese, BNB like Australia, had not experienced attack or occupation by a hostile nation, therefore, the small populace of Westerners enjoyed an idyllic life style among the Chinese, Japanese, Eurasians, Indians and local native tribes.

The Japanese invasion changed everything for about 18 months when the worm turned, and Japan found herself on the back foot.

Where Japan had introduced her agents in all guises, occupations and professions into an unsuspecting string of peacetime nations including Australia, to reverse the procedure was an entirely different kettle of fish.

When the seemingly unstoppable Japanese advance through the islands north of Australia came to a grinding halt in New Guinea, their fortunes of war took on a sour turn that introduced a maelstrom of hostile environment throughout the islands they had conquered. Created by the cruel Japanese, they suddenly became aware that subversive parties were being inserted behind their own lines. The local population, and in particular the persecuted Chinese, were subjected to increased penalties and unbelievable reprisals when insurrection was even suspected.

Furthermore, the presence of well-rewarded pro-Japanese agents among the indigenous people in coastal areas had to be considered. This was most essential in areas where 'Python', 'Agas' and 'Stallion' planned insertions by American submarines from Fremantle, Western Australia. As a result of subsequent bombing by American planes and related war damage etc, the few areas with communications before

WW2, were totally without them by the time 'Agas' arrived on the scene.

Although most party leaders were westerners - former plantation owners and oil industry related professionals etc possessing a fine grasp of the Malay language - they could not move around once having successfully landed from submarines and infiltrated the jungles where our headquarters (HQ) and radio stations were then established.

Unfortunately, westerners stood out like lighthouses on a dark night. Therefore, Asian agents had to be included with each land based operation behind Japanese lines in south east Asia.

These agents were selected not only for their fluency in the languages used in the areas where they where inserted, they had to possess the oriental appearance that enabled them to melt into the local communities without arousing suspicion. They also had to be psychologically suited for the role they needed to perform. Last but not least, they had to have the usual fighting skills of soldiers trained in jungle warfare.

The foregoing explanation is necessary to appreciate that cloak and dagger warfare in under developed BNB was entirely different to European countries where Caucasians were the norm, and where the latest in technology, communications, highways, autobahns and modern transport existed. Clandestine agents in Europe could pass messages in minutes or at the very worst, hours. They were able to travel by air, ships, trains, buses, cars, motor cycles and bicycles in the course of their secret work – even allowing for certain restrictions such as fuel rationing.

In many Japanese occupied areas of South East Asia and the South West Pacific, the aforementioned were non existent. It was not unusual for information to take a week or more to reach our headquarters in the jungle, whether by pony, native boat or 'shanks pony' (foot). For this reason, 'Agas' men while at Frazer Island Commando School (FCS), had to undergo equestrian training; as essential as folboating, both being the only means of transport in primitive BNB: weather permitting. Is it any wonder that information was sometimes out of date?

No claims are made as to the accuracy of intelligence gathered. If anything, it is readily admitted that certain information was incorrect.

However, I wholeheartedly support my 'Z' members of operations 'Python" 1 and 2, 'Agas' 1 to 5 and 'Stallion 4', who I believe have been seriously maligned by certain writers and historians. Information from them in the field would have been what they believed to be accurate and as they knew it to be. What purpose would wrong intelligence serve?

Frequently, messages had to be transmitted long distances verbally through a combination of native couriers and dead letter boxes. Even by the law of averages, some inaccuracies had to be expected. What more could we have done and how could we have done better? It was a case of modern transport versus ponies, folboats, native boats or foot, and radios versus the 'jungle vine'. The information our sigs radioed from the jungle to 'Z' HQ and subsequently Australia was what we fervently believed to be correct at the time.

I am reminded that military historians have today accepted that the landing at Anzac Cove was not a brilliantly executed operation, but was in fact a military and navy stuff-up. Nevertheless, it did not detract from the human valour of the operation and perhaps some day, the efforts of 'Z' men will – like the Anzac's – be realised. Many similar examples can be found in almost every war theatre and every conflict.

Finally, my apologies if the accounts appear complicated, over colorful or sensationalized in their presentation. How much less does one expect from an account of clandestine activities based on 9 months spent behind Japanese lines where there were never 2 days alike, and where one false move would have resulted in capture and certain beheading?

I make no claim that this book is a literary masterpiece – I am aware of my limitations. Instead, I seek the tolerance of the reader and apologise for my failings. My limited vocabulary restricts my descriptions, hopefully, without detracting from the authenticity of the stories of personal courage of 'Z' mates and the Chinese and Malay guerrillas.

Regarding the frailties of human behaviour - the almost unacceptable human endurance of POW, sufferings of indigenous men, women and children and brutality of the cruel Japanese - the reader may find some descriptions offensive.

To my readers who appreciate natural history, I trust my

descriptions do justice to the beauty of the Borneo jungles greenery, flora and wildlife.

The book is not chronologically written. In anybody's language, 55 years is too long to recall specific dates and times. Where dates have been quoted, these have only been possible by the return of a wartime diary written up in 1946, subsequently lost and later recovered.

Jack Sue DCM JP,
PO Box 490, Kalamunda
Western Australia 6076
Tel. 08 9257 1620

Letter received by Jack Sue from former Chinese guerrilla shortly after WW2

B.O.B. INTRODUCTION

Before WW2, Borneo was one of the few exciting and mysterious pioneer frontiers remaining in an otherwise civilised western world. To the average person, Borneo was where the mythical 'Wild Man From Borneo' existed, where blow pipe armed Dyak head hunters roamed, and where the mere mention of the country conjured up all manner of imaginary visions to western school kids.

That was until the arrival of the Japanese war machine and their blood lust occupation, the years 1942-1945.

During their three years, the Nipponese proved to be cruel despotic rulers who set the already primitive country back many years. Despite their claims that their Greater East Asia Co-Prosperity Sphere would release the Asian nations from the chains that bound them to the exploitation of Britain, America and Holland, they only managed to subject the indigenous races to hardships previously unknown in Borneo; a potentially rich land. The 'sons of heaven' raped and pillaged, revived head hunting with their feared Samurai swords and proved themselves to be human animals competing with the environment of Borneo's jungle animals and wild life.

Into this strange scenario, our 'Z' Special Unit party of seven men of 'Agas 1' was inserted by the American submarine Tuna following extensive training in Australia. Training in espionage, intelligence and clandestine warfare was readily available in England for operations behind German and Italian lines in European cities having communications, roads, the comforts of modern society etc and where the presence of Europeans raised no suspicion.

However, while clandestine activities were successfully conducted in Europe, our instructors in Australia made it clear at the outset that Borneo was a different proposition. While the basic principles for conducting subversive warfare remained unchanged, local topography, the lack of communication systems, jungle rentises (tracks) instead of roads, living conditions, different habits and customs of the diverse population of the Orient, all presented difficulties. We were breaking new ground in the South West Pacific Area (SWPA) and the islands of South East Asia.

In the Orient, European party leaders stood out like proverbial Australian dunnies, therefore the party leaders – most of them former plantation owners etc - had to conduct clandestine operations from jungle bases. Consequently, each party had to have an agent or two of Oriental or Malay appearance, fluent in English, Chinese and Malay. The agent necessarily had to have not only the appearance, but in addition, the correct psychological make-up for subversive warfare and have a good knowledge of local living conditions, habits and customs of the people. Last but not least, as commandos, they had to be able bodied jungle fighters.

Because of the vast distances that had to be covered on foot by couriers and between secret 'dead letter boxes' where notes were placed, information regarding the marches was more often than not, days old before it finally reached us through the native 'jungle vine' communication system. At best, that information, very often third or fourth hand, resulted in inaccuracies due to the human factor. Unlike operating a clandestine operation in a well-serviced country where good communications and roads existed and where information could be cross- checked in a hurry, such was not the case in Borneo.

Regardless, most of the details on the marches were as accurately reported as could be expected
under the circumstances. More importantly, we had the utmost faith in our own organisation.

The 'Agas' (Malay for Sandfly') party - Major Gort Chester overall Officer In Command - was one of the most successful and one of the largest 'Z' Special Unit ('Z' Force) clandestine operations behind Japanese lines. 'Agas 1', the subject of this book, covers its insertion by the submarine USS Tuna until I left Borneo and returned to Australia after the surrender of Japan.

A chapter or two is devoted to 'Agas 2' – party leader Captain Nick Combe - the second party inserted that was closely monitored by overall Operation 'Agas' leader Gort Chester. The lack of information regarding the highly successful operations of 'Agas 3' (Captain Derek 'Jock' Sutcliffe), 'Agas 4' (Major Rex Blow) and 'Agas 5 (Captain R. McLaren MC and Bar, MID) is not intended as a reflection on those parties – they were all highly successful and each deserves a book written solely on its operations. Lieut. Rex Blow and Private 'Jock' McLaren, of the Australian Infantry Forces (AIF) when captured in Singapore, typify most 'Z' men who volunteered their services behind Japanese lines in terms of dedication, courage, determination and human compassion.

After capture, both men were shipped from Changi Gaol Singapore in Japanese POW 'hell-ships' to British North Borneo where they were incarcerated in the notorious Sandakan camp. Both were early escapees from Sandakan or Berhala Island offshore from Sandakan Harbour who reached Tawi-Tawi by native prahus where they served with Philippino guerrillas before rescue by American submarine and returned to Australia.

'Jock' McLaren's name is immortalised in 'Z' history. A veterinary officer pre-war, while serving with the Philippino guerrillas he fell ill and diagnosed his problem as appendicitis needing immediate attention.

Deep in the jungle and with only one guerrilla who had no knowledge of medicine, Jock with the help of a stainless steel mirror held by his companion and a razor blade, performed an appendectomy on himself and sutured the incision with needle and cotton from his 'housewife' kit! Ironically, post war while driving a jeep as a forestry officer in New Guinea, this brave operative was accidentally killed when a tree fell on him.

Unfortunately, insufficient personal knowledge of those operations makes it impossible for me to even contemplate writing about them. We in 'Agas 1' had our hands full, particularly when another arm of 'Agas' code named 'Stallion 4' loomed on the horizon. Apart from Gort, we of 'Agas 1' knew very little of our daughter parties, and furthermore, didn't want to know. In the event of capture by the 'sons of heaven', what we didn't know could not be forced out of us under torture, and this lesson was drilled into us by our instructors at Frazer Island Commando School (FCS).

Although of short duration, operation 'Stallion 4' appears under the chapter 'Bongawan Railway Station'. Thereafter, I operated with Captain Roy McLean on the Kudat Peninsular until the cease-fire was announced when I rejoined Gort Chester for a short duration at our Pitas Headquarters prior to returning to Australia.

This book - a mixed bag of clandestine activities, guerrilla warfare, submarines, folboats, human studies, natural history, criticisms of wartime leaders, ghost stories, autobiography and human endurance - sadly, embraces accounts of almost unbelievable atrocities committed by an arrogant and cruel foe – Japan and her 'sons of heaven'. Helpless Australian and British POW as well as the brave civilian indigenous population of that realm of 'The Wild Man From Borneo', suffered badly at the hands of the Japanese.

Throughout the book, and particularly with details in connection with the marches, the escapees during those marches and those that escaped from Ranau, I have endeavoured to remain uninfluenced by books, articles and documentary films produced on the subject. My writings are in accordance with what I recall actually happened behind Japanese lines more than 50 years ago, rather than from researching the subject. In so doing, I apologise for any inaccuracies, names of people, duplications, omissions and shortcomings etc. I am only human.

Designed as suitable reading for those interested in Australian War History whether male or female, I hope the reader enjoys my stories. These stories could only occur in the mysterious and fascinating country of the 'Wild Man from Borneo', the colony of British North Borneo (now re-named Sabah) or the Land Below the Wind.

A SON'S INSIGHT

It was around noon on Thursday 2nd July 1998.

My Dad, youngest sister Aneeta and I were travelling with Malaysian Airlines from Kota Kinabalu to Sandakan, Sabah. We were seated in row one on the left-hand side of the aircraft and I was in the window seat thumbing through one of Dad's wartime photo albums. I occasionally glanced out of the window at mountainous terrain between broken cloud layers below.

We had just completed a four-day film shoot in Kota Kinabalu on the documentary film for SBS Australia by producers Carlyon and Miller. Unknown to us at that time, the film would be titled 'Jack Sue – A Matter of Honour' and we were still to spend two weeks filming around Sandakan.

Having suffered a dense stroke following a five by-pass heart and aortic valve replacement operation only fourteen months earlier, he was desperate to get back to Sandakan again. He had been back several times since WW2 leading special interest tours for Australian and overseas tourists.

This time, Aneeta and I were taking him back in a wheelchair.

For some weird reason, whilst gazing at the cloud cover below, my mind strangely drifted back to a story he told me many years earlier.

It occurred in a lush tropical beer garden tucked away in the seclusion of the Commercial Hotel Port Douglas, North Queensland. My Dad and his late wife Pam were seated with about a dozen 'Z' men and wives enjoying a quiet ale or two. The small and secluded beer garden was completely covered in creepers and was delightfully cool.

A few meters away in the rear corner of the garden sat an old man drinking alone. Lean, wiry and well suntanned, he appeared to be about seventy. Dressed in a white athletic singlet, he seemed visibly upset by my father's presence and was peering and staring at him. After some time when the old man could restrain his curiosity no more, he walked over and tapped my father on the shoulder.

"Excuse me, I do not wish to appear rude but I overheard your surname mentioned by one of your friends here. Are you really Jack Sue of 'Z' Special Force by any chance?"

"Yes!" My father replied "and I think you're bloody rude with your continual staring!"

"I'm sorry – I don't mean to be rude. No sir! You couldn't possibly be the man I have in mind. You're too bloody young" and with that, walked back to his table and continued sipping his beer. Shortly after, one of my father's friends – Cairns resident John Hay - noticed that the old man was crying into his beer, obviously quite upset. My father excused himself and approached the old man's table with two fresh beers and sat alongside him.

"Come on old timer, what seems to be the problem?"

"Are you really Jack Sue of 'Z' Force? No you can't possibly be" he muttered through his sobs. I must be seeing a ghost".

"Let me assure you my friend, my name is Jack Sue and my wife Pam sitting over there with my Cairns friends Arch and Gloria James from The House on the Hill, and John and Val Hay from Freshwater will verify that for you".

"Well then" he said "if it's really you, did you ever fly into Morotai in a beaten up Yankee Catalina suffering from dysentery and malaria during WW2? And if it's really you, how many of you were aboard the Cat? Where were you taken from the airfield? What time of day was it?"

My father replied "there were three of us dangerously ill with bacillary dysentery and malaria and we were taken to the 2/5th Australian General Hospital. Don't know what time it was, but it was bloody night and we had flown from Tawi-Tawi in the Philippines".

He cried again then composed himself and continued "well, I was one of the ambulance stretcher bearers who off-loaded the three of you. The doctor with us said that by morning two of you would be dead. How that Cat stayed in the air was beyond belief. I never saw you again after that night and now, I just don't know: please accept my apologies for staring the way I did. I thought I was looking at a ghost".

My mind snapped back to reality when the engines of the Boeing 737 were drawn back to flight idle as the aircraft commenced its descent into Sandakan. As we slipped beneath the grey canopy of cloud, my father's left hand appeared in front of my face. He pointed out the massive estuary systems that lay to the north such as the 'mudflats' near Pura-Pura where 'Agas 1' had lived for many weeks after landing by submarine in Japanese held British North Borneo.

As the 737 temporarily levelled off to break its continual descent, I could see vast areas of impenetrable jungle. I tried to visualise Gort Chester's party of seven, fifty three years earlier trying to survive in that malaria and crocodile infested area and they being hopelessly outnumbered by a cruel and barbaric aggressor.

Little did I realise that during the next two weeks I would actually travel to Pura-Pura where Dad and his mates were inserted by American submarine in folboats. Also, I would meet Chinese and Malaysian elders who witnessed first hand, terrible Japanese atrocities meted out to the peaceful and innocent locals of that time.

In a few moments we were on the ground where a welcoming committee of kindred members of our Sandakan 'blood family' the Tans, and others were waiting to greet my father.

I turned to face him as he gently placed his hand on the armrest. His eyes were closed as he rested back into the seat. A gentle smile of contentment spread over his face. He was back.

The story you are about to read is long overdue. It is his story as seen through his eyes as a highly trained member of 'Z' Special Force during his late teens. A kid of nineteen years old, yet highly skilled in subversive warfare who only nine years earlier was the president of a Junior Naturalists' club.

It all occurred in a time when most of us were not even born.

Life has its own strange ways of dishing out opportunities. Dad's stroke gave him the opportunity to write this book. The once fifty words per minute touch typist, tapped this story out with one finger of one hand over a three year period that commenced in hospital and while endeavouring to learn the intricacies of a computer.

And when 'Jack Sue – A Matter of Honour' was about to be premiered by SBS Australia wide, I was asked during a radio interview "what was it like growing up with a highly decorated war hero?"

Well reader, I grew up with a man once highly trained for a special job, who was well programmed mentally and physically, who returned from the war and was dumped back into society and expected to be a normal citizen again. And like all commandos he was never de-programmed. Maybe the Government wanted to keep them that way for future use. Who knows?

So I grew up with a man hard, tough and at times very difficult to understand. He did as he wanted and as a son, I fitted in. Children those days were supposed to be seen and not heard. Growing up with my Dad was normality for me for I knew no different.

Out of it all, I have always been very close to him and will continue to be so. I never grew up with a war hero, I grew up with my Dad. He loved, cared and nurtured me; he was my best friend and yet my strongest critic. He was there for me always, no matter what, and I could never have asked for a better Dad. That he is decorated and recognised in society is just like icing on the cake.

The effects of war can do terrible damage to certain people. Whether they ever recover from it one never knows. In my view, anyone who has been to war and survived it, is a true hero.

I hope you enjoy my Dad's story 'Blood On Borneo'.

Barry Sue, November 1999.

ACKNOWLEDGMENTS

My original enthusiastic advisors and urgers dating back to 1947 are as follows:-

Mrs. Leila Richards (Dec)

Proprietress 'Janella'Guest House, Roleystone WA

Mrs. E. Sellers (Nee Richards)

WRAN (Now resident Melb.)

Mr. Ivor Birtwistle (Dec)

Editor 'Life and Letters' West Australian Newspapers

Mr. Frank Davidson (Dec)

Chief Editor Perth Sunday Times

Mr. Ron Clarke (Dec)

Editor former Perth Mirror Newspaper

Mr. Maurie Glazier

Geraldton crayfisherman and underwater diving mate

Mr. Tommy Thompson

Motor Trimmer and underwater diving mate

Mr. Hugh Edwards

Author and underwater diving mate

Mr. Alan Hobbs

Carnarvon plantation owner and underwater diving mate

Mr. Ron Cooper

Carnarvon Retired Clerk and underwater diving mate

WW2 Ex Servicemen and Sandakan Underground Members

Sgt.Bob Pride (Dec)

'Z' RAAF Flight 200

Sgt.Les (Blue) Levett

'Z' RAAF Flight 200

Flt. Lieut. Ray Storer (Dec)	'Z' RAAF Flight 200
Flt. Sgt. Colin Ledger (Dec)	'Z' RAAF Flight 200
Capt. Sam Carey	'Z' AIF Operation 'Scorpion'
Don Harlem (Dec)	'Z' AIF Operation 'Agas 1'
S/Sgt. Graham Greenwood	'Z' RNZA Operation 'Agas 1'
Sgt. A. (Skeet) Hywood	'Z' AIF Operation 'Agas 1'
Datuk Hadji Abu Bakar Tan (Dec)	'Z' Guerrilla Leader Operation 'Agas 1'
Tun Datuk Mustapha (Dec)	'Z' Guerrilla Leader Operation 'Agas 1'
*Paddy Funk (Dec)	Civilian 'Z' Force (International) Inc.
Pte Keith (Blackie) Scarff (Dec)	'Z' AIF 'Z' Force (International) Inc.
*Dr. James Taylor (Dec)	Civilian Sandakan Underground
Pte Nelson Short (Dec)	AIF POW Death March Survivor
Lieut. Clive Boundy (Dec)	AIF POW Sandakan Survivor
Pte Ben Hart	AIF 9th. Aust. Div.
Pte Jack Bickford	AIF 2/5th Independent Commando Squadron
Pte Ken Ryan	AIF
Sir Reginald Barnewall	AIF 'Z' Force (International) Inc
A/B Seaman Bruce Inder - Smith	R.A.N. & MS 'Marina' Norwegian Merchant Navy
Doug Henley	AIF Graves Recovery Unit

Commercial etc.

Malaysian Airlines
Garuda Airlines
Government Of Malaysia
Malaysian Army
Government Of Sabah

Special Thanks

Maj. Gen. Michael Jeffery AC CVO MC KStJ CitWA	Foreword
Darrell and Lorraine MacCarthy	Computer Ed. and carers

Ross MacLennan (Color Logic)	Typesetting and Graphic Design
Jim McManus	Proof Reading (legal)
(James McManus Associates)	
Janice Fairhurst (Belmont Library)	Proof Reading
Bruce Stewart (Dec)	ProofReading
Jenny Clements	Computer Education
(RPH Shenton Park Annexe	
Education Dept.)	
Lindsay Foster	Computer Access
(RPH Shenton Park Annexe	
Education Dept.)	
Stuart Guy and	Typing
Jackie Simpkin-Brown	
Terry and Robin Miller	Promotion
(Miller/Carlyon Documentaries)	
Geoff and Carol Wallace (Colortape)	Processing and promotion
Cyril Ayris	Publishing and Promotion
(Author ex West Aust. Newspaper)	
Cliff Zerbe	Contributing letter
(retired farmer Victoria)	

General

Lynette Ramsay-Silver	Author - Sydney NSW
Betty Harlem	Retired Hobart, Tasmania
Nola and Bill Downey Retired	Caloundra, Queensland
Terry Zanetti (Dec) writer and	
Alison Zanetti	Teacher – Canberra ACT
Madam Cheong Kau Tan	Retired – Sandakan, Sabah
('Agas 1' Nurse)	
Madam Bella Tan	Investor – Sandakan Sabah
Madam Lucy Tan	Music Teacher – Sandakan, Sabah
Madam Mary Tan	Accountant – Kota Kinabalu, Sabah
Anita Webb	Morning teas and House Help
Joy Telford	Morning teas and House Help
Gabriel Farber	Morning teas and House Help

Dixie Morgan	Morning teas and House Help
Mike Harris	Voluntary Physio / Massage
(Remedial Massage Clinic)	Treatment
Steve Berndt (Acupuncture Clinic)	Voluntary Acupuncture Treatment
Wong Wui Hsien	Voluntary Acupressure Treatment
(Singapore Air Force)	
Anna Marie Thorne	VoluntaryMagnetic Therapy
Jay Salter	Voluntary Bowen/Raki Treatment
Valerie Dewar	Voluntary Reflexologist
Mark Brunt	Voluntary Assistance and
	Recreation
Allan Chang (Migration Consultant)	Volunteer Hairdresser/chaffeur
Janet Harris	Volunteer Sewing Etc.
Beryl Carpene	Volunteer Sewing Etc.
Gwen Baldock	Volunteer Sewing Etc.
John and Gladys Whyte	Personal Encouragement and
(Nee Sue – my sister)	Assistance
Morrie and Joy Bruce	Personal Encouragement and
(Nee Sue – my sister)	assistance

My Scattered Tribe:-

Barry, Glenda, Graeme, Aneeta (Broome), Kam (Mt. Keith), Constant encouragement, assistance and Kim (Edinburgh), Keith (Bunbury) love for their Dad

BLOOD
ON
BORNEO

Dedicated to the Prisoners of War who died in
Sandakan, The Borneo Death Marches, Ranau, Kuching
and elsewhere in British North Borneo and the indigenes
of the Sandakan 'underground' who now rest in the
Hero's Grave at Kuching, Sarawak plus the 171 heroes
(men and women) of the Albert Kwok rebellion of 1943
who today rest in the mass communal grave at Petagas, Sabah.

ALL OF WHOM

Sacrificed their lives in the name of freedom and the eventual
rescue of 6 Australian Prisoners of War from an estimated
number of 2,400 Australian and British POWs in prewar
British North Borneo (now Sabah).

Chapter 1

CRUCIFIED

"Christ! The poor bastard's been crucified!"

The dirty and bedraggled naked corpse of an Australian soldier lay a few metres off the rentis [bridle track]. Spread-eagled, each hand and foot was tied to a stake driven into the ground. The lifeless face stared vacantly into the fading daylight. The pitifully sunken eyes of the young soldier were expressionless in death that gave no indication of the agonising and humiliating death he must have suffered in those final moments as life ebbed slowly away. He was only young and no older than his beholder.

The open flesh of the buttock bore testimony to the cannibalism of his Japanese captors; they had made a crude attempt to take a slice of rump from the body. The long matted hair and the surround of whiskers framing the hollow cheeks and sad eyes gave the face an almost Christ-like appearance. Christ almighty!

The tissue thin covering of skin was taut all over the bone structure and the emaciated chest accentuated every rib. The legs were virtually skin-covered bone from foot to pelvis, separated only by the hideously grotesque bony knees. When alive he'd have been no more than a walking skeleton.

Bloated by the Borneo sun and the long-term effects of beri-beri, the abdomen, in sharp contrast was grotesquely full. Although he'd been dead not more than a day or two, the body showed signs of decomposition and was now no more than a host for the myriad maggots and other scavenger insects issuing from the numerous entry points of the body. Lieut Don Harlem found himself reduced to an uncontrollable fit of dry reaching.

1

A former battle hardened campaigner, and one of the Rats of Tobruk who had pitted their wile and guts against the infamous 'desert fox'- Germany's revered General Rommel - Don Harlem then volunteered his services with the top secret 'Z' Special Unit. Now he, for the first time in his army career found himself completely overcome by emotion and revile as he stared incredulously at the pitiful bag of bones that lay before him.

Don was oblivious of the brilliant tropical moon climbing into the sky, the incessant cacophony of cicadas and the calls of nocturnal birds as they emerged from their daytime hide-outs deep in the jungle. He was finally switched back to reality by the sounds of Japanese soldiers laughing in the near-by rest house, a number of which straddled the 165 mile Death March route from Sandakan to Ranau.

Hurriedly gathering up the Australian soldier's few papers that lay scattered about the scene and thrusting them into its pack - the Japanese

Front page of Camp Concert Party programme found with personal papers of unknown crucified soldier. *Image courtesy of Don Harlem*

2

had obviously ransacked his side-pack still lying near the body – Don was unable to find any personal items that might identify the young digger. No dog tags, no letters, no personal photographs of family or girl friends.

So intense was the immediate hatred that racked the whole of his body, his first re-action was to rush in to that damned Japanese rest house with machine gun blazing and rid the place of those bloody animals; those bastards! It was an insult to the animal kingdom to refer to them as animals. God's animals didn't behave in that way.

But Don Harlem had a more urgent and more important mission on his hands.

As much as he wanted to avenge the unknown POW, and his whole being ached to do just that, the unknown digger was no longer of this world and was beyond assistance. Harlem could not afford to jeopardise his mission by revealing his presence in the area. With his trusty Orang

Signatures of crucified soldiers mates on the back page of Camp Concert programme.
Image courtesy of Don Harlem

3

Tua (kampong head man) Kulang and a handful of Malay guerrillas, Don was hot-footing it for the march route sector of Ranau. There they hoped to locate four live Australian POW reported to have escaped from the Japanese POW compound at Ranau a few days earlier - four of only six who survived out of 1800 or possibly more POW. Nobody will ever know the exact number of POW that perished on that 'via dolorosa'.

The Japanese covered their tracks well. Moreover, the Japanese high command had issued orders to kill all the survivors at Ranau, so that none would live to testify against the Japanese.

A day or two later while resting at an en-route kampong, Don, unable to erase the sight of the crucified digger from his mind, decided to check through the papers that were scattered willy nilly around the body when he and Kulang found it.

He was disappointed to find nothing of intelligence value. However there was a camp concert programme that caught his eye. The front cover depicted a typical, cheeky faced young Aussie digger in shorts - not an emaciated POW - squatted over a camp fire. A separate sheet of paper in the programme bore a few names that obviously were those of his close mates in the Sandakan camp. The mystery as to the diggers identity remained as such when Don passed away in Hobart Tasmania during the 80s.

Unfortunately, the names on other papers gave no clues to his identity. It was likely that his mates had perished in the Sandakan camp as a result of aerial bombing when the American B24 Liberators commenced regular pounding of the airstrip. If not killed by bombing on the airstrip or the camp, they may have died of illness within the camp due to malaria or malnutrition when cruel camp commandant Captain Susumu Hoshijima drastically reduced the rice ration. Last but not least, they possibly perished on the Death March trail or were murdered. Who knows?

Chapter 2

THE BURNING OF TRUSAN

The strange silence of the jungle was overpowering. Don Harlem shifted uneasily in his prone position behind the large fallen hardwood tree that had lain on the forest floor for goodness knows how long. However, it was obviously long enough to have attracted a pair of palm squirrels to its hollowed interior who with their youngsters scattered as Don dived behind their refuge for his own refuge.

Both he and I and a handful of Bajau guerrillas - the notorious sea pirates of British North Borneo - had been pinned down for some considerable length of time by the Japanese soldiers who had unexpectedly arrived at the precise moment that Don had given the order to attack.

Ah Ping, the old Chinese cook and our reliable informer who had been in the employ of the Japanese force of 20 for more than two years in the small coastal town of Trusan had been unaware of the expected arrival of Japanese reinforcements.

Trusan, although a small town was considered by the Japanese garrison force to be a home from home posting.

Accustomed to living off the fat of the land and more often than not, at the expense of the indigenous population, Japanese rule within the area had been a one way street. In particular the Chinese population, had been repeatedly targeted by their Japanese warlords and no one remained safe.

And so it was with some trepidation that at long last they found that the boot was on the other foot when the 'Z' men Don Harlem and Jack Sue with their small guerrilla band surprised them; reducing their numbers by 10 in as many minutes.

Datu Mustapha, the Malay guerrilla leader, was successful in capturing one of the enemy garrison defenders before the Japanese reinforcements burst in on the scene.

The term 'guerrilla' dates back to the Spanish war days of the early 1800's and simply means 'mini war'; in our more up to date terminology 'hit and run'. The abuse of the term inevitably results in tragedy for the guerrillas should they allow themselves to be drawn into a prolonged action with good regular troops.

Given that the well organised guerrilla force employing surprise tactics is a force to be reckoned with, when faced by regular soldiers in a 'stand to and fight' situation, the regulars are usually better by virtue of their vastly superior training.

The golden rule of the successful guerrilla group is 'never take on a numerically superior force unless the planned ambush method is 'foolproof'. Any action beyond these parameters is considered suicidal.

'He Who Dares Wins' is the motto of the Australian SAS (Special Air Service) battalion, probably one of the greatest forces of its type in the world. However, while we 'Z' old-timers regard SAS as our successors, their present day role of commando-guerrilla warfare is somewhat updated from that of WW2 'Z' Special Unit, to give our unit its correct title.

In defence circles almost world wide, the unit is referred to as 'Z' force and should not be confused or connected with the Royal Navy task force of H.M.S. Repulse and Prince of Wales, the two British battle wagons dispatched from Singapore by Sir Winston Churchill to wipe out the Japanese landing force at Kota Bahru on the northern border of Malaya, present day Malaysia. Both were sunk and the result of that action rocked the world.

The Japanese entry into WW2 had been formidable and almost overnight their troops spread south through Malaya towards Singapore, Britain's 'impenetrable' far-eastern naval base. The sinking proved conclusively that the Japanese torpedo bombers were far superior to sea power of the day.

Don, who always held my admiration for his instant uncanny summation of the task in hand – probably a legacy inherited from fighting the Germans in the desert -sized up the unsavoury position in which we found ourselves at Trusan.

The Japanese house from which we had driven the 'sons of heaven' during our surprise attack was typically protected from all sides by lalang (the clearing of all jungle growth for about 50 metres surrounding the

6

building that made unobserved approaches to the building very difficult).

Having forced the Japanese over the lalang and into the jungle verge - the only direction that afforded them any hope of escape - we then found the lalang at our backs and we were trapped by the enemy reinforcements at our rear.

Don screamed out instructions for our Malay guerrillas to disperse left towards heavier jungle cover before leaping up from behind the big log sheltering him. Calling for me to join him in an endeavour to engage a small pocket of Japanese ahead of us, thereby gaining some extra time for the Malay boys to make themselves scarce, I prepared to move out and cover him.

I re-call in particular that as I was about to leap out of my sheltered spot, my attention was drawn to a tiny little humming bird that was hovering outside the bell mouth of a common jungle bloom. In retrospect, I have often wondered how the human mind could be so easily distracted momentarily by a piece of nature despite the fact that death lay all around us that glorious sunny morning.

As a boy, I had been a member of the Western Australian Junior Naturalists' Club and took an active interest in field days and other activities organised by the West Australian Museum and by the senior and junior naturalists' clubs. I guess my love of nature, be it above or below water, may explain my strange behaviour of that morning.

Typical Malay Kampong couple

Galvanised into action by Don's commands I was shortly back to reality, moving forward in the crouched position as Don climbed quickly over a log, heading for the next piece of cover between the Japanese and ourselves.

While there was still cover between the Japanese position and himself, he was unaware that one of the enemy believed to have been killed some minutes earlier was up to the 'old doggo' trick.

7

As soon as Don passed the 'dead' Nipponese, that 'son of heaven' or 'son of a bitch' was on his feet as quick as a flash aiming a 7mm Nambu automatic pistol squarely at Don's back. "Down Don!" I screamed at the top of my voice, realising that he had fallen for the oft times used Japanese trick. Don dropped like a stone as I let go a burst of automatic fire with my silenced Austen machine gun, almost cutting the enemy in half.

Left to their fate, the Malay guerrillas having obeyed Don's order to 'shoot through', did exactly that. We had extreme difficulty in extricating ourselves from our open predicament and it was mainly good luck rather than fine judgement that saved our skins on the day. We finally withdrew through the narrow escape corridor used by the Malays. Don and I had earned a cheap and valuable lesson.

Discussing the incident with the Malays later back at Jambongan Island over a cup of Tapok (a rather pleasant but potent alcoholic drink brewed from coconut plus other ingredients), I related the momentary delay created by the intervention of the little humming bird. It was then that we learned the humming bird was an omen of good luck among many tribes of British North Borneo and maybe inadvertently, the bird saved Don's life, and possibly mine. It undoubtedly had been our lucky day with a capital 'L'; we never again fell for the doggo trick.

Don, Datuk Mustapha and myself returned to Trusan some days later on a recce (reconnaissance) to find out what the Japanese were doing.

Our approach to the Japanese building was with the greatest caution, a caution that proved to be unjustified. The enemy had deserted Trusan and none of the Chinese or Malay inhabitants had any idea as to the reasons why, how, or where the Japanese reinforcements had gone. We were later told that the 30 Japanese were intended as a relief force to replace those we had so successfully attacked.

In their haste to vacate the building, little effort had been made to remove valuable maps and other materials of intelligence value that indicated Japanese strengths and dispositions. Found also was a medium sized safe that when blown open revealed a fortune in Japanese mint new occupation notes known by the locals as 'duit' or 'wang pisang' (Malay for currency or banana money respectively)

Close inspection revealed that the wads of notes – mostly in denominations of 20, 10 and 5 dollars to simulate the British Straits dollars of pre-war days but specifically printed for use in Borneo - bore no serial numbers and were probably intended as payment to the local natives for services rendered. Don and I emptied the safe completely and distributed the notes 'willy nilly' to all and sundry before we destroyed the safe.

On our next visit to Trusan we were greeted with open arms by the inhabitants who laughingly told us that a large percentage of the Japanese notes had been handed on to neighbouring kampongs all of whom had put them to use as kertas jamban (toilet paper). 'Bum fodder' was a commodity not sighted since the British walked out.

The only other point of interest lay in the fact that the hut into which we had thrown grenades, unknown to us, housed not only 'sons of heaven' but also three Japanese or possibly Javanese geisha girls. They were heavily laden with child, grotesque in appearance, faces and abdomens swollen beyond recognition from the heat of the Borneo sun. Both males and females were ready to burst at the slightest prod of a sharp instrument.

The bodies of the dead 'sons of heaven' and geishas were thrown into the atap (walls and roofing made from Nipa palm leaves) building and set alight. The burning down of Trusan at least granted the dead Japanese some dignity that we trusted would accompany their souls to the heaven or the divine winds from which they believed they originated. And so ended the saga of 'banana money' and 'the burning of Trusan'.

Typical Dusan native

Chapter 3

SYDNEY RE-UNION

The day was the Anzac Day 25th. April 1970. The location was the Twin Towers Motel North Sydney. The time was approximately 0430 and the occasion was the first national re-union of 'Z' men conducted in Australia. The re-union was well patronised by former war-time members world-wide, and more particularly, South West Pacific areas including Malaya, Singapore, the China coast, and stretching as far east as Hawaii.

Hosted jointly by the SRD association (Services Reconnaissance Department) Western Australia and the 'Z' Special Unit Association New South Wales, it probably constituted the most formidable gathering of 'cut throats', notorious 'con-men', 'black-mailers', 'saboteurs', 'clandestine agents', 'hit-men'; call them what you will. In their hey-day, any one of them could have stolen Grandma's false teeth and hocked them without her knowing!

Further augmented by wartime members of SOE (Special Operations Europe, also referred to as Secret Operations Executive), Force 136, Flight 200 and other sister unit members, they presented themselves as a sinister group. Cover names for clandestine units world wide changed daily according to the climate of events.

Offenders of British law and the bane of Scotland Yard's top brains, when WW2 broke out, the best of bank-robbers etc were offered officer commissions to instruct in breaking and entering, lock picking and all manner of nefarious activities.

Gigolos, drink waiters, transvestites, brothel keepers – not to be confused with an Australian Field Marshal - African game-farm keepers, students and as the list grew, so did the intrigue.

Then there were the usual legits. Printing process engravers turned limpeteers (men specially trained in the art of sinking enemy shipping by the application of magnetic explosive limpet charges loaded with plastic explosive) and post office telegram signalers became evasive radio operators behind enemy lines – a hazardous existence if there ever was one. The Sydney gathering heralded from all sections of the community.

I recall my post-war 'Z' mate Keith Scarff – now deceased – relating a story that took place at Morotai Island in the Halmahera group where both American and Australian bases of some strength had been established.

It seems that on this particular day towards the end of May 1945, a group of 'Z' Sergeants and Warrant officers were enjoying lunch in the mess when a dapper little 'fancy-pants' approximately four foot six inches high in the old imperial measurement, rolled into the mess.

Crossing the floor of the mess in a particularly provocative manner a la Marilyn Monroe, his 'queenie' performance drew side-glances and quiet sniggers. One of the tough 'Z' men observed casually but very quietly, the query on all lips that day, "who is the little 'Miss Fancy-pants?" The worst thing he could have possibly uttered.

One simply didn't ask such questions in a 'Z' establishment. All types of strange bods had a habit of arriving unannounced, stay a day or two, then dissolve out of the scene as mysteriously as they had appeared. Many such mystery men in fact were never seen again which only emphasised more, the strange behavioural pattern of the units members.

Whether 'Miss Fancy-pants' overheard the remark or not, will never be known. Neither did we ever find out whether or not 'Miss Fancy-pants' survived the war.

Small in stature, feminine in gait, clinically clean by front-line war establishment standards, well-groomed pencil thin moustache, perfectly manicured finger nails, he was dressed in civilian tartan pants, unobtrusive shirt, tartan forage cap and appeared to be on the way for a few holes of golf. However, he radiated the confidence of an 'unflappable' with his walking cane that never left his side and later transpired to be a lethal weapon.

A WO2 (Warrant Officer) seated with the men, was heard to whisper through clenched teeth while eyeing off his junior NCOs (non commissioned officers) "that bastard has cut more throats than you bloody mob have had good breakfasts, now bloody well shut up". The voice of authority ended any further speculation.

It was learned later that 'Miss Fancy-pants', armed to the teeth, parachuted that very same evening shortly after midnight into dense pitch-black jungle alone, a jungle that displayed only a lone recognition fire to guide him down. The eleven-man B24 Liberator crew of Flight 200 – 6 B24s, an integral component of our 'hush-hush' unit – could scarcely believe their eyes and ears as he slid out the tail chute of the kite with a "cheerio chaps" into the inky darkness. Do I hear the reader muttering "madmen dropping a madman?"

The question poses another question re the sanity of all aboard the aircraft that evening. Aircrews, like their fellow 'Z' men, were sworn to secrecy on their operations.

It was arranged that some of the West Australian contingent of 19 plus other operatives and their wives should meet in our room for toast and coffee laced with rum, before leaving for the Anzac Day march through Sydney city streets. Anzac Day in Sydney can be icy cold, therefore the rum is a 'must' before the dawn service. At least, that was our excuse.

Don Harlem was the last to arrive sparking off much handshaking and introductions. Many operatives had not seen each other since the war and in the case of our wives, most had never met Don Harlem, but like every one in the room knew him by his name and war record.

Greetings and introductions completed, Don quietly announced "if it hadn't been for Susie, your old man Pam, - referring to me - I wouldn't be here today" and in his quiet and reticent manner related the foregoing incident that took place at the Burning off Trusan.

My close mate Keith Scarff (now deceased) was a regular post-war visitor to our former wartime one-man submarine base at Careening Bay, Garden Island, a short distance offshore from Rockingham and within sight of Fremantle, the principal port of Western Australia. Fremantle was the WW2 base for a large Indian Ocean fleet of American, British, Australian and Dutch warships plus more than 100 American submarines.

A top security training centre in the late months of 1944, specially selected men were trained in the art of approaching anchored Japanese ships and attaching 'limpet' mines to the hulls. These extremely brave men – all volunteers – preferred to call their craft 'sleeping beauties' rather than by their official handle SBs (submersible boats).

Keith Ronald Donald Scarff ('Blackie'), appropriately nicknamed because of his swarthy complexion, notwithstanding his McDonald Scot background, with his father established a furnishing business in growing post-war Rockingham. He was a loyal contributor to the upkeep of our 'Z' memorial at Careening Bay unveiled in 1951, and regularly took fertilisers and other needs to the island for the lawn surrounding the memorial. He was extremely proud of the memorial and what it stood for and simply loved to see it looking good. Charitably, he funded the purchases out of his own pocket.

He was the sort of guy that attended our functions from his former home town Northam 60 miles east of Perth and thought nothing of travelling the distance just to be with his former wartime 'Z' mates. Frequently, when he came down to the unit functions, he brought a brace or two of wild ducks for the barbecue. He was a member of the rifle club in that town and was still active in Queen's Cup rifle shoots and duck shoots. A crack-shot with the .303 Lee-Enfield service rifle, 'Blackie' Scarff had won many trophies for rifle shooting as a member of the Northam rifle club and Queen's Cup events.

While serving at Morotai, he made several unsuccessful attempts to join parties behind the lines but his services as batman and runner for the Commanding Officer of 'Z' precluded him.

The initial Sydney national re-union was probably the best of many later post-war re-unions that followed. Catching up with guys that we had not seen since the war years, and in many cases had not seen since well before the WW2 era, made the event a valuable and memorable occasion.

The re-union was marred by only one incident and that was the unfortunate death of Navy Lieutenant Ted Carse, the skipper of the captured 78 foot ex Japanese fishing boat 'Kofuku Maru' of operation 'Jaywick' fame.

Converted to a clandestine operations ship by Services Reconnaissance Department (SRD) - the fore-runner of 'Z' force - and re-named 'Krait', she sailed from Exmouth Gulf Western Australia with a crew of 14 men to attack Singapore in September 1943. Seven ships - a total tonnage of approximately 40,000 tons - were sunk or damaged in Singapore Harbour by limpet mines transported by six men in three folboats from 'Krait'. After the successful raid, the folboats made the rendezvous with 'Krait' and the party returned to Australia casualty free, after 33 days cruising behind Japanese lines flying a Japanese flag and averaging 6.5 knots.

Note: for a full account of the raid see Lynette Silver's 'The Fishing Boat that went to War'.

Chapter 4

TOOLS OF BASTARDRY 'TOP SECRET'

NOTE:- This chapter is not a chapter in the true sense of the word. It is not a glossary as such, neither is it a gazetteer. It is a conglomeration of all, complete with diversions, digressions and abbreviations etc; call it what you will? To avoid later confusion, I feel an explanation in the early stages of the book is necessary. Following, are some of the secret weapons that found themselves involved in the war conducted from 'down-under'.

ALTITUDE BOMB

In appearance, colour and dimensions, it looked for all the world like a policeman's innocent truncheon minus the wrist lanyard, but this flexible little object had a hell of a punch when detonated, and what a hell of a worry it must have been to the enemies of SOE, the Germans and Italians. Likewise, the Japanese must have lost many aircraft as these sabotage bombs were also used in the Pacific theatre by the Americans, Philippinos, Dutch and 'Z' operatives.

Our demolitions instructors at Frazer Island Commando School (FCS) in 1943 never showed us the internal mechanism of the altitude bomb. It no doubt would have been under tight security. However, our class of 13 – 8 Philippinos US Army, 3 Malays AIF (ex hard hat pearl divers) and 2 Australian RAAF – were taken to the American Air Force base at Eagle Farm Brisbane, where we inspected a number of captured Japanese single and twin engine aircraft. There, an American USAAF intelligence officer pointed out the various accessible and vulnerable sections of Japanese planes where the altitude bomb could be hidden.

The most favoured position was under the pilot's seat, and preferred altitude for detonation was under 1000 ft. At this height, destruction of the aircraft was easily verified. If it was desirable that the aircraft be well away from its base when the explosion took place, the desired destruction height was manually set on the altimeter pressed into one end of the bomb.

PERSONNEL MINE

It was similar to a carpenter's expanding steel tape - found in most households these days. Approximately 3 inches diameter and 1/2 inch in width and filled with 'PE' (plastic explosive), it was usually planted under a toilet seat - depending upon the agent's mood, sense of humour and respect for the enemy at the time.

Requiring slightly more than 5 pounds of pressure to activate this ingenious invention, the tiny mine had a variety of uses. Guaranteed to give the enemy a real lift - if not in spirit.

The tiny mine was often strategically placed under office chair cushions, driving seats of tanks or any other type of motor transport, vulnerable sections of small marine craft, door mats, wheels of aircraft and were particularly effective with the latter. While not effective enough to totally destroy aircraft, undue delays in take off were assured. As the undercarriage was blown off, the aircraft hit the ground, the spinning props bit into the dirt and into the wings as well; thus the aircraft was guaranteed to be grounded.

Unfortunately for the 'Z' agents involved, who would have liked to create more damage, the Japanese during WW2 had mostly piston driven kites and very few were four engine. They were rumoured to possess a propjet but we never saw one behind enemy lines. Because the Japanese were desperately short of parts for their planes towards the conclusion of WW2, they likewise, were desperately short of front line aircraft.

Even their kamikaze drivers – both male and female – were never instructed in the art of landing a kite; three point or otherwise. As a result, theirs were mostly one way missions.

I do not wish readers to believe that I am a know-all bastard if I sound technical on the subject of aircraft. I am not a qualified pilot. I am purely an amateur. My eldest son Barry is the fly-boy of the Sue family and has some 12/13,000 hours logged, of which perhaps 2/3,000 hours were logged on kerosene (jet engines). A lot of this time was spent in piston aircraft when he was a first officer with Air Niugini flying in Papua/Rabaul/Bougainville in DC3s plus I think, a few hours in F27 Friendships.

Over the years I have learned as the father of a pilot, that once having flown in New Guinea country where clouds have solid lumps in them, the universal opinion of pilots is "drive in New Guinea, drive anywhere in the world".

My wartime flying as a passenger while in 'Z' included many hours in all types of aircraft including Martin Mariner and Catalina flying boats. Land based kites included B24 Liberator 4 engine bombers, B25 Mitchell twin engine bombers, Lockheed Electra 4 engine transports, Vickers Viscount 700 propjets, Lockheed Hudson twin engine bombers and its transport version Lockheed Loadstars. Other types included Douglas twin transports DC2s and DC3s as well as the military version Dakota twin 'biscuit' bombers, Avro Anson twin trainer bombers, 'Butterbox' Oxford twin trainer bombers at Point Cooke Victoria. In addition, I had a few hours instruction in 'Tigerschmidt's (Tiger Moths) at Maryborough Queensland – sufficient to take off and land should it ever be necessary to steal an aircraft behind Japanese lines.

We also spent a considerable number of hours both flying and on the ground at the American base Eagle Farm Brisbane. There, we inspected captured Japanese aircraft with air worthiness certificates including planes secretly coded 'Sonia', 'Val', 'Helen', 'Rufus', 'Cherry', 'Zeke' (the original 'Zero'), 'Tony' (Japan's first single in-line engine fighter, not unlike Germany's Messerschmitt in appearance and performance) and others. The Americans pointed out the various vulnerable points on Japanese planes for the placing of altitude bombs and personnel or cushion mines.

Instruction on American aircraft recognition was also included in our curriculum. We inspected all the various kites including rows and rows of Dakota DC3s that Gort told us were for an operation linked to ours, the secret code name he carefully and purposely with held from our inquisitive and eager to learn ears.

In about 1950 and well after hostilities had ended, I learned through American sources that these Dakotas were part of the Dakota fleet earmarked for operation 'Kingfisher', the proposed rescue of the Australian and British POW incarcerated in Sandakan.

The range of American aircraft was truly both awesome and mind boggling. We learned at Eagle Farm for the first time, the truth in the

WW2 slogan 'thank God for the Yanks!'

Fighters of every description were parked in scattered revetment areas, a legacy from Pearl Harbour. There they had learned a costly lesson from 'the sons of heaven' by not scattering parked aircraft, and obviously they were not going to be caught again with their pants down.

In shattering contrast, RAAF airfields were depressing. In front line areas in what had been Dutch New Guinea (now West Irian) and in Papua New Guinea, our heroic RAAF boys of those days were going to the slaughter flying Boomerang single radial engine fighters. When pitted against Japan's impressive Zeros (mis-nomer for Zekes), the Aussie pilots were shot out of the skies almost without exception. From memory, I think there were only one or two occasions where the tables had been reversed. The exceptions proved the rule.

At frontline airstrips, when Yankee aircraft landed after carrying out a bombing raid, those bombers and fighters too badly damaged to repair within a reasonable time-span, were bulldozed off the strip into a junk heap.

In contrast, the RAAF technicians had to keep every American made kite flying; kites that were ordinarily bulldozed off American strips, were being repaired and flown by our RAAF boys. Ask any 2a (airframe) or 2e (engine) fitter who served in the New Guinea area during those tough days when the 'sons of heaven' held the upper hand. He would have to admit that RAAF fitters spent a lot of their spare time salvaging parts off the Yankee scrap heaps to keep their RAAF planes airborne.

They gathered as well of course, broken windscreens from which they manufactured rings, broaches and other trinkets to send home to their families and girl friends and to sell back to the Yanks.

Even the few surviving American fighters from Pearl were battling to hold their own against the Zekes but the Yank pilots at least had fighters – which while not equal to the Zekes – were somewhere near the required fighting standard to match their counterparts. This situation was a classic example of the Chinese adage: 'fourth class ride better than first class walk' or the English equivalent 'half a loaf of bread better than no bread at all'.

Upholding the difference between fantasy and reality, on the Japanese side of the fence, one had to give credit where credit was due and admire some of their fighter pilots. Although it had to be conceded that their Zekes were superior to P39 Tomahawks, P40 Kittyhawks and

Boomerangs a poor third, bravery nonetheless existed within the ranks of Japanese fighter pilots and we should not lose sight of that fact. Our RAAF heroes would have done as well had they flown Tiger Moths in combat instead of Boomerangs.

When the worm turned, the equation became a different kettle of fish. Japanese bombers – both medium and heavy - were mostly 'tail draggers' (tail wheels instead of tricycle undercarriage) and lacked the stability of American counterparts. Little imagination is required to appreciate that when undercarriages or rear wheels were blown off, tail planes and fuselage frames were also grossly effected. The shortage of spare parts was magnified by the shortage of ground crews, both engine and airframe as well as electrical fitters.

And the final icing on the cake was completed when the Japanese became impossibly short of test pilots and crews and as in all airforces both Allied and Axis, aircraft had to be airworthy otherwise drivers (pilots) were not interested.

The shortage of aircraft and crews was partly contributed to by 'Z' men sabotaging Japanese kites with their insignificant little 'Z' tools of bastardry including the personnel or cushion mines and the altitude bombs.

AIRCRAFT
B24 Liberator

A four engine bomber used by 'Z' (Flight 200) for the dropping of agents and supplies behind Japanese lines. It was selected as a suitable aircraft for conversion to long-range flying and installation of a parachutist's slide.

The dropping of agents in the Pacific campaign – unlike Europe - necessitated flying tremendous distances and these missions were usually lone flights at night or early morning without night fighter escort, there being no fighters capable of the range at the time and aerial tankers were unknown. Consequently, the B24 was exposed to marauding Japanese night fighters; the last thing wanted by a lone bomber on a highly secret mission.

The aircraft had to be capable therefore of defending itself on the distant lone missions. That made the Liberator an ideal choice, even though some of its protective armour had to be sacrificed for a larger fuel capacity for increased range.

During the necessary conversion procedure, B24 bomb bays were redesigned to replace bombs with storepedos (solid cardboard torpedo like containers) packed with stores to support those inserted behind enemy lines. Transmitters and receivers, coding and de-coding stationery and other associated necessities, medical equipment, ammunition, small arms including automatic sub-machine guns, pistols and grenades in addition to those carried by the parachuting operatives had to be included in storepedos.

Sufficient food had to be dropped in to sustain the party until it became established in its jungle hideout complete with radio communication when back-up supplies could be dropped. When 'Agas 1' was inserted, our 'sparkies' at the 'mudflats' communicated with 'Z' headquarters, then in Melbourne, through Darwin, then the Americans at Palawan in the Philippines, Morotai in the Halmahera group of islands and possibly other stations of which I am unaware.

The 6 B24 Liberators of Flight 200 proved to be a wise choice. On most missions, operatives jumped from approximately 400 feet according to the terrain on which the DZ was located. If this sounds crazy, it probably is. Then by the same token, anyone crazy enough to jump out of a perfectly airworthy plane needs to have the sanity factor checked and deserves what follows for perfectly obvious reasons! While being crazy was not a requirement of those who made up the ranks of 'Z', it nevertheless assisted.

When the operatives had been dropped, storepedos then followed

Wartime commandos and 'Z' personnel desirous of acquiring parachute wings, undertook a mandatory six week course at RAAF base Richmond New South Wales which naturally, taught the required skills such as landings - simulated jumps made from a tower - plus other necessary skills. At the conclusion of the course, the candidate had to have made 6 practice jumps from an aircraft, usually a Dakota - wartime version of the DC3 - to qualify for certificate and parachute wings.

In the field there were many occasions however, where urgency demanded that an agent jump into an area behind enemy lines even though he had never made a practice jump of any description. This operative did not qualify to wear parachute wings. On the reverse side of the coin, another 'Z' man who had completed his qualifying 6 jumps yet had never made an operational jump into enemy territory was entitled to wear the parachute patch.

The success of the B24 was due to a very brave 'Z' man, AIF
Captain Sam Carey. A professor of geology, Sam and his wife live today
in Hobart Tasmania. This perceptibly strange and likable man, when
dining at a restaurant always ordered the fattiest steak in the
establishment, despite today's learned medical opinion that excessive
cholesterol kills.

An outstanding operative, Sam has travelled the world for a number
of years lecturing on geology associated with oil drilling.

Brave – not only because he soaks up the cholesterol, but also
because of his wartime activities, even long before he joined the 'hush-
hush' 'Z' unit.

His stories scare the pants off most listeners and yet in doing so, he
remains reticent and so matter-of-fact about his experiences. His
lectures in the 'Z' classroom at Frazer Island, held his students
spellbound.

Sam was party leader of Operation 'Scorpion' 1943, preparing for
insertion into Japanese occupied Rabaul, the pre-war capital of New
Britain when it was bristling with Japanese naval might and was Japan's
largest naval base in SWPA (South West Pacific Area). The excitingly
incredible string of events occurred at a time when Australia's survival
from Japan's vast conquering invasion forces was in the balance. Those
events are sufficient to fill a complete book.

Townsville in Queensland has good reason to remember Captain
Sam Carey's mock raid on the harbour during WW2 when a hell of a lot
of shipping would have been sunk had Sam and his team been Japanese.
But that's another story and we don't have the space here. Suffice to say
that Sam in a night raid scared the pants off everyone in Townsville, and
set off all alarms including air raid sirens.

Australia for the very first time suffered severe bombing attacks;
namely Darwin, Broome, Exmouth and across the northern areas to
Queensland. Japanese midget submarines raided Sydney Harbour, the
Emperor's planes flew recce missions over every capital city and many
regional areas of Australia, and Japanese top secret Tiger Marines -
similar to 'Z' Force operatives - landed on secret missions Australia
wide.

While it all seems unbelievable today, Japan, after commencing her
slow and long retreat from the Kokoda Trail New Guinea to Tokyo, was
subjected to exactly the same treatment as described in the fore-going

paragraph but in reverse; 'as ye sow, so shall ye reap'. Besides, war history covering these and stranger events of those dark and threatening days, has partly admitted such activities by both the Japanese and the Allies today. Our leaders of Australian youth - Army, Navy and Air Force Cadets, Scouts and similar organisations - must be imbued with these lessons.

Australia like America and Pearl Harbour, was caught with its pants down and freedom as we know it was almost lost. Without wishing to sound pessimistic, maybe we won't be so lucky next turn around.

Sam Carey's valuable work with the B24 continued. He designed, fitted and tested the first successful parachutist's slide in Liberators. Yet today, his work has never been fully appreciated. Sam Carey, is one of the many unrecognised or inadequately recognised heroes of WW2

BOOTS
('Z' Troops - For the use of)

Ingeniously designed with a moulded sole, the English designed and manufactured commando boots left nothing but the imprint of native feet in the sand.

The average Westerner suffered from tender feet problems and as a result was unable to, or found it too difficult, to walk barefooted long distances and through areas where thorns and prickles were in profusion. These areas were trouble-free to the natives and other indigenous people who after a number of years of Japanese occupation, accompanied by the resultant shortages of consumer goods including footwear, naturally enough developed tough feet.

The 'sons of heaven' were desperately short of cargo ships and warships for convoy duties following their defeat at The Battle of the Coral Sea. However, this reason could not be offered or accepted as an excuse during the first six months of Japanese occupation of South East Asia when they had the British and Americans on the run. They simply neglected and bled the countries they over-ran.

The locals' feet because of no footwear became tougher and tougher. Ours on the other hand were nowhere near as tough because of our magnificent footwear. These were mostly American commando boots and or calf length jungle boots. Both types unfortunately left unwanted tread imprints in sand, unlike the specially designed English boots that left native footprints only.

After paddling all night and beaching our craft just before daybreak,

21

we, in our weary state and stressed out condition, never did relish the task of unloading and carrying the folboat into the cover of the jungle where we slept during the day.

While we did take precautions to hide our jungle sneaker footprints and brush marks, we were never fully convinced that we had adequately concealed our entry. The last thing we needed was to be caught fast asleep in the 'fart-sack'. Often our over-stressed minds miscalculated the tide-fall after slack water following high tide. As a result we occasionally woke to find - to our horror – our entry marks exposed to all and sundry.

We tried to draw comfort from the thought that 'after all said and done, we were only human'. Now, fifty years down the track with hopefully a little more maturity behind me, plus a lifetime of living, I wonder if in fact we were.

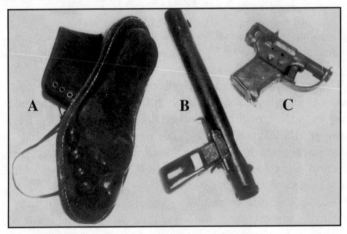

A - Special Commando Boot, B - Silence Welrod Pistol,
C - Liberator Liquidation Pistol

DAGGER
'Pigsticker'

An advanced 'Z' version of the standard American commando knife that widely speaking, was confined to the European theatre and used by the operatives of SOE, our mother unit.

To the best of my knowledge none of the 'Z' parties in Borneo had the 'Pigsticker' although there were rumours that Major Tom Harrison the party leader of operation 'Semut' (Malay for ant), a very large group whose activities were confined to Sarawak, possessed one. Although only a rumour, it could not be dismissed. As an English party leader – albeit a somewhat eccentric one – he had many contacts in SOE and undertook occasional trips to London HQ. His area ceased at the northern boundary of Sarawak where Gort's operation 'Agas' territory commenced, and embraced the whole of British North Borneo (now Sabah).

It was also rumoured that 'Mr. Fancypants', possessed a 'pigsticker' as well as his constant companion the walking stick that fired a 'L' (lethal) dart and – according to rumour – was fitted with a press button trigger cunningly let into the handle.

More information on the 'pigsticker' was given to me in the 1950s by former SOE operative Don Stewart who migrated to Perth from London with his wife Elaine (a prominent physiotherapist) and son Bruce, (all three now deceased). Bruce, a member of our association 'Z' Special Unit (International) Inc, proudly wore his father's medals on Anzac Day marches and other memorial services. He was living in the Perth suburb of Rivervale where he passed away suddenly in December 2,000. At the time, assisted by Belmont Shire librarian Janice Fairhurst, Bruce had been proof-reading the manuscript for this book

Don was a very successful SOE operative during the period Abysinia was fighting for survival after Italy invaded her territory until the end of WW2. During this period, his many escapades saw him in numerous roles in East Africa and occupied France.

On one occasion in East Africa, he and 3 other SOE men captured and sailed a 10,000 ton Italian liner loaded with Italian harlots out to sea where they met up with a British warship that provided a prize crew. The ship was then steamed to a British port where the girls provided SOE agents with invaluable intelligence.

A wild game farm keeper in Kenya pre-war, Don possessed many interesting photographs of himself and wife Elaine with prominent Hollywood celebrities including Clark Gable, Claudette Colbert and others during films shot on his property. Shortly after WW2 while living in Claremont –a suburb of Perth - Don passed away suddenly.

Within the ranks of top secret SOE, Don established the arguably famous reputation of being the only man alive who ordered King George the Sixth to "f..k off chum! This is a top security area", and got away with it.

I learned in the 1950s that the basement of the London Museum housed the SOE laboratories where the original masters of clandestine warfare designed and tested 'tools of bastardry'.

Prior to the King entering Don's domain clad in fine winter clothes topped off with a fawn-coloured overcoat and matching homburg, Don was testing the 'pigsticker'.

Just having plunged the knife into the abdomen of the target – a life-sized dummy of a man filled with sawdust or similar – he was about to depress a button, releasing a second blade at right angles to the double-edged dagger blade. The second blade - slightly lower than the hand guard – was about to drag out a great deal of the dummy victim's make believe viscera, when Don became aware of the presence of an unescorted ' someone' standing alongside him.

As the stranger had walked into a top security area unannounced; unaware of that person's identity - Don couldn't have cared a damn anyway - he blurted out in his deep vocal tone "who the f...ing hell are you and how the f... did you get in here?. F... off chum!" There was no reply from the Royal visitor who meekly turned away and left the room.

I do not know whether the King had intentions of replying or whether the King had deliberately entered the room alone. My gut feeling favours the latter, there being no escorting officer with him. He probably wanted to check the security of the establishment and his most trusted subjects. Whether or not, I'll bet he never expected the reception that Don Stewart gave him!

Don Stewart's fame preceded him wherever he moved. He was a popular guest speaker and like other 'Z' men of WW2, a part time lecturer at the Special Air Service Company (before its status of regiment) Campbell Barracks, Swanbourne.

My late wife Pam and I welcomed Don and his family on their arrival in Perth, having been made aware of their expected arrival date by the secretary of the Special Forces Club London. Today, through the portals of that club walk saboteurs, covert agents, clandestine men and women of all hush-hush units worldwide, including members of former wartime enemies Germany, Vichy France, Italy and Japan.

CAMERAS

'Agas 1' was issued with a stock standard Leichardt 35mm camera and black and white film stock when inserted into Borneo.

At a later stage as our organisation grew, more sophisticated and concealable cameras were available to parties in the field.

Mini-cameras no larger than a cigarette packet with ultra sharp lenses were available in both 16mm and 35mm formats. I still have a keyhole telescope issued to me in Morotai that was invaluable for close range work within buildings. Similar and much smaller cameras with superior lenses are now available on the open market and require no further description here.

CORDDTEX
(Top Secret)

'Top secret' newly released instantaneous high explosive fuse. White in colour, it looked like an innocent length of electric light cable or rope. When used as a primary charge in conjunction with a standard detonator and packed in a charge of plastic explosive (PE) it produced devastating results.

Commonly used today in the mining industry everywhere, it was 'top secret' during WW2.

The deadly combination was devastatingly effective in limpet mines underwater where the force of in-rushing seawater assisted the effectiveness of the implosion. One limpet would blow a hole in the side of a ship large enough for a car to pass through.

FOLBOAT

Available in two and three man models, the ingenious canoes could be folded. Pre-war, manufactured as sporting craft by the Folboat Company of England, they were widely used during WW2. When fitted with mast step, bermuda rigged sails, rudder and dagger board they could be sailed, or motored with rudder plus a well fitted in the after deck to take the British Anzani .5 hp outboard motor.

'Agas 1' used the two man model exclusively and they proved indispensable in Borneo where few roads existed between towns. At distance or first glance, they resembled native canoes under paddling, or when fitted with 'leg of mutton' sail.

Where an ultra small and light portable surface craft with a tremendous carrying capacity combining silent operation and manoeuvrer-ability was needed, the folboat admirably fulfilled the bill. Packed into two bags, one contained the rubberised heavy duty canvas skin and splash apron of the double ended canoe that was shaped like a kayak, and the second bag contained the numbered hull frame cane rods complete with joining ferrules, floorboard assembly, paddles etc.

At Frazer Island (FCS), we assembled folboats until we were blue in the face. Then the same exercise was carried out on a timber deck fixed to a large heavy rolled steel cylindrical tank – a miniature mock-up of a submarine section - anchored offshore at McKenzie's Landing on the island. It was finally washed ashore during a storm and was still visible on the beach when I last visited the island in the 1980s.

My third son Kam and his pal Jamie Hurst visited the island a month before the printing of this book and said that the abandoned rolled steel tank was still in one piece on the beach at McKenzie's Landing.

We knew we would be required to ride an American submarine even though we never knew the destination, and we knew that we had to rely on folboats to get ashore at the other end. Furthermore, we knew that the submarine would not attempt to land us in daylight and we were thankful for that. To make us proficient in assembling in the dark, our instructors had us assembling in the subdued light of the night sky and when proficient, blindfolded in a darkened room.

When it came to the nitty gritty, we were as anxious to get ashore and into the cover of the jungle as the submarine commander and crew were to get their boat off the surface, and towards this mutual end, both American submarine crews and operatives worked diligently.

Once having passed the folboats through the torpedo compartment hatches, we could assemble in minutes – two member folboat teams of 'Agas 1' had qualified to totally assemble in 10 minutes – while all our stores were brought up. By the time all stores were stacked on deck and checked off carefully, we had the folboats in the water alongside the pressure hull. When the final task of loading the boats was completed, the 'Z' men parted company with the submarine.

GAROTTE

Simply a length of extremely smooth and pliable wire with hand pull loops fitted each end. Available in two stock lengths, the professional models were made in 3mm wire and proved to be highly effective. While not as clean in operation, when made on the spur of the moment from whatever material was available at the time, they were equally effective.

Professionally made units guaranteed a silent and cleaner result.

'L' TABLETS

'L' for lethal and guaranteed to kill a person within thirty seconds.

24 hours before insertion behind Japanese lines, each party member was issued with two tablets. Roughly the size of a panadol tablet but twice as thick, the rubber encapsulated tablets were tucked or sewn into clothing seams or wherever accessible on the operatives body. It had to be readily accessible so that if captured alive by the Japanese and escape proved impossible, the operative could get to the tablet reasonably quickly.

The tablet could be retained in the mouth without harmful consequences and if accidentally swallowed it would simply pass through the human body and excreted. However, once the encapsulating rubber was bitten death followed, guaranteeing fast relief in preference to slow and painful torture short of death. The Japanese Kempei Tai and Sitjokisat were past masters in the art of positive persuasion to gain the information they sought, and provided death of the tortured victim did not beat them, the Japanese usually won out. When all persuasive methods failed, the samurai sword followed.

LIMPET MINE

A magnetic housing of about 15 inches long in the Imperial language, 10 inches wide and 4 deep, it was filled with plastic explosive (PE on the 'top secret' list during WW2).

A detonator crimped to the end of a length of cordtex buried within the plastic explosive was fired when a colour coded copper time pencil internally lined in glass that contained an acid was ruptured by finger pressure. In accordance with the colour code, once the internal glass capsule was broken by manual pressure applied by the limpeteer, the acid took a calculated time to erode a short cross-wire holding back a spring-loaded firing pin.

When activated, the pin fired the detonator attached to the cordtex primary charge that in turn boosted the explosive power of the PE in the first limpet that automatically fired the remaining two. It was impossible to detect individual explosions. The in-rushing seawater did the rest. The burning speed of the instantaneous cordtex primary charge was such that a gang – usually three limpets on an average Japanese freighter – would explode as one. It was impossible to differentiate between the first and last explosion of the gang.

On a stationary enemy ship of 1500 tons or more, the favoured practice was to apply to one side of the vessel three magnetic limpet mines about 40 to 50 feet apart according to the length and construction of the vessel. Some operatives preferred to apply the limpets on the side of a docked ship so when all three charges blew instantaneously, the ship keeled over, destroying the wharf and dockside buildings as well.

In the case of large orthodox or mid-ship tankers, charges were necessary on port and starboard sides. On the majority of tankers and other engine room aft vessels, it was preferable to apply a chain of two sets of three limpets to take out the after quarters both port and starboard, as well as the stern of the vessel which usually accounted for propellers and rudder.

Charges were normally prepared ashore, then placed in the folboat and transported to the target at night.

Most operatives experienced in limpet mining are agreed that the most dangerous part of the mission was the final few yards of the approach using single muffled paddles for silent operation.. Double-ended paddles were not favoured in the tropical regions. Experiments taught us that when one blade was in the air, the combination of reflected moonlight and bright phosphorescence of tropical water on the shining blade plus dripping water, was visible for some distance.

During Japan's victorious expansion through the South East Asian and Pacific areas, their ships were usually lit up by subdued deck lights for loading etc. Almost without fail, stray light surrounded the ship, through which the limpeteers in their folboat had to penetrate before reaching the side of the vessel.

Having reached the side of the ship, the folboat was drawn alongside the hull with the bow against the tide. The man in the bow applied a hand-held tool known as a magnetic 'holdfast' that held the folboat's bow firmly into the ship's side. The outgoing tide maintained the folboat's stern into the ship, allowing the stern man to lower the first of the three limpets underwater on the end of a rod with a hook on the end that matched a corresponding U on the limpet.

The magnetic limpet then 3 feet underwater was slowly eased on to the hull with a usually frightening characteristic resounding clang. No matter how much the stern man restrained the final inch or two as the limpet was sucked on to the hull, it was impossible to do quietly.

Those readers who served in warships or merchant ships will recall that clanging noises on ships are common and seldom arouse suspicion. Engine room noises, hammers dropped on deck during chipping operations, small boats banging into the ship's side – all daily occurrences. Re-assuring when heard from the lips of a demolition instructor in classroom, it was of little consolation to 'Z' men on the job.

When number one limpet was fixed, the folboat bow-man relaxed his hold on the side of the ship and the stern man exercising great care, paid out the coiled cordtex while the bow man allowed the folboat to drift astern to the next calculated position for number two limpet. This then would be fixed in the same manner as limpet one. The folboat would again be drifted astern where the procedure was repeated.

The last limpet fixed, a copper time pencil crimped on to the fuse end and waterproofed with a condom was activated manually by hand, crushing the inner glass capsule and allowing the acid to commence its work. It was then time for the limpeteers to haul their arses out of the area and put as much distance between themselves and the target before the three limpets joined as one by the instantaneous cordtex, exploded with an almighty bang. From memory, the slowest activating time-pencil was 8 hours delay.

While alongside the target, the folboat bow-man had to be certain of his grip on the hull. If he permitted the 'holdfast' to come away from the ship's side, the tide would sweep the folboat's bow out at right angle to the ship and the folboat, helpless with no way on, was a sitting duck to the watchmen and guards on duty aboard the target ship.

Those of us who went through the limpeteer's course at Frazer Island Queensland, Garden Island Western Australia or any other instructional venue, found the course to be very thorough. At Frazer Island we first practiced on an old railway engine. When thought proficient, we then practiced on the 'Maheno' a ship wrecked about 1936 on the north east coast of the island while under tow to Japan.

Satisfied that we were proficient, our Officer Commanding Frazer Island Commando School (FCS), the late Major Luke McGwynne – he hailed from Darlington, a hills resort outside Perth - summoned us one evening to his tent. Over a drink, he detailed 6 of us – 2 men per folboat equipped with ATR4 transmitters, emergency rations for four days, limpet mines etc for a raid. The plan required transporting us in the former Japanese pearling lugger 'Charm' (last heard of in the Geraldton crayfishing fleet about 1980) and released 5 miles off the mouth of the

Mary River, Hervey Bay Queensland after dark.

We were to infiltrate the river mouth protected on both banks by Voluntary Defence Corps (VDC) personnel armed with Vickers machine guns, paddle 19 miles up-stream to Walker's Shipbuilding Yards Maryborough. Australia's first River Class frigates HMAS Burdekin and Diamentina had been launched a week earlier by the Prime Minister of Australia and our orders were to limpet mine both ships.

One of our number Major George Leonard – a pre-war game warden in Burma - immediately said "do they know that we are coming Luke?" to which McGwynne, quick as a flash replied " of course not, you stupid bastard George. Will the bloody Japs know you're coming. If you can't do the job here in Australia, there's no f..... way you'll do it behind Jap lines. If you're seen you bastard, you will be bloody well shot!"

Tired and bored to death blowing up railway engines and wrecked ships we certainly were, but we hadn't expected to hear what we had just been told. It put an entirely different perspective on our training. What made it worse was the knowledge that our CO meant every word he said and we all knew that his every word made good sense. Not one pulled out of the exercise.

Due to a miscalculation in tides, instead of arriving about 2000 hours off Walkers Shipyards, Maryborough at slack water and before moonrise, we arrived after midnight with the full moon high in a cloudless sky and the tide fairly ripping out.

The plan of attack had to be revised, our party leader Captain Noel Robinson called the other two folboats in under a casuarina tree overhanging the river where a new approach was discussed; it no longer possible to attack the ships from the middle of the river. Instead, it was decided to approach both warships from under a long land-backed jetty on the bank of the river. The approach commenced.

Seemingly miles long, the folboats in line ahead – Robinson/Leonard, Bird/Robertson and Wong/Sue – were about 100 yards from the nearest frigate Diamentina when the word of caution was passed from the leading craft that a guard was approaching on the jetty overhead.

All three boats held on to the nearest pylon, keeping the bows of our craft into the surging tide to lessen the noise of the outgoing water contacting the folboats beam on. The approaching footsteps overhead stopped abruptly above boat number 2 – our RAAF Scotsmen Flying

Officer 'Dickie' Bird and Pilot Officer Jamie 'Robbie' Robertson.

Instead of hearing a rifle shot or the bark of a sub machine gun as we expected, the sound of trickling water came as a surprise. 'Dickie' Bird the bow paddler wore a beret as all of us did which protected his head from the unexpected overhead stream of warm piddle. Unfortunately, his typical RAF handlebar moustache copped the lot. Afraid to move his head lest he created a change of sound in the accurately directed stream through the jetty above, he had to grin and bear the ordeal. What a co-incidence! His partner Jamie Robertson later claimed that 'Dickie' Bird was impossible to live with for the next day or two as 'Dickie' was really on the nose.

After the guard had passed and his footsteps were no longer audible, we carried on. As we drew level with HMAS Diamentina, word was passed back from the two folboats ahead wishing us the best of luck, then they were lost in the darkness as they approached HMAS Burdekin tied further upstream.

My RAAF pilot cousin Peter Wong and I fixed six limpets – filled with kindergarten moulding plasticine instead of PE, otherwise the limpets were correctly assembled and to all intents and purposes, 'ridgy dig'. In our folboat Peter was bowman and attended to the holdfast duties while I attached the limpets. The two sets of three, one set portside and the other starboard that almost reached the stern, together would have taken out the engine room of Diamentina, sunk her and possibly destroyed the section of the wharf to which she was tied.

The two Scotsmen, RAAF Officers 'Dickie' Bird and 'Robbie' Robertson fixed 6 limpets to HMAS Burdekin.

The crew of the remaining folboat – army Officers Noel Robertson and George Leonard AIF - using climbing equipment, boarded Burdekin and placed large chalk crosses on gun emplacements, radio installations and last but not least, the Captain's cabin. All 3 folboats individually escaped undetected out of the river to Duck Island offshore where we radioed HQ Frazer Island and reported 'mission successfully completed' and other information.

This was the first of many Captain Sam Carey (Townsville) style practice raids carried out by 'Z' men on Maryborough. The English Navy Officer in Charge (NOIC) Maryborough when notified the next day by Luke McGwynne at FCS and invited to remove the limpets, was not amused. Navy guards supposedly on duty – AWL at the local dance

– forfeited pay and spent time in the brig as a result. The name of 'Z' in Maryborough stunk for many moons thereafter.

During my last visit to Frazer Island and Maryborough during the mid 1970s, I visited Walkers on a Sunday morning not expecting to see anyone there. Instead, a security guard answered my call and when he learned of my identity, insisted I wait while he called the assistant manager at his home who very enthusiastically came down and took me into the yards. I once again saw the jetty where we had technically sunk HMAS Diamentina and Burdekin, the first Australian built frigates

I can still vividly see the explosives instructor telling us in his very convincing words, "when behind enemy lines, remember that the safest place to hide is right under the enemy's nose, because, that's where he least expects to find you". For further interesting reading on limpeteering see 'The Heroes' by Ronald McKie and 'The Fishing Boat that went to War' by Lynette Silver.

THE ELIMINATOR

A small, short, menacing and ugly in appearance, cheap looking, big-punch packing, highly effective automatic pistol used in the extermination of the dispensable or no longer required character. It was not particularly effective for anything other than the quick disposal of an unwanted person. Both, in its 45 calibre fire-power and recoil, the Eliminator had no peer – it was almost as devastating to the user as the victim

Though scarcely used in the SWPA, I do believe they were used in the China, Burma, Italy and occupied France theatres. Whether they were used or not in the SWPA, there were quite a number of them about among the 'Z' operatives of the larger operations.

Favourite targets were the 'Judas' operators; those who swore allegiance to both sides and were paid by both. Greed alone was their downfall, irrespective of the rewards won.. The appaling and heartbreaking losses suffered on both sides as a result of a 'Judas' in the organisation - and they did exist – was positively frightening.

No effort was spared to find and eliminate a proven traitor! Every party whether big or small, could not continue to operate until the 'Judas' was run down and eliminated.

Attracted by the big money, the 'Judas' invariably finished up as a 'bad penny' and invited his or her own disposal. They were found in operations 'Python', 'Lizard', 'Semut', 'Agas', Robin', to name just a few. These parties operated in Borneo through to the Solomons. How many of the bad pennies were disposed of by the 'eliminator' – also called the 'liberator' and many other names in the European and American theatres - I do not know.

I understand that a collector of firearms in USA has a comprehensive collection of 'eliminators' from WW2 and Korea donated by 'incognito' agents and commandos. I don't think I would care either, to be identified with the disposal of a man or woman who had been blown away with a 'liberator'/'eliminator'. In the case of a woman, even less; although I guess it would be a case of 'he/she who does the work gets the pay', which saying gives thought to 'money-hungry' people and the obvious rejoinder 'you can't take your money with you'.

Wrong! You can in fact physically take it with you but it's bloody hard to spend! Obviously in warfare, the 'Judas' does not think of that.

Special note: For the benefit of the 'Doubting Thomas' reader confined to tunnel vision thinking, who thinks that members of 'Z', 'M'(coastwatchers),'AIB', 'MI5', 'Force 136', and other such sister units were playing at 007s, here's an interesting thought on which to ponder.

After hostilities were over, at least two 'eliminator' pistols were found at the former 'Z' base Careening Bay Garden Island Western Australia. Concealed or buried after having been wrapped in oil proof silk cloth for protection, these obviously had been the property of two 'Z' men. Whether they were operative or base shiny bums, whether they were used; we will never now ascertain, but obviously the eliminators

Garden Island 'Z' Nissan type hanger for storing Welman Midget Submarines - Sleeping Beauties.

were forgotten when the war ended.

The one - man submarine training base on the island was wound down and eventually closed after the end of WW2. The buildings were auctioned off to the West Australian community for removal or use as weekend cottages and this was when the 'eliminators' were dug up.

Garden Island is a holiday paradise. Its breath arresting sunrises and sunsets, superb white sandy beaches, good surfing and swimming beaches, excellent fishing both from boat or shore and its free (snorkel) and scuba diving in the island's crystal clear bays makes it any red blooded person's holiday dream. Endless delightful walk trails meander through pine and ti-tree groves and sandhills, in which a variety of mammals and bird-life abounds. Today, the Navy's jurisdiction of the island precludes private homes, camping etc and therefore there is no night entertainment which is instrumental in retaining the pristine charm of the island.

When the Royal Australian Navy took over the island in 1972, a two mile long causeway was constructed connecting the southern point of the approximately 8 mile long island to Point Peron on the mainland. This was done with the minimum amount of disturbance to the underwater environment. The depletion of seagrass in Cockburn Sound had been for some time and is still, a source of concern to the environmental authorities.

The historical landmarks and features connected with the landings and exploratory expeditions of the early Dutch, French and British seamen and sailing ships, have been carefully preserved. Visiting groups are permitted to visit the island on certain days by arrangement with the Navy authorities at HMAS Stirling on the island.

While most of the northern section of the island and specific historical venues is open to the boating public, the Navy cares for the whole island and commendably rules it in such a way that history, fauna and flora is protected. The environmental care must please the 'greenies'. HMAS Stirling, Australia's Fleet Base West has proved to be – at least in my opinion – a bonus to Western Australia.

At this point I must add that the 'Z' memorial in Western Australia is situated on a hill overlooking Careening Bay and Cockburn Sound in which waters, our Welman submarines (one and two man), Welman freighters (4 man) and folboats trained during WW2. It is within sight of the guardhouse and main gate of HMAS Stirling.

The base cares for and maintains the memorial and the lovely landscaping of the precincts, and continues to do so today. Flags are raised to the mastheads of the flagpoles daily and the senior sailors' mess has always been our hosts on the one day of the year that we visit the island. Annual wreath laying services to commemorate Remembrance Day 11th November have been conducted since the unique memorial was unveiled in 1952 by the two 'Z' Associations that exist in Western Australia.

It is of further interest to note that numerous bodies – some Asian and never identified - were unearthed there when the base was under construction during the early 70s. The latest remains were located during the last five years when base extensions were in progress. Details of the news story appeared in 'the West Australian' and The Navy News. A Japanese Tiger Marine's helmet was also found on a remote part of the island after a bush fire had gone through. The Sound Telegraph 12/04/1989 featured a front-page story and a pic of Conservation and Land Management Park Ranger Wayne Taylor with the helmet.

Z's top security base in 1944/45 was situated in Careening Bay on the sheltered east coast of the island where the 23 man operation 'Rimau' trained, and from where serious breaches of security occurred that resulted in the loss of all 23 operatives. When HM submarine Porpoise sailed, the training of one man subs ('sleeping beauties') to attack Singapore and the highly confidential subsequent departure of Porpoise were topics commonly discussed in mainland hotel bars at Rockingham and Fremantle. It left a lot of room for thought and conjecture.

Tunnel view readers – even one or two 'Z' operatives residing in Perth today – find it difficult to accept such stories, but the fact is undeniable. Then again, it takes all types to make a world and possibly those same people still believe that the televised first landing on the moon was a mock-up done in a Hollywood studio.

On behalf of a surviving Perth 'Z' man whose name cannot be divulged, an eliminator pistol was presented by my late 'Z' pal Keith Scarff and myself some years ago to Arch and Gloria James, co-owners of the historic 'House On The Hill' (THOTH) Cairns.

Mysteriously burnt down after the ownership changed hands, the historically rich national heritage home – it was the boyhood home of Australia's famous pioneering aviator Sir Charles Kingsford-Smith before it ultimately became Z's advanced training base 1943/45 ('Z'

Experimental Station) – housed in its museum for some years, the 'eliminator' and a silenced 'welrod'.

Before or during the fire, both weapons mysteriously disappeared and today, it is still uncertain whether they were ever recovered by the Queensland police. For the sake of posterity, the missing 'eliminator' pistol unfortunately became involved in a different story and rumour has it today in the possession of a certain person, and only time may finally reveal its whereabouts. The whereabouts of the Welrod is anybody's guess.

WELROD
(Top Secret)

A 32 calibre silenced pistol approximately 12 inches long and 1.5 inches in diameter. At first glance one could be excused for thinking that it was a piece of heavy duty rubber hydraulic hose with a tiny pistol grip and mini firing mechanism on one end.

I do not remember the official weight of the weapon but it was much heavier in comparison with other pistols we used such as Smith and Weston 38 revolver, Luger 9mm, Browning 9mm, Nambu 7mm and 45 colt. Most of the weight was contained in the silencer. Trying to remember the exact dimensions and weights of top secret weapons after 50 years is not easy.

When the Welrod was issued to me, I managed to locate a pouch that could be worn strapped to my inner leg and within the leg of my green

Welrod

American jungle overalls. When we left the US Submarine Tuna, all 7 'Agas 1' members, carried Welrods, plus a revolver or automatic pistol of personal choice. We each had a few grenades and a 9mm silenced Austen sub-machine gun that proved useless for extended jungle operations. The Austens were exchanged later when Owens became available and that turned out to be a very wise choice.

I distinctly remember that the Welrod was deadly in aim. I recall that the trigger action made a barely audible click that sounded like the breaking of a match and so unlike the Hollywood silenced pistols of today with their characteristic 'phut' sound of recoiling gases. Again, unlike the Hollywood model's characteristic jerk of the wrist recoil, one was unable to detect in the Welrod any report as it was fired, or any recoil on the wrist to suggest that a round had been fired or that the projectile had left the silenced barrel.

Having fired the first round from the Welrod at the firing range on Frazer Island where I first tested it, I simply had to apply the 'safety catch' and walk up to inspect the dummy target man. To say that I was speechless when I found the bullet hole in the dummy man is an understatement. The natural accuracy and silent operation astounded me. It immediately set me to thinking about the criminal potential of the weapon. Perhaps there are connotations to the stolen Welrod from THOTH at Cairns.

The only entry on the debit side that I could find was the fact that the magazine only held five rounds. However, after some thought on the

Submerged Welman 'Sleeping Beauty' in Careening Bay, Garden Island

matter I settled for the fact that it was not a combat weapon but a silenced eliminating weapon and as such, an agent would have to be in a worse than desperate situation if more than five rounds were required.

PLASTIC EXPLOSIVE (PE)
(Top Secret)

The latest in explosives, it was developed shortly after WW2 began. Perfectly safe to handle, it did not create headaches to the demolition user as was the case with gelignite. It would not explode without a primary charge such as a detonator, even if accidentally dropped into a fire. The explosive force was much higher than an equal quantity of gelignite or dynamite. Unlike these two explosives, 'PE' was not expected to deteriorate and become unstable.

When exploded by a standard detonator and combined with another newly released product named cordtex (instantaneous fuse which like 'PE' was top secret) the resulting explosion was far more devastating than any other known product during WW2. A quarter pound block of 'PE' detonated by cordtex and a standard fuse would cut through a New South Wales train line like butter. NSW train line was one of the heaviest in the country. Likewise, two strands of cordtex around a six inch diameter tree dropped it with ease.

WELMAN SUBMERSIBLE BOAT (SB)

Twelve foot three in length and about eighteen inches across the beam this amazing metal craft could and did operate to 60 feet in depth although this depth was not recommended.

Welman 'Sleeping Beauty' on surface under tow in Careening Bay, Garden Island

Known to the men who rode them as 'sleeping beauties' rather than the official designation of SB 'submersible boat', they were an incredible craft.

A 'Z' mate of mine living in Kalamunda Western Australia rode 'sleeping beauties' at Garden Island during the final 12 months of WW2; Bob 'blue' Wood a RANVR (Royal Australian Naval Volunteer Reserve) member and a volunteer to 'Z' is one of the luckiest men to be alive. 'Blue' it appears, lost control of a 'sleeping beauty' (SB) and this apparently was very easily done as the craft was still somewhat in its experimental stages and ordinarily would have been classified as experimental or for testing purposes only. However, the urgency of the day won out against safety.

Be as it may, 'Blue' commenced spiraling to Davey Jones' locker some

10 fathoms deep and apparently regained control just before he lost consciousness, sending the craft back towards the surface. He broached – laid on the surface with no headway – before being picked up by the instructor.

Fortunately, it was during training. Had it occurred during operations, 'Blue' would have been captured and met his maker via the samurai sword as was the fate of most 'Z' captives. Broaching in a submarine was feared by all submariners irrespective of whether the craft was a 300 foot long American submarine or a 12 foot long British 'sleeping beauty". Few submariners caught in that predicament lived to tell the tale.

Despite its problems, it was the most advanced and last craft of its type to appear in WW2 operational theatres. It far outperformed Italian chariots or any other similar craft produced by the Germans, Italians or Japanese during the closing 12 months of WW2.

CD Sury Worn by RN "Operative" of a "Sleeping Beauty"

39

Located rusting away in a marine dealers yard by the late Bill Escott, an English member of our 'Z' Association living in Dorset, he secured it and with the help of many experienced in that field, restored it to send to our association.

Bill was an MI5 man, a Royal Marine Sergeant who with his wife Shirley and young family was posted to Singapore following WW2. They spent 15 years there including the period of the Malayan jungle communist confrontation that led to Malaya's gaining of independence when the name of that nation changed to Malaysia. He spoke Malay and during his years there, became interested in operation 'Rimau' to the point of being haunted by his inability to put the jigsaw puzzle together. There were a few parts missing.

Bill was so obsessed with the whole operation - he was the first of a long line of writers to follow - he spent almost all weekends among the many islands of the Rhio Archipelago - now Indonesian territory - retracing the footsteps of the 23 'Z' men who disappeared mysteriously and whose disappearance was covered up by the Australian Government of the day after WW2. The Japanese remained silent and evasive on the matter.

Only a few years ago, others became interested in the subject and the trail became so hot, the Australian Government leaked limited details to silence the mouths of insistent relatives who craved the truth. Still, Japan remained silent, or the little that was said meant nothing, and some of it was decidedly a fabrication.

Sadly, Bill Escott died before his book could be published.

I suppose one could rightfully claim that the relatives of the 2,400 Australian POW of the Borneo Death Marches, were treated with the same indifference as the relatives of operation 'Rimau'.

My personal friend of many years standing – Mrs Roma Page of Canberra - lost two husbands, both 'Z' men, due to tragic circumstances.

Her first husband, Captain Bob Page AIF, and folboat partner Able Seaman Arthur Jones RAN, of Perth, were part of operation 'Jaywick' and both were highly decorated. Bob Page was later captured during operation 'Rimau', tried in a Japanese Military Court and was the first of the captured 10 survivors beheaded by Japanese samurai swordsmen at Bukit Timah Singapore July 7th 1945, 5 weeks before the surrender of the Japanese.

His lovely widow re-married after she met Dick Greenish, a folboat instructor at Frazer Island, Queensland. Dick, founder of the 'Z' Special Unit Association Canberra, was seriously injured in a bus roll-over in

Queensland after the war and died as a result of his extensive injuries.

After Bill Escott's death, his widow Shirley took possession of the 'SB' and the spare parts that Bill had hoarded, and finally donated the lot to our association in Perth and that's where our difficulties began.

Our association wrote to Australian airline Qantas hoping they might fly it out for the sake of posterity. Our request was refused. They were indifferent about flying the 'SB' out of Heathrow England, despite its historical value to Australia. They offered us 20% off the regular freight rate. Our association patron Sir Charles Court AK KCMG OBE former Premier of Western Australia took up the cudgels on our behalf and Qantas agreed to further reduce the charge to 50%. However, Sir Charles felt that the new quote added insult to injury. Qantas at the time was flying England/Australia with a seat occupancy of 22%.

Numerous other airlines were approached and most were willing to up-load it for us at no cost but all expressed the difficulty of overcoming the image cast by Qantas. Our old friends the US Army Air Force agreed to fly it out if we could get it from Heathrow to Frankfurt. Eventually, we were unofficially approached by Japan Airlines who offered to up-load the 'SB' at Heathrow and off-load it at Perth; an offer that proved too embarrassing to accept.

In desperation we finally wrote to Prime Minister Bob Hawke for assistance. With his blessings and the co-operation of the RAAF we had the 'SB' in Perth within 6 weeks after 6 years of frustrated attempts.

It is now on permanent loan to the Western Australian Army Museum, North Fremantle where it is on display with other 'Z' memorabilia.

With further assistance from the Western Australian Government and Australian Shipbuilding Industries, Cockburn Sound, two exact replicas were built from the original, one of which is on display at the Rockingham Historical Museum opposite Garden Island, the wartime home and training ground of the 'SB'.

The second 'SB' toured the schools of Western Australia during 1995, the 50th anniversary of the end of WW2. When no longer required for this purpose, arrangements have been made to place it on permanent display at Fremantle's Maritime Museum of Western Australia.

Chapter 5

SUE – A SPY FOR THE JAPANESE?

"During WW2 my parental home was listed with the Australian comforts fund as suitable for R&R of service personnel.

It was through this that I became acquainted with Jack Wong Sue. This would have been late '43 or early 1944. I was the same age as Jackie, being 18.

Jackie was as far as I knew or was concerned, a member of the RAAF, holding the rank I think of corporal or sergeant.

At that time I was a member of an Army amenities (civilian) concert party, playing piano accordion and stuck in a reserved occupation as an apprentice toolmaker.

I worked at Kingsford-Smith Engineering (Smithy's brother), and in those dark days we were told to keep our mouths shut about our work and other things we may have known.

Being in this concert party necessitated my transport home by taxi from Melbourne to 290 Whitehorse Rd. Blackburn in the early hours of the morning.

This, I think was the first time I wondered about this Chinese bloke (Jackie) and his RAAF credentials because, in the early hours one day, around 2am, in the headlights of the taxi – there being no street lights – the driver and I saw this figure jogging along the side of Whitehorse Rd. Blackburn, near my home.

I recognised the figure and said nothing, but re-call the taxi driver commenting "that bloke's keen".

Looking at only 4 hours sleep myself, I was quickly in bed but I believe I heard Jackie come in.

So, minding my own affairs, I was off to work later that morning and consequently thought little more about it, as my father, when I told him at breakfast, merely said he (Jackie) must have felt like a run.

I believe my parents were aware of his role at that time, but had no detail. Only much later did they tell me what little they knew.

My cousin Gwen MacKinlay and her mate Kath Gedye – who were both AWAS (Australian Womens Army Service) – decided Jackie was a Japanese spy due to his strange comings and goings. They therefore, due to these strange patterns, emptied his kit bag looking for proof. Needless to say, they found nothing. I don't know what else they may have done to check him out, but they lost interest.

However, Jackie (as we knew him) continued to come and go at all odd times, and then pop up when least expected. My mother called him a 'little rabbit' because of this.

Only at the end of hostilities did I learn that Jackie was, and had been a member of 'Z' force. A cairn with 'Z' force names, including 'Sergeant Wong Sue can be seen at Tidal River, Wilson's Promontory, Victoria, where commando training was practiced.

Over the years since then, I gradually learned of his wartime activities on behalf of Australia, as we have been distant, but firm friends ever since. Jackie in Western Australia and me in Victoria.

Jack Sue, *(left)* - aboard RAAF Crash Launch, Matilda Bay, Perth October 1943

I am now more aware of his dangerous, personal observation of the 'Borneo Death March' at close quarters, having just recently read a new book which covers all Australians as POWs.

The inhuman treatment of that group of POWs was so far removed from our western thinking, it was only from Jackie's observations as I understand it now, that this terrible treatment was verified, at that time.

I felt a remark in that book that Jackie 'could have wirelessed a report out', was very harsh on him.

After all he was just dressed as a native of Borneo, a local, and any sign that he was any other than that, I have no doubt, would have cost him his life, as was the fate of so many of those POWs.

As I understand it, Jackie's job was to go in, observe, get out alive, and report.

Now as I write this, I hope he can get out of hospital after many weary months of illness, and continue for many years yet, being proud of the fact he achieved what he did then, and has done so in other peace time activities since then."

(signed) Cliff Zerbe,
7 Gordon Avenue, Inverloch. Victoria. Jan. 98.

Melbourne was in one of its temperamental weather patterns as the Dakota transport approached the airfield. The flight from Brisbane had been uneventful and the flying weather had been perfect until nearing the Victorian capital city when it decided to sour and give us a hard time.

A flight lieutenant alongside me wore pilot's wings and I think must have been a close friend of the ATO (Air Transport Officer) in Brisbane where I had boarded the aircraft, as he was anxious to engage in conversation and was talkative during the flight. Most commissioned officers remained aloof from NCOs (Non Commissioned Officers) and ORs (other ranks) and only spoke when necessity demanded.

He was particularly interested in learning how the only NCO on the aircraft had managed to be flying on a priority 1 ticket while he was on a much lower rating of 9. He explained that he was behind me in the queue at Brisbane and spotted the priority number as I was being weighed in and also had been intrigued at the American hammock pack I carried. Those days, air travel priority numbers ran from 1 to 14 and the high priorities 1 to 3 usually were reserved for top commissioned officers. NCOs and ORs usually travelled on 10 to 14 , consequently 'Z' men travelling on high priority aircraft raised many an eyebrow.

In fact this was a common occurrence when we were travelling on aircraft or rail whether travelling alone or accompanied by Gort. On trains and particularly troop trains, a RAAF AC1 (aircraftsman) travelling with an Army Captain as Gort was then, and in the carriage set aside for officers only was a point of conversation throughout the carriage. However, when travelling with Gort, no questions were asked by superior officers of the Navy, Air Force or Army who were passengers on that train; security was so tight in those grim days.

At the Melbourne airport of Laverton, I discovered that my main gear contained in a RAAF sausage bag secured by a 'D' handle and lock was not on the aircraft. The ATO (Air Transport Officer) learned that it was still at our small staging camp in Urangan on the mainland opposite Frazer Island where I had just completed a jungle survival course.

This posed a bit of a problem as I had fully intended going to the Elizabeth St. Services Canteen for a night to get organised for a few days of leave. I was not regimentally dressed and my garb was American green jungle gear and a RAAF peaked cap as worn by RAAF marine section members. I remained a member of the RAAF for the duration of the war; the RAAF unwilling to transfer me to the Army just in case my services were required by the RAAF intelligence section. Gort told me later that I would have been promoted to a commissioned officer – probably Lieutenant – had the RAAF transferred me to the Army.

Feeling a little disappointed in the knowledge that my gearbag would be a day or two late, I wandered into a small Australian Comforts Fund hut in Collins St. and sat there observing other service men and women and wondering what I should do. An announcement came over the public address system inviting service folk to a weekend at a private home. Something within me said "go for it".

In response, I applied to the reception officer and was given a rail travel voucher to a place called Blackburn where my hosts, a Mr. and Mrs. Fred Zerbe would meet me at the station and take me to their home.

After a relatively fast train journey to Box Hill, the electric train was pulling in to Blackburn station when I peered out through the window to see if my hosts were there.

The station was almost deserted save for a very tall elderly gentleman and an elderly woman as short as he was tall. This was not surprising, but what was astounding was the number of young people with them, many of who were in uniform.

While the introductions were in progress, I became acutely aware of the body language given off by some of the folk of whom there had to be at least ten or twelve including two civilian girls about 17 or 18. The two were introduced to me as Gwenda MacKinlay and her girl friend Kath Gedye. One of the RAAF men, a Clarrie Hall from Perth I had previously met at dances conducted at the Railway Institute Perth, and we were destined to meet several times after the war was over when he was taxi driving back in the west.

The group of us walked back to the Zerbe home at 290 Whitehorse Rd, just a pleasant walk from the railway station. During the walk home I was very conscious of the stares from my newly met companions. I sensed the unasked questions of "what sort of outfit is this?" And "what sort of guy do we have here?"   Lace-up American green leech-proof jungle boots almost knee length, Yankee jungle green overalls with pockets galore and topped off with an RAAF khaki peaked cap!

In hindsight I suppose one could scarcely blame them for their thoughts yet not one uttered a word about my uniform or lack of uniform.

All three services were represented there. Naval ratings from HMAS Flinders, RAAF personnel 2a (air frame fitters), 2e (engine fitters) and WAAAFs (Womens Australian Auxiliary Air Force) all of whom were based at Ascot Vale and some Army men from various locations.

The week-ends activities of bush walking, walking around the Zerbe fruit orchard and community singing around the family piano accompanied by son Cliff Zerbe, an accomplished piano accordionist were very enjoyable and provided that touch of home that all WW2 servicemen and women came to miss.

None the less, I knew that my identifications were under query by most of the company there that Saturday night and Sunday. Much of the conversation and discussions that took place were based on their units activities and where they were expecting to be posted. My silence as to what unit I was a member of and matters pertaining to my duties did nought to improve the doubts in all minds. All in all, while a war was on one was supposed to act in a tight- lipped manner, so nothing was voiced.

All excepting myself returned to their respective bases that Sunday.

As I was officially on leave in between training courses – altho we were never issued with leave passes which at times proved to be an embarrassment, particularly when a 'Z' man was confronted by MPs (Military Police), SPs (Special Police- Air Force) or NPs (Naval Police).

I was invited to stay on with the Zerbe parents for an extra day or two, which I gratefully accepted. I had seven days leave before I had to report to our headquarters which was a large old home and formerly the Dutch Consulate situated in Acland st, opposite the Melbourne botanical gardens. The Zerbes made me very welcome and asked no questions. However, I shall never know if my identity was discussed between Fred and Gladys Zerbe those first few days of our acquaintance. Neither do I know what the servicemen and women staying there that weekend might have discussed with them.

I continued to come and go with no particular leave pattern. The Zerbes were like second parents to me and I respected and loved them dearly as though they were my very own. My Mum and Dad were not aware that I had joined 'Z' and believed I was with the RAAF in Rathmines, New South Wales doing a navigation course commensurate with my Air Force classification which officially was 'marine section, motor boat crew'.

The Zerbe family allocated a verandah room for my personal use in their large country style home and their acceptance of me – without questions – was highly valued. This happy situation persisted for close on 9 months but I fully expected that I would have to give an acceptable "please explain" one day.

Meanwhile, I was never aware that son Cliffs cousin Gwenda MacKinlay and Kath Gedye had been through my belongings in an endeavour to find out who I was and where I fitted into the war picture until I received Cliffs letter as per the commencement of this chapter.

Then it finally happened one cold wintery Sunday night. All the service folk staying for the weekend had left for their respective bases. Fred, Gladys and myself had just returned in the family car a Graham Page, from a service at the Blackburn Methodist Church where I read the bible lesson for the night and was guest speaker.

Cold, wet and miserable as it was outside, there was a glorious inviting open log fire burning in the lounge room and Gladys suggested that we three have hot chocolate and biscuits before going to bed. While sitting in front of that fire and sipping chocolate, the inevitable came.

To fully appreciate the situation one needs to understand that Mrs.Zerbe, although a smallish woman wore the pants in the family. Her husband Fred on the other hand, was an extremely tall man and, if anything, took a back seat in matters of family life and the household. He was very active in the family orchard and in the Fruit Growers Co-Operative of Blacburn and other bodies where he compensated for the back seat position he occupied in the home. The name of Zerbe was highly respected in the Templestowe/Blackburn areas.

Gladys broached the subject with the opening remark and it went something like this:-

"Jackie, you know that we are not the interfering type of people, and we have not asked any questions of you over the period you have been coming to our home. We love you dearly and the last thing we want is for you to misunderstand what we are about to say.

As you are possibly aware, the regular servicemen and women who regularly stay in our home over weekends have been discussing you since the first day you arrived.

They are somewhat suspect of you in many respects as a number of them believe that you may be engaged in some sort of activities detrimental to the war effort and to Australia.

Jack Sue 19 years old at the Mount Matha Agriculture Reaseach Station, acover name for ;Z; intelligence school

48

This afternoon, Eleanor is as you know, a member of the WAAF. With some of the others she went into your room while you were out and systematically went through your kit bag hoping to find your paybook, leave pass and any other documents to establish your identity, your unit and where you are based. Because they found nothing this has made them even more suspicious.

You come and go in strange ways, your dress is unorthodox and you never discuss your activities as the others do.

Fred and I cannot but help feel that there is an explanation to your strange behavioural patterns and while we do not need to know your activities, we will feel more comfortable if you can assure us that the others are wrong in their judgement.

Cliff said he saw you running along Whitehorse Rd, recently at about two o'clock in the morning as he was coming home in a taxi from a camp concert and could not understand why you would want to get out on the road at such an hour in freezing cold weather. He believes there is a good reason for your strange activities and we hope you can alleviate our concerns"

Unfortunately, there was little that I could tell them other than that I was engaged in activities of a security nature, pleading with them to trust me implicitly until at a later date I could explain further.

'Z' was going through a very difficult period at the time with parties being captured on landing at the various insertion points behind Japanese lines and security within the unit was on with a vengeance.

To the credit of the Zerbe clan, no further questions were ever asked of me and I do not know how the situation was handled by them when my name crept into conversations among the other service folk in the house. When I finally sailed from Australia on the American submarine 'Tuna', nobody – not even my own parents and family – knew.

In 1948 when my citation for the DCM (Distinguished Conduct Medal) was publicised throughout the Australian media, I received a congratulatory telegram from the Zerbe family that simply read "congratulations on your bravery award stop now we know and understand the truth you young rabbit".

Chapter 6

CLEAR THE BRIDGE!
"DIVE! DIVE!! DIVE!!!"

The United States Fleet class submarine Tuna (Captain Stephanides) cleared Darwin Harbour – or what remained of it - on January 16th 1945 after loading a motley crew of seven 'Z' men. We 'Z' men and our mysterious packages of waterproofed cans and sealed bags of what appeared to be secret stores, aroused the curiosity of those ashore and on Tuna. Anything to do with 'Z' was not intended for the eyes of the uninitiated, or the enemy agents known to inhabit the northern frontiers of Australia.

Escorted by the USS cruiser Chanticleer, Tuna was chaperoned to safe depths well out to sea; anything less than 40 fathoms unwelcomed. The cruisers signal lamp flashed out 'good hunting' and the two vessels parted company; Tuna for British North Borneo (BNB) and Chanticleer for her home-port Darwin.

My diary entry for the day made interesting reading:-

"Weather good and calm. It's a real novelty to travel on a submarine. Made three 'trim dives' this morning to test diving control. Submerging in a submarine is a strange sensation. Dives were to 180 feet and the submarine was deathly silent and still while submerged. God knows what we would have done had the so-called 'trim dives' failed and we were unable to re-surface – it had never occurred to me".

Post-war records revealed that lurking Japanese submarines and German U boats at that time, were more interested in allied commercial shipping that circumnavigated 'down under' than submarines. Unless presented with 'certainty kills', Japanese submarines both the 'RO' class and larger ocean going float plane equipped 'I' Class, preferred to prey on the easy targets in their combined efforts to strangle Australia, by denying Aussie the overseas and coastal supplies of essential war commodities.

Isolation of Australia by German U boats, Japanese submarines and axis surface raiders, had both American and Australian 'big brass' worried following the fall of Pearl Harbour. How and why surface raiders both German and Japanese, plus U boats and Japanese submarines, failed to totally dominate the Pacific and Indian ocean theatres, will remain forever anybody's guess. Some 210 allied ships were sunk in the Indian Ocean in a 9 month period during those desperate years following Pearl Harbour, the fiasco of Singapore and Japan's lightning strike and expansion through the Dutch East Indies (now Indonesia).

Prior to enlisting with the RAAF Marine Section (air sea rescue), the RAN refused to enlist me because my father was born in China, despite the fact that I was born in Aussie. My work-mate at Attwood Motors Perth, Bruce Inder-Smith and I served nine months in the Norwegian Merchant Navy, enlisting at the age of 16.

A thoughtless woman near my parents' home who had two sons in the fighting services, posted me a white feather – a sign of cowardice - that incensed me no end; I told Bruce of my intentions and that influenced his decision to join me. At that age I looked older than my actual years.

We signed on as crew aboard the Norwegian aircraft octane tanker Marina – the second largest at the time and a new ship on its second voyage - and served in the Indian Ocean theatre and near Middle-East from December 1942 to August 1943. During that time we carried cargoes of octane from Abadan in the Persian Gulf to South Africa, Portuguese East Africa (now Mozambique), India and finally back to Australia.

Both loaded and unloaded, Marinas cargo of aircraft octane virtually labelled her as an explosive bomb. Even when empty, the gas within the holding tanks branded her as a floating bomb until totally flushed – which took days - lifeboats were useless. As parachutes were far more appropriate, we necessarily had nine months of constant tension at sea. German and Japanese submarines in the Indian Ocean had been ordered to seek and sink allied tankers, these being their priority targets.

Of the seven 'Z' men aboard Tuna, only two were experienced submariners.

Our party leader, Major Gort Chester and Lieutenant Fred Olsen had landed on the east coast of Borneo by U.S. submarine during the middle of 1943, south of the notorious Sandakan POW camp.

The most advanced 'Z' party operating behind Japanese lines at that juncture, Gort's 'Python 1' and 'Python 2' parties were probably the bravest of the brave. At that time the Japanese were at their dizziest heights of success; their agents in Borneo pre-war had convinced the native population that a new era was on the way. That was to be The Greater East- Asia Co-Prosperity Sphere that would free the chains that bound the exploited Asian races to Britain, America and the Dutch nations. The 'Python' parties were nine months ahead of their time. The indigenous populations were still waiting for the wonderful prosperity promised them by the 'sons of heaven' that finally failed to eventuate.

Operation 'Python' was on the back foot from the very outset. With only the limited support of the Chinese population who the Japanese ensured were completely neutralised from the very first day of Japanese occupation of BNB, the party was lucky to survive.

Forever on the run, three 'Pythons' were eventually captured by the 'sons of heaven', tortured and finally beheaded by samurai sword. Unsuccessful attempts were made by US submarines to extract the rest of the party.

Eventually one submarine, one of America's most famous submarines of WW2 - USS Harder - evacuated them during which she suffered the most horrific concentrated pattern depth charging attack, but succeeded in returning them to Australia.

On a later wolf pack patrol, Harder was sunk with all hands outside the Truk Island lagoon. She was valiantly protecting a member of the same wolf pack by interposing herself between the disabled submarine and an attacking Japanese destroyer. To make it even worse, a Nipponese Rufus floatplane joined in for the final kill. The US submarine fleet heard with disbelieving ears the last moments of Harder, who had sacrificed herself while protecting her sister American submarine that survived to fight another day.

Those submariners and 'Z' men were the toughest of tough nuts. Our operation 'Agas 1' was a piece of cake in comparison.

The day after departing Darwin my diary entry read:- "At 1400 a

USS Tuna (SS - 203)

periscope was sighted astern off the port quarter where one shouldn't be. It is thought to be Japanese as we are travelling alone now since saying goodbye to Chanticleer. Course was immediately changed and 'battle stations' was sounded throughout the ship. Tuna submerged for two hours to elude the Japanese submarine. Surfaced approx 1750 and continued on the surface heading towards Timor".

The following day's diary entry read "struck fairly rough seas today. Expect to ..." and there the diary entry abruptly ceased. From memory, one of Tuna's Junior Officers suggested to me that it might be extremely dangerous to take the diary ashore should I be captured. Even though I had no intention of doing so, it was finally returned by Tuna along with my other personal possessions and uniform to 'Z' stores quartermaster at Batman Avenue Melbourne for safe- keeping until my return to Australia.

The journey nor- west towards the Dutch-East-Indies was uneventful. By day Tuna cruised along on the surface of the oily smooth tropical sea, the monotony broken only by flying gurnards taking off ahead of the submarine and landing in the water further ahead, plus pods of dolphins and the occasional game fish leaping out of the water.

Surface speed was reduced so that Tuna would arrive at Lombok Strait at the appropriate time to make the passage through the strait in darkness and with the current running northerly to drive us through. There always was a strong north or south current in the strait - usually about 10 knots - and a slow moving craft incapable of a better speed could actually go astern trying to negotiate the short passage.

Our 'Z' force 78 foot Krait (6.5 knots) - former Japanese fishing boat Kofuku Maru - carrying the 14 members of operation 'Jaywick' was a typical case when they attempted to penetrate Lombok Strait en-route to attack Keppel Harbour Singapore September 1943. They found themselves going astern for some time, and the ship's log entry showed that they passed the same landmark several times until the current slackened off.

To make matters worse, the 'binatangs' (Malay word meaning animals and used to describe the Japanese troops) had destroyers and heavy gun batteries on the Lombok Island side of the strait. These were to prevent allied warships and submarines transiting from the Indian Ocean to the Japanese territorial waters of the Java Sea.

The following afternoon in smooth surface conditions, Tuna's watchmen on the bridge reported the sighting of two land features ahead that marked the strait entrance. Standing out like sentinels guarding the Lombok Strait, Gunung [Malay for mountain] Agung (Malay for King or great) stood off to port on Bali Island while Gunung Rinjani (a Malay Queen) on Lombok Island stood off to starboard, allowing the narrow treacherous strait to flow between.

Both mountains were actually volcanoes. Rinjani was totally extinct but Agung had been known to erupt occasionally during the 20th century. Mt. Kinabalu in British North Borneo is the highest mountain in south-east-Asia at 13,450 feet and the two Indonesian monoliths of Agung and Rinjani rank not far behind.

Tuna remained on the surface cruising at reduced speed for a further hour or two. I was permitted to go onto the bridge to enjoy the late afternoon sunshine where I admired the two mountains from afar, both bathed in brilliant sunshine, although at sea level we were about to enter the twilight zone.

After about half an hour on the bridge we were all ordered below decks. Tuna submerged to approach the entrance to the strait. As we drew nearer to the Gunungs, a careful periscope reconnaissance was made by the Captain and duty executive officer as Japanese destroyers were always in the narrow strait to trap unwary allied submarines and surface warships endeavouring to get through.

While on the bridge I was amazed to see butterflies flying across the submarines path and yet we were still some 10 to 15 miles off shore. Furthermore, they certainly were not headed for either Bali or Lombok, but appeared to be flying out to sea, although it was obvious, that they must have come from one of the islands.

Sea birds were plentiful also. They were mostly gulls and gannets but, quite a few colourful tropic or bosun birds hovered above Tuna squawking their approval or disapproval. According to the Yankee crew the bosun birds were always in the Bali/Lombok area. About the size of the silver gull, they were easy to distinguish by the twin feathers trailing from the tail, and the addition of pink/red plumage on the white body. The perching of a Bosun bird on a ship during WW2 was considered an ill omen by seamen..

The Japanese were well aware that the only entrances to the Java Sea from the Indian ocean were Lombok Strait and Sunda Strait, the latter being the fatal escape route taken by the cruisers USS Houston, HMAS Perth and accompanying destroyers, American and Dutch. After the inglorious defeat of Singapore, the remnants of the allied fleet ran the gauntlet of the Japanese Navy and Air Force, in its dash through the Sunda Strait to the freedom of the Indian Ocean and Australia.

The Allied fleet was almost through the strait when it ran into a vastly superior Japanese armada, and in the ensuing night action, the total allied fleet was sunk.

Having entered the passage under cover of darkness, Tuna surfaced and made a dash through the Lombok Strait with the following current. In this manner, she was able to make better than thirty knots on the surface while re-charging her batteries. Japanese patrol boats and destroyers were known to regularly patrol those waters but no difficulty was experienced, and by daylight, our sturdy submarine was well clear of the strait.

Following our transit from the Indian Ocean to the Japanese controlled waters of the Java Sea, the next day was a typical tropical ocean surface. There was no wind, the sea was like a piece of glass, the sky was cloudless, and surface fish were everywhere. Furthermore Tuna was cruising along on the surface with about ten of her crew on the bridge. Nothing could have been further from the hostile atmosphere of warfare.

Likewise, the atmosphere among the officers and crew on Tuna was akin to nature. It was unbelievable that there was a war on and that we were behind Japanese lines. I certainly could not believe what my eyes witnessed or what I was hearing on the bridge that morning.

One of the officers on the bridge was speaking into a microphone, and I assumed that he was conducting a conversation with someone aboard Tuna in the control room or elsewhere on the ship, but that was not the case. The subject of the conversation was a good-looking 'gal' back in Perth and her address was in the process of being communicated, plus, she was getting the best possible reference. Tell her "Hank sent me" and give her my love.

Imagine my surprise when I passed a jocular remark about 'the broad' to one of the motormen standing alongside me - Jimmie Hellisen. He immediately laughed and said that the address was being passed on to another submarine in a wolf pack returning to Fremantle after a successful patrol of Siamese waters! They believed in looking after the interests of their shipmates!

I immediately gazed around me but could see no other submarine and I was then told that the recipient of the 'gals' delightful measurements was over the horizon. Furthermore, I learned that American submarines used the Java Sea with almost complete immunity as their crews used St. Georges Terrace -Perth's main street - when on furlough. One had to admire these cool Yank submariners.

A day or two later, I had cause to think again. I still did not doubt the bravery of the Americans but I did think that foolhardiness nearly cost us the boat and the crew, including Mrs. Sue's little boy.

Tuna was running on the mirrored surface of the Java Sea again. She had made one or two 'trim dives' only. Suddenly, smoke was spotted on the horizon and the boat increased speed to overtake the coal burning Japanese smoke-belching freighter.

As we drew within about seven miles of the enemy ship – estimated tonnage of 5,000 - she began to belch even more smoke, and it was obvious that her watchmen had spotted Tuna on the surface, rapidly overhauling them. The engine room stokers were pouring on fuel to get an extra few knots out of the old girl, and I imagined that the Japanese crew could almost see 'Davey Jones' Locker beckoning them.

Batavia – Jakarta today – was within sight on the horizon and the old freighter was hell bent in getting to the safety of the harbour before the American submarine closed within torpedo range. If Tuna could run the 'sons of heaven' down before entering the harbour, Tuna was certain to dispatch the freighter to Davey Jones Locker under such ideal conditions, but this was not to be.

Tuna's delightful full-throated diesel engines thrust her through the water at top speed. Meanwhile, a number of us were standing on the bridge watching the race as we would have watched a horse race. The old freighter belching black smoke like hell from the stack, had about 5 miles to go to safety when out of the sun directly above – it was about noon – screamed a Japanese Rufus floatplane.

Deliberately coming out of the sun, it had escaped the close attention of the watchmen on the bridge, and somehow, the radar men below in the control room. Urgent orders from the bridge mingled with the frightening urgency of diving klaxons as they sounded throughout the boat. Urgency was the keynote of the orders. "Clear the bridge! Dive! Dive!! Dive!!! Take her down "!

There was no mistaking the urgency of those orders from the bridge and conning tower. Klaxons echoed and re-echoed their terrifying sounds throughout the steel hull of the submarine as Tuna suddenly crash-dived in the all too shallow waters of the Java Sea in her endeavour to escape the Japanese float plane.

The order had barely died away before bodies scrambled through the conning tower from the bridge. The last man down slammed and sealed the conning tower hatch as Tuna crash-dived. This man was the stern gunner who had the longest distance to run, and it was an accepted fact among submariners that stern gunners had on odd occasions not made the conning tower in time, resulting in the submarine crash diving without them. Better to lose one or two men rather than the boat and crew of 90 or more men.

Before Tuna was more than a few feet below the surface, two horrifying explosions occurred a few seconds apart. Fortunately they failed to blow us back to the surface. Had this occurred, the boat with no way on - forward movement - would have been a sitting duck for Rufus. This very scary situation spelled the death knell for many a submarine in WW2 both allied and Axis. Seemingly, the explosions were towards the stern of Tuna, one off the port and one off the starboard quarter. Believe me, a submarine is my last choice when being attacked at sea. At least when on the surface, one can see what is going on and use one's judgement to take evasive action. Whether this judgement is correct or otherwise, remains in the lap of the gods.

And yet, submariners have a philosophy of their own; concealment, hide and seek. We were close to the Batavia coast and in shallow water. We were on the bottom and taking evasive action to get Rufus off our backs, but had there been deeper water we would have gone much deeper. The clear shallow waters of the Java Sea offered little protection.

The clearer the water, the easier it is for an aircraft to spot a large submerged submarine.

As Tuna went this way and that in search of deeper water, and yet put as much distance as possible between the sub and where she crash dived, what appeared to be cork dust ceased to fall from the roof of the submarines interior. However, the horrifying reverberations of the depth charges seemed endless. Depth charging in a submarine while submerged can be compared with being locked in a 44 gallon drum and someone lobbing a grenade close by. And yet, my good friend motorman Jimmie Hellisen turned and confidently said to me, "Jack, we're as safe as the Whitehouse down here".

Whether Jim's words were meant as comfort to me I will never know. With 140 feet of water above and a hard bottom immediately below Tuna, I felt as though I was in a steel coffin with no visible means of escape. Jim's next mouthful did little to further comfort me, if that was remotely possible.

"We submariners have our own philosophy Jack. We firmly believe that having got off the surface safely, they have to find us before they can sink us. When that 'son of a bitch' up there runs low on gas, the Nips will probably send out another aircraft to keep us down until dark when high speed anti submarine attack boats will come out to prevent us from surfacing to re-charge our batteries". I felt like saying to him "thanks Jim for nothing".

When we joined Tuna in Darwin, we four 'Z' men – all NCOs – were allocated bunks on top of torpedoes in the forward torpedo room during 'action stations' where we were instructed to remain lying or sitting on our bunks. It was not exactly what one would describe as comforting, knowing that one was lying on top of a lethal explosive charge.

From the time we sailed from Darwin, New-Zealand signaller Sergeant Vic Sharpe was violently seasick. He was never comfortable in Tuna and after the depth charge attack, he grew steadily worse and became a pitiful case of jaundice. In colour, he was more yellow than the atebrin tablets we took daily to build our immunity against malaria, when we eventually left the submarine for the swampy jungles of BNB.

My Malay mate, Sergeant Kanun Bin Garfu, a former hard hat pearl diver of Broome North Western Australia – a man obviously not scared easily - confided in me later that he sat on his bunk unable to move, even if he wanted to, and prayed quietly to Allah. He said in jest a little later

58

that he was unsure as to whether his legs had turned to jelly, or whether he was unable to move because of his soiled trousers! I must admit, I also had to check my own after the attack.

Sergeant signaller George Nash (AIF) a 'banana bender' (Queenslander), seemed unshaken after the attack but we knew very little about him as he was a last minute inclusion to 'Agas'. He replaced Kiwi signaller Staff Sergeant Graham Greenwood who was left in Darwin hospital suffering from acute food poisoning after we spent a night at the Broome Roebuck Hotel during our flight from Perth. The RAAF Dakota – twin engine but single toilet only - bore testimony to the violently disturbed stomachs of we 'Z' men plus its RAAF crew for the remainder of the flight to Darwin. On landing, the interior of the plane was bad enough, to say nought of the smell, accentuated by the tropical heat and had to be hosed out..

There were some interesting statistics about the depth charging that were explained to me later. The Japanese Rufus floatplane at 100 knots could cover the radius area bounded by the point of the crash dive to Tuna's maximum escape point in virtually minutes. Tuna was only capable of about 9 knots flat out submerged, and at that speed for only a limited length of time before her batteries needed re-charging. From memory, her submerged cruising speed was approximately 6.5 knots so that in 8 hours she could not be further away than about 90 miles, and that was dependent on the evasive measures taken. Rufus was able to cover the same distance in a fraction of the time.

That 'son of heaven' kept us submerged for the rest of the day and when the aircraft had to return to base, the patrol boats took over to prevent us from surfacing to re-charge batteries. However, they were unable to pin point our position and no further depth charging occurred. It appeared that the submariner's philosophy of "they've got to find us before they can sink us" had paid off.

As the air within the submarine had become quite fetid by mid afternoon with 90 or more sweating bodies in a confined space despite the 'no smoking' order, white chemical granules were scattered throughout Tuna to absorb the excess carbon dioxide.

When no further activity could be detected on the surface, Tuna cautiously rose to periscope depth. The order was given for "up periscope" and after a careful sweep around the night horizon that revealed no patrol boats, the executive officer gave the order to "blow bow buoyancy tanks". This was followed by the order "blow main ballast tanks" whereupon 'Tuna' headed for the surface, switched from electric propulsion to diesel and she was away to a flying start. Orders were issued to "open all hatches and ventilators" followed by "watchmen to the bridge" and with the submarine under way greedily recharging her spent batteries, all aboard gulped in the clean fresh air of the Java Sea.

Obviously the Japanese had alerted all aircraft and patrol boats in the vicinity to the presence of a submarine, for the following morning shortly after breakfast, the "action stations" order was again given and Tuna went deep. Then the order went throughout the submarine for "silent ship" which indicated that surface craft were searching for us on their echo sounding devices and strict silence had to be observed throughout the boat.

Resting on my bunk, I reflected on the previous day's events wondering what the hell I was doing in the Java Sea aboard a steel coffin when I could so easily have been back in the comfort of Australia. My sentimental frame of mind was not made any easier by the piped music that came from the radio shack via the intercom

The beautiful sound of Artie Shaws big band going through its paces of the delightful 'Frenesi' was most disturbing. And if that wasn't enough, it was followed by the haunting sound of Kay Kuyser's band in a heart rending sentimental version of the slow foxtrot 'Humpty Dumpty Heart'.

At a later stage, I checked with the radio shack and found 'HDH' was a Regal Zonophone recording. It was the exact replica of the record that the Edwards sisters - Joan, Pearl, Marjie, Gretta - and I danced to in the ballroom of the Marybrook Guest House at Sherbrooke in the Dandenong Ranges. 'HDH' was one of our favourites and one I still favour. It also became one of the favoured numbers of my late wife Pam.

Marybrook on the edge of the lyre-bird sanctuary of Sherbrooke Forest was managed by the late Alan and Pearl Edwards. Former Lake Eildon strawberry farmers, they were a lovely Victorian country couple who conducted the house in a homely atmosphere. They were like parents to me, as were the Zerbe family of Blackburn. An 18 years old 'Z' Force trainee, I was grateful that both families treated me like one of their own; a comforting feeling of 'home from home' I never forgot.

As I lay atop the torpedo musing in my sentimentality, Tuna was forced to submerge again. However, lady luck was with us thank the lord, and after a couple of hours, we surfaced and headed through the Karimata Strait and northwards up the west coast of Borneo, submerging only when necessary. Regular sightings occurred of all types of sailing craft from humble fishing prahus to junk like vessels used in the archipelago trade of the islands south of Singapore. Within another couple of days or maybe more, we would leave Tuna to land behind Japanese lines.

Our American friends of ten days had been wonderful hosts to us. Washing and ice cream machines, and many other forms of luxury that we had only heard of in Australia but had never seen, were to be discarded by us for the harshness of the Borneo jungles.

The executive officer Tom Gardener who married a West Australian girl from Claremont after WW2 and took her back to the States, said to me as he eyed off the enemy coastline through the periscope "Jack, why don't you stay aboard and come back to Australia with us? There are no friends ashore in this hostile territory" and I vividly re-call my answer as if it was yesterday and not 55 years ago. "Thanks Tom for all the hospitality and lovely attention we have received while aboard, but just put us ashore safely. Without wishing to sound ungrateful, I would prefer to take my chances in Tojo's territory than another depth charging". And there I rested my case.

Chapter 7

SUBMARINE INSERTION

Like a monster from the deep rearing its gigantic head out of the water, the American submarines bow broke the mirror calm surface of the Sulu Sea. Often referred to as the Celebes or Makassar Sea, tons of its phosphorescent water cascaded from the pressure hull and deck in the darkness and ran off harmlessly into the sea. Without losing any headway, she switched from electric propulsion to 'half ahead' on her powerful diesel engines and surged towards the eastern coastline of BNB barely visible in the gloom.

For more than two hours before nightfall, USS Tuna had been lying at periscope depth like a cat observing a mouse hole, waiting for the precise opportunity to pounce.

In relatively shallow water and within a mile or so of the beach, Captain Stephanides the commanding officer of Tuna and our commanding officer of operation 'Agas 1' Captain Gort Chester were studying, the shoreline and surrounding waters for signs of enemy activity through the periscope. At the same time, the radar men were intent on picking up any signs of enemy aircraft or surface craft. They didn't wish to be caught flat footed again as was the case on Tuna's previous patrol that day out from Batavia when chasing the Japanese freighter, hoping to get within torpedo range to sink her before she reached the safety of harbour only a few miles ahead.

With the last of daylight and satisfied that no enemy activity was present, Tuna retired into the deeper waters where she rested on the bottom to allow us to prepare our boats, supplies, weapons etc ready to pass through the deck hatches later that evening in readiness for landing.

The couple of hours were probably the shortest that I have ever experienced in my entire life.

Gort Chester and our signals officer Lieutenant Fred Olsen had been through this experience in 1943 during operation 'Python 1' further south on the same east coast where we proposed to land that night. It was 'old hat' to them. To the rest of us it was to be a new experience.

Captain Jock Sutcliffe, Lieutenant Don Harlem and myself while being old campaigners had never been in a clandestine landing from a submarine. Jock had seen battle experience in Malaya/Singapore, Don was a very experienced veteran from the Middle East and I had served in the Norwegian Merchant Navy in the Indian Ocean and near Middle East waters.

To the best of my knowledge, the remaining two of our number had not served in battle zones. Staff Sergeant Graham Greenwood and Sergeant 'Skeet' Hywood were highly trained signalers but this was to be the first occasion where they would possibly face real live bullets.

I was not conscious of a fear of dying, but I have to admit that a thousand and one thoughts passed through my mind during those couple of hours before Tuna surfaced under cover of night to land us. These included my boyhood days with my wonderful Mum and Dad, my brothers and sisters, my clan cousin Peter Wong who had resigned from 'Z' because his religious conscience would not permit him to do certain acts required of him. Perhaps Peters decision had been the correct one to make. Who could have known?

I had never been faced with anything like this before. Even joining the Merchant Navy in wartime with my pal Bruce Inder-Smith never brought forth such thoughts, and that was a momentous and a very responsible decision for any two sixteen year old boys to reach. But for some inexplicable reason, this seemed different. What was I doing here? My mind was like a bucket of worms.

Over-riding these numerous thoughts, one factor remained clear. The fact that I knew I was meant for this job and that nothing short of death would deter me from it.

I had faced the possibility of death many times in my life. I was mindful of the normal rigours that a youth faced in life, accidental death at school or on the roads etc; I always elected for excitement, and simply revealed in such activities as cross country bike-riding, sea scouting and diving, canoeing, yacht racing etc, that finally led to the Norwegian Merchant Navy.

My sea-scouting days were a perfect example. As a ten year old, I was always bound to boats, sailing them on the Swan River across to Garden Island (the future 'Z' Force one man submarine training base established late 1944) and wreck diving at Cottesloe. I had my first dive in a hard hat helmet (traditional pearl diving helmet of pre-war days) under instruction from scoutmaster Hal (Tinnie) McKail before my twelfth birthday at 1st. WA Sea Scout Troop headquarters based at Pelican Point, Crawley Bay near Perth.

While sitting on my bunk above the torpedo, various thoughts raced through my mind as I checked out my silenced Austen machine gun, ammunition, grenades, 'L' tablets and other personal effects ready for the night.

All the while, subdued sounds of the big American bands came through the near-by inter-comm from recordings played in Tuna's radio shack. When it was time to move, one of the last numbers I remember hearing as I made my way down towards the control room was my favourite 'Humpty Dumpty Heart' by Kay Kuyser's band:-

> "Don't mean to criticise or say I'm wise, but if
> you will just recall,
> You sat on a garden wall and you know, yes you
> know what happened,
> You'll still take a chance wont you, you still want
> romance don't you,
> I hope you're lucky, Humpty Dumpty Heart"

The music and lyrics are as fresh in my mind today as they were then when fleetingly, they took me back to Marybrook Guest House, Sherbrooke Forest, Victoria and I had to brush them from my mind as I hurried through the submarine to the control room.

Once all the gear was ready to go it was just a matter of waiting until sufficiently dark when Tuna would break surface, knowing her low silhouette was safe from detection and that she could charge her batteries under cover of darkness. She had been submerged all that day and needed to top up her exhausted batteries as she headed inshore to drop us off.

I had developed friendships with a number of the American crew over the two special missions we had been aboard Tuna, and during that afternoon they passed remarks such as "Jack. Why do you want to leave us and go ashore into unfriendly territory? You've got friends aboard here, but when you get in to Japanese territory, buddy, you wont have a friend in the world. Stay aboard and go back to Fremantle with us".

They were probably right, but the inescapable fact remained. I had enjoyed the time spent on the submarines Bream and Tuna and the accompanying comforts of both boats, to say nothing of the wonderful hospitality extended to us by the American crews, but the possibility of taking another pasting under depth charging was never far from my thoughts. The long and the short of it remained; I preferred to take my chances ashore.

As we passed through the control room, the lights were dimmed to an eerie blue/green to prevent extraneous light from escaping through the conning tower hatch that might be detected by the enemy. The officers and watchmen of the watch, wore red goggles to acclimatise their eyes to the darkness before emerging through the conning tower into the darkness of the bridge and night. Strange noises came to my ears from the myriad of whirring mechanisms and instruments that only submariners understood. The combination of strange sounds and subdued lighting reminded me of space age movies when I was a lad. It truly presented a ghostly scene with an eerie atmosphere.

Yankee hands reached out from all directions grasping ours mid wishes of good luck as we prepared to climb the ladder to the conning tower and out on to the bridge. To this day, I feel sure that they half expected us to remain aboard Tuna and return to Fremantle with them. They were so sure that as they wished us well, they were nonetheless consigning us to a one way street that led to certain death.

In the back of my mind, the teachings of New Zealand Major Don Stott and Captain Peter Moyes in the classroom at Frazer Island rang loud and clear. "Check and double check" and "the safest place to hide is right under the noses of the enemy because he least expects to find you there". Ironically, after meeting him, party leader Don Stott and other members of operation 'Robin' were ambushed by the Japanese shortly after the American submarine inserted them off Balikpapan, Dutch East Borneo and all members were lost. Maybe they did not "check and double check".

In addition to the officers and the watchmen on the bridge, only a certain number of the crew was permitted below on the deck casing. They were instructed by the Captain to assist in the passing of our boats and other equipment up from the forward torpedo room, through the escape hatch to the deck of the submarine.

The night was perfect for our landing. The mirror calm waters were disturbed only by the phosphorous flashes of darting fish in the water as they shot off to port and starboard of Tuna's bow wave as they sought to avoid the oncoming hull. Cirrus clouds were in abundance as they scudded across the sky, periodically permitting the moon to shine through and illuminate patches of the ocean, otherwise shrouded in the darkness of the night.

While we worked quickly on deck, nocturnal sea birds gave vent to their mournful wailing as they wheeled and turned in their flight above Tuna. For some strange reason, the sounds of nocturnal sea birds are far more blood chilling than sea birds of the daylight.

Even today, this still seems to be the case. Mother Nature has not changed her ways. Mutton birds off the many islands of Western Australia's Abrolhos Archipelago, Curlews in the paddocks of Australia's vast agricultural areas, Mopokes and Owls on the coastal plains or the night sea birds of Borneo; all have one thing in common – their mournful tone.

While four of us assembled the two folboats, the other three unpacked the inflatable boat from its carry bag, inflated it and checked it for oars, rowlocks and other ancillary equipment in readiness for launching.

Within a few minutes of the submarine coming to a stop all three boats were afloat and tethered to Tuna.

Meanwhile, our canned stores, personal equipment, arms and ammunition to last us for three months were passed up through the submarines hatches and the loading of the boats commenced. The plan provided for all seven of us to ride in the 7 man inflatable with as many of the stores as it could safely carry plus our weapons, and to tow both folboats astern of the inflatable loaded choc-a-bloc with the balance of the stores.

Although his attitude showed no signs of impatience, Captain Stephanides understandably, was anxious to get us away so that Tuna could clear the areas of the shallows to seek deeper waters. The waters through which we were approaching the shoreline were barely 100 feet deep. If the 'binatangs' appeared, the submarine would have insufficient depth to submerge and take evasive action. Besides, there was no way that Tuna wanted to attract attention to the area in which they were about to insert us. Without doubt, her crew of almost 90 men would have shared his thoughts; a surfaced and motionless submarine is a vulnerable target.

With the able assistance of the Yankee crew, the loading was completed within minutes and we were aboard our 7 manner inflatable boat ready to 'shove off'.

Final calls of 'good luck guys' and handshakes were interrupted by several large bottles of Johnny Walker Black Label Scotch passed down to us by Captain Stephanides and other officers on the bridge. These were hurriedly stowed aboard the 7 manner or as in my case, thrust into the American flying jacket issued to me back in Australia.

The flying jackets, considered an absolute luxury by Australian troops who envied the quality of American issued equipment, were only one item of Yankee G.I. gear to which 'Z' had access. In addition to clothing, our unit was able to draw on any American equipment including weapons, jungle hammocks, jungle kit bags, food supplies etc. When we left the submarine, we were all clothed in American multi-pocketed

Jack Sue - Mock Submarine landing off Mount Martha Agriculture Research Station - cover name for Mount Martha Intelligence School. Seven man inflatable boat and stores.

jungle overalls, lace-up leech-proof commando jungle boots almost to the knees, gaiters, flying jackets plus numerous other items of equipment.

We wore no badges of rank or any other positive means of identification. In fact, we could so easily have been mistaken for American troops.

Once aboard the inflatable, the American deck crew passed the towlines of the folboats to us that in turn were made fast to the transom of the inflatable boat. Finally, after a brief last minute check, the bowline of the 7 manner was tossed from Tuna to Jock in the bow. We were free of the submarine – we were on our own.

As though impatient to get on with the job, the inflatable drifted quickly away from the side of Tuna. The two folboats almost automatically took up their stations astern as we watched the deck crew go onto the bridge and down the conning tower followed by most of the officers, leaving only the officers of the watch and watchmen on the bridge.

Drifting quickly apart, the last thing I remember identifying in the gloom was a pair of chequered black and white gingham shorts going through the conning tower that my particular friend on board Tuna, motorman Jimmy Hellisen was wearing that night. In short time Tuna was no more than a sinister silhouette in the dark and when safely clear of us, her powerful diesel engines moved into slow ahead so as to lessen the noise and avoid detection by the Japanese. Soon she was well out of sight when the dying throbs of her engines indicated that she was clearing out to sea.

Tuna had dropped us approximately seven miles out from the coast of BNB and slightly north east of Pura-Pura Island and we were alone in enemy territory. Our only contact with the outside world had disappeared and in its place there was nothing but the slowly settling wake of the submarine.

How different this departure was, compared to the last time we left Tuna to board Bream 100 miles out from the west coast of Borneo late at night and during a 'sumatra' (rain squall). On that occasion, the seven of us in the inflatable were half way between the two submarines when a Japanese plane passed overhead forcing both submarines to submerge. We were left alone like the proverbial Australian 'dunny' in the hellish rough South China Sea mid heavy rain. The feeling of emptiness as the waves closed over where Tuna had been resting is indescribable. The two submarines – our only friendly contact until minutes before, disappeared from sight as the unfriendly waters of the South China Sea filled the void that had been Tuna. Fortunately both submarines had us pin pointed on radar while submerged and when the Japanese plane had passed, Bream surfaced and took us aboard.

Wasting no time and anxious to get ashore and into the safety of the jungle, we prepared to take up the oars and head towards the coast. There was no time for past thoughts; our very lives depended on reality.

It was then discovered that while we were drifting clear of Tuna, an oar somehow had slipped overboard and drifted away in the darkness never to be recovered.

Taking up the remaining single oar and the folboat paddles – not meant for use with the inflatable - it fell to Graham and I in turn, to scull over the transom. We were the only two who could scull with the single oar. Assisted by the other five who shared the four folboat paddles, we headed for the shore. The combined efforts of the four muffled paddles plus the scull over the transom provided some propulsion and limited steerage. It was a case of 'half a loaf of bread better than no bread at all' but what else were we to do seven miles offshore in Japanese patrolled waters?

As we slowly approached the white beach clearly visible in the darkness, it became obvious that we had the benefit of the in-going tide. Very little effort was required to propel the inflatable. Instead, we were slowly but surely drawn towards and over the treacherous sandbanks across the entrance into the little river according to plan – or perhaps it was according to Hoyle! Four of us were later to learn more intimately about those treacherous sandbanks when we endeavoured to leave the river mouth for the open sea.

Crouched as low as possible to reduce our silhouettes, our silenced machine guns cocked at the 'ready' to fire, we expected a volley of rifle shots or the chatter of a machine gun from the beaches. Making no effort to steer the inflatable, our boat was silently and effortlessly drawn into the river's main channel as we slipped through the heads of the river. Surprised that neither headland of the river was guarded, we allowed the current to sweep us well inside the river before a word was spoken and then only in whispers.

Fortunately, other than losing an oar accidentally, getting ashore was incident free but it had taken more than five hours of back breaking hard paddling before safely entering the Sungei Tagahang Kechil, a tiny river that did not even appear on maps.

Obviously, God had beamed on us benevolently as we approached the treacherous entrance.

Further up the river and just prior to daybreak, we found what appeared to be a small tributary leading off the main river on the northern bank. On closer inspection of the barely discernible entrance of the stream, we found that it was screened off from the main body of water by overhanging jungle vines about 80 feet high, reminiscent of a giant curtain. When parted, it revealed a fair expanse of water beyond, affording perfect protection.

Physically tired out and mentally exhausted by our hours of constant vigil and nerves on edge, we gratefully parted the jungle creeper curtain and ventured further into the creek where we found a suitable landing spot. After concealing the boats, we took out some field rations and enjoyed the first bite since leaving Tuna followed by a swig of scotch. Graeme being the only abstainer, took to his Yankee water canteen.

It was too hot and muggy to sleep. Instead, we took what rest we could in the shade of the jungles trees before setting out to find a permanently dry camping spot high enough to guarantee it unaffected by high tides. The perfect permanent site needed to have trees suitable to suspend our American jungle hammocks, be reasonably free of mosquitoes, have a reliable fresh water source and a suitable site to set up the radio shack, transmitter and aerial.

It was imperative that we carry out a recce patrol at the earliest possible opportunity to satisfy ourselves that we were relatively 'alone' and that we were not doorstep guests of the 'sons of heaven'.

Folboat - As used by 'Z' Force Operatives

Chapter 8

'TUNA', MEN AND COOKING.

The intervening days between our arrival back at the 'mudflats' and our departure for our pre-arranged RV with Samak was a mixed bag of uncertainty, experimentation and argument.

Uncertainty, was a state of mind the four of us in the folboat team shared in common and would not be dispelled until our RV with Samak occurred. The days of worry in this matter hung heavily on us, not knowing the answer to the big question 'would Samak come alone or come accompanied by the Japanese?' The anticipation of what might be, made the time drag by, creating a feeling of uneasiness that was shared by the whole party.

Human weaknesses show up under stress, and the fact that we were behind enemy lines made little difference; if anything the danger factor probably exacerbated the situation. Looking back today on that worrying period of time, I have no doubt that it was a case of fear of the unknown.

The domestic duties around the camp area were generally carried out by Fred Olsen, Don Harlem and Skeet Hywood – two Lieutenants and a Sergeant – while the cooking duties were shared by Graham Greenwood and myself: Graham and I also doubled up as hairdresser's when required.

Following the settling in period of establishing the campsite at the 'mudflats' and acclimatising ourselves to the new environment, Graham and myself quickly realised that despite the copious quantities of food supplies there was little room for variety.

All our meat, eggs, vegetables and numerous other lines the average housewife regarded as fresh supplies were in our case, de-hydrated. This meant that all dehydrated items had to be soaked in water for varying times from half an hour to four hours. Graham and I who were the 'babbling brooks' (cooks) found this soaking procedure to be a real bloody pain in the neck.

Initially at the 'mudflats' we were somewhat short of freshwater– relying partly on rainwater we managed to drain off the ridge top covers of our brand new jungle hammocks, that tasted strongly of rubber at first, but perfectly drinkable. We were also short of dishes suitable for soaking dehydrated vegetables, meats, etc and other purposes.

Our shallow American army issue dixie's cum frying pans were ideally suited for general army camp life in civilised Australia, but months at a time in the jungle was an entirely different kettle of fish. Our food supplies represented three months of living in the jungle and presented a number of difficulties and inconveniences.

Despite the versatility of Graham and I, as our supplies were entirely dehydrated, minced beef, potatoes, carrots, parsnips, onions and powdered egg, all required special preparation before cooking. We soon learned that the American dixie's were too shallow for soaking dehydrated foods.

The dehydrated fare was very practical but left little room for variety. Those back at headquarters in Melbourne responsible for equipping parties going behind enemy lines were obviously sadly lacking in certain respects and in particular, imagination. A woman's hand there was urgently needed.

Eventually, we found a small jungle soak that proved sufficient for our immediate water needs when sterilised. Even when augmented with rainwater, it was not long before we realised that a more reliable source had to be found before the real dry season set in. We often joked about the huge fortune awaiting the person who could invent water tablets – provide water without having to soak them in water initially!

The deeper Australian issue mess kits would have been more practical for soaking purposes and while having certain advantages over the American mess kit, lacked in other ways. Generally speaking, the Yankee dixie was more versatile, better in design, lighter in weight and was easily packed into our jungle hammock back packs. At least, this was my opinion and I believe that most of our crew shared my thoughts on this matter.

Our popular party leader Gort Chester realised the difficulties the cooks operated under and set a fine example by his thoughtful actions and was never beyond bogging in to assist where possible; even to the extent of scrubbing and scraping burnt cooking vessels. He, being our party leader and a Major, he outranked us all and therefore, if anyone was to be excused from these humble and mundane duties, it should have been Gort. He carried an enormous responsibility on his shoulders and his mind at all times was overloaded with planning plus a myriad of other thoughts relative to our operation, safety and welfare.

The dubious honour of 'bludger' in our midst and the only member of our party guilty of 'bludging' on his mates was our second in command and rank, Captain Jock Sutcliffe who most of us came to despise in a very short space of time.

He was never known to lift a hand to assist in any of the domestic duties around our campsite and spent most of the early settling in period sitting around paring and manicuring his toe and finger-nails. In a small group such as ours, this was considered by army and most other service units to be the certain way of earning the dubious reputation of 'bludger'. My reader's immediate question might be 'why the hell was such a man taken into an operation of that nature?'

The explanation is simple. Our party who were inserted by the US Submarine Tuna on March 3rd 1945 off Sandakan, differed from the personnel involved in the earlier attempt of January 1945 to land on the west coast of BNB from the same submarine. This forced Gort to abort the landing and return to Australia in the Bream to re-plan the operation.

Because of the aborted attempt, Gort decided to make the landing on the east coast. This change of insertion point also required a change of personnel, hence Jock Sutcliffe's inclusion. Jock and Don Harlem became the replacements. As commando specialists, their inclusion was deemed necessary in view of the still proposed attempt to rescue the POW at Sandakan - operation 'Kingfisher'.

Our first insertion by Tuna was planned for Kimanis Bay or an alternative insertion point on the west coast of BNB. This attempt was thwarted by the fact that the Japanese had constructed what appeared to be a DF station on the very point of land on Mandahan Estate where we proposed to establish our first headquarters and radio transmitting station.

A few weeks prior to our departure from Darwin aboard the Tuna, Gort and our second in command, Captain Nick Combe made a reconnaissance flight over the proposed insertion point. It revealed that the point of landing was uninhabited and almost virgin jungle. Nick, formerly a district officer and magistrate in BNB, had served in many areas including Sandakan the pre-war capital on the east coast and the wartime site of the notorious POW camp. He also served in a similar capacity at Kota Kinabalu the post war capital on the west coast of BNB - renamed Sabah after the Malay's gained independence in the mid 1960s.

After Tuna arrived off the coast of Kimanis Bay in daylight and approached the beach submerged, great caution was exercised. The depth of water was less than 200ft – far too shallow for the likes of submariners in large submarines like Tuna – and strange radio signals were emanating from our proposed insertion point.

With utmost caution, Tuna made her way back to deeper waters where the rest of the daylight hours were spent, allowing Gort and Nick to decide on the next move and to radio back their findings to headquarters in Australia.

Left to right - Sgt Graham Greenwood on Boston generator and Lieut. Fred Olsen on transmitter in radio 'shelter'

With memories of operation 'Python' fresh in the memories of Gort Chester and Fred Olsen, plus the chilling reminder that somewhere in the organisation of SRD (Services Reconnaissance Department later renamed 'Z' Special Unit) there was a 'Judas'. He or she had engineered the loss of a number of 'Z' parties as they landed in occupied territory. Japanese reception parties sitting right on the insertion point where 'Z' operatives were landing were too frequent for coincidence.

In Malay, 'binatang' is an animal. 'Bintang' however is a star and this latter term was used to describe the Japanese at the time of the occupation when Japan claimed the end of the domination of the Americans, British and Dutch and their exploitation of the coloured races of South East-Asia. The Japanese troops wore a yellow star on their caps hence the adopted term 'bintang' – stars. Being referred to by the locals as stars pleased the Japanese hierarchy immensely, but their subsequent cruelty however, quickly earned them the change to 'binatang' – an animal which naturally enough displeased the Nipponese hordes.

In occupied Timor the Japanese captured a number of anti-Jepun locals who were active in clandestine activities. These locals comprised the reception group for small parties of 'Z' men inserted behind Japanese lines by submarine, parachute or surface craft. Captured locals were tortured, blackmailed etc., and by using these methods the Japanese learned the recognition signals to be used at the insertion point where one of the first parties, operation 'Lagarto' was to land.

Compromised in this manner, 'Lagarto's initial party was dropped in by Flight 200 aircraft from an altitude of 400ft after correct recognition signals had been passed only to find as they neared the ground that instead of friendly indigenous people to meet them, the Japanese were there in large numbers.

The operations radio operator was captured alive with all equipment and under duress was made to transmit to Australia advising that the drop had been successful and that all was well and to drop in the second party 'Lagarto 2'. This procedure went on and on and many 'Z' men went to certain deaths in Timor. An extremely woeful tale of continuing errors that did not win bouquets for 'Z'.

Finally when the Japanese nation surrendered, SRD learned the sad truth when they received a radio message from the Japanese thanking SRD – then 'Z' Special Unit – for their "wonderful support of officers, arms and other supplies for the last few months". They even had the audacity to thank the "lovely lady radio operators" working the transmitters at the Australian end. (for more information on this operation see the book "Silent Feet" by G.B.Courtney, a former commanding officer of our unit when it was operating out of Labuan Island).

Returning to our aborted landing, after recharging batteries at sea over night while surfaced – this allowed the submarine to refresh the air within after being submerged all day - the submarine submerged again the following morning. In daylight, Tuna slowly made her way inshore for a closer inspection. Lying offshore in shallow water at periscope depth, we watched bemused, as the Japanese on the beach enjoyed swimming, sun-baking, washing dishes, horse racing, etc.

Having finally established that the Japanese were well under way with the construction of the DF station that we learned post-war was an advanced mobile unit, Tuna again retired to the safety of deep water. Gort decided that we should return to Australia to re-plan. Accordingly, an RV was made for that night 100 miles off the coast of BNB with an American submarine wolfpack returning to Fremantle from the Gulf of Siam where the pack had been raiding enemy shipping during its six week patrol.

At the appointed time – around midnight - the RV was made with the U.S submarine Bream in fairly rough conditions and light rain falling. The seven of us took to an inflatable boat, bade farewell to the crew of Tuna and in what were fairly rough conditions for a 300 ft submarine were simply impossible for our inflatable boat.

All our personal gear and operational equipment was left aboard Tuna. The strong wind was lifting the tops of the waves in the form of continuous spray. The sky was heavy with cumulus clouds scudding across the moon while endeavouring to get its light through the soupy mess. When the inflatable was in the troughs of the waves, nothing was visible other that the menacing sky. When on the wave peaks, a hurried look around 360 degrees revealed naught but Hughie's threatening seas and white capped waves, many of which were breaking; even the two submarines could not be seen.

While Bream appeared to be only half a mile away from Tuna when we set out to bridge the gap, I doubted whether we had made any worth while head -way in the prevailing seas, even with four of us paddling. With its shallow draft and wind catching areas, the inflatable was not the ideal craft for windy conditions. Our bodies that almost acted in a sail like manner, only further exacerbated the situation.

As though we didn't have enough to contend with, when midway between the two submarines, the unmistakable sound of a Japanese multi-engine aircraft became audible, although not visible in the cloud strewn canopy: possibly a transport aircraft, a recc plane, a twin engine night fighter or bomber.

Submarines don't favour an encounter on the surface with an enemy aircraft. Probably as a result of the dirty conditions and low ceiling of the cloud cover, neither submarine picked up the intruder on radar until almost too late.

Both immediately crash-dived, leaving us floating around in the middle of the South China Sea like the proverbial Australian country 'dunny', not knowing the whereabouts of either submarine. It was indeed one of the more lonely experiences in which one could ever expect to find oneself.

Unknown to us, both submarines had the situation well in hand. Keeping track of us at periscope depth by radar, to them we were never far away. After what seemed like an eternity, Bream – when happy that the Japanese had not seen us and had left the area – re-surfaced about half a mile away. She then made slow headway toward us, coming to a stop beam on and to windward of our position. This afforded us some wind protection, allowing us to bridge the gap between the inflatable and the submarines pressure hull.

As we came within hailing distance, raucous voices – unmistakably Australian – carried across to us on the wind, "come on you f.....king bastards; you're holding up the bloody show."

Many willing American sailors' hands reached down from the casing decking with grappling hooks and lines and despite the high rise and fall of the inflatable, they soon had us aboard. The inflatable was left to the mercy of the angry seas. In wartime, abandoned inflatables, rafts, dinghys and similar rescue craft raised little suspicion.

In Japanese occupied waters, ships were regularly sunk by Japanese, German, American and Dutch submarines and none wanted rafts or lifeboats aboard – subs just don't have the space. There had been reports that enemy subs had actually used the ruse of putting a periscope up through a small unoccupied craft to lure unsuspecting ships into close range only to be sunk by torpedoes from the submerged submarine.

The raucous Aussie voices turned out to be those of Lieutenants Johnny Sachs and Alex Hawkins, 'Z' men who were part of operation 'Politician'. This operation involved the posting of two 'Z' men as part of the American crew to each of a number of US submarines. As such they qualified for Submarine Combat Pins, a highly sought decoration by US submariners.

The 'Z' men were equipped with folboats, limpet mines, radios and other specialised equipment, enabling them to sneak into enemy harbours and areas protected by anti-submarine nets and where the parent submarine could not enter. The scarcity of Nipponese shipping during the last few months of the war in the Pacific necessitated new attacking strategies, hence the development of operation 'Politician'. The operations party leader was the highly successful and respected Major Bill Jinkins who had escaped from Ambon.

Limpets with time pencils affixed to fuses proved very effective when attached to Japanese ships and other worthwhile targets on shore. The attacking folboat then cleared the target area and sought the RV with the submarine. Almost without exception, these 'Politician' raids were carried out under cover of darkness, and by pursuing the strategy of 'Politician', their contribution played a big part in the overall contribution of 'Z', in bringing WW2 to a successful conclusion.

The morning following our transfer at sea from Tuna to Bream, we learned from the crew of Bream that one of the boats of the wolf pack of which Bream was a member was lost overnight. It was believed that she had crash-dived with the conning tower main hatch open. Not a very comforting thought. Unfortunately, I was unable to identify the boat although I was told after WW2 that it may have been the USS Grayling, one of the 52 American subs lost in WW2.

On arrival at the newly established submarine base of Onslow, North Western Australia, Gort and Nick Combe went ashore and flew off to Melbourne to plan a second insertion. The rest of us remained with Bream, and completed the journey to Fremantle where we immediately boarded a plane for Melbourne.

Although Fremantle was the port serving Perth – Western Australia's capital city – and my home was in Perth, I was not permitted to phone my parents and family; the strict observance of security for our highly secret mission was essential.

On arrival at Adelaide, South Australia, we were ordered off the Dakota aircraft and Fred Olsen and I were handed 'must fly' tickets to Darwin. We had no gear other than the clothes in which we stood, and most of that was American rig issued by Bream. Plans had changed considerably and so had the composition of our party.

Nick Combe became party leader of 'Agas 2' – to parachute in when 'Agas 1' had been inserted successfully by submarine. Sergeant Kanun bin Garfu the Malay agent, Queensland Signaller Sergeant Nash and the New Zealand radio operator Sergeant Vic Sharpe – the last named admitted to Hollywood Hospital in Perth with severe jaundice - were replaced. Kanun – now retired and living in the Melbourne suburb of Thornbury – returned to Melbourne to await further orders, and the replacements were Captain Jock Sutcliffe and Lieutenant Don Harlem.

It was usual for a party to train together in order that members would have the opportunity to prove their compatibility, however this never occurred. Time was the lynch pin of the operation. Jock and Don were virtually strangers to us, such was the urgency of the situation.

Continuing the saga of Bream, she had a two-week refit in Fremantle enabling her crew to take a well-earned liberty. She then sailed for Indonesian waters in search of suitable targets. Near the small island of Lambrongan Kechil in the Masalembo Group, an enemy ship was spotted that succeeded in making the safety of harbour before the submarine could come to grips with her.

With the onset of darkness, Johnny Sachs and Cliff Persche – who had replaced Lieut. Alex Hawkins - set off in the folboat to attack the ship within the anchorage but were never seen again. They failed to keep the RV with Bream. The submarine remained in the area and made the alternative RV pick-up position in the hope of picking up the 'Z' men but without success.

Radio contact on the men's frequency was later made and a voice that sounded like Johnny Sachs operating under duress was heard calling the submarine into a particular area to pick them up. This RV had not previously been planned with the Bream and as it did not conform with the pre-arranged alternative RV for extraction, understandably, Bream cleared the area immediately. She ran a huge risk in the shallow waters surrounding the island to say nothing of the ship and crew of approximately 90 at stake.

There was little doubt in the mind of Breams skipper that both men had been captured and that Johnny Sachs had been forced into operating his radio set. The strange RV may have been John,s warning to Bream to haul her arse out of the area quick smart.

A year or so after hostilities had ceased, John Sachs' young brother went in search of John and Cliff after exhaustive correspondence to Japanese and Allied sources failed to produce any worthwhile clues. At the time, Japan, with looming war crimes trials on the horizon, was saying nought about anything to do with POW and was tight lipped regarding missing 'Z' men.These captured 'missing' men were obviously guilty of espionage and or sabotage, almost all of who had been beheaded or executed without trial. The Japanese have remained stubbornly mute over these matters for some 50 years and it is only since the 1980s that a new generation of young Japanese is demanding explanations for Japanese war atrocities. The new generation had been brought up in the belief that their nation had fought an honourable war.

If my memory is correct. John Sachs' brother returned to Australia none the wiser for his time spent in Indonesia other than the fact that he had found John and Cliffs names scratched into the wall of a cell in Surabaya. The Japanese Kempei Tai and the Sitjokisat (military police intelligence) used the cell during WW2. Both men had obviously been held captive in the cell at one stage in 1945, but again according to my memory, the trail ended there.

Some many years later, a news item appeared in a leading Eastern States newspaper to the effect that two headless bodies were found in an unmarked grave on an Indonesian island south of Singapore, believed to be those of Johnny Sachs and Cliff Persche.

Those responsible for the deaths of the two brave 'Z' men and many others were never brought to trial. Instead, during the early fifties, Australian Prime Minister Bob Menzies discharged remaining Japanese war criminals awaiting trial. The enormous build up of trade between Japan and Australia took precedence over such trivial matters as men's lives and the manner in which those men were slaughtered.

The foregoing lengthy explanation of changes in the personnel of 'Agas 1' and the saga of Johnny Sachs and Cliff Persche and the US Submarine Bream are interesting facets of our 'Agas 1' operation.

This digression also partly explains the reason why we were unable to spend training time in Australia with Jock Sutcliffe and Don Harlem. The incompatibility of the former was thus discovered after insertion behind enemy lines.

As stated earlier, Gort Chester set a fine example for those in the party of 'Agas 1' and never did shirk the simple boring domestic duties around our 'mudflats' headquarters campsite.

Jock on the other hand was the opposite of Gort. When assistance was needed, he sat around trimming his fingernails and toenails, cleaning his weapons or trimming his handlebar moustache. He refused to lower his dignity to carry out menial tasks.

I recall signaller Graham Greenwood having an altercation with Jock over these matters one day, whereupon I said to Graham – an extremely polite person and a great product of his New Zealand parents – "had it been me Gra, I could never have acted in your polite and well restrained manner". In reflection, I had to admire Graham. On that occasion his usually placid manner was noticeably heckled and his eyes were afire.

Gort in his wisdom – having heard the altercation – said nought but it was obvious that he agreed with Graham's grievances in total.

My turn to have words with Jock came about much sooner than my companions or I expected. It was my day of cooking and I had done quite a stint of experimenting with our dehydrated supplies in an attempt to produce some new dishes. By the time the food was ready to eat, the last of the daylight hours was upon us. Realising what I had been endeavouring to do all afternoon, nobody complained about the lateness of the hour but Jock had to have his little say. "Come on Jack. How much bloody longer will dinner be? Do we eat tonight or tomorrow?"

Jock's remarks couldn't have come at a less appropriate moment. I was ruffled and my usually calm Chinese equilibrium urged me to let fly "if you did something to help matters instead of sitting on your bloody arse all day, you'd have something to complain about you lazy bastard".

Complete silence followed. One could have cut the stony silence with a knife. All present expected Gort to have a piece of me. All 6ft 5in of Skeet stood nearby. He despised Jock's laziness and his glassy eyed stare at Jock spoke far more than words. I believe Fred, Graham and Don in a discussion later agreed that I had spoken in the most appropriate manner and tone possible under the circumstances, notwithstanding Jock's superiority in seniority. Normally, sergeants just don't talk to Captains in that way.

After what seemed to be a long uncomfortable silence, Jock replied with "mind your bloody language Wong or I'll have you Court Martialled smartly". In the short few weeks that I had known Jock, he had always called me "Jack", but now it was "Wong" and my first thought was that he had played his hand as I had expected the moment I first set eyes upon him. My assessment of the moment – English Capitalist to Oriental Coolie – complete, I casually turned on him and said, " I couldn't care a stuff about you Jock. Have me Court Martialled as soon as you like."

In my family and among my large circle of friends, I believe they regard me as being fairly tolerant and I have always been that way; the long fuse has to burn away completely before my charge explodes. The charge when exploded is severe but short in duration, and there is no sulking or bearing of a grudge towards the other person.

On the mention of 'Court Martial', Gort immediately broke in with "right! That will be enough on the matter from both of you", signalling the end of our altercation. However, I felt that I had cleared the air on behalf of us all and that my action was completely justified. The short but sharp dual made no difference to Jock's attitude towards the doing of his fair share of domestic duties.

Chapter 9

JUNGLE NOISE AND OTHER NOISES

I never envied our three hard working radio operators and their lot. When we left them I feared for their survival; not for any other reason than that the whining noise set up by the Boston generator might be picked up by the Japanese.

The Boston was an American manufactured portable transmitter comprising two principal components; the first a transmitter that sat flat on a bench top and the second a tripod mounted generator. Two opposing folding seats opened off two of the legs of the tripod. A handle finally fitted to each end of the generator head. In operation, two operators sat face to face and produced power by winding the handles. This power was transferred to the transmitter operated by the 'sparks' (radio operator). When the unit was generating power to transmit, the winding of the handles that activated the guts of the unit set up an unbelievably loud whine.

Our three 'sparks' seemed unperturbed about the racket. The other four of us literally chewed our fingernails off to the elbows with every revolution of that damned generator. Sound in the jungle – and particularly at night – seemed to travel vast distances. In fact, dense jungle absorbs noise and our 'sparkies' knew it.

The continuous cacophony of cicadas that occurs in the daylight hours is mostly absent at night. In our camp area the only noises were the nocturnal birds giving vent to their territorial claims, the snorting of wild boar as they pursued their females or fought with other boar over them, or their crashing through the thick jungle undergrowth. Combined, it all broke the complete silence of the area. Finally, one day when Gort's curiosity got the better of him – despite Fred's assurances that all was well – he and Jock took off into the ulu (jungle) to listen out for our whining generator. Only then did we four relax when they said that the generating noise could scarcely be heard.

After leaving the submarine, the little river that we had penetrated was situated midway between two main rivers approximately three miles apart. After hostilities had ceased, we learned that the Japanese had a motor torpedo boat base at the mouth of one river and a Kaitan training base at the mouth of the other, both heavily damaged by American bombing and strafing.

During our entire training, our instructors drummed into us the lesson 'the best place to hide is right under the enemy's nose because that is where he least expects to find you'. Whether at Frazer Island's Frazer Commando School (FCS), The Cairns Queensland The House on the Hill (THOTH) or the official name 'Z' Experimental Station, Mt. Martha Experimental Station Victoria, or for that matter any training base in Australia, we were constantly told this and the lesson was never forgotten.

It must be very obvious to the reader after my description of the radio set-up that our lives were dependent on good communications and thoroughly dependable operators. In fact, they were the unsung heroes of operation 'Agas 1'.

Gort Chester's judgement in selecting our insertion point had been uncanny. I believe our radios location remained safe for this reason and more so when one remembers that the Japanese had a large DF (direction finding) station at Sandakan about twenty miles away as the crow flies and another at the MTB base.

While we never envied their work we admired the diligence of our radio team in everything they did. They were glued to the one location by virtue of their necessity to be reasonably static. Re-locating was Gort's decision entirely, and then only in an extreme emergency or a change of HQ location.

I recall that when we were about to leave them to make contact with Jambongan Island, Gort, Jock, Don and myself were heavy of heart, realising the extreme danger that faced our radio operators in the event of their being picked up by the Japanese direction finder.

Generally speaking, our boys transmitted at night when the reception was better. HQ Australia and 'Agas 1' could however, transmit at any time outside agreed transmission times in an emergency by following the pre-arranged call sign with the letters 'QSQ' which in plain terms meant 'break radio silence and come on air – I have an urgent message for you'. As 'Agas' radio traffic grew in volume the sigs had to be on vigil all hours of the day and night.

I am reminded that frequently when listening in to World News London on our American receiver at nights we heard strange messages in plain language (PL) over a background of constant morse code after the BBC news. The set was approximately the size of a carton of Chesterfield cigarettes and was considered to be one of the smallest long-range receivers in the world at that stage. We regularly heard the oil silky voice of 'Tokyo Rose' telling the Aussie soldiers to lay down their arms and go home as the Americans were having a grand time with their wives and girl friends back in Australia while the Aussies were risking their necks fighting a losing cause.

Furthermore, we were acutely aware that in the event of the capture of our three operators and the Boston radio, there was no survival for we four. Our RAAF ATR4 transmitter – while it was a wonderful and rugged unit – it was only designed for use between our outlying groups and our Boston. There was no likelihood that we could radio Melbourne or Darwin for extraction. We would be stranded in hostile territory, unable to get intelligence out and for that matter unable to receive messages from headquarters in Australia or get ourselves out.

We were very aware of this precarious situation, particularly as we soon would have to leave the three 'sparkies' – Fred, Graham and Skeet - to fend for themselves while we searched the land for some of Gort's former contacts of pre-war years or those of his earlier 'Python' days.

During my early training at Frazer Island commando school was joined by my clan cousin Peter Wong from Perth – an accountancy student prior to enlisting in the Royal Australian Air Force, where he graduated as a bomber pilot. He – like myself - was interviewed by a London representative of the hush-hush Services Reconnaissance Department (SRD) later renamed Z Special Unit, and volunteered his services with the newly formed Australian cloak and dagger unit.

Peter and I were closely associated as boys and grew up together – I always looked upon him as an elder brother. We regularly attended the Chinese Methodist mission Sunday school together and Wesley Church Perth. Peter lived with his father; his mother and two younger brothers having been stranded in China after the Sino Japanese war erupted. He regarded my mother as his second mum, hence our closeness. We only separated when he turned 18 and joined the RAAF and I, only months later, enlisted with the Norwegian Merchant Navy at the age of 16.

The tide was beginning to turn. Japan had suffered major defeats at the Coral Sea and Midway and the allies were now on the offensive. General MacArthur's island hopping strategy was proving itself again and again, resulting in the perfect climate for the introduction of clandestine or 'dirty' warfare into the Pacific theatre just as Japan had done with Australia, America and Britain pre-war.

Training at Frazer Island completed, Peter and I volunteered to join a small group – mainly Englishmen, plantation owners in Malaya, Borneo etc. Peter finally withdrew from the party because his strong religious beliefs forbade him to carry out activities conflicting with his conscience.

Snapping human necks, cutting throats, numerous other unsavoury methods of disposing of unwanted people, additional forms of bastardry that constituted 'dirty warfare' and blackmail, finally compelled him to resign from 'Z' and return to the RAAF.

Meanwhile, I continued to train with the group until I tired of being treated like a coolie. If it was going to be like this during training in Australia what could I expect after insertion behind Japanese lines?

Finally, I requested an audience with the then commanding officer of FCS (Frazer Island Commando School) Captain Luke McGwynne a West Australian from Darlington, a hills suburb of Perth, to whom aired my grievances. As our services in SRD were entirely voluntary, I withdrew from the party of Englishmen and was immediately approached by Captain Gort Chester seeking my services. Within minutes I felt at home with my new commanding officer and never ever regretted my decision to make the change.

Gort's plans to get to the Sandakan POW camp were governed by the need to establish a permanent base in place of the 'mudflats' with a suitable DZ (dropping zone). That established, we could then be supplied with sufficient arms, ammunition and supporting stores to form a guerrilla force. If SRD were unable to arrange stores by submarine, a United States Army Air Force base (USAAF) in the Philippines would arrange an airdrop.

The recently captured Japanese airstrip of Porta Princessa, Palawan was quickly upgraded by American Seabees and within 48 hours of the landing of American troops, had extended it to take four engined B24 Liberators. Palawan, a large island in the south Western division of the Philippines was separated from the northern tip of BNB by a narrow strip of water, the Balabac Strait.

General MacArthur's island hopping strategy included Palawan and excluded BNB. According to Gort Chester, MacArthur considered it unwise to attack oil-rich Borneo. MacArthur believed that the allies could completely by-pass Borneo on their drive towards the Japanese mainland, thereby possibly preserving the oil wells of Brunei, Dutch Borneo's Balikpapan and Tarakan, BNB's Labuan, Sarawak's Miri, and other additional oil producing areas of Borneo. Such a move would also isolate thousands of Japanese forces, then desperately short of a Navy and Air Force.

To a very large extent, this was the point over which MacArthur and Australia's General Blamey disagreed; the other being the Australian and British POW camp at Sandakan. Until their argument, MacArthur fully supported Blamey's plan to attack the Sandakan Peninsular thereby liberating approximately 2,500 Australian and British POW. General MacArthur had pledged the support of Dakota aircraft for the transport of Australian paratroops specially trained for the operation and the necessary landing barges for an assault by sea.

Gort Chester always maintained that these were the two points that created the bitter feud between the two leaders that was never amicably resolved. The feud cost thousands of Australian lives and casualties, fighting for former British and Dutch territories that resolved nothing. The Japanese in those war zones were already a beaten and isolated force with nowhere to go.

Blamey, unwilling to accept the role of second fiddle to MacArthur, broke with the American Supreme Commander and invaded Tarakan in Dutch Borneo. Australians who fought there know that Tarakan and Balikpapan were near disasters and that had the Japanese been able to put some aircraft into the skies, our troops could have been repelled and driven from the beach back into the sea. Although successful, both were costly lessons.

Gort Chester had little time for Blamey, who he maintained had an interfering hand in Gort's previous operation 'Python' in July 1943 to locate the whereabouts of Australian and British POW transferred from

Changi and thought to be in BNB. Operation 'Python' established that they were incarcerated in Sandakan. The planning of Operation 'Kingfisher' to rescue the POW then began.

'Python 1' landed in the Lahad Datu area south of Sandakan followed later by 'Python 2'. Gort established many excellent contacts in Sandakan, some working for the Japanese within the POW compound. He also established runners and dead letter post offices – where messages etc could be safely deposited – and was well on the way to setting up a strong and reliable guerrilla movement. Somehow, the 'Binatangs' learned that they were in the area and 'Python' was compromised. This then brought the Japanese Kempei Tai on their trail and they were indeed lucky to get out with their lives. Constantly on the run from the Japanese, the operation achieved little and cost 3 Australian lives.

Other than intelligence gained, 'Python' had been expensive. The three Australian 'Z' men Rudwick, Brandis and McKenzie were captured, interrogated and tortured before their supposed trial at Jesselton on the north west coast - now Kota Kinabalu, the capital of Sabah – and finally beheaded towards the end of 1944 near the notorious execution site of Petagas. Here some 171 local Chinese, Malays, Eurasians, Indians and other indigenous patriots, were slaughtered for their involvement in the west coast uprising led by Lieutenant Albert Kwok US Army, - 10th October 1943 - known throughout Sabah today as the tragic 'double tenth'.

Gort Chester claimed that General Blamey was responsible for the lack of back-up for his already committed 'Python' operation. The later bitter feud between General MacArthur and Blamey was at that early stage already simmering and was destined to boil over in the not too distant future. Had it not been for the fine relationship set up between the US Navy and Gort Chester, the total 'Python 1' and 'Python 2' parties would have been lost.

Gort was like a father to me. We spent many hours together folboating; many of those hours under perilous circumstances. During the course of time together, we naturally discussed many things including my family ties etc.

By the way we accused each other of bludging on the.job when folboating, one would never guess the disparity of rank between us. As I have so often remarked over a lifetime, "the easiest way to make your best friend your worst enemy, is to take him folboating". However, at all other times I respected and admired him as we all did. Without exception, we all appreciated his fine and uncanny judgement on all matters, and admired the popularity he enjoyed and as well, the beautiful manner in which he was received everywhere by the local population.

He often spoke of Blamey in not very glittering terms. He maintained that Blamey was interested in only his personal promotion, irrespective of the cost to others. Blamey's eventual promotion to Field Marshall in the early 1950's by Sir Robert Menzies was at the cost of many Australian and British POW lives plus other campaigners, unnecessarily lost in the various Borneo battle zones.

According to Gort, MacArthur's successful campaigning completely overshadowed Blamey. Consequently, Blamey felt that he had to get out on his own and in doing so, he unnecessarily committed Australian forces to fight and die on former British and Dutch soil in the furtherance of his own reputation.

A number of unsuccessful attempts were made by American submarines one of which was lost while endeavouring to extract the 'Python' parties who had been on the run for some long weeks, always just one jump ahead of the Japanese. Their survival was little short of miraculous.

Eventually, the submarine USS Harder was sent from Fremantle and under very trying and dangerous circumstances succeeded in extracting the total party.

USS Harder was lost some months later at Truk Island. Harder was one of the US Navy's most famous submarine of WW2, hence her most fitting title of 'hit 'em again harder'; a slogan prominently displayed at the US submarine school in Pearl Harbour in commemoration of her and her brave crew. She was the only submarine of WW2 credited with sinking 5 destroyers in one patrol including a 'down the throat sinking'; a bow to bow torpedo shot! Submariners regard the destroyer or tin can as their worst enemy.

At the time of 'Python's' insertion, no American and certainly no Australian aircraft with sufficient range were available to drop supplies to 'Python'. They were solely reliant upon the US submarines for their back-up supplies and in particular, the Fremantle submarine base with which Gort Chester had set up such a wonderful rapport.

It therefore requires little imagination to realise the extent of the chaotic situation created by Blamey's personal feud with MacArthur who finally told the Australian General to "go his own god damn bloody way". Thereafter, US support virtually fell away to almost nothing.

37,000 Japanese troops could have been by-passed in Borneo. The Japanese were virtually without a Navy or merchant shipping so necessary to supply their vastly spread troops. They were thus relegated to a non - combatant role.

Likewise, the Japanese Air Force had been all but totally destroyed and was no longer an issue. They had the oilfields and refineries but no aircraft to use the fuel and no tankers to transport the fuel elsewhere to use. Japanese headquarters in Borneo had been moved inland to the Sapong estate near Keningau and should have been left there until doomsday. They had no-where to go, were hopelessly cut off from their main forces preparing to defend the Japanese mainland and their fighting forces wherever they existed, were desperately short of food supplies and other necessities.

It is also feasible that the extensive oil wells in Borneo would have been saved from destruction. Certainly, superficial damage had been done to oil well installations by the concentrated bombing by B24 Liberator and B17 Fortress bombers from nearby Palawan, but no effort had been made to fire the wells by the Japanese. Just before the Nipponese surrendered unconditionally to the allied forces, they fired the wells. When the British were unable to extinguish the fires after the war, ironically, they had to call in American experts.

Had 'Python' succeeded and Blamey kept his nose out of it, operation 'Kingfisher' would have been a re-sounding success and the majority of the POW – approximately 1800 Australians plus 600 British – would have been saved.

As Gort had often maintained, 'Python' was in place south of Sandakan. Operation 'Kingfisher', a joint US/Australian operation was planned for September 1944 to land Australian paratroops on the Sandakan Peninsular by US Dakotas, thus sealing off retreat to the west coast of Borneo by the Japanese. 'Kingfisher' was ready to go.

Specially trained troops both American and Australian had completed their plans on the Atherton Tablelands of Queensland and it was purely a matter of setting a landing date. The POW were at that juncture still fit and well enough to give a good account of themselves with arms planned to be dropped into them by American Dakotas.

Additionally, an Australian beach group was to be landed by Yankee LSTs – landing ship troops and tanks – following a joint naval bombardment by allied warships. Gort believed that once ashore, the Australian beach group would seal off the peninsular preventing Japanese escape to the west.

The POW were transferred from Changi POW camp Singapore in 1943 for the specific purpose of building an airstrip at Sandakan for the Japanese emperor. In September 1944, the airstrip was still in reasonable condition and was not subjected to saturation bombing until well into October.

Although 'Python' 1 and 2 had failed and had been extracted from the area, Gort Chester had set up a reliable organisation who were ready to move against the Japanese the very moment that leadership and continuity of supplies in the form of 'Agas' could be re-established.

While there is more regarding 'Python' and the POW camp elsewhere in this book, it is perhaps appropriate to add here that operation 'Kingfisher' was abandoned after the MacArthur/Blamey blow-up and the two leaders went their separate ways.

It was a sad day for ' Z' Special Unit and the POW at Sandakan.

Without wanting to be politically involved, one needs to point out at this juncture that the Australian Parliament in Canberra denied on several occasions over several years, the true circumstances of the Borneo Death Marches. It also denied that operation 'Kingfisher' was planned, troops trained and the real reason for its cancellation.

These denials were typical of many that occurred at that period of time. Whether these denials through the House were in the best interests of the people or for security reasons, we probably will never find out but one thing was certain, it rang in the death knell for the Sandakan POW.

General Blamey held the Americans responsible for the cancellation of 'Kingfisher' and continued in this vein to his deathbed. He maintained that the operation failed to take place because the Philippine landings overshadowed 'Kingfisher' resulting in the US withdrawal of support, Dakota aircraft and LSTs. Nothing could have been further from the truth. There were Dakotas and LSTs to burn.

Following the loss of Pearl Harbour, the US was never at any stage of WW2 short of equipment until the Normandy landings in France when the Americans ran out of fuel – their back-up supplies could not keep up with the headlong advance of their forward troops.

91

Another of many denials concerning 'Z' activities was operation 'Jaywick' that struck the first blow to the invincible Japanese who captured Singapore shortly after their infamous attack on Pearl Harbour and their subsequent relentless drive through South East Asia and the Dutch East Indies towards their ultimate goal; Australia.

The former Japanese 78 foot fishing vessel Kofuku Maru - operating out of Singapore when Japan entered WW2 - was captured by an Australian corvette.

The 6.5 knot Kofuku Maru was re-fitted as a clandestine ship under the cloak of 'Z's former cover name 'SRD' (Services Reconnaissance Department), that was part and parcel of 'SOE' (Special Operations Executive) based in London.

Carrying 14 'Z' men, Krait sailed from Potshot in Exmouth Gulf, Western Australia September 1943 to raid Singapore Harbor (renamed Shonan or Syonato by the Japanese – a difference of opinion exists among historians)

Operation 'Jaywick' leader, Major Ivan Lyon – a Highlander – and five other of the Kofuku Maru (renamed Krait – a small vicious and deadly viper of south east Asia and Burma), left the ship 80 miles south of Singapore. Paddling their three folboats into Keppel Harbor at night, they limpet mined 7 Japanese ships totaling 40,000 tons in round figures. The Japanese feeling totally secure in Singapore did not even have black out restrictions and were staggered by the attack. The moral victory far outweighed the material damage

Lyons folboat party escaped from the target area and made a successful return to the RV (rendezvous) with Krait; the ship having spent the ten days cruising in Borneo waters disguised as an innocent fishing boat. Having taking the folboat team aboard, Krait escaped to Australia unscathed after sinking seven ships and steaming 33 days behind Japanese lines at a top speed of just under seven knots while flying the Japanese 'poached egg' flag.

News of the highly successful raid was not released to the Australian people, even though most of 'Jaywicks' members were Australian.

This was in stark contrast to the Doolittle surprise raid on Tokyo in 1942 when B25 Mitchell twin engined bombers released from the USS Aircraft Carrier Yorktown managed to sneak into range of the Japanese capital city. The blow to the Japanese morale was far greater than the material damage to the city and the Americans made certain the whole world knew about it. It was a great morale booster for the allies.

After Japan's surrender, Britain's Lord Louis Mountbatten described the 'Jaywick' raid as "the most audacious and the longest sea-raid in the history of naval warfare", and yet the Australian Government remained tight lipped about the raid even in the Canberra House of Representatives.

A year later, intending to give the Japanese a repeat dose, Ivan Lyon led a second raid on the former Singapore Harbour. Operation 'Rimau' numbering 23 men sailed from Garden Island, Western Australia on the British mine-laying submarine HMS Porpoise. Off the south-west coast of Dutch Borneo the submarine surfaced and the 'Z' men captured a Chinese junk, the Mustika. The Chinese crew transferred to the submarine and returned to Australia where they spent the balance of the war years as the guests of the Australian Government at the Adelphi Hotel Perth, Western Australia – one of Perth's leading hotels during WW2.

The 'Z' men transferred their cargo of 16 SBs (submersible boats nicknamed 'sleeping beauties') – one man submarines 12 feet in length – complete with limpet mines and all necessary support equipment from the Porpoise to the Mustika, hoisted a Japanese flag to the mast head and sailed off for Singapore. They were never seen again by the Western world.

Luck did not favour Rimau. The Mustika arrived uneventfully in Singapore waters where it dropped anchor off an island not far from Dongas Island where a year earlier the three folboats of operation 'Jaywick' had camped for a few days while observing the shipping movements before making their attack.

Mustika was discovered at her anchorage by a Japanese Naval police patrol boat, a fight broke out, the patrol boat was sunk and her crew killed except one who was injured but managed to swim off into the gathering darkness and raise the alarm. Within hours, thousands of Japanese including small ships, planes and troops were out searching for the 'Z' men. Memories of the havoc created twelve months earlier were still fresh in their minds. The Japanese still did not know who had sunk their ships.

Post war evidence revealed that at one stage the Japanese firmly believed that the ships sunk by operation 'Jaywick' were sabotaged by Australian POW and local Chinese working on the Singapore wharves. This could have had some bearing on the shipping of POW to BNB to build the Sandakan airstrip for the Japanese Emperor.

Ivan Lyon realised that Rimau had lost the element of surprise, scuttled the Mustika and her cargo of top secret 'sleeping beauties' – still not recovered today - and ordered all personnel to take to the 11 folboats. They had to make their individual escapes back to Merapas Island – the RV arranged with HMS Porpoise – and await the arrival of the submarine to return them to Western Australia.

The Japanese chased the 'Z' men relentlessly during their retreat through the islands of the Rhio Archipelago. Lyon and a number of his men were killed in running battles, 2 trapped men took their 'L' tablets (lethal tablets) rather than be captured and the remaining 11 were captured alive and imprisoned in Outram Road gaol Singapore, where one of their number died of malaria.

The 10 surviving 'Z' men were tried by a Japanese Military Court on charges of sabotage and clandestine warfare, found guilty and beheaded just weeks before Japan capitulated to the Allied forces.

Time and space do not permit a full account of operations 'Jaywick' and 'Rimau' however a brief mention is necessary here to illustrate my point that the Australian Government unreasonably withheld considerable information on certain operations, years after hostilities had ceased.

Note: For the full account of Ivan Lyon's two raids on Singapore, see Lynette Ramsay Silvers books 'The Fishing Boat That Went to War' and 'The Heroes of 'Rimau' and 'Krait'.

If one does not feel proud to be an Australian after reading these two books, then that person has not a trace of patriotism in his or her body. I believe these stories should be part of history education in our every day schools as are the Gallipoli landings.

Scant thought and consideration has been given to the families of those men who gave their lives for their country for Australians of following generations, most of whom have passed on without ever learning the truth about their loved ones.

Chapter 10

ORANG HUTAN AND GRAHAM

Shortly after breakfast, I turned my jungle hammock upside down to shake out loose particles of sand, twigs etc and to air the inside.

I was resting on the outside of the lower section so that the mosquito netting sides and the lean-to roof sheeting with its tension straps and ties were hanging below me. I was enjoying the sunlight streaming through the jungle tree-tops while admiring some white jungle orchids very similar to some I had seen growing around 'the house on the hill', our Cairns advanced training base and the former childhood home of Australia's famous aviator Sir Charles Kingsford Smith.

The very same orchids also grew in profusion at Frazer Island where our initial training base was situated - FCS. (Frazer Commando School). The small blooms - about the size of the Cooktown orchid and similar in shape - grew on tree trunks and more often than not, high in the trees.

Out of the corner of my eye my attention was drawn to a small animal that was moving along a bough that was approximately 15 to 20 feet away. My immediate thought was 'fresh meat', always high on our priority list of foods. What a change it would provide after being on dehydrated meat for a while! My quarry was a small striped squirrel with a particularly bushy tail that I figured would make suitable soup, there being insufficient meat to share between the seven of us.

My welrod was hanging almost beside me on a tree branch. I had not used it since landing in Borneo from Tuna and I felt that a round or two would clean out the cobwebs.

Reaching across to the welrod hanging in its holster, I slipped it out, lined up the squirrel and dropped the poor little devil. Replacing the welrod, I got down from my hammock, retrieved it from the ground where it lay, gutted and cleaned it ready for cooking. When souped with dehydrated onion, carrot and other vegetables flavoured with vegemite, pepper and salt, all agreed that it was tasty soup made tastier by the addition of army carrot biscuits but the meat was as tough as old boots. But it was 'fresh meat'. Our last fresh meat meal was aboard Tuna.

Before we were anywhere near established at 'the mudflats' - we had only completed the burying of the inflatable dinghy, having no further use for it - Gort made a ruling that the campsite must never be approached from a particular direction as a further measure of security. Anyone coming from that direction could safely assumed to be enemy.

The morning before we left 'the mudflats' for the RV with Samak near the Kampong of Menunghutan (Malay for fragrant jungle) we were all about the campsite doing various chores. Again it was a delightful morning, a real sunny balmy day and Graham was missing again. I had on several occasions reminded him that he was going unarmed but I did appreciate his point that he felt 'like a hypocrite' carrying a firearm and a bible.

Suddenly, we were all alarmed by a noisy approach through the undergrowth from the forbidden direction. Gort immediately ordered us to take up weapons and stand by for action that was done within the time it took to blink. All realised that it was hardly likely to be a wild animal creating such noise in broad daylight.

Don Harlem and Jock Sutcliffe had taken up positions behind the stacked up wall of 4 gallon supply tins while the rest of us were scattered around the campsite behind trees; all of us wondering who or what the intruder could be. All of a sudden, Graham Greenwood burst into our clearing and it was very fortunate that no one opened fire with a silenced Austen sub machine gun. Before Gort or anybody could utter a word, it became obvious that Graham was very agitated. His colour was starkly white, his lips quivering and he was unable to get an intelligent word out. So unlike the composed Graham Greenwood we had become accustomed to know.

Quickly rendering safe our weapons, Gort ordered Fred Olsen to take out a flask of brandy from the medical kit and within minutes we had Graham seated comfortably and a small swig of the contents was poured down his throat. Graham being a non-drinker, it straightened him out very quickly after which he was told in no uncertain terms by Gort that he was indeed fortunate to be alive and that he had almost been filled in by six sub machine guns. Then Graham poured out his incredible story.

He was out for his usual morning jungle stroll and bible reading - his thoughts no doubt with a particular passage of the holy book or some associated matter. Following the track that he had created by daily use through the jungle undergrowth, he negotiated a bend to be confronted by an Orang Hutan ('Orang' meaning man and 'Hutan' jungle in the Malay language), commonly known in English as 'Orangatang'.

The Orang was as tall as Graham who was about six feet high in stockinged feet. Bearing in mind that we were in country not previously frequented by man, the man of the jungle was as astounded as Graham, and no doubt the factor of fear was mutual and the other factor 'to get away' was likewise mutual.

We had no means of knowing what transpired in the Orang Hutan's mind but we were amazed at the story from Graham who we knew to be as honest as the day was long and his behaviour always indicated it. As a matter of fact, he was barely back on planet earth and I am sure he has often thought of the experience in the intervening years.

It appeared that man and Orang Hutan eyed each other off for starters.

Feared by almost all creatures in his jungle environment, the Orang Hutan had the advantage of being on his own home ground. Graham on the other hand was in strange surroundings.

Possessing superhuman strength – yes, an Orang Hutan of the size confronting Graham could have torn a jungle cat apart in its powerful hands and arms – it could so easily have reduced Graham likewise and I am certain that Graham would have realised it.

From there on, just what the adversaries thought of each other can only be a matter of conjecture. Graham, stark white when he burst out of the jungle was completely incoherent when we endeavoured to get the story out of him and little wonder. Naturally, it was impossible to interview the Orang Hutan, not that any of us wanted the dubious honour of such an opportunity.

To Graham, instantly forgotten was the beauty of the morning jungle. The soothing sound of cooing fruit pigeons broken occasionally by the cough-like sounds of monkeys in the mangroves as they searched for mud crabs and the overall continuous humming of cicadas in the treetops didn't soothe Graham's fear. The jungle, swathed in glorious sunshine that concealed the many small audible animals and the colonies of small honeyeaters and humming birds in the secondary growth would have been lost to both man and beast.

In mutual fear, both were transfixed where they stood. Staring in disbelief at each other, undisputed ruler and man of the jungle versus man of New Zealand. Certainly, Graham was staring at the first Orang Hutan he had encountered in the wild and more than likely; the Orang Hutan was staring at the first Homo Sapien he had ever seen.

Graham - clutching his bible - knowing there was no earthly chance of outpacing the man of the jungle by running, said a prayer and bravely took a bold step forward. To his amazement, the Orang Hutan did the same. Two paces closer to each other - and I could imagine the fear that must have been in Graham's mind - he said another prayer and took another step ahead. To Graham's horror, the Orang Hutan did the same. The moves were repeated by both man and beast, both realising that there was no turning back. Eventually, they passed each other, a step at a time while looking back over their shoulders until safely apart when both took off at express speed for the cover of the jungle.

If the truth was known, the Orang Hutan was still in full flight while Graham was pouring out his story. Lucky to be alive to re-count his story, he began to settle down as we listened intently. Probably as confused as Graham, the Orang Hutan, driven on by his fear of a strange animal he had never previously seen in his domain; the domain he thought he was undisputed King of and feared ruler.

We were completely unaware that Orang Hutans were in residence in that particular area. Today of course, the famous Sepilok Orang Hutan Rehabilitation Reserve is close to the 'mudflats' area and is the exact type of jungle, tall timber, undergrowth and jungle floor as that of our campsite.

Back in 1945, Borneo and particularly the east coast of British North Borneo - now Sabah - where few roads existed, was still largely virgin country and the most that anybody knew about that inhospitable land was that it was the home of the 'wild man from Borneo'. Beyond that, it was anybody's guess.

Since about 1979 when I first returned to Borneo and Sandakan to search for my very good friend and the leader of our wartime Chinese guerrilla section Tan Teck Bak, there are jungles still as virgin as those of 1945 albeit the logging of giant trees and forest fires.

Post war, Tan Teck Bak married and converted to the Muslim religion and as a result of his wartime record and successful business career, was elevated to the status of Datuk. Later, he made the pilgrimage to Mecca and was entitled to the addition of Hadji to his title, making him officially Datuk Hadji Abu Bakar Tan. I must confess my ignorance as to the change in his Chinese name from Tan Teck Bak to Bakar Tan. Be as it may, I last saw him in 1945 at our Pitas HQ in the extreme north of BNB before I left Borneo to return to Australia after the cessation of hostilities.

After the war he left Kudat and returned to Sandakan where he eventually became a very wealthy merchant with timber holdings and a three-ply peeling mill in the hinterlands and an export office in Sandakan. He was also recognised as one of BNB's cattle barons, possessing some thousands of beef cattle on Bangey Island in the north-east of BNB.

Early in his business career, he experienced hard financial times and according to the story he related to me on our first post-war meeting at Sandakan, he fully expected to declare himself a bankrupt. He had become a victim of the financial situation brought about by the Malayan political situation and subsequent confrontation with Indonesia

By chance one day while strolling down the main street of BNB's capital city of Jesselton - Sandakan was the pre-war capital - he met our Malay guerrilla section leader Datuk Mustapha who invited Teck Bak to coffee at a nearby 'kedai kopi' (coffee shop) for old times sake.

Mustapha asked after Tan's post war activities and Tan answered to the effect that he was about to declare himself a bankrupt. Mustapha listened intently and sympathetically to Tan's problems and suggested that Tan only needed bridging finance to get on the right side of the ledger. Mustapha already a millionaire as a result of his parentage and his own successful business investments, took Tan to meet his (Mustapha's) bank manager.

Without even as much as an agreement, Mustapha gave Tan a chequebook and authorised him to advances from Mustapha's account reserves to bide Tan over his problems. Thereafter, Tan and Mustapha became business partners in many large ventures including the pioneering of the Australian wild buffalo meat import industry into BNB, flying the product in on their jointly owned Boeing 707 from Darwin.

Mustapha went on to become Tun Mustapha and the Chief Minister of BNB - equivalent of Prime Minister of Australia - and as previously mentioned, Datuk Hadji Bakar Tan became a millionaire in his own right after repaying his lifelong friend and wartime compatriot the monies he had borrowed. Both men have since passed on leaving their legacies to families and charities etc. Consistent with the Muslim religion, both men had four wives apiece, each with her own home and children. Both men were fearless guerrilla fighters and featured prominently in the defeat of the Japanese within their own country. In recognition, both men were sent by BNB to London to participate in the Victory Parade after the war.

I never had the pleasure of seeing Mustapha again after my return to Australia, although we did correspond, but fortunately, I caught up with Tan Teck Bak in 1979 - who according to a friend had died since the war's end - and on many occasions since, both in Borneo and during his visits to Western Australia.

Accompanied by his number one wife and often with his families, - some of them studied in Perth universities – he enjoyed his frequent visits to Perth. Tan was a kind and friendly man and I was proud to have him serve with distinction in 'Agas 1' and doubly proud to call him one of my best post-war friends. In fact, following our 1979 re-union we proudly referred to each other as 'blood brothers'.

S/Sgt. Greenwood inspecting a 'Yaw' on a baby's head

It was Tan and some of his family members who first introduced me to Sepilok Orang Hutan Rehabilitation Reserve shortly after its modest opening.

At a later date, Tan applied to the Immigration authorities for Australian citizenship for he and his wife as retirees on the strength of his wartime services in Borneo. He was advised later that the application had been approved in principle and that it was only a matter of time for the processing of his application.

Meanwhile, as required by the Immigration authorities, he had transferred a large sum of money for the purchase of a home and additional funds for a proposed business venture in Western Australia. He subsequently purchased a home in Kallaroo, a new northern suburb of the state's capital city of Perth. The balance of monies remained with the bank to meet Government guarantee requirements and other contingencies to prove that he and his wife would not be dependent on the social services of Australia.

Once his citizenship was granted, he proposed to purchase a large tract of coastal plain bordering the Indian Ocean north of Jurien Bay to establish a cattle ranch for future export of beef and other Australian products to Borneo.

The ranch was to be named 'the lazy Z' and he invited five 'Z' men to join him on the basis of six equal shareholders. They were the late business man Keith Scarff of Rockingham, 'Z' operative Sarawak cum former Yalumba Wines state manager Ross Bradbury, the late Flight 200 RAAF navigator wireless air gunner and retired engineer Colin Ledger, ex 'Z' 'snake boats' Able Seaman Gordon Hamilton and myself. Our 'peppercorn' ingoing was to be $10 per man. Tan just wanted the 'Z' men around him and he would provide the capital.

That was Tan's way of showing his thanks to Australia and 'Z' whose association he was extremely proud. He estimated that the ranch would provide employment for a staff of about twenty Australians, plus indentured Malay slaughter-men to dress the carcasses in the Muslim accepted manner.

In addition to the cattle ranch, he proposed to develop a beche-de-mer industry on the shores of the ranch. Again, his plan was to bring indentured Malay workers if aboriginal labour was unavailable to collect and sun dry the sea slugs before exporting to the profitable Asian markets.

101

On his first visit to Perth he marched on Anzac day with our unit 'Z' International. He, Madam Tan and eldest daughter Bella attended the following year with two of our 'Agas' guerrillas from Sabah and the Tans were special guests on the official dais.

Then the muck hit the fan. The Liberal Government was defeated in a federal election and the ingoing Labor party cancelled all pending decisions including Tan's application. No explanation was given.

Tan had returned to Sabah for a few weeks to attend business matters. While there he received a letter from the new Australian Commissioner at Kuala Lumpur instructing him and Madam Tan to present themselves at his office for an interview - re their application for a retiree's visa to live in Perth.

Tan, Madam Tan and their daughters Bella, Lucy and Mary attended the commissioner's office only to learn that he was not available. In his absence a female officer – new to the position and who so obviously was ignorant of the Muslim way of life - interviewed the Tans.

The fact that the High Commissioner was not there was in itself an unforgivable breach of Malaysian protocol. Top order Malaysian citizens – Tan had been invested with the Australian equivalent of KCMG - do not expect to be interviewed by 'sit in officers'. This is purely and simply a matter of courtesy and the same protocol would apply in Australia.

This officer was thoroughly disgusted when she learned that Tan had four wives and made no effort to hide her disgust, and was even more disgusted when Tan was unable to furnish the full names and ages of his seventeen children without referring to a written list! She actually said to Tan that she thought he was 'positively bloody disgusting' and ushered him out of the office and that was the end of the interview.

Tan could not believe his ears. He rang me immediately after flying home to Sabah and instructed me to sell their Kallaroo home and added that he would arrange for the transfer of his ANZ funds to Canada where he and his wife would take up retirement. He added that he was finished with Australia and felt very hurt, particularly in view of his wartime efforts to assist POW as a member of 'Agas 1'. Who could blame him?

When he finally arrived in Perth to clean up his affairs, he and Madam Tan were further humiliated at the Perth airport when immigration officers down graded his visa. The visa had been issued years earlier as he frequently went to eastern states capital cities selling timber logs from his mill, finished doors and other products from his numerous factories in Sabah.

After WW2 a number of Eurasians, Chinese and Malays who like Tan, had served with 'Agas' in BNB were offered and accepted Australian citizenship in return for services rendered to POW during the Japanese occupation.

Other resistance fighters like Tan, had elected to stay in their own countries at the cessation of hostilities. However, those who chose to stay in their own countries and who had earlier been offered Australian citizenship and who later wanted to retire in Australia, were more often than not, refused. All were very successful and wealthy business - men. Tan said to me later that he believed Australia had forgotten the debt it owed to Chinese, Malay and other indigenes of Asia who had succoured Australian POW during the war and that it had returned to its old ways of racial discrimination and the hated White Australia Policy.

Yet, in Australia we have it rammed down our necks that there is no discrimination in the country. Ask the Tan family for their opinion. Needless to say, Canada welcomed Tan and his wife with open arms and laid out the welcome mat.

On frequent occasions, I have flown over our old 'mudflats' area but try as hard as I know how, I have to admit that I cannot identify the area from the air. Sad as it is, I daresay it would be impossible to locate today without specially designed search equipment. Out there lies an inflatable dinghy and in a hollow tree trunk only a short distance away, a quantity of gold sovereigns that I was unable to get back to retrieve.

Somebody one day will strike a small fortune. In the fifty years that have elapsed since we buried the dinghy and planted the English sovereigns, the jungle has resumed itself and the hole in the hollow tree-trunk could today be 150 feet up in the air. Alternatively, the tree may have died and the jungle has swallowed up the remains of the tree in much the same manner as it did some of the missing POW of the Sandakan/Ranau death marches of 1945.

To complicate matters, it is not inconceivable that the small water tributaries - one of which we had settled close to - may have altered their courses and the 'mudflats' could today be underwater. From the air it would appear that no land has been taken up in the area, it seems to be as pristine as ever.

On one occasion, I spent ten minutes in a helicopter flying around and hovering over possible spots. Alas, it all looks different. Even the mouth of our small river where we capsized the folboats appears quite different. The Malaysian Army helicopter was made available to me by the Malaysian Government who has always been extremely helpful in such matters.

Graham Greenwood described his experience with the Orang Hutan in a limited edition book printed in New Zealand - only ten copies of the book entitled 'No Turning Back' by joint authors Frank WigZell and Graham Greenwood were produced. Frank was another 'Z' man who was an operative in operation 'Semut' (Malay for ant) in Sarawak, south of the 'Agas' area of BNB.

In that book, Graham in his usual quiet unassuming manner merely stated that he "almost ran into the man of the jungle" as if it was a daily performance. We six - his companions - knew better.

I have been going back to that country for some twenty years and have never heard of anyone going through such an experience in the wild! Teck Bak Tan when told of Graham's experience shortly after I met him in 1945 at Lokopas said that the experience had to be a first. At the same time, Datu Mustapha was of similar opinion. When I related the incident to a zoologist at the Sepilok Orang Hutan sanctuary Sandakan in the early 80s, the officer said that it was indeed rare and that Graham was lucky to be alive to talk about the incident. God certainly took care of Graham that day.

At the time of writing this chapter, due to circumstances beyond their control, Graham and his lovely wife Olive left Perth Western Australia for the second time to return to New Zealand to spend their retirement years.

Chapter 11

THE BANK IN THE JUNGLE

The day had been one of pristine beauty in the jungle. Birds were calling in the treetops, honey eaters and humming birds were in profusion in all the secondary jungle shrubs and butterflies in hundreds seemed to fly through our vision continuously. They brought repeated remarks from Jock, Don and myself regarding colours and the number of varieties including many Birdwings and Glasswings. Gort was blasé about the birds and butterflies, having spent so much time in BNB.

On our way down the Sungei (river in Malay) Tagahang Kecil (small or little) from our 'mudflats' headquarters (HQ), monkeys were very active in the trees searching for fruit and other delicacies. In and around the mangroves, others were hunting small crabs, mud-skippers and shellfish before settling down for the night.

As darkness set in to hide us from Japanese patrols – if any were about – fireflies by the thousands became visible on all the trees overhanging the river. They were so dense, it was possible to navigate through the increasing darkness by the extent of the fireflies on the extremities of branches overhanging the water on both riverbanks. It was a simple matter to keep the bows of the folboats in the middle of the darkness zone between the concentrations of fireflies where we also sighted numerous crocodiles by their golden red eyes on the surface.

Occasionally, we rested under the branches to discuss directions. This was our first excursion downstream as a two folboat team after leaving Tuna and getting ashore, settling in to the new surroundings, acclimatising ourselves to the environmental changes, searching for a permanent water supply and setting up the radio station.

It had been a beautiful day and night, enchanting in fact. Little did we know then that we were in for a hell of a night that proved worse than the previous two – if that was possible.

The original folboating plan - suggested by Jock – was for Gort, Jock and I to travel as a three-man team in the one two-man folboat. When the plan was first unfolded to me, I expressed concern on the basis that safety would be jeopardised by the additional weight of the third body plus weapons, food supplies etc.

I also pointed out to Gort that the boat would be very irresponsive, particularly in strong currents and that provision for the third man was only an extreme emergency measure and was never intended for any distance or for rough surface conditions. This much had been drummed into us at Frazer Island where we had undergone comprehensive training in folboats.

Jock told me that I didn't know what I was talking about and eventually convinced Gort that he knew what he was talking about. Without a rudder and hopelessly overloaded, I foresaw disaster looming as I had been through that experience years earlier in my own 16 foot double ended maple built clinker canoe 'Water Spray' while in the Sea Scouts. Its dimensions and design were almost identical to our folboat.

On the first attempt, the night of the 19th March 1945, after an early evening meal with Don, Fred, Graham and Skeet, we said farewell to the boys and set off in the folboat for the river mouth as darkness fell. It was very obvious to all of us that Don was disappointed that he had been left out of the party; it was originally planned for the 4 of us to go in the 2 folboats.

I favoured taking Don with us, but who was I – a mere RAAF motor boat crew Sergeant – to argue with two British Army officers, one a Major and the other a Captain? I eventually kept my counsel to myself.

The tide was on the way out and we had little trouble in making the river mouth but we immediately ran into trouble when we cleared the river mouth and attempted to cross the sandbars and through the surf chop to head north. The current refused to allow us to do other than it had decided, and in about half an hour we had swamped in the surf.

Laboriously, we swam and dragged the folboat ashore. Fortunately, it was purely a swamping and we managed to keep the boat upright so that none of our gear was lost.

The boat and our gear emptied of sand and water and dried out, we made two more attempts to get across the sand bar and swamped on both occasions. With dawn not far away, Gort decided that we should drag the boat into the cover of the jungle fringing the shoreline, cover our tracks across the beach and rest up in the jungle for the daylight hours. I had won round one.

The day was a mixed bag. In between sleeping with one always on watch, two Japanese sailing boats were sighted within a mile of shore, and with our binoculars we could see that a crewman on the boat had the coastline constantly in view through a pair of binoculars. Both boats were equipped with a machine gun mounted on the forehead deck. Later that afternoon from the shelter of the jungle, through binoculars we observed native footprints in the beach sand near the headland 300 yards away. Staying within the jungle fringe, we approached the point and on its far side we watched as two native girls, unaware of our presence, happily gathered shellfish on the reef. During that day, I again attempted to dissuade Gort from the concept of '3 men in a boat' but he had made his mind up to try again.

When sufficiently dark, the boat was dragged out of the jungle for the second attempt. The gear re-loaded, we shoved off again and promptly overturned in the rip and surf. Round two to me.

By this stage Gort was furious. When drying out the boat and our weapons, in addition to overturning, Jock discovered that his American water canteen was missing. This was the final straw for Gort. Drying the boat out once again, we immediately backtracked to the 'mudflats' where we arrived after midnight severely mosquito and sandfly bitten, our bums sore and wet and thoroughly miserable. The boys climbed out of their hammocks and immediately set about preparing hot chocolate and biscuits for us while we strung our hammocks up in the trees again and poured out our tale of woe.

The next morning Gort drew me aside and apologised for having listened to Jock's drivel about his experience in folboats and added that in his opinion, Jock had proved himself to be a 'bloody awful canoeist'. Gort then called Don over and told him to pack his gear and prepare to leave in the second folboat with me as his partner. I thought I had proved my point.

With darkness approaching and the advantage of slack water, Fred, Graham and Skeet bade us 'good luck' as we pushed off to negotiate the curtain of vines concealing our little creek from the main water of the river. We later learned from the natives that our river was known as Sungei

Tagahang Kecil (little Tagahang river). They watched us until we were out of sight, then breathed a sigh of relief as they did not wish to have Jock around the 'mudflats' camp-site longer than necessary.

We reached the mouth of the Tagahang Kecil in about 2 hours where Gort decided that we should tie the folboats under overhanging Casuarina trees, go ashore and have a look out to sea for Japanese boats and beach patrols before venturing out in the folboats.

Our small river did not appear on normal maps of the area that merely listed two larger un-named rivers north and south of us with enemy strong-posts at the mouth of each. Gort and Captain Nick Combe had flown over the area shortly before we departed Darwin aboard Tuna. Nick, like Gort was a very popular man in the eyes of the Malay and Chinese people. He had been a district officer and magistrate in Kota Belud on the northwest coast of BNB north of pre-war Jesselton, and he and Gort Chester were old buddies. Nick had also served in the same capacity at Sandakan the pre-war capital of BNB on the east coast.

Just off the coast and slightly south of us were Pulau (island) Pura-Pura and Kaniogan and by climbing a tree it was possible on clear days to see part of the Sandakan peninsula where the POW camp and the airfield were situated.

One could scarcely believe that carnage beyond comprehension was existent only a few short miles away. POW and civilians were being slaughtered almost daily. Torture, rape and other atrocities were rampant in Sandakan, yet while we were free men, we were unable to lift a finger to assist. The frustrating knowledge left us with an empty feeling in our stomachs and an uneasy mind, feelings that would become much stronger in the near future.

We had an outgoing tide when we left Fred, Graham and Skeet at the 'mudflats' and the last hour of paddling was in slack water prior to tethering the folboats.

Having satisfied ourselves that the coast was clear of enemy traffic, we returned to the folboats and headed outside the protection of the river mouth into the open sea against a strong incoming tide and immediately ran into difficulties. A large sandbar stretched across the river mouth that we had to cross before reaching the safety of deeper water but the force of the eddies created by the main sandbar plus smaller ones scattered about the entrance to the river, made steerage quite impossible without a rudder. The folboats swung violently from port to starboard incessantly almost within their own length, and within about half an hour of hard paddling, Gort and Jock overturned. The language that came from that folboat almost turned the air blue.

Although we had succeeded and were through the worst eddies and over the sandbars into safe water after hard paddling, in going to their assistance, Don and I broached our folboat between the white capped eddies and were finally overturned as well. The water was no deeper than about a fathom, and it was not until our folboat and ourselves were washed into about half the depth of water, we realised that between the white capped waves breaking over and around us, streaks of phosphorescent trails were everywhere in the water.

It did not take us long to realise that the phosphorescence was caused by dozens of small sharks about 3 to 5 feet in length that constantly bumped against the folboat and our trouser covered legs. There was the lingering concern that with such numbers of small sharks about, the presence of a few mums and dads could not be discounted. We wondered how Gort and Jock were faring. They told us later that they were also scared to death when they became aware that they were among dozens of small sharks. The drift carried them further down the beach and after dragging their folboat ashore, they came to our assistance.

The remainder of the night was spent recovering equipment that had fallen out of the folboats when they capsized, even though we had fitted cock-pit splash cover sheets. The sheets proved useless in a capsize. It was almost impossible for us to get out while underwater. Had we overturned in deep water one of us could have been drowned.

As the first streaks of dawn stretched across the sky, we dragged both folboats into the cover of the jungle and carried out a detailed stock-take of the folboats and our equipment. Miraculously, we had recovered everything except one of Don's American commando boots, obviously still underwater somewhere. The missing boot, oar and Jock's water canteen haunted us for the full time of our stay at the 'mudflats'.

If washed up on the beach and recovered by a Japanese beach patrol, or, if handed in by a pro-Japanese native, it would be the end of 'Agas 1'. The Japanese were certain then to institute a land and aerial search, putting us on the run constantly. When forced to flee from the enemy one has no time to think about gathering intelligence; it is an achievement just to stay alive and 'Agas' did not want to start on a new role where 'Python 'had finished. Gort had been there in just that situation with operation 'Python' over a year earlier in the Lahad Datu area south of Sandakan and that had cost the lives of 3 'Z' men Don McKenzie, Bill Brandis and A.J. Rudwick; all captured, tortured and executed.

So insignificant was our Sungei Tagahang Kecil (little Tagahang river) that it did not exist on pre-war lands and survey maps or our silk army maps which fact -from our point of view -provided an additional protection for ourselves. The enemy least expected us to attempt entry into such a non-descript river. We later learned that the Japanese, as a result of the sandbars, considered the small river un-navigable.

At a considerably later date we learned also that our silk maps were in big demand by the nurses at the 2/5th AGH (Australian General Hospital) Morotai. Whenever 'Z' men were admitted as patients, they were pestered for silk maps. Apparently, the American manufactured maps made beautiful underwear and scarves, as did our nylon parachutes. The material had become a forgotten luxury, unprocurable since the war commenced. My BNB map is almost as good today as it was when first issued to me on the submarine despite having been through all forms of hardship in the jungle and dunked frequently in sea water over a period of nine months.

On the night we left 'Tuna' and entered the Sungei Tagahang Kecil, perhaps our highly tensed nerves at expecting to find a Japanese reception committee on the beach - as had occurred on numerous insertions of 'Z' parties in New Guinea and elsewhere - contributed to our failure to observe certain features as we approached the river mouth.

At that point of time, security at the top level of 'Z' was at its lowest ebb and many operatives lost their lives as a result. We later learned to recognise these reference features when entering or leaving the river in darkness.

One needs to bear in mind that as we had capsized in enemy held territory, and because of the close proximity of Japanese out-posts, we could not use waterproof torches in the search for our lost equipment.

Waterproof torches and pressure proof torches – the latter for underwater work – were available in 'Z' during the war. Some underwater pressure proof torches were also equipped with a Morse key suitable for atmospheric use and were standard issue on 'sleeping beauties'. Used also by folboat crews of operation 'Politician' - operating from U.S. submarines - they were a WW2.luxury dreamed up by our technical section in London responsible for the designing of 'tools of bastardry'.

When we capsized we were headed for Jambongan Island. As a result, a complete day and a half was lost at the river mouth while the folboats were emptied of sand, water and checked for damage. The same applied to weapons, clothing, field and emergency rations and other gear, much of which had been waterproofed for such a contingency.

There being no other way of travelling at night, we had to rely on the folboats and only towards the end of the Borneo campaign were we able to travel safely in daylight on rentises (jungle paths) connecting towns and kampongs (villages).

Gort Chester and I set up an unofficial record in 'Z' by paddling our folboat 640 miles in 6 weeks at night, after I designed and made a timber yoke rudder controlled by the stern man – number one.

Two separate lengths of light cotton rope were knotted on one end and passed through holes drilled on each end of a yoke fixed across the top of the rudder at 90 degrees that led into the cockpit through screw eyes on the after deck and combing. Screw eyes and pintles were fitted to the stern and rudder and finally, the rope ends in the cockpit were looped on the ends and passed over the feet of number one to effect steering. It proved to be a great success. It was even possible for both paddlers to paddle on one side of the folboat when negotiating eddies and currents and still maintain a steady course.

In addition to drowned equipment, we had to dry out gold sovereigns and a stack of paper currency including American dollars, British Straits dollars and Australian pounds.

During the following day, Jock and Don made frequent searches using binoculars from the cover of the jungle in the hope that Don's boot and the oar – previously lost near the submarine - might have washed ashore but it was not to be. Jock and Don extended their search for about half a mile north and south of the river mouth where the capsize had taken place. Any of our tracks on the beach we had failed to smooth out, had been obliterated by the intervening tides.

The monotonous observations of the beach that day were broken by the fascinating behaviour of thousands of soldier crabs. The tiny blue and white crabs were very appropriately named and I am told that they are identical to those that exist on our northern beaches of Western Australia. Apparently they extend from Coral Bay in the west across the sandy beaches of the north of Australia to Hervey Bay opposite Frazer Island on the east coast.

Resplendent in their blue and white, armies of them – possibly 500 or more – marched up and down the golden sands of the Borneo beach wheeling and turning like a well drilled army. At the slightest cause for alarm, they broke formation, scattered in all directions for cover only to re-form when the cause for alarm had passed. They then resumed their orderly marching

Meanwhile, Gort and I concentrated on the drying operation. In addition to drying and folding clothing, cleaning weapons etc., we played the game of 'bank johnnies'. Carefully, we separated the soggy bundles of notes, laying out the individual notes interspersed by many light hearted ribald remarks about presidents, treasurers and 'bank bastards we had met'

Fortunately, there was not a breath of wind in the jungle that day. One fallen tree trunk was literally covered with drying gold sovereigns that had to be individually wiped and polished with a dry cloth to remove the dullness created by the dry sediment of sea-water. Additionally, bank notes were everywhere, almost as far as the eye could behold. As we counted and re-counted the notes then stacked them neatly into bundles, we cursed the day we were born for allowing ourselves to be beaten by the sea. The loss of time created by capsizing could never be re-gained.

With the Japanese 'binatangs' so close, we knew not what to expect. We also wondered how our sigs were faring as this was the first time we they had been alone since leaving Tuna.

By the time that Jock and Don returned, having found no sign of the boot or oar, Gort and I had completed the drying operation and had launched and re-loaded the folboats. We were less concerned with Jock's missing American water canteen. When lost, it was three parts full of water and probably sank. It would take ages to wash ashore, if ever.

Experience at Frazer Island had taught us that it was a big mistake to lift loaded folboats when out of water. The hulls became stressed and the cane rods that formed the shape of the craft developed twists causing the boats to behave strangely in the water. The boats yawed to port or starboard and never righted themselves.

Satisfied that all was in readiness with both folboats, we moored them under the overhanging mosquito infested Aru trees in readiness for a second attempt to get out of the river when sufficiently dark.

Our hammocks and field rations were left out so that we could have a short kip, a meal and a cuppa before shoving off.

Jock and Don reported having seen two Japanese powered and armed patrol boats and a Tongkang (sailing craft) with a machine gun on the fore deck close in-shore flying poached egg flags, but no patrols on the beach. A number of Malay fishing Prahus was also sighted. In addition to the boats, they had sighted a flight of American P38 Lightnings low flying across the sea to the north and headed in the direction of Tawi-Tawi.

After a short well-deserved kip in our hammocks, we lit up a smokeless 'canned heat', brewed some coffee and after a quick meal followed by a fruit bar, we smeared our exposed faces and hands with mosquito repelling citronella. We were ready for the new night's activities.

It was truly amazing the difference that a rest and a meal made. We all immediately mellowed and while enjoying our coffee we were able to reflect on the previous night's unfortunate capsizes and gear losses as well as the unavoidable loss of time.

Gort and Jock were openly apologetic to each other regarding the bad tempered remarks made just prior to their capsize. Remarks such as "pull harder for f...... sake" and "I'm pulling as hard as I can go you lazy bastard" came to our ears from their boat prior to capsizing.

While they worked individually in folboats at Frazer Island they lacked team experience. However, it was great to hear them making light of the incident. At Frazer Island during training, we deliberately rolled folboats so that we could practice the technique of righting the craft. In operations and riding heavily loaded folboats, once having capsized, it was virtually impossible to right them.

There was no questioning the popularly held belief among folboat crews that the fastest and most certain method to make one's best pal one's worst enemy, was to take him folboating. It had been a convincing experience.

Being at the river mouth as darkness fell gave us a huge advantage. We were able to wait until slack water before pushing off and crossing the sandbars without difficulty. We then headed north towards Jambongan under a starry sky surrounded by phosphorescent streaks in the water as fish streaked away in front of our folboats. Numerous flying fish took to the air ahead as we sliced through the mirrored water, once having cleared the river mouth; one even struck Gort on the left arm and fell into the boat. Contributions of gurnards for the morning breakfast were eagerly accepted.

Chapter 12

BANANA MONEY

On the 2nd January 1942, the Japanese occupation forces moved into BNB (British North Borneo), completely unopposed by the Malayan Volunteer Force who had been instructed by British war-time Prime Minister Winston Churchill to offer no resistance? Needless to say, the small but valiant Volunteer Force was disgusted, but orders were orders.

The Japanese quickly called in all the old British currency of Straits Dollars and Yankee Dollars, then replaced them with Japanese dollar notes.

The new Japanese bank notes very quickly won themselves the tag of 'banana money' because of the bananas, coconuts and palm trees adorning the notes. The 'banana money' was printed on poor quality paper, cheapened further by the second class quality artwork that did little or nothing to enhance the bank notes or the confidence of the BNB people. Strangely, none of the notes had serial numbers.

Generally speaking, the indigenous people refused to do business other than on a barter arrangement when trading among themselves; such was their faith in Japanese 'wang pisang' ('wang' Malay for money and 'pisang' banana). However, the Chinese and Malay guerilla's and others employed by 'Agas1' eagerly sought our Yankee Dollars, Aussie Currency, Straits Dollars or gold.

All our payments to the local people for information on Japanese troop movements and other intelligence, were initially made in gold sovereigns taken ashore from Tuna. However, it did not take long for the locals to realise that we Australians were there for keeps and that our Australian pound notes could be used with limitations within 'Agas'

territory. After the establishment of Jambongan Island our second headquarters (HQ),
supply drops were more frequent.

The proof of the pudding was in the eating, and this was realised shortly after the local guerrilla families actually witnessed Flight 200 B24 Liberators arriving overhead dropping arms, ammunition and urgently needed goods including medical supplies, rice and clothing for young and old. Thereafter, the local people were happy to receive their wages in Australian currency that they hoarded until Australian troops landed at Labuan and Brunei on June 10th 1945 when the Australian Government honoured the currency.

Towards the end of the war in BNB, the local people of all nationalities avoided working for the 'sons of heaven'. Whenever local workers (usually Malay) were employed by the Japanese, they avoided the 'binatangs' (Malay for animals) like the plague, knowing full well that the Japanese 'banana money' was worthless: it was impossible to spend, and the Japanese had no goods to sell anyway.

On the other hand, there were those who worked as spies for the Japanese and amassed huge fortunes in 'banana money', only to learn after the defeat of the 'binatangs' that those fortunes amounted to nothing other than bum-fodder.

In Trusan where we first gave away 'banana money', not only were the large denomination Japanese notes being used as bum-fodder, the smaller denomination notes were preferred as a substitute for cigarette paper, lighting fires and numerous other uses. Fifty-five years on, I still like to believe that we started the rot off in BNB; a bum-fodder practice that spread throughout Borneo!

After we - Don Harlem, our guerilla's and I - cleaned out the Japanese at Trusan and blew the bank safe, we freely distributed the banana money to every Tom, Dick and Harry. Said bank notes – preferable to jungle leaves - were used by all and sundry as an acceptable substitute for toilet paper; toilet rolls had not been available since the British left the scene. What a bummer!

Following the 'burning of Trusan' saga, the Japanese sent a small investigation team of three to check the reasons for the lack of communi-cation between Trusan and Japanese General Headquarters (GHQ) at Sapong Estate on the west coast.

The Japanese team arrived to find none of their troops in the town, and commenced an investigation into their whereabouts from the Malay residents who pleaded ignorance. Refusing to believe the Malays, the investigation team made further enquiries and learned from neighbouring kampongs that a large force of Australian commandos had annihilated the Japanese.

After a few days in Trusan and meeting with no success, the team of three returned to Langkong from whence they had come. They never made it. Instead, they fell foul of the Malay kampong people en-route and were very efficiently dispatched. Parangs (machetes) had many uses and told no tales

To remind me of this event, I still have a small bundle of brand spanking new ten and five dollar bills among my souvenirs from behind Japanese lines in BNB.

Chapter 13

SIAPA ITU? (WHO'S THAT?)

It was about 10am when we were rudely awakened by Jock Sutcliffe's loud voice "Siapa Itu" (who's that?) followed almost immediately by "Murri Sini" (come here). Jock's Malay was pretty rough but it got its message across to the intruder: I believe it was the first opportunity he had to converse in the language since he left Malay classes at Frazer Island.

Our unwelcome visitor was an elderly Malay man whose face was just peering over the tops of nearby jungle undergrowth when I first heard Jock's voice.

Jock apparently had woken earlier than the rest of us and was musing in his hammock when he became aware of the gentle rustling of the surrounding undergrowth. Thinking it was probably a wild pig or a Pelandock (mouse deer) – both were very common in the area – he was horrified when on looking out through the mosquito netting wall of his hammock, he was almost fact to face with the unwanted intruder.

In a flash we were all out of our hammocks, hurriedly taking up Austen machine guns as we gathered near Jock's hammock to find Jock standing nearby in his singlet and underpants. His height of about six feet plus, and his reasonably good physique despite the full time soldier's life he had led, accentuated the shortness of the Malay. It is uncommon to find a very tall Malay; when one encounters one, he is usually super tall.

In retrospect, the scene was quite comical. Jock in his underwear towered over the poor little old Malay unable to control his emotions. Jock's towering frame, firm voice and welrod - only an inch or two from the forehead of the little Malay -commanded the situation.

117

The Malay appeared to be about 50 years of age but one needs to remember that unlike Caucasians, Orientals ages are difficult to guess. The poor little man's fear was evident in the fact that he was shaking uncontrollably, even his thick medium length handlebar moustache was very noticeably quivering, so great was his fear. Jock 's cocked pistol aimed at the centre of the little man's forehead did nothing to improve the situation.

He was eventually summoned into the centre of our small clearing whereupon Gort took command of the situation with his delightfully full-faced smile. A smile style that could only emanate from Gort Chester but a certain winner – and after greeting the man in flawless Malay and chatting with him for a few minutes, the little Malay commenced to recover his normality.

His name was Samak, 72 years of age, married with wife and three children and lived in the Kampong of Menunghutan (fragrant jungle) on one of the many tributaries of Sungai Trusan (Trusan River) where he had spent the latter part of his life. Most of his working life had been divided between Sandakan and Kudat, the most northern town of BNB.

Following much discussion, Gort discovered that Samak was definitely anti Japanese and had lost relatives after persecution by the Kempei Tai.

Many times since the end of WW2 I have thought of him. Many times I have imagined that I was in fact Samak. While one can only guess at what must have flashed through his mind in those terrifying few minutes, regardless of whether one is a Malay, Australian or other nationality, his fear could be appreciated.

When a man of that age is confronted by four tough looking commando types – three Caucasians and an apparent Oriental – one of whom had a pistol aimed at his forehead, it's a tough world. I believe that his entire life would have scrolled back in his mind in similar manner to that of a computer. Understanding and language ability run a poor second when ones life is threatened and hangs precariously on the trigger pressure of a pistol; be it friend or foe.

Regrets, recriminations, worries etc must have flashed through his mental monitor screen. Samak – I feel sure – thought that he was facing the end of his life when eyeballed by Jock Sutcliffe, who when occasion demanded, could be merciless and it certainly showed in his cold, pitiless eyes. I had cause to remember those cold steely eyes when Jock and I had words over the cooking duties and his laziness. Only one factor differed – I had no fear of Jock.

It must have been sheer terror to Samak. What will my wife and children think of my strange disappearance? How will they fare in troubled times of Japanese occupation with whole families throughout the country on the move, just one step ahead of their oppressors and the very next meal and bed in doubt? Why did I decide to beach comb this morning? And there must have been endless thoughts racing through poor Samaks mind.

After having been re-assured that he was with friends and the situation was not as bad as it appeared, he was thrown into confusion a second time when Gort asked Samak to remain seated. He then called Jock, Don and myself aside to discuss the unexpected situation and what to do with the Malay intruder.

Jock did not mince his words. In his mind there was only one solution; liquidate the man. Both Don and I felt that this drastic action was not necessary and that if Samak was in contact with some of Gort's pre-war pro-British friends he might be a decided asset. Gort in his usual style gave the opportunity for all to voice an opinion before weighing up the situation and making the ultimate decision.

Unless security demanded – and this was often the case – he always believed that 'two heads were better than one'. We knew of course and respected the fact that his ultimate decision was final. Although I never heard Gort express it in as many words, I'm certain that he felt as the rest of us did that our small party's success or failure behind Japanese lines was reliant on each and everyone of us. Gort Chester – a bachelor – nonetheless, was both understanding and compassionate.

The end result was that Gort asked Samak if he was interested in joining our clandestine movement. We all knew that unless he was agreeable to do so, we would have no alternative other than to liquidate him on the spot and safely dispose of his body before we left. Our total security at that very juncture rested on Samaks decision. However, there was no question of coercion. He was either a willing party or not.

After returning to the tree stump on which Samak was seated while we four decided his fate, Gort immediately launched into discussion with him. He began by asking him if he knew the whereabouts of a certain Malay headman – Datuk Mustapha – and whether or not Samak could and would contact him. To both questions, Samak's reply was in the affirmative. When asked if he was prepared to act as a contact, he could not accept fast enough. Jock's attitude to Samak remained aggressively adamant and he maintained that we should dispose of the poor man.

Samak indicated that he and 99% of the indigenous population were just awaiting for an opportunity to overturn their Japanese warlords, but could not do so unless they were assured of allied support from outside BNB and guaranteed continuing support at that. The indigenous population could not afford another uprising like the Albert Kwok rebellion eighteen months earlier. He knew of the executions of almost 200 civilians who were part of Kwoks guerrilla force plus other non-combatants.

He informed us of the never ending and regular reprisals that had been perpetrated and were in fact still in force against those families of the executed warriors of 'the night of the double tenth'. Albert Kwoks successful opening ambush fell apart when promised reinforcements and weapons failed to arrive. The nation of BNB had not forgotten the incident and felt overwhelmingly that Kwok had failed; but not for the want of numbers or for that matter, courage. Promised support of Philippine guerrillas and an impressive cache of weaponry for Albert Kwoks men did not arrive from Colonel Suarez, leader of the Philippine guerrilla movement in Tawi-Tawi: the ship had been detected and sunk by the 'binatangs'.

Samak was aware that the leader of the POW group, Australian AIF Captain Lionel Matthews of South Australia had built up an underground organisation within the Sandakan camp including a radio receiver, built with the outside assistance of Australian civilian doctor Jim Taylor and locals. Permitted to continue his pre-war practice because of the shortage of Japanese doctors, with assistance from a civilian group under the leadership of Alexander Funk, a young active Chinese Eurasian, Taylor smuggled medical supplies and radio parts into the POW camp.

Funk and Albert Kwok on the west coast were former members of the BNB Volunteer Force that was ordered by Churchill to "lay down your arms and offer no resistance to the Japanese" when the 'sons of heaven' invaded BNB on January 2nd 1942. The underground organisation outside the POW compound comprised Dr. Jim Taylor, Alex Funk, Heng Joo Meng and many other Chinese, Malays, Eurasians and Indians.

Gort Chester's unsuccessful operation 'Python' 1943 in the Lahad Datu area south of Sandakan – due largely to a security lapse in our headquarters 'L' room (top secret planning room) in Melbourne – did not auger well for indigenous groups planning insurrection. Add to this the failure of Albert Kwoks 'double tenth' uprising in the Jesselton area and it was easy to understand the reluctance of local groups to take up arms against the Nipponese without assurance of continuing assistance from a reliable external source.

The Chinese in particular, suffered worst of all the indigenous people under the pressures of Japanese reprisals. Their leaders were compelled to fly the Japanese flag over their homes daily and take the Japanese newspapers. Their young daughters were raped at every opportunity. They were at the beck and call of the Japanese whose hatred of the Chinese was of course reciprocal.

The Chinese remembered the cruelties imposed on their countrymen during the Sino-Japanese war in China when the Chinese nation, lone-handed, blunted the tip of the Japanese sword for six years before the commencement of WW2. The rape of Nanking and Shanghai, were just two of the many incidents of atrocity. The Chinese world wide, seethed for revenge. Those in countries closer to the Chinese mainland, seethed even more; particularly under Japanese oppression of their everyday life and looked forward to the day when they could retaliate.

Under these cruel and oppressive conditions, the multi-lingual races of BNB longed for the opportunity to strike back at the 'sons of heaven', the 'binatangs'. This was the reason why Samak appeared so anxious to join us and do his part.

We learned that shortages of every food commodity imaginable were commonplace every day and everywhere throughout BNB. To aggravate the situation, farmers – whether Chinese or otherwise – were forced to turn over their rice crops, beef, pork and other staple items to their un-reasonable masters. Clothing, medicinal supplies, spare parts for agricultural and other types of machinery were unprocurable.

Poor little Samak sat on the tree log, his eyes welled with tears, his destiny in the hands of four men. In later discussions, Gort, Don and myself were still of the same mind. We three had felt great sympathy for Samak and the position into which he had innocently blundered. Jock was adamant that the wrong decision had been made and that liquidation of Samak was the simple way around the situation and guaranteed our security.

After the incident, I often wondered what reasoning was foremost in Jock Sutcliffe's mind when determining Samaks fate. In my own mind I was completely convinced that we had made the correct decision. Had we taken the other direction of liquidation, the fact that Samak was missing would undoubtedly have been reported to the Japanese.

Japanese suspicion would then be focussed on his family and they in turn would attract the attention of the Kempei Tai who were still on the alert after the defeat of Albert Kwoks 'double tenth' uprising. The memories of the 'binatangs' and their reprisals were still fresh following the expulsion of Gort Chester's operation 'Python' and the capture of the three 'Python' men who were beheaded. The mortally feared Kempei Tai would have focused smartly on the east coast to carry out a thorough investigation into Samaks disappearance.

The discovery of 'Agas 1' in their midst would have brought unbearable reprisals for both the indigenous people and the POW in Sandakan. This would have created a 'double edged sword' effect on our operation 'Agas'. We would possibly be hated and probably hunted by both the locals and Kempei Tai.

We were all the more concerned that Don's missing boot may have been picked up on the beach by Japanese beach patrols after our folboats capsized on the first attempt to get out of our home base river. The Nipponese were not dumb in such matters. There were numerous points that had to be considered in regard to Samaks unexpected intrusion.

The decision having been made, we returned to an anxious Samak who was sullen faced and no doubt expected the worst. Gort's face broke into a beautiful broad smile – one of the best I've ever seen on a man's face and one that was undoubtedly appreciated by Samak. He briefly said to Samak in Malay "we are brothers in a fight against the 'binatangs', whereupon Samak again broke out into tears, so great was his relief.

I need to again explain at this juncture that the Japanese troops wore a khaki peaked cap bearing a yellow star on the cap front. The word for 'star' in Malay is 'bintang' and the word for animal is 'binatang'.

When the Japanese first invaded BNB – a bloodless take-over - and announced that they were liberating the population of their British rulers and British exploitation, they were applauded by the majority of the indigenous races and referred to as 'stars'; a promise that never eventuated.

To promote themselves further, they even produced a series of cheap quality matches with appropriate propaganda matchbox covers. The first into circulation and certainly the one that was best known by the indigenous people depicted the nations of South East Asia connected by chains to the British Isles. Hovering above the chained mass was a giant pair of scissors reaching down from Japan and an obviously delighted Japanese Prime Minister and warmonger Tojo, about to severe the chains.

After some six months of Japanese occupation the bestial 'sons of heaven' were beginning to be despised by the indigenous population of BNB who then referred to their masters as 'binatangs' (animals) instead of stars, 'bintangs'.

A relieved Samak asked Gort for permission to smoke and took from his woven palm leaf basket a home made rolled leaf cigar and a box of the cheap Japanese matches described, and lit up. I have no idea what the taste was like but the smell was not unlike burning cow manure.

Intrigued, Don went to his hammock and produced a packet of Lucky Strike cigarettes and a box of Australian matches which he gave to Samak after lighting up one of the American cigarettes which, with Gort's approval, he handed to Samak. Our new contact looked at it lovingly before placing it between his lips and taking a long draw. By the expression on his face, one would have thought that he had been given a bar of gold.

To cut a long story short, after much lengthy discussion – mostly confined to Gort and Samak – we gave Samak various small items that his family could use and that he could conceal on his person or in the small Atap (palm leaf) bag that he carried. He was invited to take coffee and army issue carrot biscuits - which we detested yet he thought delicious – plus issue chocolate and fruit bars that he had not seen since the days of the British.

Gort gave Samak 'x' amount of Straits Dollars with promises of more to come on an agreement that Samak contact the Tuan Hadji (head man) – whose name I have long forgotten – of Jambongan Island and Datuk Mustapha. We arranged a return RV (rendezvous) with Samak at that very same spot for seven days hence when Samak would have arranged a day and time for us to arrive at Jambongan to meet the two Malay headmen.

Our arrival at Jambongan – for obvious reasons – had to be as soon as possible and when the Japanese were not about. We were uncertain of our arrival time there, folboat travel being governed by a number of factors including tides, weather conditions, enemy intervention and human factors of which there were many. Accordingly, danger signals for day and night from folboat to shore and shore to folboat had to be arranged should the 'binatangs' be on Jambongan Island.

Samak was made fully aware of the task he was taking on. Should he carelessly talk, the risks involved and most of all, the reprisals on his family members in the event of detection by the Kempei Tai would be horrific. It was impressed upon him that careless talk to irresponsible people would result in betrayals, the cost of which in turn would mean his arrest by the Kempei Tai and probable beheading without even a trial.

After plying him with other small gifts that he concealed in his basket, Gort told Samak he was free to leave adding that we would next see him on the appointed day. Gort warned him to say nothing about the morning's incident and to take great care when using the gifts given for his family.

Should there be others on the beach, to distract attention from our hiding spot in the jungle fringe bordering the beach, Gort instructed Samak not to glance back as he walked up the beach on his return to his kampong.

Thanking Gort for his compassion and kindness, Samak bid us all 'jumpa lagi' (see you later) and disappeared up the beach towards the nearby headland without looking back.

Chapter 14

SAMAK NO JUDAS

On the appointed day, Gort Chester, Jock Sutcliffe, Don Harlem and myself were back in the area of Kampong Menunghutan to keep the RV with Samak.

Treating the RV area and the appointed time with extreme caution, Gort and I left Jock and Don to guard the folboats in their place of concealment - the folboats being our only method of escape should there be a foul-up.

We purposely arrived one hour earlier and took up separate positions where we could observe the RV area, and at the same time, cover each other.

At the precise time, we observed Samak approaching the RV tree alone. After giving him a few minutes waiting time and completely satisfied he had come alone, I came out of hiding, approached cautiously and greeted him in Malay.

I then lead him well away from the RV area, noting as I did so that Gort, completely unknown to Samak, had come out of his hiding place and followed Samak and I at a safe distance astern. Satisfied that the coast was clear, I gave Gort the pre-arranged signal that all was well, whereupon Gort caught up with Samak and I, and we went into hiding in the thick of the jungle to enable Gort to discuss matters with Samak. I immediately took up a position to cover any unexpected approach.

Samak had handled his tasks to the letter and thoroughly at that. His information included details on the POW at Sandakan.

According to Samak, the Japanese chose the fittest 500 for the first march, if one could describe them as fit. Most were suffering from under-nourishment caused by the starvation diet that had been forced upon them by the Japanese. Samak said the Nipponese had large reserves of rice stored in a number of officers' houses at the Mile 8 camp and because there was no shortage, the POW should not have been deprived of the rice.

Beri-beri, malaria, dysentery, yaws (a tropical form of ulcer) – and other diseases were rife among the ranks of the POW who comprised the first march that left Sandakan POW camp from the 8 mile peg on the 29th. January 1945 bound for Ranau, an inland town 165 miles distant.

No constructed road existed between the logging centre of Beluran about 30 miles from Sandakan and Ranau, merely a jungle rentis (jungle track) which was suitable for ponies only. The rentis by-passed Beluran to the north – there was a connecting rentis to the timber kampong – and was about 6 feet wide. At frequent intervals, it narrowed to 3 and 4ft through thick patches of greasy mud, jungle and heavy rain forest, through terrain varying from 500 feet above sea level to 7,000 ft, often with gradients as steep as 1 in 3.

A number of the POW - too physically weak to march any distance let alone ford swift running streams - were swept to their deaths at the treacherous and swift running Muanad River crossing, west of Beluran. The Japanese guards made no effort to rescue those swept away and would not permit other POW to attempt rescue. Westward from the Muanad the real hard slogging commenced. The rentis had been neglected since the 'sons of heaven' occupied BNB some three years earlier.

Samak revealed that most of the POW wore ragged clothing, many in loincloths only and very few wore boots. They had left Sandakan in groups of 50 POW daily, accompanied by Japanese guards numbering up to 100 in some groups. It was impossible for sympathetic natives and Chinese kampong residents akin to the track to render assistance of any kind, and escape from the rentis was virtually impossible. The Japanese guards shot those that attempted escape, or for those that succeeded, the thick jungle afforded a slow but certain death to the already half dead POW escapees. Sympathetic locals, who were caught attempting to pass food parcels to POW, more often than not were beaten to death by the guards.

Each prisoner carried his daily rice ration of 2 ounces per day and was expected to supplement the meagre rice ration with fern shoots and obi kayu (a wild tapioca which when eaten excessively, soured the stomach and caused numerous other health problems). Lizards, worms and other small insects available in the jungle were relied upon to augment their daily food fare. Occasionally the prisoners were able to kill a snake, squirrel, pelandok (mouse deer) or jungle rat en-route that proved to be a bonus to their meagre food ration.

In addition to their personal belongings, the POW were cluttered up with gear such as bed rolls and kit bags or other gear that the Japanese guards chose to hoist on their already overburdened unfit prisoners.

At night, the POW slept in the open propped up against trees, or in hastily erected shelters while the Japanese guards were housed in permanently built atap huts at the various staging camps along the rentis. The Japanese had set up local forced labour groups who built the huts long before the POW marches commenced.

Before the POW were force-marched from Sandakan to Ranau, numbers of Japanese had marched over the same route. On one occasion at least, almost 1,000 foot slogged right across Borneo from Lahad Datu south of Sandakan to Jesselton (now shown on modern day maps as Kota Kinabalu the capital city of Sabah). The additional distance from Ranau was approximately 70 miles. The Japanese soldiers involved in the march were passed as medically fit, and yet hundreds of them died on the march of approximately 3 00 miles, as did the Australian and British POW who were nowhere near as fit as their Japanese captors.

Without exception, each morning revealed a number of POW dead, having died during the night or who were too weak to march and simply refused to move. Accordingly, a number of guards were detailed by the Japanese officer in charge to remain behind with those that were unable, or refused to continue.

Those capable of carrying on were forced to march off after their dying mates had passed their food ration and prized personal items on to those still able to continue. Knowing that death was only a few minutes away, the only request was that the continuing soldier – if he survived the march and made it back to Australia – pass on the prized possessions to the respective next of kin. . When beyond sight of those left behind, the sound of rifle or machine gun fire signified the end of their sufferings. Samak was unable at the time to ascertain the name of the Japanese OIC (officer in charge) of the first march.

As we listened unbelievingly to Samak's information, Gort realised and said aside to me, that on the extraction of the Python parties by U.S. submarine, only a small number of POWs had died in the Sandakan Camp. Those deaths obviously had occurred before the rice ration was reduced to almost nothing, along with Japanese refusals to supply medical necessities. Further, atrocities beyond description, bashings, the cages and finally the Death Marches were proving far too much for the already sick and weakened POW.

What a wealth of information was pouring forth from Samak's lips!

According to Samak, west of the notorious Muanad crossing the rentis split into two routes; both converged again, east of Ranau. The northern track passed through Lingkabau and the southern through Boto, another small timber town. According to prevailing weather conditions and other contingencies, the westbound locals from Sandakan and Beluran had their preference of rentises while the reverse applied for east bound foot traffic from Ranau to the east coast.

The two rentises had been in use for many years before the arrival of the Japanese hordes;

Weeks after our RV with Samak, Jock and Don with supporting Malay guerrillas were in the Death March area about 50 miles east of Ranau. They confirmed that on the first march, it was certain that at least three and possibly four groups of 50 POW plus some Javanese labourers, had taken the northern route.

In reply to Gort's queries as to the positioning of the groups en route in respect to their dates of departure from Sandakan, Samak said that it was not uncommon for a group to overtake a slower moving group ahead. Over the total distance of 165 miles, leap-frogging by parties was common.

Samak also advised that Australian civilian doctor Jim Taylor who had lived in BNB prior to the outbreak of war, was permitted by the Japanese to continue his private practice because of the shortage of Japanese doctors in Sandakan. However, Taylor had been imprisoned on charges of smuggling medical and other supplies into the POW camp.

In particular, he was found guilty of smuggling radio parts and turtle eggs to Australian Captain Lionel Matthews, a signals officer who with fellow Australian Lieutenant Rod Wells and others had built a radio within the camp from the parts. According to Samak the contents of the turtle eggs were blown for the benefit of the sick POW and the outers were dried and used in the manufacture of some vital piece of radio equipment or material.

A subversive civilian group led by Eurasian Alex Funk, a former member of the BNB Volunteers, had united its efforts with the Sandakan Underground Movement under Australian doctor James Taylor.

As part of his punishment, Dr. Taylor was force-marched through the streets of Sandakan naked, whipped along by Japanese guards. He carried a waist length double-sided sign slung over his shoulders and waist length, purportedly confessing his guilt as a traitor to the Japanese Emperor and the Japanese war effort

After discovery of the radio, Captain Lionel Matthews, other Australian officers and ORs (other ranks) involved in the underground movement within the POW camp were arrested and imprisoned in Sandakan's Kempei Tai gaol. Shortly after, Doctor Taylor and the members of the Sandakan Underground Movement including Alex Funk, a Chinese named Heng Joo Meng and several other civilians were arrested and imprisoned .

Further, during October 1944, the Kempei Tai arrested a number of civilians suspected of anti Japanese activities. All were held in custody in Sandakan while the Japanese weeded out the 'sheep from the goats'. A number of them were eventually beheaded in a rubber plantation in outer Sandakan.

On the completion of questioning - along with the usual forms of torture that the Japanese were past masters of - those obviously involved, and those even suspected of some minor involvement in subversive activities, were held for further questioning. Those involved, included a reported 30 plus Australians and an unknown number of civilians including the three Funk brothers Alex, Paddy, Johnny and Doctor Taylor. They were then shipped to Kuching the capital of Sarawak for further questioning, torture, trial and sentencing; usually death by execution, and for the unlucky ones, varying gaol sentences that virtually meant lingering death from starvation and torture anyway.

The Japanese, believing that the construction of the radio and the subversive movement within the camp were planned by the 'intelligentsia', shipped all the officers from mile 8 camp Sandakan to the POW camp at Kuching (Sarawak) adjoining the civilian internees camped at Lintang Barracks. Only a handful of medical officers remained at the Sandakan compound to care for and to be in command of the Australian and British prisoners, most of whom were ORs.

Morale within the camp had deteriorated since the first march left;

their date of arrival at Ranau and the surviving number was then unknown.

Since the arrest of suspected civilians, smuggling food and produce into the POW camp had ceased; all former helpers and supporters feared for their very lives and the horrific reprisals they knew would follow if arrested. Never a tooth for a tooth but instead, a head for a tooth.

They came even sooner than expected. The already meagre daily rice ration of one-cup per prisoner was reduced, resulting in the increase of the daily death rate. Samak reported that since October, up to 25 deaths per day was not uncommon. Remaining POW were existing on obi kayu (wild tapioca), kangkong (swamp spinach), rats and snakes and anything that moved within the camp. On one occasion a pet 'anjing' (Malay for dog) - Japanese owned - wandered into the camp and it was quickly captured and dispatched to the POW cooking pots.

Arrangements had been made by Samak with the Orang Tua (headman) of the Jambongan Island kampong to receive us shortly. The OT pledged the full support of his villagers, who like all other civilians during the Nipponese occupation, longed to see the overthrow of their captors. We were particularly pleased to hear that Datu Mustapha had been contacted and that he would arrive at Jambongan within days to renew his pre-war friendship with Gort Chester. Mustapha was in the Philippine islands of Tawi -Tawi seeking the support of Colonel Suarez who was the leader of the Philippine guerrillas: they had been giving the Japanese troops curry.

Gort was very pleased with all the information that Samak had produced even though there was no way of checking the accuracy of the report at the time. We were at least in possession of the very latest information re the plight of the POW in Sandakan and the Death March. It was now up to us to get those details back to Fred, Graham and Skeet at the 'mudflats' for transmission to Australia.

We also became aware of the betrayal in the civilian underground movement in Sandakan that automatically led to the discovery of the POW camp radio. The enormous amount of work done by Samak was indeed an eye-opener.

The outback full blood Aboriginals of Australia are noted for their ability to communicate over vast distances without the sophisticated communication systems of the white race. I do not claim to know how it operates; I only know that it does – and very successfully. The jungle people of the Asian countries have the same ability in a totally different environment, hence the well-known term 'heard on the jungle vine'. This was particularly applicable in Borneo.

There were no made roads between Samak's home kampong of Menunghutan and Sandakan; only bridle tracks. No communication system existed such as telephones, radios etc. As we were later to learn, most of the outback indigenous people had never experienced the novelty of hearing music and an announcer's voice coming out of a box, the sound emanating from a source several hundreds or thousands of miles distant. Yet, without this sophistication, they were able to communicate just as effectively over vast distances: 'A la pointing the bone', even though a little slower.

The task of establishing the very first agent in enemy occupied territory is the most difficult. Had Samak placed a foot incorrectly, it most certainly would have cost the lives of his immediate family. The Kempei Tai would have forced Samak to witness the snuffing out of his loved ones before torturing him. When he could withstand no more, the Japanese, en masse, would joyfully witness his blissful death, thus putting an end to his earthly suffering.

Yet, while aware of these consequences, he agreed to act for us knowing full well that he could have gone the other way and betrayed us to the Japanese, who undoubtedly would have rewarded him well.

The Japanese did not have to be reminded of the dire consequences of the unsuccessful Albert Kwok rebellion, or Gort Chester's unsuccessful operation 'Python': often victory was found in defeat. Both left a nasty taste in the mouths of the 'binatangs' who realised that their rule of BNB was vulnerable. Samak added that posters dating back to 'Python' days offering a reward of 50,000 Straits Dollars for Gort Chester - dead or alive - were still existent throughout BNB.

Because of the speed of following events, the transfer of our 'mudflats' headquarters transmitter to Jambongan and other factors, I seldom saw Samak again but he continued to work effectively for us until the end of hostilities.

For his splendid work, Samak was well rewarded financially. He probably gained 'independence for the term of his natural life'. Gort, - always a kind, compassionate man of his word - gave Samak a parcel of sarongs for his family, rice and other staple food needs plus basic medical supplies. However, Samak was more grateful for the opportunity to serve Gort and the cause of ultimate freedom from his Japanese oppressors. He continued to serve us handsomely in numerous ways, including information, acting as a live letterbox (receiving messages from other sub agents and passing them on to Gort) and the identification of Japanese informers.

A month or two later, after we formed our first groups of guerrillas at Jambongan Island, Samak approached Gort, requesting that he be permitted to serve as a guerrilla and get his bag of Japanese heads. Cool eh?

He was heart broken when Gort pointed out to him that his age precluded him from this activity. He, being the Orang Tua (literally 'old man' in Malay but the accepted term for headman) of kampong Menunghutan, his absence from the kampong would be noticed by the Japanese or their paid informers in the area. Such absence would undoubtedly arouse the suspicions of the Kempei Tai. Gort quickly reminded him that his contribution in terms of intelligence was invaluable and that his continuing work in this field was vitally necessary. Gort also made it perfectly clear that we were particularly anxious to learn of the physical condition of the remaining POW at Sandakan. If physically strong and able to use weapons dropped by air, perhaps Operation 'Kingfisher' might still be a goer.

Finally, he was reminded that the new sarongs and other gifts from us should not appear in public gatherings for some time as this would be tantamount to a 'lighthouse on a dark night'.

The four of us took leave of Samak and headed for Jambongan Island after Gort instructed Samak to go independently to the island in his own prahu (small boat) and meet us there.

Chapter 15

"SUPERIOR OFFICER - NEVER" !

We were extremely cautious when we left 'the mudflats' headquarters the first time, particularly after our capsizes when attempting to get out of the river; we therefore hugged the coastline from one headland or prominent coastal feature to the next. However, it did not take us long to realise that having to navigate in this manner in darkness was a pain in the butt and distances could be reduced drastically by heading from headland to headland direct across large bays and inlets. The risk of running into a Japanese patrol boat increased as a result of our decision, but time was against us and our increased confidence in handling the folboat, enticed us all the more.

The urgency to develop 'Agas' and the need for additional intelligence on the POW at Sandakan impressed on Gort the desperate need to establish our first 'DZ' (Dropping Zone), more suitable headquarters and guerrilla training areas. As a result, we gambled on the fact that our folboats would present a very low profile to the enemy and particularly at night.

We arrived off Jambongan about midnight on the 11th April 45 and cautiously approached the kampong beachfront from seaward. It was a starry night and the moon had just about reached its zenith with light wisps of cumulus cloud passing across its face. Flying fish were leaping out of the mirror calm water in all directions, leaving short phosphorescent trails in their take-off paths to again alight in the water, well ahead of our craft.

At the kampong, three burning lanterns had been placed at strategic points and at different levels as arranged by Samak with the Orang Tua, indicating that all was well and that no Japanese were on the island.

As our two folboats nosed their way into the beach at low tide, our recognition torch signals were received and answered by the lighting of a separate 'all's well' signal lantern displayed outside the Orang Tuas beachfront home. It was not long before the action commenced.

After an uneventful journey from the 'mudflats', the bows of our folboats had barely grounded on the wide expanse of beach when we became aware of voices approaching from the direction of the Orang Tuas home. We expected to be greeted by the Orang Tua and one or two others, however, long before we sighted anybody we detected the sound of approaching people that later proved to be at least 70 or more, talking in subdued voices.

We were somewhat alarmed and were not the least surprised to hear Gort give the command to take up defensive positions close to the folboat bows with our Austen sub machine guns. Should the locals prove hostile, we were thus prepared, to push both craft off the beach after spraying the oncoming mob with automatic fire that would have been considerable from four sub machine guns firing at relatively short range. Spare magazines were kept at the ready to re-load immediately. If need be, we would sell our lives at great cost!

Captain Dereck 'Jock' Sutcliffe

It was indeed a frightening moment for us and a situation that was completely unexpected. The factors of weariness from long hours of paddling, the moments when nerves - already on edge as a result of exercising caution avoiding Japanese patrol boats - and other stressing factors, took its toll. Further aggravations resulted from accusations in both folboats "What the bloody hell are you doing? Pull you bastard; are you blind? Can't you see the bloody boats going round in circles you lazy bastard!" did little to lessen tempers. This is only a mild sample of the impatient remarks and criticisms passed between the members of each folboat as the currents and eddies yawed the craft port or starboard.

Add to this situation sore bums from hours of paddling in the one position, clothes wringing wet from the spray off the bows blown back over the canoeists unable to wear waterproof gear because of the heat factor. Despite the cold stinging spray from the bows, extreme discomfort was suffered by each of us as continuous rivulets of sticky sweat trickled down our backs and into our trousers. Last but not least, one or other of the two men passing wind - considerably more unpleasant when both men have been on field rations consisting of dried fruits, hard high protein biscuits and army style chocolate. The odours that wafted out from below our waterproof cockpit covers was, to say the least, simply revolting.

Lieut. Don Harlem (left)

In a crowd when someone farts, it is a simple matter for the perpetrator to 'pass the buck' by accusing the nearest, but in a folboat when two canoeists are paddling 'passing the buck ' is out of the question.

Strangely, it was rare that both men in the same folboat would pass wind simultaneously. Almost without exception it was always one or the other and seldom both, on any one given night

Back to the beach and the approaching throng of Malays. At the height of the moment, Jock decided to test everybody with a command to Don. "Don! Get out in front some 10 yards or more while we cover you from behind", to which Don replied "Get stuffed Jock! I'm not going to take the chance of being mown down by you bastards from behind spreading fire. We're better off maintaining a line of fire knowing there's no one behind, and also, if the natives are hostile, the pushing astern of the folboats into water deep enough to get away will need all four of us!".

Don was perfectly right in what he had said, even though his remark constituted refusal to accept an order. Gort and I agreed later that Jock's command was foolhardy. However, Jock in his usual manner had to have the last say. "You do as you are bloody-well told Don: I'm your superior officer and that's a bloody order." If you don't I'll have you court martialled". Don immediately came back with "Court martial me as soon as you bloody well like Jock: I'm not moving. Senior Officer you maybe, Superior Officer, never!". Gort and I inwardly agreed in tote.

By this time the horde was almost upon us and our Austen safety catches were off and ready for automatic fire when from out of the darkness came a single voice. Translated from Malay to English it meant "Welcome Tuan Chester and welcome to your companions. Seeing you is like seeing one's grandfather coming back from the grave".

Realising that the crowd had alarmed us, the Orang Tua ordered his throng to halt while he alone approached Gort. The next moment he was embracing Gort in a very touching moment of genuine friendship followed shortly after when the four of us were subjected to a long bout of handshaking that almost wrung our hands off to the elbow.

More excited people from the kampong arrived on the scene. The altercation on the beach quickly forgotten, the four of us were invited to refreshments at the head man's home while a number of Malay boys were ordered by the Orang Tua to unload the gear from the folboats

Chapter 16

WHAT'S IN THE JARS

Within a short space of time we were conducted inside Orang Tua Hadji Pangiran's home where another endless round of welcoming and hand shaking commenced. It seemed to be without end and I'm certain we must have shaken the hand of every male member of the large kampong of Jambongan and introduced to the leading ladies who were mostly 'binis' (wives). After what seemed like ages of the various forms of welcome including a ceremonial dance staged by the young men and young ladies of the kampong, it became obvious that refreshments were next on the list.

With the hour around 0200 hrs (2am), it was a battle to keep our eyes open, especially after pigging out on lovely Malay cakes and numerous drinks of borak and tarak. The tasty spirits made from the sap of the coconut tree bled during the early morning hours, possessed a kick equal to that of any mule and I remarked to Don that it would make ideal aviation fuel. Hadji suggested that we must be very weary – an understatement – and invited us to take rest.

Gort – ever cautious – suggested that Don and I should take a couple of hours off while he and Jock discussed with Hadji our immediate requirements and the formation of a guerrilla group. Don and I welcomed Gort's suggestion as one would welcome the flowers in springtime.

Reed mats were hastily produced and laid out for us by the village maidens (dusky, shapely attractive girls of about 15/16 and fully mature, who in Western dress would never have failed to attract the eye of any western male worth his salt). In the middle of the community floor of Hadji's home and in full view of the large gathering watching our every move and obviously discussing our commando jungle greens, American lace-up green canvas jungle boots and weapons, we immediately fell asleep.

A couple of hours later, still short of rest but somewhat refreshed, we were wakened by Jock and our sleeping mats were taken over by he and Gort who must have felt like walking zombies. Jock was extremely red-eyed but Gort who must have been as tired as Jock, was still smiling and appeared tireless. When occasion demanded, he was the perfect example of friendliness. He had a delightful smile and won all hearts both male and female: the kampong youths of both sexes simply adored him and later, followed him like faithful puppy dogs. In short time Gort and Jock were in the world of sleep while Don and I took over their roles, endeavouring to maintain the status quo that Gort and Jock had established.

All doubts as to the intentions of the Hadji and his Kampong faded into oblivion. Come mid morning, the four of us had taken a refreshing bath. Other than a dip in the 'mudflats' crocodile safe creek where we kept the concealed folboat, or when the heavens poured refreshing rain, it was our first real opportunity to wash in a rumah mandi (Malay for bath-room or house) since showering aboard the American submarine 'Tuna'.

Feeling like a million bucks again and aware that breakfast served by the kampong's dusky, shapely, attractive maidens awaited us, we could hardly be blamed for thinking that we were guests at a pre-war Bali guest house instead of hunted men behind Japanese lines in Borneo..

To Australians pre-war, Bali-Bali (the original name of the island) was unheard of. The romantic island was mainly patronised by the world's millionaires and Hollywood's prominent and wealthy stars who popularised the island in films, musicales and a number of popular hit songs. In 1934 the late Bing Crosby and Dorothy Lamour co-starred in a film in which they sang and recorded 'It Happened on the Beach at Bali Bali', a smash hit that continued well into the post war years.

Today the lush green volcanic island Bali is a popular resort for Australians and in particular West Australians. The now affordable exotic, tropical and over-commercialised venue is attended by every

Tom, Dick, Harry and Jane from 'down under'.

Had the 'binatangs' realised that the residents of Jambongan were hosting us as they would have hosted their own Sultans, they would have been there within the blink of an eyelid. After having located and eliminated us – at a guaranteed heavy cost of Japanese lives despite there being only four of us – unimaginable carnage would have reigned. Men, women and children would have been slaughtered much in the same way that they were slaughtered on an island in the Mantanani group off Jesselton (now Kota Kinabalu) on the west coast. Following Albert Kwok's unsuccessful rebellion of the 10th October 1943, the 'Double Tenth' observed by the Chinese as a National Commemoration Day of Dr. Sun Yat Sen, the male islanders suspected of participation were executed. Not content with that, a company of Japanese soldiers were sent to the island where they rounded up and slaughtered every male in sight regardless of age excepting one 11 year old boy who became the Orang Tua of the island. The Japanese issued orders that male visitors were banned from the island and the penalty if caught, was instant death.

None would scarcely have thought that only a few miles away the 'binatangs' were there in their hundreds subjecting the locals and particularly the young attractive women to revolting forms of bestiality.

Our lovely breakfast consisted of freshly picked pineapple, bananas and or mango, eggs and fish lightly fried in coconut oil, the sum total of which was washed down with sweetened super strong Borneo grown black coffee; very palatable despite its strength.

Breakfast over, plans were discussed to form a guerrilla force, develop a DZ (dropping zone) and defences for the kampong. The Hadji then invited us to accompany him to view some of his wartime collection of Japanese items. Leading the way, he walked out on to a decking of split jungle bamboo laced together with strips of ratan (jungle cane vine). A large atap (roofing slats made from Nipa palm leaves which provided an excellent waterproof cover with insulating qualities) covered verandah adorned with numerous earthenware jars. These displayed some delightful jungle type orchids of all colours that impressed us all.. He proceeded to another one of the same type of vessel (similar to Chinese manufactured Soya bean jars about 3ft in height and about 20 inches in diameter at the widest point) covered with a large inch thick cork cover.

Without any hesitation or further word, Hadji removed the cover and invited us to peer inside. I half expected to see a conglomeration of Japanese side arms, weapons, uniform buttons, match boxes etc., that were in evidence in almost every kampong in Borneo. Imagine my shock and revulsion when I was confronted with about 7 or 8 Japaneses skulls, complete with green moss or something similar to moss growing on what must have been slime, still clinging to the obviously decapitated skulls, the odour of which was absolutely horrendous.

Don apparently sensed my revulsion. I fought hard to show no weakness as such behaviour would have been frowned upon by these warriors. He took a swift glance at the contents before backing off and congratulating the Hadji who stood there beaming with pride.

These were the first Japanese heads that we had seen 'in the flesh', or should I say more correctly, 'without the flesh': they were not to be the last. I hasten to add that these were the first of a long line of Japanese heads that we were to witness in the following months. I had always been under the impression that only the Dyaks took these trophies. These Jambongan people were predominantly Bajaus (sea pirates) with more than a trace of Philippino blood. We were to learn in the following months that what had been a Dyak custom originally, was practiced by most Malays and Chinese in Borneo since the Japanese occupation of their country.

Provided the heads were Japanese, they were considered fair game. This practice was in retaliation for beheadings carried out by the 'sons of heaven'

However, irrespective of their tribal background, headhunting seemed to be the 'proof of the pudding'. Don – despite his experiences in the middle east campaigns that were known to be bloody – had turned away slowly to conceal his facial expression. 'a lighter shade of pale' scarcely did credit to Don's look as his face passed through that phase and slowly took on a decided hue of light green. This, I can vouch for, was not due to envy on my part. Our hosts – proudly smiling – then led us into the community room of Hadji's home where the male and female young bloods were entertaining Gort and Jock with songs and dancing.

With the exception of Gort who had spent many years in Borneo and was familiar with the traits and customs of the people, to us, Borneo was still a pretty wild country in 1945 and that had been made very evident to Don and I that morning. From our experiences during the WW2 years in Borneo, trophy hunting of Japanese heads was not confined to any particular race. The longer we remained in the country, the more convinced we became that racial origin played little or no part in this horrendous activity. It appeared to us that the locals looked at it as a case of 'tit for tat'.

Pre-war, the Ibans and Dyak young bloods were expected to produce heads (not necessarily Japanese) before proposing marriage. The more heads the greater the status of the young warrior: perhaps even verging on the old adage 'the more the merrier'.

The natives of Borneo applied the 'tit for tat' to the Japanese taking of heads and who could blame them? To them, it was merely a matter of returning to the pre-war days.

The treatment of heads varied from area to area and tribe to tribe. Some smoked and strung them or shrunk them and strung them on long lines within the communal meeting place. Others did likewise but displayed them in what I would describe as a shallow cane basket hanging in the communal room of the longhouse. In areas where the Japanese did not frequent – mostly thick jungle areas - skulls were displayed on pickets or stakes. Many of the hill's tribes preferred to smoke and shrink skulls while others stored them in earthenware jars.

In many cases during WW2, Japanese heads adorned stake tops driven into the ground at the common entrance to kampongs and even in reasonably large 'civilised towns' including Jesselton, Sandakan, Beaufort and wherever the Japanese 'did their damnedest'.

Where oppressed civilians had the opportunity to reverse the tables despite the terrible and tragic cost of reprisals, 'binatang' heads adorned fence picket tops with the blood seeping out and running down the pickets. Shortly after the Japanese captured Singapore, this was commonly practiced on the 'big lights' of the local anti-Japanese Chinese and other nationalities that made up the population of that great city.

Interestingly, one of the names given to Singapore by the Japanese after they had captured it was Syonato – the light of the south.

The kampong people spared no effort to provide a dinner fit for kings. Beautiful Chinese willow patterned crockery and vases appeared on the table. These had been recovered from the jungle where they had been buried after the Japanese occupied BNB and pillaged the homes of the prominent and wealthy people. Bearing beautiful hibiscus, red, orange, yellow, white and even a smaller wild variety of a blue colour, the crockery, vases and flowers were nothing short of spectacular.

The four of us occupied a table at the top of the room and on the floor before us sat circular groups of the more prominent members of the kampong, where food was set up in the midst of each group in true Muslim custom. At both ends of our table stood two beautiful shapely Malay girls in attractive sarongs recovered from the jungle where they had obviously been hidden, waiting for the day when they could again be used in a free and liberated world. Each of the girls held a palm frond fully 4ft long and a spread of about 2ft that when constantly waved in long sweeps provided us with cool fresh air. They spared nothing in the way of comforts for Gort 'the grandfather that had come back from the grave' and his three companions.

The occasion was a bit un-nerving with dozens of other locals both male and female standing around the group on the floor, feasting Muslim style. Just peering at them, it reminded me of spectators at the Perth zoo standing about witnessing the feeding of the lions.

After enjoying the sumptuous meal of chili hot curries – bloody hot - fish, poultry, meat, vegetables of all kinds (some strange to us but very palatable), Malay cakes, sweets and fruit, we rested a while before accompanying the Orang Tua on another tour of the kampong.

In the front of Tuan Hadji's home and parallel to the beach was a large area of Lalang (cleared secondary jungle) that had been a soccer and community ground in pre-war years. As it was the potentially perfect DZ, Gort suggested to the Hadji that it be cleared of the long grass as quickly as possible. Although badly overgrown with light (secondary) jungle growth, Tuan Hadji said it could be totally cleared in a day or even less if a supply drop was imminent.

Having made all the necessary arrangements for construction of the DZ and organisation of the guerrilla training, Gort decided that Jock and Don should remain at Jambongan while we returned to close the 'mud flats' HQ.

Our return folboat journey was uneventful except for the fact we again ran into a Japanese night patrol surface craft that like ourselves, was on a southerly course but was to the east of us and further out to sea. We first recognised the pulsing vibrant sound of her engines - an unusual sound for a diesel powered boat - as she sped through the darkness on a glassy smooth surface. The lack of moonlight prevented us from identifying the type of craft, its length and its armament. When it was at its nearest point of approach to us, we could distinctly see the bow waves as it sped through the darkness.

Suddenly its searchlight switched on. Obviously pointed in our direction, the stabbing finger of light seemed to illuminate us in its path. Within a split second we swung the folboat hard to starboard presenting our backs only to the light and our faces away from it, thus reducing what would have been a full length folboat target to a relatively small silhouette.

In almost the same split second, I immediately got off the after decking where I always sat to paddle – the position gave me more leverage - and resumed my seat inboard, further reducing our silhouette. Gort fortunately had his beret on that prevented any reflection of light off his bald head. Instinctively, we shipped our single paddles inboard and rested them, blades flat on the gunwales to prevent the highly phosphorous water dripping that might be picked up by the light and crouched head down motionless in the cockpit.

After what seemed like hours but in reality was probably only seconds, the light never moved off the set trajectory it must have been set on, and nothing further eventuated. With our hearts pounding in our chests like a sledge-hammer not knowing what might follow, we waited for several minutes, half expecting to hear the chatter of machine gun fire

When it did not eventuate and the sound of the diesel engines did not fluctuate, we began to realise that the light's beam must have been over our heads and that the crew may have been testing the light. We breathed a sigh of relief when the light switched off but we maintained our crouched position for several minutes as the sounds of the diesel engines began to fade before taking up our paddles again and heading inshore to widen the distance between the 'binatang' patrol boat and ourselves

Two or three hours later and still thanking our lucky stars that we had not been in the direct beam of the searchlight, the fading of the night into dawn was apparent on the eastern horizon as we negotiated the shallow waters of an island that may have been Torongohok.

Two very tired men climbed out of the folboat after finding a safe and heavily timbered headland that was uninhabited judging by the lack of crowing poultry and barking dogs, unloaded our gear, carried the folboat into the jungle and covered our tracks across the beach. Too exhausted to even string our hammocks up, we laid them out on the jungle floor, made a brew of hot chocolate, changed into dry clothing and after a cuppa and hard carrot biscuits, threw ourselves down on our hammocks. Covered by our lightweight Indian rugs, the beautiful sounds of the nocturnal jungle birds intermixed with the commencement of the day's constant humming of cicadas and the fading stars of the heavens, we were lulled into blissful sleep within minutes.

It must have been mid to late morning that I was wakened by the rustling noise of dry leaves in the jungle nearby. Scarcely daring to breathe for fear of seeing another Samak peering at us, I slowly slid my right hand down under the rug, grasped the silenced welrod pistol and disengaged the safety catch simultaneously. I half cocked an eye open to look at the intruder on my right and immediately thought I was in the world of dinosaurs or was I dreaming?

Less than five feet away from me on all fours stood a giant monitor lizard at least seven feet long. The first I had encountered in Borneo, it was not unlike the Australian monitor of Queensland or its smaller cousin the Racehorse Goanna of Western Australia. The Borneo model seemed to be miles longer! Probably, it was more like what I imagined a Komodo Dragon to look like.

Thrusting its tongue in and out, right and left, and with its strange menacing gait, it was quite frightening at first as it drew nearer. Then I realised that the monitor was not interested in us but its intentions were focussed on the basket of eggs and cakes near my head. As soon as I moved to render the basket safe, the monitor scampered away at a tremendous speed, notwithstanding its awkward gait. A kind kampong lady at Jambongan had given the goodies to us for the radio boys back at the 'mudflats' and made me promise that we would deliver them safely. I was so glad to have beaten the monitor to the punch.

Captain Gort Chester with three Guerrillas Lto R Indian Mohommad, A Malay Dusan, Chinese leader Tan Teck Bak

Sorely tempted to wake Gort, I restrained myself as I felt that it would be 'old hat' to him. As it turned out, when I later told him about the incident he confirmed my thoughts by saying that he had seen many and even larger monitors during his years in BNB. The Borneo of WW2 never failed to relinquish surprise after surprise for the unwary!

Later that day as we were preparing to pack our hammocks and gear, a large wild sow with about half a dozen squealing piglets at heel crashed through the jungle at full flight and across the area where we were camped.

As luck would have it, I was wiping my silenced Austen machine gun down with an oily rag as the pigs went through. Quickly slamming a loaded magazine in the gun, a single round picked off the last of the piglets 'tail end Charlie' as it endeavoured to follow its mother into the cover of the jungle. More fresh meat for the 'sparkies' and ourselves!. We hurriedly dressed and washed the carcass after burying the entrails etc and waited for sufficient darkness to make the last lap home.

No difficulty was experienced in entering our small river, the tide being full and on the slack. The sig boys who no doubt had spent some anxious moments during our absence wondering whether we were alive or dead and whether we had established any worthwhile contacts, eagerly awaited our mid morning arrival at the 'mudflats'.

Great was their joy when they learned that we had made what we believed to be a reliable and fruitful contact and that a further RV had been arranged with Samak.

They showed extreme concern when they realised that Jock and Don were not following behind our folboat until Gort told them that we had left them at Jambongan to arrange the building of huts for the sigs, a DZ and the formation of a guerrilla outfit. Furthermore, Gort told Fred, Graham and Skeet they were to close down the 'mudflats' pronto and that boat transport was on the way to pick them up and transfer them to Jambongan. The thought of getting back to some sort of civilisation was good news to their ears.

They were even more overjoyed when Gort and I presented the goodies from Jambongan. Unbelievably, not one of the 'cackleberries' was even cracked and the cakes, two fresh coconuts and the piglet were soon greedily consumed. Little did they realise the trials and tribulations we had experienced since leaving them.

Chapter 17

VULTEE VENGEANCE DIVE BOMBERS

Gort Chester was a man of many skills. The pre-war manager of the Lokawee Plantation, a short distance out from pre-war Jesselton (now Kota Kinabalu the capital city of Sabah), did not suffer fools or foolish actions. He was extremely tough physically, he possessed a face that was full of character, strength, and had a great sense of humour.

He was a highly intelligent intelligence officer and into the bargain was a good soldier. He was the ideal party leader for clandestine operations behind enemy lines, one who held the respect and love of the men serving with him, whether 'Z' men or guerrillas.

While he was a man of far more than average tolerance, his fuse could be extremely short on certain occasions when he would 'go off the deep end'. Gort was very mindful of the fact that 'HQ bunglers' as he variously described the shiny bum 'top brass' of SRD (later 'Z' HQ), had almost cost him the total force of operation 'Python' and carried those feelings with him to the grave.

His beautiful countenance and mannerism endeared him to all the indigenous races. They never disguised their love for him and spoke of him in the highest terms, irrespective of their ages from children to adults. He was probably one of the most popular party leaders to grace the threshold of 'Z' HQ and ladies simply adored him whether black, brown, brindle or white.

Shortly after getting ashore and into the river tributary in which area we established our first headquarters (HQ) the 'mudflats'. Then all of us assisted the sigs rig an aerial across two trees selected by Fred, at right angle (90 degree) to a beam transmitted from Melbourne.

146

Prior to our departure from Australia, Gort sought and received the assurance of the then Commanding Officer (CO) of our unit - then known as Services Reconnaissance Dept (SRD) and later renamed 'Z' Special Unit - that a strict radio silence would be observed until 'Agas 1' was firmly established. Gort would advise HQ accordingly. Only then was HQ Australia to call us on air.

The first few weeks ashore for all parties behind Japanese lines were tantamount to their operations ultimate success. Such worries as security from the enemy, locating a reliable water supply and finding a suitable spot in the jungle to set up camp plus the radio station for transmission to Australia, were matters of importance and on which our lives depended.

The morning was a typical Borneo jungle paradise for that time of the year, March until August / September. They are normally delightful months and that day was no exception.

Sunlight was streaming through small gaps in the verdant treetop canopy, cicadas sang in their usual ceaseless cacophony, the carolist birds of the morning – Whip birds and Fruit Pigeons - gave chorus in the treetops and secondary jungle. Colourful butterflies including Emperors, brilliant blue Skippers and Glasswings, flitted around.

Gort was pacing up and down outside the newly established radio shack – a tarpaulin strung between trees providing a lean-to roof over a bench made from jungle timber – deep in thought, his spectacles hanging from the corners of his mouth as was his usual habit.

The idyllic scene however, was unexpectedly broken by a radio signal from HQ in Australia calling us on air. Our call sign followed by 'QSQ' virtually meant "urgent stop I have an urgent communication for you stop".

The unexpected instruction infuriated Gort. However, realising that the communication could be urgent and could possibly endanger our location, relented to go on air.

Gort exclaimed 'why are these useless brothel bred bastards calling us to come on air? Those f....ing idiots agreed to lay off transmission until advised by us that we were happy about our location, security and radio; they wouldn't know how to organise a good shit-house. Is it any wonder that we are losing parties on insertion and even those who get in successfully are being compromised after establishment?"

The glorious morning and jungle beauty provided the perfect

scenario that justified the humourous old adage 'not a leaf stirred, not a bough stirred, not a dog stirred'. Stony silence reigned as Gort continued to pace up and down outside the radio shack. Six pairs of eyes fixed themselves steadfastly on our leader whose annoyance knew no bounds.

After lengthy consideration that seemed like hours instead of minutes, Gort reluctantly instructed Fred, our sigs Lieutenant, to go on air and take the 'QSQ'. The possibility that the message may be related to the POW in Sandakan had not escaped his mind; only the thought of those poor sufferers persuaded him from ignoring the call sign.

Still in the establishing mode, we had been unable to do anything constructive in the matter of the POW and all felt badly about the sufferings of those poor devils – the forced starvation, beatings, tortures and the dreaded 'cage' treatment etc.

'The cage', feared by the POW, seems to have been solely confined to the Sandakan POW camp during the Pacific and South East Asian campaign. It was without roof, too low for a person to stand erect, too short to lie down. 'The cage' constructed of rattan (cane) was a typical well-designed Japanese torture contraption and was open on all four sides, top and bottom. The prisoner was compelled to urinate and excrete through the rattan strake floor. He was seldom allowed out and on the rare occasions that this was permitted, was thrashed and thrown back in the cage. As a result few survived the cage treatment. One prisoner actually survived 40 days and nights before mercifully dying.

The daily rice ration was drastically reduced to the barest survival minimum and with 'kangkong', (swamp spinach), was tossed on the floor of the cage where the POW was expected to take his food like an animal.

Frequently, passing Japanese guards and officers urinated and spat on the prisoner and according to the Japanese whim, taken out and severely beaten or burned with hot coals, then put back. Many POW were subjected to this treatment and several perished in 'the cage.'

Shortages of food and the non-existence of clothing and medical supplies had its disastrous effect. It was unbearable for us to accept that here we were just miles from the camp and unable to assist in any way to alleviate the daily death rate, approaching 20/25.

The 'cage' appears to have been a progression of the 'chook pen', one of which was discovered in the Sandakan camp near the pigpen after their surrender. They were known to exist also in the River Kwai camps and one was found in the Ambon POW camp

Constructed in the same manner, the 'chook pen' was a miniature of the 'cage' but instead of human inhabitants, poultry was substituted. Apparently the 'chook pen' was highly regarded as a sport by Japanese soldiers who took it in turn to pierce the eyes of the unfortunate birds through the sides of the pen with sharpened slithers of bamboo while spectators cheered and laid bets. Only the Japanese could dream up such cruelty and regard it as an entertaining sport.

Is it any wonder that we at the 'mudflats' were anxious to see the POW at Sandakan liberated at the earliest possible date by operation 'Kingfisher'?

The three sigs Fred , Graham and Skeet moved into action and within minutes the familiar sounds of the Boston generator moaned into the glorious cacophony of natures overtones.

We were all trusting that the noise would not be picked up by the enemy only three miles away.

Jock, Don and I had no part in this task other than to admire the smooth operation of our sigs group. While we 3 were competent to operate radios and knew how to decipher our code, when compared with the sig group, our efforts were amateurish in both speed and style. Jock was quick to observe that they were a "flawless bloody sig group and we are fortunate to have such a team".

The time to decode the 5 letter groups was the bugbear of the signals operation. While the three sigs sat doing their chore, Gort continued to pace in silence like the proverbial tiger, his bald head reflecting the sunlight filtering through the treetops.

Gort continued to pace back and forth. Meanwhile, we three sat aside discussing the tomato seedlings that Fred had managed to propagate from seeds brought from Australia.

Fred had selected a small plot of soil near the mess table to plant the seeds. The sigs had built the table from jungle timber and in fact, it might still be there. When we left the 'mudflats' for Jambongan the legs of the table had sprouted leaves and the table may now be way up in the air. Who knows?

The tomato seedlings grew at a remarkable rate of about 3 inches daily and were about 2 feet high after the first week. We had already anticipated the glorious taste of fresh tomatoes, but one morning after breakfast we noticed that there was not one plant remaining. The jungle rats had eaten them down overnight. Fred made several attempts to grow the plants but was outsmarted by the rats and finally gave it away as a bad job.

All radio messages required a double transposition of the five letter groups: a time consuming job. Meanwhile, all seven of us – three sigs and four observers – anticipating anything, curiously awaited the decoded signal.

Finally, the message in plain language was handed by Fred to Gort who read it quickly while pacing, re- read it twice, not believing what his eyes revealed, then vocally exploded. The small amount of hair surrounding Gort's bald pate stood erect and his complexion slowly reddened until almost scarlet as it spread down his neck.

"A thousand immaculate bastards. Christ, Jesus, God almighty! What in the name of Christ do those brainless pricks back there mean by dragging us on air against our security arrangements and jeopardising our existence with this bloody rubbish? They're just a bloody lot of incompetent schoolboys playing at a game of intelligence. There would not be a single brain among the bloody lot of them. To call them arseholes would be doing a grave injustice to an arsehole"!

Clutching the document in his hand, Gort's pacing speed increased while cursing, unable to accept the impossible, the utter stupidity of the document he was holding.

All the while, poor Graham, whose hackles had been raised by Gort's unchristian like ranting was slowly regaining posture. With his religious background, on the occasions when Gort exploded in that manner, Graham's feelings were easily understood, feelings he could do little about; after all Gort was our commanding officer, senior rank and the authority of the party.

Despite the personal hurt suffered by Graham, his respect for Gort never wavered. He, like the rest of us, had over the period since joining 'Agas 1', developed a very strong and lasting respect for Gort Chester whose previous record with SRD in operation 'Python' was beyond criticism.

His involvement with other operations only added to his reputation as a worthy leader. When I first joined Gort he was Captain Gort Chester OBE (Order of the British Empire) vested on him for operation 'Python'. Since the insertion of 'Agas 1' he had been promoted to Major. After operation 'Stallion 4', he was posthumously decorated with the

Distinguished Service Order (DSO), Skeet Hywood and I, as Sergeants, the equivalent Distinguished Conduct Medal (DCM).

Even Captain Jock Sutcliffe 2ic (Second In Command) of our operation 'Agas 1', while not always in agreement with Gort's decisions, ideas and recommendations, never the less accepted his authority knowing full well that Gort was seldom wrong.

Jock, who had served with the Gordon Highlanders in Malaya pre-war was a very proud man in his own way, and did not normally accept decisions that were in variance to his own, of this we were all painfully aware as later events proved. However, in Gort's case he always accepted and respected Gort's experience and judgment.

Gort Chester had a charisma of his own. His smile and beaming countenance plus his charming mannerism won him unbounded popularity among both men and women. In fact, where the ladies of our unit were concerned he was tops. I never ever met anybody that spoke of Gort in terms other than good. Even the epitaph on his tombstone in Kota Kinabalu bears the words 'a most lovable man'.

Fred, who had been in Borneo as a Sergeant signaler in Gort's operation 'Python 1' was accustomed to Gort's idiosyncrasies. On the other hand I, who had been the next longest serving with Gort, was experiencing my first occasion of Gort's verbal outbursts, but it was not to be the last.

On a later occasion when he and I were sneaking through the jungle adjacent to a Japanese establishment, Gort unfortunately blundered into a ' nante dahulu' palm spike, a very painful experience at any time, and more so in Gort's case as the spike had penetrated his eye. In the Malay language 'nante dahulu' literally means 'wait awhile'.

Gort immediately exploded into his usual opening phrase when cursing. "A thousand immaculate bastards, Christ, Jesus, God almighty" which brought forth Japanese soldiers who fired on us as we fled through the jungle. We were both very fortunate to be alive. Gort had a sore eye and I was nursing a sprained ankle, injured in our hurry to get away. Gort was apologetic about his outburst for days.

Fred Graham and Skeet were a jump ahead of Gort, Jock Don and myself. Incredulous, dumbfounded they were, but at least they were right up with Gort's reasons for his agitated behaviour while we could not guess at the contents of the signal.

Having finally regained his normality, he put us in the picture by reading out aloud the signal "Can you build airstrip suitable for Vultee Vengeance dive bombers stop so many hundreds of feet long and so many feet wide?". The authority for the message was Flight Lieutenant Bartram. We could scarcely believe our ears, but knowing some of the inglorious history of earlier SRD operations, the failures and loss of life caused by administrative bungling, nothing surprised us.

Appreciating the fact that Paul Bartram was a senior officer of our 'L' room (top secret – planning) and who was supposed to have a good knowledge of the terrain in which we had located ourselves, the message was too stupid to even contemplate.

First and foremost we were only 7 men not 70. We were in jungle that white man had previously never penetrated. The terrain varied from sea level to 3000 ft and one was battling to find 50 feet of level ground suitable for a chopper, let alone Vultee Vengeance dive-bombers. I am no aviator but my first guess would be that at least a strip of 3,000 feet would be the barest minimum required to get a Vultee Vengeance airborne and back on the deck.

Gort was almost back to his usual equilibrium after a lot of joint discussion about certain personalities who would have been more gainfully employed running a brothel than as a planning co-ordinator for clandestine operations. At 'Z' HQ, their ears must have been burning that memorable morning. Gort decided that the signal had to be some form of joke. Accordingly, on Fred's assurance that a quick reply would not compromise our radio location, Gort decided the following reply was appropriate. After encoding by the sigs it read: -

"Re building of air strip suitable for Vultee Vengeance dive bombers, regret we cannot help stop have no bulldozer stop Gort"

The following night, despite our calculations that our reply would have acknowledged the HQ message and the matter would be at an end, we were called on air again 'QSQ' and the message read when decoded "Can arrange for bulldozer stop Paul Bartram stop".

Gort's reply in the next radio transmission read "Message acknowledged stop even with bulldozer we have no qualified driver".

Not content with what had transpired, back came another 'QSQ' message "Re bulldozer, can arrange for qualified driver also stop Bartram".

The matter was becoming a farce. However Gort – not to be denied - sent back the next piece of bait "Have no shovels, other tools or men stop Gort". When would this stupidity end? The bait was snapped up immediately.

From Bartram at HQ came "Captain John Chipper on way to Palawan stop have arranged LST (landing ship tank) to transport bulldozer, driver, 20 men and tools stop Bartram".

This was the last straw and it certainly did break the camel's back, motivating Gort to explode again. "F...ing arseholes! These idiots are for real! A thousand immaculate bastards! Christ, Jesus, God Almighty! This f...ing bastard is not joking, he is dead serious!" Gort became so agitated we felt he would leave the planet.

After a long spell to calm down and resume his normal pacing speed, Gort had the sigs send back "Re bulldozer, driver, men and tools stop forget the matter we are only having you on stop Gort".

Reflecting on the matter today, I can see in my mind's eye a picture of the 'L' room at 'Harbury' our then newly established HQ opposite the Botanical Gardens Toorak Melbourne.

I see also a number of agitated, pompous, authority inflated, beer bellied officers ranging from army Captains and Colonels to message boys in the form of lowly Lieutenants and Sergeants lurking in the background awaiting orders to carry out the jobs of drudgery and unimportance. Holding the centre of attention, I see none other than Flight Lieutenant Paul Bartram Royal Australian Air Force. Nicknamed 'the kangaroo' at Frazer Island Commando School (FCS) by the operatives and sigs because of his approximate height 6 foot 5 inches, thin frame plus his lean and hungry look, he seldom smiled and oozed with authority, rightly or wrongly.

Never to be denied the last word, Bartram's authoritative rejoinder to all his former 'QSQ' messages was amusingly received by Gort who responded in like manner. Gort knew Paul Bartram and was not particularly impressed by him.

Bartram's anticipated reply read "Please restrict your humour whilst in the field or be withdrawn" to which Gort immediately replied 'QSQ' "Withdraw us all immediately". To Gort's terse reply we heard no more.

Gort had won the battle for words and there was much laughter in our camp thereafter. The unexpected happened when considerably later, having arrived back at Morotoi aboard an American Martin Mariner Flying Boat on a mission for Gort, I was shown the 'Agas 1' back order list. A typewritten foolscap document listing thousands of rounds of ammunition, weapons, grenades, medical supplies, rice, sarongs plus even toys for the children of our guerrillas, hung on a clip-board on the wall of the Q store for all to see. The Quartermaster and his staff – like the rest of the staff from highest to lowest – knew the story as described above. It spread through 'Z', Flight 200 and sister units like the proverbial bushfire.

On the very bottom line of the back order was listed one bulldozer, qualified driver, 20 men plus shovels and assorted tools.

Mercifully the said machine never did arrive. Furthermore, Gort Chester and we six representing 'Agas 1' were never withdrawn. Needless to say not another word from Paul Bartram was ever received regarding "building an airstrip" and the offending bulldozer plus extras remained on the back order list forever.

Come 1974, my 'Z' buddy Keith Scarff and I were staying with my former sister-in-law Nola Downey (nee Sheahan) and her husband Bill of Rabaul. Nola was the Harbour Master's secretary and after relating the story to them over a beer in their garden hacienda one night, they said there was an ex-army man John Chipper in the marine business in Rabaul. Appropriately aged, they wondered if their John Chipper was the man in question.

Imagine my surprise when I visited him and found that he was the Captain John Chipper involved, and he was still cackling over the incident almost 30 years later. It seemed like a fitting end to an almost unbelievable story of an intelligence??? officer and an air-strip for Vultee Vengeance dive-bombers. It makes one wonder how in hell we ever won a war.

Towards the end of hostilities and prior to establishment of 'Z' HQ at Labuan Island, I recall that Don Harlem – in the Death March area – sent a radio message to HQ Morotai. It simply read "Have captured two Japanese Geisha girls stop very clean, very hygiene, very symmetrical stop what shall we do with them?" stop. Harlem. Obviously, someone with a streak of humour – probably a radio operator - replied poste haste thus "Message re Geisha girls acknowledged stop will swap for Flight Lieut. Paul Bartram" stop. The message naturally, bore no name of sender. We did not have to wonder why.

Chapter 18

MUSA AND THE JAPANESE RAFTER GHOSTS

With the sigs firmly entrenched at Jambongan after months in the stinking 'mudflat' area, it must have been like heaven to them with plenty of fresh coconuts, paw paws, other fruits and vegetables, fish, meat and poultry. Furthermore, they were no longer alone. They had the protection of the newly recruited guerrillas that Jock and Don were training, as well as the friendly kampong people and their lovely children who were always a delight.

Although their stay there was only for a short time, and this they were unaware of at that juncture, better still was to come at Lokopas on the mainland. Security on Jambongan Island could not be guaranteed as had been proved by the visiting Nipponese patrol craft, whereas Lokopas was relatively safe from land and sea. It was completely ringed into the coast by impenetrable mountains to the north, south and west and was also protected by the endless shallows of Musa channel to the east.

At the 'mudflats' HQ, the sigs had Japanese strongposts a couple of miles north and south of them and it was always a lingering worry to us knowing full well that Jock and Don were at Jambongan, we were always on the move and this left the sigs alone. Our meagre force of seven was separated. Additionally, we were still worried that the oar we had lost the night we left Tuna, or the equipment washed out of the folboats on our first attempt to get out of our small river might be found on the beach; this would spell tragedy for the sigs.

While at Jambongan helping to set the sigs up in the new headquarters, two events of importance occurred. From Samak came the news that a former wealthy Chinese trader whose name must remain anonymous, had turned pro-Japanese and was working in conjunction with the Japanese Sitjokisat. This was a MI6 type of organisation that was feared by the indigenous people even more than the Kempei Tai. Rumour had it that he was being sent to the east coast to enquire into reports that an Australian underground movement was alive and well, and that its clandestine activities were responsible for the loss of Japanese patrol boats and personnel plus attacks on outlying Japanese posts. Gort sent a message via the grape-vine, asking Samak to keep us informed as to Judas' movements and, particularly if he arrived in Sandakan.

Gort and Nick apparently knew him pre-war or knew of him and neither had a good word for the man.

The second event surrounded another wealthy Chinese merchant who had arrived from the northern island of Bangey with two accomplices. To me, it was obvious that while Gort was his usual pleasant outward self towards him, he was none the less very guarded in conversation with the man and asked the Tuan Hadji of Jambongan not to allow the man or his accomplices to wander around the island alone. Hadji was to keep a close record of their activities,

The Japanese were slowly but surely moving their scattered pockets of troops to a central area on the west coast north of Jesselton – possibly Tuaran – near where their intelligence information had indicated that the allied troops proposed to land. Other than the POW being in Sandakan, it was pointless landing on the east coast. There were no roads out of Sandakan westwards or anywhere else. It was impossible to move large concentrations of troops inland, particularly, since the airfield at Sandakan had been all but totally bombed off the face of the earth by the American saturation air raids since September/October 1944.

The Japanese intelligence didn't need to be very intelligent to recognise hard cold simple facts.

Toward the Lokopas end of our journey, encountering strong headwinds and a savage current against us that entailed navigating through the shallow channel that separated Musa Island from the mainland, we realised too late to turn back that we would not be able to get through the channel before daylight.

Our guide's small native Prahu and its crew of three were considerably slower than our folboat, and had difficulty negotiating the numerous shallows through the channel. Even our folboat that drew so little water had to be walked through a considerable distance of the channel, frequently compelling the heavy Malay Prahu to be dragged through a much longer distance while seeking deeper water to enable the Prahu to negotiate the maze of sand banks.

Despite the weight of the Prahu, the problems of currents and wind, fatigue and the possibility of treading on stone fish that were prevalent in the channel, the Malay boys never uttered a complaint. They only had one advantage over us; they could afford to be seen in the area without arousing suspicion whereas our folboat and ourselves stood out like a lighthouse on a dark night.

About 0300 we spotted a long penghalen (jetty) reaching out through the darkness from the shore. A long meandering snake like kilong (picket like fence constructed of long stakes that trapped fish in the long maze-like structure as the tide fell) shielded the short tee ended jetty. The kilong stretched for some distance north and south of the jetty and had received no maintenance for a long period. Knowing that a dwelling or kampong had to be in the vicinity of the kilong, Gort decided that we should discuss the situation with our Malay guides before venturing shorewards.

After what seemed like ages, the Malay boys arrived along side when the discussion revealed that at the beach end of the jetty there was a large solid timber godown (warehouse). While in good condition, no one had lived in it for some time; the nearest kampong was some three miles or more from the jetty. Our extreme weariness and being fed to the teeth with the long night journey over-ruled our senses of curiosity and caution.

Normally, it would have registered to us both, that a good warehouse and jetty so far from a kampong was just not on, and certainly not compatible with Malay life. The lovable Malay people in those days were not known for their activity and industrious ways as is the case today; even their language until they gained their independence was like their lifestyle – lazy and suggestive of "why do today that which can be done tomorrow."? No way would they establish a kampong so far from a godown where they would purchase every day household needs, and where they would trade their fish and other sea products, and the availability of such a damn fine jetty on which to unload their catches. No way!

Taking up our paddles again, Gort and I took the lead and propelled the folboat a short distance north along the meandering kilong until we eventually found a section where a number of stakes were missing. This gap allowed both craft to enter with ease – it was almost as though someone had thrown us an open invitation to come on in.

Arriving under the shelter of the jetty, our shielded torchlight on the oyster covered piles revealed that there was still considerable clearance at high tide to tie the boats, rendering them fairly inconspicuous from land and sea. Leaving the Malay boys to guard the boats and satisfied that both craft were securely tied, Gort and I took our weapons and cautiously made our way down the jetty towards a large building, barely visible in the lingering darkness - to check it out.

Nearing the building, we noticed first that there was a verandah fronting the typically Malay styled godown under which was a large round table with a number of mahogany chairs – neatly positioned and all in perfect condition. Most odd for a supposedly deserted building! Behind the round table were a pair of solid mahogany doors leading into the building which when pushed, readily opened and we found ourselves confronting a counter in what we assumed was the main part of the shop.

An area of about 25ft x 20ft faced the front door, and over the narrow section was a mezzanine serviced by a flight of stairs. Gort and I went up the stairs, hurriedly peered around the floored area and satisfied ourselves that the place was deserted. We then returned to the boats to fetch the boys, hammock bags and personal gear to enable us to change into dry clothes before settling down for some well-earned sleep.

On our way back along the jetty, when peering through the darkness towards the building we noticed that the jungle surrounding it appeared to have been cleared which was not out of place for a godown – probably owned by a Chinese towkey (shop owner). By clearing the land around the building – the cleared section known as lalang – protection was provided against the secondary jungle growing back to reclaim the warehouse, preventing monkeys and other animals from entering the building via the roof.

Although the risk of fire in rain forest areas was minimal, squirrels and other animals similar in their habits to our Australian possums, accessed themselves through overhanging trees, fouled up water run-offs with leaves and other matter.

The guerrilla boys appeared strangely uneasy when we announced that the building was ideal for our purpose but offered no explanation, neither did we seek one, their uneasiness misinterpreted as weariness. We were completely buggered by this stage and sought only a dry spot to get the head down for a few hours.

Setting our hammocks flat on the floor near the side wall, the boys took up the opposite wall where they squatted on juke bags brought from their prahu – I often wondered how they managed to sleep in that position. In next to no time Gort and I were fast asleep. The boys apparently fell off to sleep not long after.

We had been asleep for probably an hour or so when we were all rudely awakened by what could only be described as blood curdling screams that appeared to emanate from the rafters of the building. The screams continued for minutes – or so it seemed – while we lay awake before I switched on my torch. The screaming switched off. The guerrilla boys were by now huddled together in one corner, the whites of their eyes prominent in the torchlight and stark terror spread across their faces.

Not feeling too happy about the strange situation myself, Gort broke the silence with "what the f.....g hell is that Jack"?. Then to the boat boys "apa itu yang bunyi besar?" (what's that making the loud noise) to which they stammered out in unison and in shaking voices "Hantu Jepun Tuan" meaning "Japanese ghosts Sir" in Malay. One could not but notice the terror in their eyes, given that the Malays and Chinese are upholders of ghosts and their like. Gort looked at me almost quizzically before saying "sounds like a lot of balls to me Jack; but stranger things have happened in this bloody country. I must say that I don't believe in ghosts" and in so saying, re-iterated my feelings, although I had only been in British North Borneo for weeks compared with Gort's many years. Nonetheless my inexperienced youth shared the same un-easiness as did the wisdom, experience and maturity of my senior and father figure.

The decision to get out of the bloody joint was unanimous and less time was spent getting out than getting in! We started making our way back down the long jetty when the screaming re-commenced and must have continued for a minute or two before we got into the boats. We were content to spend the remaining darkness hours there, during which the screaming continued intermittently for an hour or more. The Malay boys were well ahead of us and in their boat by the time we had arrived, so great was their fear. They were very reluctant to discuss the matter and wanted to get to sea immediately. However, Gort and I were convinced that no bird or animal could emit such a sound, and that the sounds were definitely of human origin: we finally agreed that the blood-curdling screams suggested a bout of throat cutting.

It was a crying shame that the night's work was completely ruined by the sandbanks, the delays caused by the Malay prahu through no fault of the great little crew, and finally our sleeping hours that were so badly interrupted by the unexplained and yet horrifying screaming human-like noises. Sitting in the folboat endeavouring to get some sleep as hoards of mosquitoes attacked us mercilessly, and while my sore bum was seeking the most comfortable position on the bare timber slat-seat, I had sufficient concentration left within me to reflect on the night's activities.

It had been a beautiful sunset as we prepared to leave the mainland on our night's paddle to Lokopas. The red and gold of the waning sunset gave way gradually to a pale silky green canopy through the silhouetted coconut palms along the shoreline. This in turn was displaced by an almost ultra marine dark blue that was finally absorbed by the black of the night sky, glittering with a marvellous display of studded diamonds as the heaven's lights reached their maximum in brilliance.

The overhead brilliance was matched only by the phosphorescent beetles in the ocean below, seemingly endeavouring to compete with the overhead jewelled cover as the bow of the prahu and the folboat sliced through the water setting up brilliant phosphorescent trails. These trails were interspersed with circular glows set up in the water as alarmed flying gurnards panicked and took off from the surface in their flights to safety.

From under the jetty where our boats were riding with their tired human cargoes, I noticed that the piles of the jetty near our folboat were covered with large oysters and what I assumed were some type of phosphorescent shellfish, nudibranchs or similar small marine creatures. Whatever they were, they set up a decidedly eerie green glow. I looked towards the shore, swatting mossies all the while and noticed that all the small shrubbery cum secondary jungle was covered in fireflies resembling fairy cities where the concentrations were the thickest.

As the darkness was replaced with the pre-sunlight of dawn, the Malay boys chose to 'let sleeping dogs lie' and stuck to the boats. Gort and I, armed with our silenced Austen machine guns, side arms and torches and all the while re-gaining our confidence as daylight approached, made our way slowly back along the jetty towards the godown.

Having convinced ourselves that nobody was about, we set about making a closer inspection of the premises.

Over the edge of the jetty and on the beach sand well above high tide mark were a couple of broken chairs of the same design as those surrounding the round table on the verandah front. A closer inspection revealed a huge stained area almost as large in area as the top of the table. Creeping up to the double mahogany doors in the crouch position and with the safety catches on our Austens in the 'fire' position, with one simultaneous action we thrust both doors open with the flash compensating muzzles of our Austens. Bloody marvellous how two human minds could re-act as one when the chips appeared to be down.

Inside the double doors were traces of what appeared to be dark paint drips leading to the mezzanine stairs and at the foot of the stairs we found another pool stain about half the size of the one under the round table. More drip marks led upstairs towards the corner of the mezzanine where the last stain was found, again of pool dimensions but twice as large as that under the table

After much discussion, we decided that while the Chinese towkey would have stocked paint for the maintenance of boats and for domestic purposes, the stains were definitely those of human blood. But what was the story behind all the stains and were they connected with the human screams we had witnessed? Even today more than fifty years later, those screams are etched deep into my memory as though it had happened only yesterday.

An inspection around the outside of the godown yielded nothing that could explain the strange happenings. There were no overhanging trees or even shrubs that could harbour any creature of reasonable size capable of such noise. The lalang while not kept mown was less than two feet high, which itself indicated that it had probably been mown less than one year ago but no shrubbery was present. The more we thought about it, the more puzzling the problem and further more, we knew that we had to get on our way as we were expected at Lokopas the previous evening.

With no further enlightenment on the subject and the boys not prepared to discuss the matter beyond the point that the place was riddled with 'Hantu Jepun', as soon as night had fallen sufficiently to conceal our movements, we pushed off from the Musa Island jetty.

The night was another memorable one following a beautiful clear day completely free of wind, similar to the previous night. The air all that afternoon was somewhat steamy and heavily scented with frangipani and other jungle blooms, and if there was one butterfly there, there had to be

161

thousands; all brightly coloured against the lush green background. Small Skippers similar to our Australian common brown Skippers - aptly named for their skipping motion in flight – flitted everywhere. Measuring only 5 inches from wingtip to wingtip, they were resplendent in their blues and yellows as they mingled in flight with Glasswings of numerous varieties and sizes. The unbelievable varieties of butterflies ranged from tiny lavender blue Grass Blues that were smaller than the Skippers through to the colourful Birdwing Rajah Brooke of approximately 6" that occasionally flew through our line of vision.

Whether or not the lalang was an attraction to the butterflies I still do not know. I could see that they were in plague proportions, the like of which I have never seen again.

In 1979 I was invited by Malaysian Airline Services to spend some days at the newly constructed Merlin Samudra Hotel on the then little known pulau (island) of Tioman off the east coast of Malaysia. My purpose was to check out the underwater world for overseas diving tours pioneered by our family business W.A. Skin Divers established 1951.

After free-diving alone there for a week in the glassy smooth clear waters, I found it to be a diving paradise with its exquisitely coloured staghorns, tree gorgonians, cabbage, plate, soft and other varieties of corals and coloured anemones. Through the numerous anemones swam schools of clown fish, parrot fish and wrasses of all hues and others I had not previously seen in our tropic or sub-tropic waters in Australia. On the ocean floor looking like a pumpkin farm were closed anemones of all sizes, purple, blue, orange, yellow, green, and brown.

Not only had I discovered a divers dreamland but I had also found an entomologist's paradise with Tioman's unbelievable array of butterflies, day and night moths and other interesting insects including fire flies.

Having accompanied me in the fishing boat that serviced the island from Mersing on the Malaysian mainland, long before the arrival of ferries and light aircraft. a very young Chinese Singapore Airlines pilot and his newly acquired attractive bride were spending their honeymoon there. We were the first three guests to stay in the newly opened Merlin Samudra Hotel.

Although not generally known to the film-going public, most of the backdrops for the Hollywood musical 'South Pacific' was shot on beautiful Tioman Island, which interestingly enough, is almost in the same tropical zone as Musa Island. This possibly explains the profusion of butterflies and similar small animal and bird life common to both islands.

The heavily scented air hung off Musa Island as we made our way seawards. The silky green sky of the twilight had turned to blue black studded with myriads of diamond-like stars. The ocean was calm as a millpond, mirroring the maze of stars that seemed to increase in number as the sky darkened before moonrise. The mirrored image was spread around our two boats, disturbed only by the phosphorescent trails of surface fish avoiding the intrusion of our craft. With this entire God given splendour, it was inconceivable that we were in a hostile environment.

Negotiating the shallows approaching Lokopas was no mean task, and without the expert guidance of our Malay boys we would have been in big trouble. It was little wonder that the Japanese feared negotiating the channel separating Musa Island from the mainland.

At approximately 0200 we entered a small bay hidden from seaward, beached our boats and were preparing to make our way with the boys to the nearby kampong when the populace – men women and children – began to drift out to welcome us after having been aroused by the kampong's look-out.

The very first impression gained by Gort and myself was that these people were predominantly Chinese; the first Chinese guerrilla group we had encountered.

By now we were growing accustomed to the overwhelming greetings of the suppressed peoples of the Nipponese occupied territories. Not only were they impressed by our equipment, equipment the likes of which they had not seen since the British left, they already knew that the new friendly faces and mannerisms were largely Australian, rather than British.

Even though the new faces were represented by Gort and myself, the tall Chinese self professed leader – who accompanied the welcoming party- had spread the word throughout the kampong on his return from Jambongan that he had met four Australians there.

He added that there were three radio operators hidden in the 'ulu' (slang for jungle) 'somewhere in BNB' so secret that he did not have the faintest idea. It later transpired that he had told them that our tiny ATR4 transmitter was capable of transmitting over thousands of miles; the three radio operators could be anywhere. The truth re the ATR4 was carelessly handled or exaggerated out of all proportion for while it was a wonderful little set, it had its limitations as Fred, Graham and Skeet had repeatedly warned us.

Gort put on his best face for the Chinese; he had that winning charm and charisma that never failed to create the best of first impressions. After the welcome and the introductions were behind us, the Chinese gentleman who we shall refer to as Lim, expressed the concern of all the kampong people when we failed to arrive the previous evening. We explained that the elements were against us and that we were forced in to Musa Island. Lim felt relieved, knowing full well that the pro-allied kampong on the island would have welcomed us with open arms and cared for us.

The benevolent smiles however, turned to looks of stark horror when it was pointed out to them that we had avoided the kampong – not knowing whether the Japanese were about – and had slept in the jetty godown. They were even more horrified when we poured out our strange experience involving the screaming 'Hantu Jepun' and they were not surprised by the fact that our boat boys – scared to death -would not discuss the matter. One of the Chinese guerrillas we had just met, Tan Teck Bak – we will learn a lot more about this brave man as our experiences unfold – related the story of the Musa Island ghosts.

It transpired that a couple of years earlier, only small Japanese vessels would attempt to navigate through the Musa (Malay for deer) Channel and then only when there was a Chinese or Malay pilot to take them through the maze of channels. The Chinese towkey who owned the godown on the Musa jetty conspired with the young Chinese bloods of the kampong who unanimously agreed to a plan to 'do over' the next 'kapal binatang' (kapal meaning ship in Malay – animal ship) seeking a pilot.

The day eventually arrived when a Japanese MTB (motor torpedo boat) tied alongside and sought a pilot from the towkey. The appointed Chinese pilot pointed out that the tide had already commenced to fall and that it would be impossible to make the passage until slack water following high tide, after which the tide would commence to fall again. All the attractive Chinese and Malay girls were conveniently about at the time with the older folk of the kampong.

The officer commanding the ship was invited ashore with his crew to enjoy some 'makan dan minum' (food and drink), dancing and singing. He showed no hesitation: the girls – believe me when I say they were beautiful - no doubt provided the extra bit of enticement.

A freshly slaughtered pig was brought in from the nearby kampong and placed on a spit. Meanwhile, the captain of the ship and his crew of eleven were invited on a short tour of the surrounding areas and kampong, and finally back to the godown verandah, arriving there a little worn out and anticipating a lovely meal and sojourn.

The round table on the verandah of the godown was invitingly set up with a table-cloth and the necessary trimmings. The drink was served along with nuts and other pre-dinner titbits by the attractive girls who in the eyes of the Japanese – they were no different to any other hot blooded males of any race – became all the more attractive and alluring as the alcohol took the desired effect.

Tan Teck Bak was particularly descriptive of the reigning scenario. The air was balmy, the scenery along the foreshore with hundreds of tiny blue and white soldier crabs marching and wheeling in unison on the golden sands was a picture any artist would wish to paint. Overhead, the coconut palms swept their lofty heads over the exposed undulating sandbanks and remaining shallow pools following tide fall.

The lingering aroma of frangipani with intermittent tantalising wafts of barbecued pork; the anticipation of good food, more drink and prospects of laying some pretty and shapely maidens was not difficult to imagine. Mother nature had set the stage beautifully as per the night before. Ours while still balmy was minus drink, dusky maidens for the laying, but with the Japanese ghosts.

Suddenly and at the precise moment when the drink had taken its toll, some fifteen Chinese young bloods leapt out from all surrounding points of concealment – Tan Teck Bak leading them. Brandishing long sharpened parangs, they pounced upon the unwary, unsuspecting and alcohol befuddled Japanese. Any ideas harboured by the 'binatangs' of laying the lovely Chinese and Malay girls disappeared in a flash as the roles became reversed.

With Japanese heads rolling across the deck both port and starboard, blood everywhere and all retreat seaward cut off, the only escape from the macabre scene was through the shop for the few Nipponese still retaining heads. With nowhere to turn they took the only route possible, the mezzanine floor stairs. At the foot of the stairs the parangs took their further grizzly toll while the remaining guerrillas chased the surviving few 'binatangs' into the exit-less mezzanine where they were finally butchered.

As the story unfolded through Teck Bak's lips, it was particularly noticeable that by his gesticulations and expressive face, he was joyously re-living the experience as were his listening compatriots who had taken part in that day's activities.

Fearing the inevitable discovery of the missing MTB by the Japanese Navy and subsequent 'preksa' (investigation) by the Kempei Tai or the Sitjokisat, plus the inescapable reprisals that would undoubtedly follow, the Chinese deserted the island. They sought the protection of Lokopas on the mainland while the Malays shifted their kampong from the precincts of the godown.

The Malays in particular, being more superstitious than the Chinese – and that's really saying something because the Chinese were also fairly superstitious – believed that the ghosts had to be appeased. They kept the godown and verandah tidy as part of the appeasement plan. Since the massacre on the island, the 'Hantu Jepun' had been heard on many occasions; their screams indicating – so the Chinese and Malays believed – that they were still not happy with their lot. It was little wonder that they were not happy!

Strangely, the wrath of the Japanese did not eventuate. The expected routine investigation by the Kempei Tai never materialised and there the matter died a natural death.

When two Japanese Kempei Tai officers finally visited the island to half- heartedly investigate the matter, the kampong people of Musa and the Chinese towkey denied any knowledge of the MTB having called in to the island's jetty. More than likely, the MTB may not have been in radio contact with its home base thus compelling the Kempei Tai to accept the assumption that it had been sunk by American aircraft or surface vessel.

Perhaps the craft had been lost with all hands as a result of foundering on a reef or lost as a result of accidental explosion. Who among the Japanese was found guilty of 'neglect of duty' or held responsible for the loss of the MTB, none seemed to know; the islanders being the last to care. To Tan Teck Bak it seemed the lack of follow-up on the matter positively suggested that all suspicion of the island folk's involvement had been lifted and the Japanese had looked elsewhere for the answers.

Whatever the outcome of the Kempei Tai's enquiries, no further Japanese patrol craft ventured through the channel.

What should they do with the Japanese MTB? The final coup de grace had yet to be played in the bizarre action.

As nothing could possibly look less like a Malay fishing craft, in order to protect themselves, Tan Teck Bak and his cohorts, much against their grain, wisely decided to take the craft well out to sea at night and open the sea cocks. Secretly, they wanted so badly to crew the craft and use the MTB against selected Japanese targets.

Steamed out into deep water and safely consigned to Davey Jones' Locker, Teck Bak and his crew were taken aboard a Malay fishing boat and returned to the island.

Musa was abandoned and Lokopas was established. All the Chinese and many of the young Malay population deserted the island for the mainland area of Lokopas, shortly to become our third headquarters.

Lokopas consisted of a good boat landing, spacious level ground for a DZ, excellent fertile land admirably protected on all sides by lofty mountains. Numerous permanent streams irrigated the beautifully fertile volcanic agricultural valley, including some small patches of padi (rice) fed by waters from the outer ring of high densely forested mountains that surrounded the valley and its contained smaller hills. The mountains constituted a natural protective barrier against the Japanese.

The evening spent there on our first visit was well worth the time. Gort, having noticed Lim's reluctance to include Teck Bak in conversations, suspected that Lim might appear to be the spokesman for the kampong yet felt that there was a gulf between Lim, the older folk of the kampong and the younger guerrillas led by Teck Bak. These young potential fighters were the people that attracted us and we needed to recruit them. These were the people who had killed the hated Japanese on Musa and we needed to encourage that hatred; we were not the least interested in their local politics. The Lokopas Chinese, unlike most of the Malays of the area, had a proven record against the 'binatangs'.

Being much closer in age to the guerrillas, I naturally was able to discuss with them – free of politics – the progress of the war in the Pacific and their approaching involvement now that 'Agas' was in their territory. They needed to understand the part they would play by sabotaging the enemy from the rear – typical guerrilla activity –as the allied advancing front neared the Celebes (now Sulawesi) and BNB (now Sabah) and what that meant to them in real terms. A very close association was set up between Teck Bak as the leader of our Chinese guerrillas and myself which was to prove a life-long friendship, that extended to his families and mine to this very day.

Again, Gort's hunch that there was a feeling of uneasiness and factionizing in the area proved to be correct; the old or not so old and the young. However, believing that the situation could be contained with delicate handling, Gort made the decision to move headquarters to Lokopas. The enthusiastic Chinese guerrillas were immediately signed up and commenced work building a suitable house for us on the slope of one of the inner ring of small hills overlooking the ocean and clearing a DZ. The only direction that the hide-out could be approached from was the east – the shallows of the bay that had virtually claimed the Japanese MTB and its crew.

Within two days the DZ had been cleared, recognition fires had been established and the atap roofed house completed. The total house,boasted solid mahogany one inch thick flooring. Having been built on the side of a hill, the house undercroft served as a cool and spacious area for the medical stores that would provide a stop-gap until a small hospital was built.

The DZ was a two-purpose ground suitable as a dropping zone and training ground for the guerrillas. The way was now prepared for Captain Nick Combe and his 'Agas 2' team to be inserted by Flight 200 Liberator. Arms, ammunition, guerrilla clothing, food, medical supplies and personal requirements were high on the priority list. Even badly needed clothing was on the order for the guerrillas' wives and families etc. Gort was most adamant that happy guerrillas produced the ultimate results and we had learned that in these matters, he was an unerring judge having been through the ropes of the game earlier.

The morning after the night before, I was awakened by a glorious chorus of what I thought was bird-song. Gort was up and about a few minutes before me. Lying on my hammock I listened intently to the beautiful sounds that obviously came from the trees surrounding the valley.

The song – as near as I can describe it – comprised one word "kelawott" repeated over and over commencing on a low bass note and the word being tunefully and slowly drawn out as 'k…e…l…a…w…o…t…t'. Gradually it increased in pitch and rapidity until going through more than an octave, it hit the ceiling with a crescendo when it just became a fast succession of "kwott, kwott, kwott." Yet it maintained its beautiful tone, even in the top register a la Benny Goodman's clarinet – beautiful tone in both low and high registers. There was not just one of the songsters but hundreds of them, the sounds emanating from treetops surrounding the valley. There was only one way to describe the melody – plain bloody beautiful, beautiful beyond belief and had to be heard to be believed.

I learned later that the songsters were not birds but gibbons of a particular family when Nelson Short (one of the 6 survivors of the Death Marches) and I went to Borneo with Ian Leslie and a documentary team to shoot 'Return to Sandakan' for 60 minutes. Nelson remembered that during the Death March from Sandakan they often woke to the beautiful sounds of the 'kelawott' gibbons in the deep parts of the mountainous rain forests, but seldom saw them. Despite their pains of beri-beri, stomach cramps, malaria, dysentery, desperate hunger etc and sleeping in the open, they were still able to appreciate the beautiful singing of the kelawott gibbons.

Beyond their trials and tribulations, they still had the appreciation for the beautiful wild life that surrounded their every painful night hour and daily killing slog through mud and other difficulties during that hideous march. In fact, he added "I had one given to me as a pet after you blokes rescued us from the Nips and I simply loved it. It broke my heart when I had to leave him behind in Borneo. I knew I would be prevented from landing back home in Aussie with the little bastard".

I found Gort about to sit down to breakfast and immediately joined him. The menu included glorious tasting pineapple that surpassed any I had ever eaten previously and today, the same Sabah pineapple retains its reputation in Japan, mainland China, south to the Indonesian archipelago and other Far East nations. A little more expensive than pineapples grown elsewhere, the exquisite taste of Sabah grown pineapples owe its popularity to the volcanic soil in which they grow and they are occasionally available in Australian markets to connoisseurs. Once eaten, never forgotten.

On the menu also were very tiny golden bananas the flavour of which could only be described as 'delicious banana', Jack Fruit and another fruit new to me - Rambutan. Fish followed the fruit and the sum total was washed down with fragrant Chinese tea. The fish 'Ikan Puti' (white fish) was as the name implies, beautifully white flesh and was of a delectable texture and taste and quite similar in shape to our 'Dart', a mid-water swimming fish, fairly commonly distributed over a wide area of Australian waters.

The Chinese guerrillas and their families always referred to me as

"Wong Sin Sung", 'Sin Sung' being the equivalent of the Malay word 'Tuan' which the Malays used when addressing Gort or myself. The English equivalent was 'Sir'. Both the Chinese and Malays referred to Gort as Tuan Chester. I found the people of Borneo to be most courteous at all times irrespective of race, and this was always evident despite the fact that in most instances, I was junior to them all. I could only assume that Gort had placed me on a fairly high pedestal in the eyes of the indigenous people and it was a promotion I always tried to maintain; no way would I let Gort down.

Following breakfast, Teck Bak asked Gort if two Chinese girls (pre-war school - teachers of the Chinese language) would be useful to the organisation. When Gort said he would like to meet them prior to making a decision, Teck Bak proceeded to lead us through lalang over a small brook to a small atap hut on the other side of the valley confronting a crystal clear gurgling spring.

There he introduced us to the two attractive Chinese girls. I guessed that they were in the twenties. They were simply and cleanly dressed in Cheong Sams; one was of average height by Australian standards, build and weight, somewhat curvaceous and wore her beautiful hair 'page boy' style shoulder length. The other girl, unlike the first, was of frail build, considerably shorter and flat chested; she had plaits to the waist. They both sported beautiful glossy jet-black hair.

Both were charming, unassuming girls and had to flee their homes after the Japanese occupation or run the risk of assault or worse, rape. The first one was introduced as Cheong Kau Kan but the second girl's name escapes my memory. I have kept in contact with Miss Cheong since the war years. Her name changed to Madam Cheong Kau Tan when she married Tan Teck Bak after WW2 and assumed the title as fourth wife. Subsequently, Teck Bak became our Chinese guerrilla leader and my 'blood brother' after the war. Gort appointed Datuk Mustapha – his friend of many moons – to lead our Malay guerrillas.

The girls shared the small home confronting the delightful gurgling watercress lined mountain stream with an old couple who were both pre-war 'tukang jahit' (Malay for tailor). I have reason to remember all four of them for they collectively made me a beautiful pair of Chinese style pyjamas out of a bottle green nylon parachute I gave them. The Mandarin styled (flared) legs were almost wide enough to go around my waist and shaped high collared coat had Chinese rolled white tape embroidered buttons and loops down the front. They were my pride and joy for many years after the war. I gave the rest of the huge chute to the girls and the old couple who were very appreciative of the material. Nylon was very much sought after at that stage as it was relatively new and not available on the civilian market. Following the occupation of BNB and the exhausting of British and foreign stocks of material, clothing, footwear, medicines and drugs, food, vehicles, machines and parts thereof etc., the Japanese literally replaced nought.

Invited to take morning tea with them, we conversed in the Malay language. They did not speak English and I could not understand their Chinese dialect, but we all understood Malay – the common denominator. Gort explained to the girls that we had a Chinese doctor due to arrive from Australia and needed two young ladies to train as first aiders to care for the needs of the guerrillas and their families: they excitedly accepted.

'Yaws' (a form of highly contagious weeping tropical ulcer) was rampant in the kampong and mainly confined to the Dusans whose hygiene left a lot to be desired. Once having established itself however, it spread through the whole community. There was no racial discrimination with 'yaws'. It attacked young and old including Europeans, Eurasians, Chinese, Indians and the Malays – even us, in spite of our many inoculations, vaccinations and injections etc. However, the Dusans were the worst cases of 'yaws' we were to see in BNB. Commonly, a sufferer would have a 'yaw' drip and where the weep set, another would shortly emerge.

Popular with the Dusan community, Graham Greenwood who was always about the area – being a radio operator – was commonly referred to as 'Tuan Dokteur' before the arrival of Doc May. I remember him treating a Dusan guerrilla's baby boy in arms suffering a 'yaw' that covered almost the top of the child's head. It was approximately 1/8" deep, gave off a foul smell and would have been fatal had Graham's sulphanilamide treatment been unavailable. The child's head had been swathed in filthy rag and when Graham removed it he found a poultice of cow-dung on the wound which was popularly believed by the Dusans to be a 'cure-all'.

Graham covers this incident more fully in his own book 'No Return' that unfortunately was a limited edition published only in New Zealand.

Both Chinese girls were thrilled to be given an opportunity to contribute in no uncertain manner towards the betterment of the local health and in particular, the fighting men and the eventual defeat of the Japanese. Along with the guerrillas, the girls' names were placed upon the payroll.

It was obvious to me that once having arrived at Lokopas our immediate task was to reach an agreement with Lim. He still came across to me as an arrogant man full of his own importance. Gort later confirmed that my first impressions of him were accurate as Gort and Nick had known him for many years pre-war. He sounded like a very important person with his utterings of "I am this and I am that", despite his annoying idiosyncrasies and habits.

He was forever relating how he had been continually on the run from the Japanese for the past two years, and how he had managed to slip through their fingers so often at the crucial moment. That there was a reward offered by the Japanese of 50,000 straits dollars for him dead or alive and that he had finally fled to the east coast to escape his enemies. How and where he had set himself up in a hide-away – Lokopas - in deep rainforest country that he considered his personal valley. He related how he had recruited a band of Chinese guerrillas who had to, repeat had to, obey his every command or be banished from his territory. Alas, it went on and on like a phonograph.

His endless claims of personal fame were to say the least, extremely boastful and tiresome. When one could finally get a word in edgeways, I found difficulty in restraining myself from asking him at point blank range "are you related to God?"

He claimed to have had connections with the famous guerrilla leader Colonel Suarez based in the Philippine islands of Tawi-Tawi, plus a supporter of Lieutenant Albert Kwok. He claimed Suarez had agreed to supply him and his followers with unlimited arms but we were never able to confirm his claim.

Despite all his claims and his urgings, we were later to learn that the young Chinese guerrillas had indeed been talked into joining him, but had to learn what patience was all about. His followers lost faith in him. However, with their families, they continued to live in the valley where they planted successful crops of vegetables and rice and became self supporting.. Lim was regarded, as everyone's senior father figure and that I recognised and accepted, although there were many occasions when I had to bite my tongue.

In our home in Perth, we Australian-born Sue children were educated by our parents in the Australian way of life, exactly the same as our

Aussie peers. However, Chinese family culture was strictly adhered to by my father – Perth's leading Chinese herbalist with his practice in prominent London Court when war broke out – who considered Chinese family life to be very much closer than the Australian.

Even today, two generations further down the line and with less Chinese blood content, the closeness of our families in moments of need is so obvious and draws many favourable remarks from friends and observers. My mother was Australian born Chinese and possibly half Pom/Scot, supported my father and believed firmly in the Chinese family philosophy and instilled it into us.

The teachings of my father including "respect your seniors" prevailed when the tall Chinese Lim was about. I was never guilty of arguing with him or showing any disrespect even when I knew him to be wrong, but there were times when I could have slaughtered him. Gort in his usual manner of wisdom pointed out particular failings in the man.

Jock and Don meanwhile were flat out on Jambongan Island preparing their weapons, communication system, food and selecting the top 50 Malay guerrillas to go across to the mainland. From there they proposed to march through the mighty Paitan River estuary system to infiltrate the areas through which the northern routed POW traversed as they approached Ranau where the Death Marches were reported to have ended.

Although we were far too late to do anything for the POW from the Sandakan end, their progress had to be reported regularly and where possible, action taken.

Reliable reports had also been received through our contacts on the west coast – the shades of our unsuccessful first attempt to land from Tuna in Kimanis Bay, north of Labuan on BNB's west coast some months earlier. The reports indicated that 'small working parties' of Australian and British POW had been seen in the west coast towns of Kota Belud, Jesselton, Papar, Kimanis and Bongawan. The reports all stated that the condition of the POW was poor. Little was known of their exact numbers and how they came to be at those destinations.

US forces had landed and captured the Philippine islands of Tawi-Tawi, Sanga-Sanga and Bongo. The Americans were getting closer and closer and it was obvious to all that their westward advance would shortly envelope Palawan, the largest of the west Philippines before their spearheads turned north towards the home islands of Japan. Gort predicted and felt certain that the Americans would not turn south to take Celebes,

Borneo, Singapore and other South East Asian areas (all principally British and Dutch pre-war territories).

The fracas between MacArthur and Blamey was bearing fruit for the former, but headaches, frustration and a second class role for the latter. Gort likened the island hopping strategy of MacArthur and its resultant situation to a giant killer; wipe out the head and the body would automatically follow; history has proved conclusively that Douglas MacArthur's strategy and Gort Chester's summation were right on the ball.

Come the 20th April 1945, punctually at 0520, a Flight 200 Liberator arrived and flew down the length of the DZ at about 500 feet to identify our recognition fires and ground signals. When satisfied and to divert Japanese attention to the area, the B24 Liberator disappeared into the distant south, returning in approximately 30 minutes.

On its second pass at almost hedge-hopping altitude – we reckoned we could see the whites of the pilots eyes – a small parcel with a white streamer tail was thrown out of the aircraft that was quickly retrieved by the guerrillas, once having realised the B24 was not crashing. The small parcel was hastily opened and the enclosed note offered congratulations to Gort (Order of the British Empire) and Fred (British Empire Medal) on their newly won decorations earned during operation 'Python' and was signed 'Nick'. He also advised that he was aboard the Liberator making the drop, wished us all the best of health and good luck and hoped to join us soon. Good old Nick! He was always quick to recognise when a good job had been done and showed his appreciation. Nick had been in the original 'Agas 1' party on Tuna when the insertion had to be aborted. We eagerly looked forward to his arrival of 'Agas 2' and the rest of his party.

A perfect drop of 8 storepedos and 14 free drop packages followed from 400ft before the aircraft made its final pass, wiggled its wing tips in salute and climbed into the blue beyond on its lone journey back to allied lines. We hoped upon hope that no Japanese air dawn patrols would be encountered on the Lib's long unescorted flight back to Morotai. At that stage, Flight 200's Commanding Officer Wing Commander Graham Pockley's aircraft and crew had been the squadrons only loss; lost without trace.

Meanwhile at Jambongan, Jock and Don received their first airdrop of 3 Brens, 15 Austens, 60 .303 Lee Enfield rifles and ammunition. The Flight 200 Liberator also free dropped a stack of parcels including rice, clothing for both the guerrillas and their families and medical supplies. Since leaving Jock and Don at Jambongan they had recruited 150 Malay guerrillas, and while awaiting their first drop of weapons, had been subjected to intense training using sticks as mock rifles.

Two or three days after the drop, Jock and Don with 50 of their well armed and best trained guerrillas set out for the mainland and Sungei (river) Paitan itching to come to grips with small parties of Japanese. More 'Z' operatives arrived at Jambongan to continue training the balance of guerrillas until they had reached the required standard when they would be sent to reinforce Jock and Don's parties in the Death March areas.

Information also came to hand that Gort's 'Python' agent Chinese Sandshoe Willie had been captured, tortured and thrown into the Japanese gaol at Beluran about the end of March 1945. Gort was determined that we should free him and towards that end, ordered an airstrike on the town making sure that the strafing American planes avoided the gaol.

About to set off to RV with Catalina off Musa Island for for the flight to Porta Princessa. Palawan. *Left to right* - Capt. Gort Chester, Sgt. Maa'ruff bin Said (later beheaded operation 'Platypus'), Sgt. Skeet Hywood (back to camera), Sgt. Jack Sue and two Malay boatmen.

Chapter 19

THE NORTHERN AND SOUTHERN ROUTES

Little or nothing has been mentioned in the 55 years that have elapsed since the end of WW2 1945 - the year of the infamous Borneo Death Marches – regarding the lesser used northern Death March route. The numerous writers of books on the Death Marches, have referred only to the southern route through Boto and Tampias and their reference maps likewise, support their stories.

However, Gort Chester, Nick Combe, Geoff Ripley, Jock Sutcliffe, Don Harlem, Datu Mustapha, Tan Teck Bak and I knew that the northern route through Klagan, Lingkabau, Murud Kurud and Parenchangan to Ranau existed, and that it was occasionally used by the POW and Javanese labourers. Interestingly, not one of the aforementioned men of 'Agas' was ever summoned to give evidence at the War Crimes trials and yet almost all had many months in the areas concerned. Bodies of the POW must still remain along the northern route, if it could be re-traced today. Just how many, nobody knows.

I understand that when Major Harry Jackson and WO Bill Sticpewich re-traced the Death March Route after the war – they were the first to do so - Sticpewich either didn't want to re-trace the northern route or just didn't know it existed. Unaccountably, he had been acting very strangely which must have been very disconcerting to Major Harry Jackson and other members of the investigation and graves recovery team. Maybe it was because of his 'fed up' state of mind and his desire to return to Australia that precipitated his firing a gun down the main street of Sandakan one night. Fortunately, no one was wounded.

A Chinese resident of Sandakan informed me that Sticpewich was 'not in his right mind'.

I guess it would have been a very difficult period for Sticpewich. Irrespective of his reported closeness to Captain Hoshijima, and the fact that he was known in the Sandakan camp among the Australians as the 'white Jap', the psychological effect on the poor man must have been absolutely horrific. He must have been well aware of the hatred the men held for him and yet, there he was back in Borneo on the Death March rentis helping to locate and recover the bodies of the men who hated his very guts.

Even we of 'Agas 1' were psychologically affected by frustration knowing full well the extent of their sufferings, and that we had been inserted near the camp for intelligence purposes and yet were helpless to assist the POW. I can well imagine the state of Bill Sticpewich's mind and I had not been subjected to three years of incarceration, or the almost fatal tortures of that 165 mile jungle march

Whatever the reasons for his strange behaviour and reported lack of co-operation with the investigation team and the graves recovery unit, I felt I was able to understand that he had 'had enough'. Who can possibly know the story from both sides now that Bill Sticpewich has passed on?

On the few occasions I referred the matter to Nelson Short, he thought he had heard of the northern route while in the mile 8 camp Sandakan but according to him, one heard so many rumours behind the barbed wire that it was difficult to separate truth from fiction.

The proven results of the swiftly advancing American troops under MacArthur in his island hopping strategy and the argument between the American and Australian commanders caused them to split and go their separate directions. The landing at Tarakan by Australian troops was the forerunner of later beach landings at Labuan, Brunei and Balikpapan that ultimately proved to be the final beach invasions carried out in Borneo by Australians during WW2.

For the 'Agas' parties it signified considerable changes. The deployment of Captain Jock Sutcliffe and my mate Lieutenant Don Harlem to the Death March area bounded by Beluran to the east, Ranau to the west, Boto and Telupid in the south and Lingkabau to the north. This virtually meant that their guerrilla troops straddled both northern and southern routes of the Death Marches. The section Sandakan to Beluran in early 1945 had been under observation by 'Sandshoe Willie' (B.S. Willie) until first imprisoned at Beluran by the Nipponese, released and

177

imprisoned a second time.

According to Gort Chester, 'Sandshoe Willie' was a close friend pre-war when Gort was on Lokawee Estate and was a valuable contact during the tragic days of Operation 'Python'. He would have been invaluable had operation 'Kingfisher' gone ahead as planned.

Unfortunately 'Sandshoe Willie' had no means of getting information out as 'Agas 1' was not inserted until March 3rd and 'Kingfisher' was still pending. Since that morning on Jambongan beach when Jock threatened to court marshal Don, friction between them continued to build up to the point where they could no longer work together.

Shortly after reaching their area of operation, parties were sent out to investigate the northern route. Kampong natives said that some Australian POW had been seen on the rentis accompanied by Japanese guards and that many atrocities had occurred. They said that large numbers of Javanese prisoners had also gone along the northern route, a route even worse than the southern, and only used when heavy rains rendered the southern route impassable. Blowpipe armed natives and uncertain food supplies along the route presented further problems for the 'binatangs'.

As impossible as it was for Jock and Don to work together, separation did not improve matters. However, individually they were both doing some sterling work and it was always a mystery to Don and myself, right to the day he died, why they had never been summoned to give evidence at the war crimes trials. Both men knew far more about the routes, the POW and the atrocities committed by the Japanese than any other living person.

In reflection, and knowing the shocking truth that was revealed in later years, maybe they knew too much and their knowledge was deliberately hidden from the Australian community. The atrocities that had occurred at the mile 8 camp Sandakan was kindergarten stuff compared to the bestial treatment meted out on the march routes and at Ranau, the end of the marches.

Is it any wonder that the whole saga of the Death Marches appeared to be a deliberate conspiracy of the truth from 1945 to the present day, and possibly will continue to be so forever?

As late as 1953, the Australian Government was still denying they were concealing the fact that almost 2,000 POW lost their lives on the Borneo Death Marches.

Meanwhile, Gort Chester who should have been one of the principal witnesses against the Japanese, passed away in February 1946 at the age of 46 as a result of a relapse of bacillary dysentery that he, Skeet and myself picked up at Bongawan during operation 'Stallion 4'. Skeet and I recovered from it, probably due to our youth and fitness, but Gort suffered a couple of relapses and at one stage was flown to Melbourne for urgent treatment and briefing before returning to Borneo. He never recovered and died only months after hostilities had ended.

Not one member of 'Agas 1' was asked to testify against the Japanese and yet we were the first party landed in Borneo to locate and feed back regular reports on the POW. Was this co-incidental or part of the great conspiracy?

Don confided in me that their partnership was unworkable and that the whole efficiency of the operation rested on a knife's edge. Jock continued to treat his guerillas as tools of trade and ruled them with fear. He believed that natives should be treated as such and made to realise that they were subordinates with a capital 'S'.

Don on the other hand was dearly loved by the very same guerillas and mainly because he treated them with respect and as equals. Don retained authority without having to assert his authority to get results from his Malay guerrillas and this fact was difficult for Jock to accept. While Jock and Don were still together, Don was virtually making his own decisions and could no more work in conjunction with Jock than fly in the air.

The following extracts taken from a letter dated the 29th July 1945 written in the field by Jock to Don speaks for itself.

"It is obviously ridiculous for me to continue my idea of controlling your operations except in a strategic sense (as opposed to tactical). I will therefore inform control that I want you to have two (2) skeds a day to be mutually arranged between you – I want our 7am sked to stand and scrub the 1200 hrs sked".

And further on in the same letter under general orders for Don:-

1. Keep an account of money spent.
2. Never treat a native as an equal and don't be too friendly with them – if you want to halve your worries.
3. Don't take orders from Geordie but do ask for advice. He didn't get this MM for nothing and his ideas may be helpful. Indulge him a little cos he is a different type to others you have had to work with.

4. Remember my previous advice about .... Don't stand any nonsense.(sorry old pal. If it wasn't that I felt we must get cracking quickly I'd fix him myself and I'm not shifting the buck).

5. If Kulang comes back send him on that mission to Telupid and or Boto. Tell him the sun shines out of his backside, that he is doing a great job and it will be better for him if he goes on doing it!

6. Sabrang I want this bird if possible and he can get down to Nelepak from Meridi via Merungun and Kirokut.

7. Stores remaining here – there are two ground to air signalling appliances – these can be sent down to O.T. Adjak for safe keeping together with anything else you consider worth salvaging. You yourself will be able to call on coolies from Kaingaran to carry your stores and use the spare blankets for wages before you use the money or cloth.

Just received your letter and 3 men – I didn't realise from Mac that he left before my letter arrived – I take back what I said about not reading my notes.

Yours aye
Derek (Jock)
See you at the Australia if not before.

Unfortunately for Derek, the contents were leaked. Whether the contents were read before Don received the letter we will never know, but in a conversation I had with Don after the war, what little faith the guerillas (mostly Malays) had in Jock (Derek) disappeared out the window.

The numerous letters written by Jock to Don – one or two of which I have today – could only be described as being stamped with rank authority and his antagonistic attitude towards Don and all others subordinate to him. Proof was evident in the fact that he never spoke in the same manner to Gort, and while I do not know, I feel sure that the same would have applied to Nick.

Without going into a lengthy explanation of the letter and its orders, it is suffice to say that O.T. (Orang Tua) Kulang, a leading Malay headman and Don had a mutual respect for regard and ability that was evident many years after the war when they continued to correspond. Kulang admired Don and literally worshiped the very ground on which he walked. Don was proud of the fact that Kulang would have given his life for him.

During the years before Don's unfortunate death when we were researching our joint-written book on events relevant to The Death

Marches, Don was still receiving a letter or two per year from Kulang. Don always spoke fondly of Kulang and it was perfectly clear that the feelings were mutual.

Although I never met Kulang it was obvious that there was a 'blood brother' relationship between Don and Kulang that was similar to the father/son feeling that I felt and hoped existed between Gort Chester and myself.

In clandestine, covert or call it what you will activities behind enemy lines, it was essential that one was popular and held in the highest respect by the guerillas. Because we were very much in the minority as numbers go, they could have disposed of us at any moment. We were seven among hundreds of guerillas.

Unfortunately, Jock did not possess this quality and I believe that had the Japanese not surrendered when they did, he would have been extracted from the 'Agas' operation.

Back in 1980 while staying with Don and his wife Betty in their Sandy Bay home Tasmania, Don related an incident that occurred just prior to his separation from Jock. The story readily spread throughout the 'Agas' organisation.

Apparently they had just received a fairly substantial drop from a Flight 200 Liberator. On the evening following the drop, Don was lying in bed in his half of the hut separated from Jock's half by an atap partition. He was almost about to drop off to sleep when he heard a soft rap on Jock's door.

Jock obviously had ordered the person to come in. The next moment, Don overhead the subdued conversation between a female voice that he recognised as that of a young attractive unmarried Philippino woman and Jock, and the conversation – though only brief – went something like this:-

"Oh Captain Sutcliffe. This morning we had a big drop of stores including many sarongs, cloth and food supplies. My two small children are starving and without clothes, and I wonder whether you would be kind enough to allow me to take a sarong for each of them, a sarong length for myself which I will sew, and some rice for my family - please Captain Sutcliffe. If you will allow me these few things, I will give you a-n-y-t-h-i-n-g- and the voice trailed away.

The next moment, Jock's light was doused. By the sounds issuing from the bed on Jock's side of the hut plus the ominous creaking of the floor timbers, Jock had agreed to give the very attractive Philippino girl what she sought, and she was living up to her side of the bargain. She was giving her a-n-y-t-h-i-n-g and the debt must have been substantial by Don's account, because he fell asleep some time later while repayment was still in progress..

For the next few weeks, poor old Jock paid dearly for his folly. He finished up with a pretty severe dose of 'the clap'.

Approximately the 20th May 1945, quite un-expectedly, Gort told Skeet and I that HQ in Morotai had sent him a message asking him if he would be prepared to take a small party of volunteers into the west coast area directly opposite Labuan Island to cross check Dutch intelligence. He asked us to join him. Skeet and I had no hesitation in volunteering.

The first sea-borne invasion of Dutch Borneo by Australian troops took place at Tarakan on the east coast south of Sandakan and was almost a disaster. Our troops were at their extended best to hold the beach head they had established, and battled to avoid being driven back into the sea each time the Japanese counter attacked. The Australian troops won out in the long run but had little left to spare against the fierce counter attacks of the 'sons of heaven' who were virtually without air power.

Further south at Balikpapan in July 1945, again in Dutch territory, Australian troops made another beach invasion – the last of WW2 - and while eventually successful, again they were lucky not to have been driven back into the sea. Again the 'binatangs' were sadly handicapped by the lack of air power.

In his strategy of island-hopping, MacArthur wanted to by-pass the newly captured ports of Balikpapan and Tarakan - major oil producing and export centres - in his drive towards homeland Japan, thus isolating thousands of Japanese troops en-route. The destruction of the Japanese Air Force and shipping, both   merchant and Navy, meant that the Japanese troops were then redundant and no longer presented a challenge to Allied forces. Furthermore, assuming that the atom bomb had not been dropped, and that all Allied forces had concentrated on the drive to the Japanese home islands, the duration of the war would ultimately have been shortened and it would have been unnecessary to fight for the possession of the oil centres..

Both oil centres were Dutch territory pre-war and MacArthur could see no sensible reason why good Australian lives should be risked when the 37,000 Japanese troops bottled up in Borneo were unable to leave. The many rich oilfields on the east and west coasts of Borneo while deprived by the Japanese to the Allied forces, were of little value to the Japanese. They had no tankers available to ship the finished product to Japan or elsewhere and few ships or front line aircraft to use it, even if they could.

Blamey obviously reasoned otherwise. He certainly won the accolades of those who supported his views. He never won an ounce of oil and he cost a number of good young Australian lives un-necessarily. However, he won for himself Australia's highest military promotion – the title of Field Marshall.

The war was approaching the final stages. Australian forces in Borneo were engaged in fighting mopping up actions and steadily losing men to no purpose.

On the 20th May 1945, an Australian crewed RAAF PBY Catalina landed off Lokopas to transfer 2,600 lbs of stores, weapons and ammunition and to take Gort to Morotai for briefing on the coming 'Stallion 4' operation. The dispatching 'Z' officer aboard was Flight Lieutenant Paul Bartram of "Can you build airstrip suitable for Vultee Vengeance dive-bombers?" fame. Understandably, Gort was somewhat cool towards him when he boarded the aircraft.

Going back to Morotai with Gort on that flight was Malay Sgt. Ma'Aruff bin Said who had been parachuted in with Nick Combe's party, 'Agas 2'. Ma'Aruff unfortunately had proved unsuitable for our type of operation. He was probably one of the most popular of the Malay pearl divers who had served with Army Water Transport and then volunteered their services to SRD around about the same time that I had transferred from RAAF Air Sea Rescue. We were all sorry to see him leave including Gort.

Both Sergeants, Ma'Aruff bin Said and Kanun Bin Garfu trained with me at Frazer Island and played a major role in teaching me to speak Malay. For security reasons they had been assigned to my care at one stage when we spent a three weeks leave session between training courses. During the time spent at the home of my parents and my younger brothers and sisters, they all found both men to be charming and well mannered and they were always welcomed in the Sue home.

The brothers and sisters listened eagerly to their stories of their exciting lives and incidents during hard hat diving in the waters out from Broome while chasing the elusive pearl. Their stories of almost daily shark experiences kept my brothers and sisters sitting wide-eyed on the edge of my mother's lounge chairs.

Ma'Aruff was extracted to Morotai for security reasons. Unfortunately, his friendly nature and natural desire to fraternise with the guerillas and their families exceeded his ability to observe security: essential in enemy territory. If captured, what we didn't know about, we could not divulge under torture.

After his extraction from 'Agas 2' and return to Morotai, he was quickly snapped up by another party leader. With three other 'Z' men, he was dropped behind Japanese lines by a Flight 200 B24 Liberator in former Dutch Borneo territory in the Balikpapan area. Of the four men, only the party leader Alan Martin a West Australian RAAF member of 'Z' got out alive. The late Alan Martin post war became a highly respected meteorologist and blue water yachtsman. Warrant Officer Jim O'Dwyer, Ma'aruff and one other 'Z' man whose name escapes my memory were captured and according to the reports we received, beheaded by the 'binatangs'. We were all very saddened by the unfortunate news. Despite Ma'Aruff's lack of security, he was great company and had he remained with us, he may have survived the war. Kanun bin Garfu was towards the end of hostilities, inserted into 'Agas 4' territory, lived through the experience and is today retired in a Melbourne suburb.

After the stores were transferred to the two native Prahus that Gort and I had taken to sea at daybreak that morning to RV with the Catalina, Gort took off for Morotai while I returned with the Prahus to Lokopas arriving there at about 0800.

When the stores were immediately unpacked and checked against documentation we found that the shipment consisted of arms, ammunition, rice, medical supplies and other urgently needed commodities. The arms amounted to 10 Bren guns, 5 Owen and 5 Austen sub machine guns, 18 .303 rifles, 48 hand grenades plus 14,800 rounds of ammo.

On the same day, our guerrilla ranks were joined by the enrollment of a fine contact possessing a wealth of information. His name was Chong Buck Ngee, a former bosun on the last Japanese tongkang (sail patrol boat) operating on the east coast. It came as a surprise to us that the Tongkang called in to Musa Island where the Malays on the island killed the Japanese captain and his crew of six 'binatangs' after releasing the Chinese and Malay crew.

According to entries in my diary it was a very active week beginning with Gort and Ma'Aruff's departure for Morotai, followed by the loss of a Flight 200 Liberator the next day plus the loss of Captain Tom Eltham and his signals officer. On the 22nd May, the building of Doc May's hospital at Lokopas got under way with more than 20 locals working on the job. The 23rd saw Doc and some of the guerillas head off for nearby Molobong on matters concerning the crash of the Flight 200 Liberator. The entry for the 24th recorded the arrival of Nick Combe and Jock Sutcliffe for Gort's expected return and conference later that day at Lokopas

After long discussions with Gort on the 25th, Jock Sutcliffe sailed for Jambongan, then to the area of the Paitan River in Death March territory. The following day the 26th saw the first guerrilla admitted to the newly completed hospital. Entry for the 27th recorded Nick's return to Molobong taking Captain Roy McLean with him and the buzzing of Lokopas by a lone Australian Beaufighter, the first we had seen. We presumed that it came from Tarakan.

Nick planned to attack the Japanese outpost of some 30 'binatangs' on Banguey Island off the north east coast in about a week's time and invited me to join him. I readily accepted. Gort however, intervened and told me that he planned to leave with Skeet and I within a few days for Palawan and not to make any arrangement to join Nick and Roy. Instead, Gort suggested that we should prepare our gear immediately as we were then already on stand-by.

Sure enough, on the 28th without any warning whatever, an American Catalina landed off Lokopas at 1300. Gort, Skeet and I were ferried offshore in a native Prahu and we boarded the Cat; it immediately took off for Porta Princessa at Palawan where we landed at 1630.

The airfield displayed more than 400 planes! What a boost to one's morale! The sight was simply awesome. As far as the eye could see, the field was just like a sea of aircraft. B17 Fortresses, B24 Liberators, B25 Mitchells, P38 Lightnings, Black Widows, Dominators, Marauders and others we had not even heard of, graced the field. Only the day before, we felt thrilled to see a lone Australian Beaufighter in the sky!

Before our arrival at Palawan, an Australian Catalina had touched down from Morotai carrying our equipment for operation 'Stallion 4'. Skeet and I still knew nothing of the details of the coming operation.

Chapter 20

GETTING INTO THE LION'S DEN.

The little Chinese guy was a veritable roley poley. A 'Mister Five by Five' by any standards. He had the habit of rolling his eyes in much the same manner as Stan Laurel of Hollywood's Laurel and Hardy fame of the pre-war years. Whichever way you viewed him, he was a Chinese version of the Hollywood comedian pair.

When he arrived at Lokapas, he requested an interview with Gort, who in his usual friendly manner made the visitor very welcome.

In his inimitable way, the Chinese guy - probably in his early twenties – offered his services to our guerrilla force. It was an unusual approach and had to be treated with caution, just in case he was a 'plant' from the Kempei Tai. Having no letter of recommendation or personal references, only served to cast further suspicion on him, and likewise, all the more caution from Gort.

However, he did not lack in enthusiasm and spirit was written all over his face. An unlikely looking guerrilla physique was more than compensated by the work he performed and where he worked.

He was a cook at the large Pitas Rubber Estate where more than 80 Japanese troops were based, and he had acted in that capacity at the former pre-war British owned Pitas Estate of a Mr.Coleman. He had been in the employ of the Japanese for almost two years, and according to him, hated the 'sons of heaven', or as he preferred to refer to his masters – 'binatangs' (animals).

His approach was to say the least, unorthodox.

"Tuan Chester" said Mister Five by Five in Malay, "Why are you and your men content to live in this atap house like binatangs when there is a beautiful house at Pitas available for you all?"

Gort's reply was simple and right to the point. "We are not yet ready to take on a fight with a Japanese force of 80 regular troops. We would have little chance of defeating them, and for what purpose? We don't need a comfortable house at the price of heavy casualties among our own men. How can we possibly justify such a cost?"

Cookie came back with - "It is not very difficult Tuan. It just happens I am aware that all the Japanese troops stationed at Pitas, whether in the home or camped around the rubber estate, are being recalled to Langkong within a few days. Most of their heavy weapons have been transferred already, and   Japanese headquarters at Sapong estate near Keningau, intend to replace the 80 front line fighting troops with about 50 Formosan or Korean law and order guards"

This information was of immense value to Gort who was aware of the original plan to land Allied troops on the Kudat Peninsula. According to Gort, that invasion force was to cut the peninsula off at the base thereby isolating Kudat, the most northern port of BNB and its important airfield. The plan was to capture the major town of Jesselton (Kota Kinabalu today), thereby cutting off retreat to thousands of Japanese troops on the peninsula and denying the Japanese the use of the Kudat airfield and the coastal railway line between Jesselton and the major southern junction of Beaufort.

Servants quarters Pitas, HQ of Operation 'Agas'

Such a move would expose the whole of BNB and Brunei to mass bombing raids from Palawan, which island the Americans had re-captured.

Even more importantly, the loss of the railway line would have the effect of isolating Japanese General Baba and his command at Sapong Estate serviced by a branch line leading from the coast into the eastern agricultural areas.

Whatever and wherever the Japanese intelligence emanated from, they were always accurately informed on allied invasion plans.

The move to transfer fighting troops west from Pitas towards the Kudat Peninsula was in the same pattern as the transfer of troops from Sandakan to Ranau; there they were dispersed to the west-coast by Baba. It differed in only one respect. The troops moving from Sandakan were taking allied POW with them in the full knowledge that few would survive the march of 165 miles, and those that did survive would eventually be systematically liquidated anyway.

Meanwhile, the Japanese had a pretty thin cover story to justify the transfer of the prisoners: their top brass could not be accused of ditching the POW at Sandakan. Every indication pointed to the fact that the Japanese were reinforcing the western coastal areas of BNB in readiness for the allied landing.

After the MacArthur / Blamey fiasco and the 'hold' of operation 'Kingfisher', any likelihood of a major landing on the Kudat Peninsula – still in the discussion stage – faded into oblivion.

According to our Chinese Cookie friend, only five Japanese including a First Lieutenant remained at the Pitas Estate house until the arrival of the law and order Japanese troops. The main body had left Pitas and were heading for Langkong to the west by foot; there being no roads those days.

Setting the wheels of action into motion, Gort immediately dispatched two Chinese and two Malay guerrillas to the Pitas area to cross check Chinese Cookie's claims. The four guerrillas duly returned to Lokapas, advising Gort that all the Japanese troops had left leaving only five in occupation.

Chinese Cookie had remained as our guest while the four guerrillas were cross checking the information and the existing situation. Meanwhile, he had drawn for Gort, a mud map of the Pitas home which was apparently a spacious two level building with all the live-in areas on the upper level. A central staircase from ground level opened into the middle of a huge open living room with

The Coleman Estate Home, Pitas, British North Borneo - Base HQ of Operation 'Agas' 1945

188

numerous bedrooms bordering the living space.

Cookie had obviously spent much thought on the matter of getting rid of the Japanese troops and fairly impressed Gort and Nick Combe with his ingenious suggestion. Nick was about to leave on a separate mission to set up a secret jungle training area with suitable DZ somewhere in the Molobong area where an air drop of training staff from Morotai and appropriate weapons, supplies etc for the families of the guerrillas could take place.

Cookie was prepared to return to Pitas to his regular job so as not to arouse the suspicions of the five Japanese who had granted him a number of days leave to visit his family.

His plan of action was all the more appealing because of its simplicity. He would return to his work place and at the appropriate time and moment, with chalk provided by Gort, he was prepared to outline the beds of the upper level bedrooms on the timber ceiling of the lower level, these being the beds occupied by the five Japanese.

The operation required precise timing. He explained that he would have to outline the beds after he had prepared the evening meal for his Japanese masters, and added that our attack would have to take place before sunrise the following morning. Understandably, Cookie was concerned that if the raid was ill-timed, the chalk outlines could be discovered by the Japanese during the following day and his head would be off.

After much further discussion and plans to overcome any likelihood of pitfalls, and the unexpected factors that can and do occur, even in the best of plans, a date and time was set for the operation.

It was agreed that Cookie would be paid a certain attractive fee for his information prior to the attack, and further payment at the successful conclusion of the shooting match. It is inappropriate to state the total amount paid, but suffice to say that he was well rewarded for his efforts.

On the other side of the ledger, while no threats were made, Cookie fully realised that betrayal on his part would mean instant death. Plans were finally set and all concerned were happy with the arrangements.

Our 'Agas 1' sigs Fred, Graham and Skeet were fully occupied in dismantling and packing the radios etc for the big move overland to

Pitas. They looked forward to the anticipated attack, knowing it would succeed and that at long last they could set up their transmitters with some permanency and that some degree of personal comfort for all of us would result.

The sigs had experienced an interesting progression of radio station changes since leaving the submarine, commencing with the 'mudflats' that provided initial safety for the seven of us, albeit very primitive. The welcome transfer to Jambongan Island had been an enjoyable although brief stay before they had to pack up again and move to Lokapas. Comfortably established there and anticipating some permanency, they had to move yet again.

Gort decided that the sigs would proceed by foot with a party of guerrillas to assist in the humping of the radio equipment, and to provide protection should the necessity arise. The rest of us representing the attack party plus a handful of Chinese and Malay guerrillas led by Tan Teck Bak would proceed to the planned entry point of Pitas estate by native boats.

The distance was approximately forty miles as the crow flies. As stated earlier, Lokapas was completely surrounded by almost impenetrable mountains so we had no conception of the distance up and down in terrain ranging from approximately 2,000 ft to 7,000 ft. Neither were we interested in finding out the hard way. Urgency demanded that we get there quickly so that the operation would be completed by the time the sigs arrived at Pitas. If my memory serves me correctly, Captain 'Doc' May was included in the overland party and was – as a result of the tough slog – laid up for a few days after, nursing sore feet and legs.

Skeet, was the tallest man in the entire 'Agas' operation – about 6'5" - and like many tall men tended to be slightly stooped in the shoulders, probably conscious of their height and not wanting to accentuate the fact – had a step about twice as long as mine. As a result, he invariably finished up carrying the biggest load, yet I cannot re-call him ever complaining. He was brave and tough. He had an incredible resilience and just kept coming back for more.

When Skeet maintained that it was a tough march, one could rest assured that it was no exaggeration. Doc May – like Cookie, another roley poley - on the other hand was unfit, had a stride half the length of mine and could barely carry his own weight. While Skeet and I marched many miles on operations together, I was somewhat glad of not having to witness the hardships that Doc would have gone through on that cross-mountains trek.

Our sea journey was quite the reverse of the overland march. Boring and monotonous, much of the time was spent lolling on a calm sea without wind. Becalmed at sea at the close of the wet season was not unexpected; somewhat similar to the weather pattern of Perth offshore areas when summer sea breezes made way for three or four weeks of calm, before autumn and winter sea trends took over.

Geoff Watts and I were in the boat skippered by Mohd. Sariff's boatman, lying on a sail to keep out of the sun, cursing the lack of wind. All of a sudden, the young skipper leaped to his feet and without hesitation exclaimed "God Save The King, Bugger America" and sat down again. That was his total knowledge of the English language, and when asked how and where he had learned it, he didn't know: and worse, he had no idea what it meant.

The night of the operation was noteworthy for its quietness. Few nocturnal birds were about and only the occasional bark of a distant crocodile, or the crashing of a wild pig through the undergrowth, disturbed the silence as we approached the RV selected by Cookie. Even the dogs and roosters in the kampong that Cookie said was near Pitas, obliged us by remaining mute at the appropriate time.

Our party was huddled in two groups under cover of coffee trees when a lone figure appeared out of the surrounding darkness that transpired to be Cookie, right on time. He greeted us with a "Selamat pagi Tuan" (good morning sirs) and without further ado, said "Ikut saya" (follow me) and led the way through the trees surrounding the large expanse of lalang (clearing), until we had skirted the area where a halt was made.

At this point, Tan Teck Bak went in one direction to position his guerrillas at selected observation points where they could cover any escape from the building. A former Malay police boy - he had served with the British and was known for his soccer skills – was armed with a .303 rifle and posted almost on the back door steps of the building leading to the servants' quarters.

Even the possibility – as remote as it appeared at the time – that one of the Japanese might escape and get back to Langkong to raise the alarm that would result in hordes of Japanese descending on Pitas

191

to wipe us out, was unthinkable.

Dawn was about to break. A rooster was crowing as Cookie led the remaining four of us towards the front of the house, the shape of which was beginning to materialise with the approach of daylight. Wherever one finds habitation in Borneo, it is inevitable that chooks or dogs or both will be present.

There were four of us but five beds to cover. Geoff – Nick's radio operator – was allocated the task of covering two beds in the one room. Armed with Austen machine guns, each weapon having a shaded torch attached to the underside of the barrel to sufficiently illuminate the outlines of the beds, we lined up the targets.

When all four were positioned and Geoff gave the pre-arranged signal, the crowing of the rooster and the otherwise reigning silence of the dawn hours was shattered by the bolt actions of the silenced Austens on automatic fire. Volley after volley of 9mm bullets and the occasional whine of ricocheting rounds as the targets were sprayed, created a strange sensation and sound in the confinement of the basement area.

The shooting completed, all ears were strained for human sounds from above but none issued. Gort and Nick took to the front stairs leading to the centre of the living room while Geoff and I headed for the back door leading to the servants' quarters.

We were completely dumbfounded to find the body of the Malay police boy lying crumpled near the steps of the rear entrance with a neat single bullet hole almost dead centre of his forehead, and his rifle alongside him. We found it almost unbelievable, that a shot could have been fired without us hearing the report, but recognised that he may have been shot during the automatic fire of the Austens, despite the silencers: the bolt actions were noisy and could not be silenced. It was obvious that the police boy had been shot with a 7mm rifle or pistol.

That nobody had heard the shot was the puzzling point. It was all the more puzzling knowing that Japanese pistols and rifles were not equipped with silencers. A thin trail of blood led past the body, indicating that whoever fired the shot had been wounded.

Wasting no time, we cautiously made our way into the living room area where Nick quickly advised us that the other four Japanese were dead in their beds and that it appeared that one had escaped. This was evident from the trail of blood leading away from the bed towards the rear door of the house.

What we had feared and yet believed most unlikely, had indeed become a reality. Maybe the survivor was now making his way towards Langkong and the wrath of the Japanese would soon be upon us.

By this time, every dog for miles around was registering its disapproval of the disturbance of the usually tranquil pre-dawn hours, supported of course by the incessant cackling of chickens and the crowing of roosters.

The occupants of the few surrounding houses began arriving to find out what was happening in their usually quiet neck of the woods. These were warned not to stay around should there be cause for additional shooting. They quickly returned to their homes rejoicing in the fact that the Japanese 'binatangs', with the exception of one - yet to be located - were no more.

Tan Teck Bak and his guerrillas had been instructed to maintain their positions surrounding the lalang to ensure that no possible survivor could cross the cleared land without being seen. Teck Bak was called in and he was most adamant that no one had got across the lalang, not withstanding the half gloom of the early dawn, and we accepted that: the locals were very observant and extremely keen of hearing.

When the light had improved, an all out search around the house took place commencing from the end of the blood trail that yielded nothing.

Still fearing the worst, all hands were diligently searching for the surviving 'binatang' through the servants' quarters and toilet, the basement of the house and across the lalang, without success.

The sun was well above the horizon when Geoff and I – acting on a hunch - approached the doorway of the servants' toilet where Geoff gingerly prodded the door ajar with the barrel of the Austen until the door backed up against the toilet wall; still nothing.

Still acting on the hunch,, Geoff edged across to the dunny seat, turned the torch on – still attached to the barrel of his Austen – and flipped the lid open with the barrel of the Austen, illuminating the open dunny pit. There, with his back to the side of the pit and taking what little advantage there was of the shadow cast by the dunny seat above, stood the missing Japanese Lieutenant with his 7mm Nambu pistol at the 'ready', chest deep in the contents of the pit. He was literally in the shit!!!

In his weakened condition and unfortunately for 'the son of heaven', the 'Z' man let fly first with a burst of automatic fire from point blank range and wrote 'finis' to the mystifying search.

The Japanese Lieutenant uttered not a sound and slowly sank into the mire. The four Japanese who had died earlier, were removed from their beds, tossed into the latrine trench with their superior officer and the whole establishment was set afire, burning it totally to the ground. It is possible that their remains are still there, I have heard nothing to the contrary.

No effort is made to portray this incident as any heroic action, no one felt very good about the incident.

Unfortunately, in our type of warfare where we were the minority against foes numbering many thousands, it was a case of kill or be killed and ethics ran a poor second.

As pointed out earlier in this book, many 'Z' men operating behind Japanese lines came from religious, God fearing families but were compelled to change their way of thinking within a short space of time after seeing some of the atrocities committed by our Japanese enemies. No doubt, many of those enemy soldiers were good clean living men – possibly of a religious faith, including Christians – and it is possible that they regarded us in exactly the same light. Who could afford to take the gamble?

It is difficult to re-call specific details of some of the actions that occurred 55 years ago. From memory, our sigs Skeet and Graham slept on mattresses that bore the evidence of that attack for the whole time they spent in the Coleman house at Pitas Rubber Estate. I cannot remember where Fred slept but in any case, nothing worried him. Fred was only a little guy but with a ton of guts, as he proved in operation 'Python' for which he and Gort were decorated. I doubt whether much sleep was lost as a result of the previous occupants, the Japanese.

In guerrilla warfare, I personally found the Chinese to be superior in fighting quality to the Malays. Experience taught me that the lovable Malays were very efficient in training, great showmen who liked to display their prowess as soldiers and generally very reliable. However, I found on the other hand, that where a given number of

Malay guerrillas were required to carry out a fire-fight, the Chinese would do it with half the number, as we will see further into the story.

As claimed by Cookie, the Pitas home turned out to be a luxury home. Beautifully constructed in expensive Borneo hardwood and softwood timbers, the home had mahogany flooring, a number of the internal walls were lined to frieze height in mother-of-pearl, including the huge toilet that sported bookshelves and pictures on its walls.

Since the war, the house has held many memories for me, and yet I believe that Gort and I probably spent the least time there. The sig boys and Doc May spent the most.

I cannot remember who dubbed Mr. Five by Five 'Cookie', although I fancy it was Fred Olsen. Be as it may, Cookie became a firm favourite in our midst and shortly after the take-over of the home, he approached Gort seeking to act as our cook thereafter; and what a brilliant cook he turned out to be.

Every few days, Cookie in his wide long legged shorts that reached to his knees 'Bombay bloomer' style that we described as 'short longuns', went 'shopping'; his broad woven reed coolie hat perched on his head to protect him from the sun,. A couple of the boat boys took him up the river that flowed along the side of the estate to purchase fruit, vegetables and meat from the various kampongs that provided the quality supplies he demanded. He was very fastidious in his choice of produce.

He earned our implicit trust to the point where Gort gladly gave him a 12g shotgun and ammo he used in his frequent forays into the surrounding jungle, thus keeping us well provided in beautiful venison – deer steaks.

In particular, I recall walking into the dining area one day to see Cookie slowly edging his way along the wall with ear hard- pressed to the beautiful timber and listening intently. He wore a smile from ear to ear, and when I enquired in Chinese as to what he was doing, he told me that he thought he had located a huge beehive in the wall cavity. The following day, with the assistance of two guerrillas, the lining was removed and the bees smoked out. Cookie then drained a huge quantity of wild jungle bee honey, both clear and tasty, from the wall cavity. That honey proved to be an unexpected luxury for all of us.

On another section of the wall hung an old-fashioned cuckoo clock that would be regarded as a priceless antique today. The clock persisted in running 'slow' and was re-adjusted daily by the sigs Fred, Skeet and Graham, who referred to it for their radio schedules.

Eventually, Graham lost his patience with the timepiece and took it down from the wall. When opened, it revealed a family of miniature banana bats. After he had flushed them out and re-assembled the clock, it ran perfectly.

The occupation of the home completed, Gort instructed our Malay guerrilla leader, Datu Mustapha - he became Chief Minister of Sabah post-war – to send a number of the Malays to various kampongs en-route to Langkong. There, they were to spread the rumour that a large force of Australian commandos had landed at the Pitas Estate, annihilated the resident Japanese force and were preparing to attack Langkong.

Those Malay guerrillas did their work well. The plan worked like the clock on the wall. The Japanese – taking into consideration mysterious losses of personnel and equipment at Musa Island, Trusan, Jambongan Island and finally Pitas - decided against replacing the Japanese force there, and left us in possession to pursue the war from our latest advanced base.

Chapter 21

JEFF WATTS NOT SHORT OF GUTS.

Although we were together in Borneo and post-war as neighbours, until his premature death in Kalamunda, a hills resort out from Perth, I never did know whether it was Geoff or Jeff.

To briefly recap on his background, Geoff was a West Australian who came from the Perth suburb of Mt. Lawley. He was a corporal signaller in the AIF and it was suggested to him that he volunteer his services with 'Z'. He transferred from his regular army unit – it could have been an armoured unit but again, I am not sure – and commenced his training at Frazer Island Commando School (FCS).

He excelled in his 'Z' training class and was selected by Major Nick Combe (British Army) – then a Captain – as principal signaller for 'Agas 2', promoted to Sargeant and was inserted by parachute along with his party leader Nick. Others in the jump were Captain (British army) 'Doc' May a Chinese gynaecologist – he acquired a number of nick-names - from Shanghai's leading women's hospital pre-war and Malay agent Sargeant Ma'Aruff bin Said (AIF) a former hard hat pearl shell diver from Broome Western Australia.

Geoff was a happy-go-lucky type and always had a cheery grin and a hearty slap on the back for his companions. In his own particular way, he was a spectacular person. He habitually had a cigarette tucked behind his left ear – either new or a mere butt - and was a person who could never be disliked, such was his disposition.

Within a couple of days of his insertion we became the best of mates, although we were not destined to see a lot of each other behind Japanese lines because of our different roles and different parties.

197

Even his insertion could only be described as spectacular. Jumping from the Flight 200 Liberator at 400 feet, his three companions made the middle of the DZ [dropping zone] with comfort. Geoff however, when approaching tree-top height, was picked up by a puff of wind that carried him towards the edge of the DZ where his 'chute' fouled a big mahogany tree, tearing four panels out of his canopy at about 80 feet. He luckily, made the ground without injury other than hurt pride. The supporting drop of storepedos and free drop parcels went off without a hitch.

A few days later, while using a pair of leg irons to climb the trunk of a tree for the purpose of rigging an aerial for his newly installed transmitter, one iron became dislodged and Geoff slid down the trunk about 10 metres rendering his chest red raw. Still, he scarcely complained. I thought to myself at the time "you're a better man than I, Gunga Din".

A real 'dead-eye dick' with his Luger 9mm pistol, Geoff could be relied upon always to give a good account of himself in a fire-fight and preferred to get into a scrap with the enemy than tap a morse key. He was the only man I ever saw draw from the hip and drill a tobacco tin 9 out of ten times from about 20 feet away when the tin was tossed up in the air for him. He was a natural with weapons, and was an unerring shot with any firearm as he proved post war when a member of the Wiluna Rifle Club (a goldfields area of Western Australia), the club he represented in Queens Cup shoots.

And that precisely was how he came to be involved in a 'shoot' that cleared out the enemy post near Molobong. The 'binatangs' threatened the establishment of our secret training base for further development of a guerilla force in that area.

The Japanese seemed reluctant to send forces east from Langkong as their losses at Trusan, Musa Island and Jambongan had proved very costly. I believe at that stage, the 'sons of heaven' accepted that Australian commandos were operating on the east coast in fairly large numbers, whereas in actual fact there was barely a handful of us. We envisaged the necessity to set the rumours flying in all directions that Australians were existent in large concentrations, and our Malay boys saw that those rumours were efficiently spread via the jungle vine. They did a fine job of distributing the propaganda.

At that stage there was little the Japanese could have done anyway. There was no shipping available to transport their troops, no planes to fly them and no road system to use. To worsen matters, they were aware of an imminent invasion on the west coast by Allied troops. Desperate attempts were under way to bolster their defences by marching troops overland from the eastern and south eastern theatres, to the west coast areas of Labuan Island and Brunei Bay to Jesselton on the mainland.

Nick and Geoff had the Japanese post under daily observation for a few days prior to the attack as it was their fervent desire to rid the area of Japanese. Not only was it desirable to ensure security for the guerilla training base deep within the jungle, it was also necessary for the protection of Pitas and our 'Agas 1' sigs, Fred, Skeet and Graham, who at that time, were on their way overland from Lokopas. Gort felt sure at the time, that our sigs would be permanently based at Pitas for some time to come.

In addition, downstream from Pitas where the river entered the bay there was a perfect area suitable for the landing of PBY Catalinas and Martin Mariners. There was no suitable landing strip for land based aircraft, and yet aircraft were so essential for the transport of our 'hit and run' guerillas against the Japanese. Even though fast Yankee PT boats were available to us from the American base at Tawi-Tawi in the Philippines, very often they were not available when required.

There were instances when Gort, Nick or others of 'Agas 1' or 'Agas 2' had to be extracted for consultations, supply of specialized equipment, change of codes and discussions with HQ in Morotai. Those extractions could be promptly expedited by PBY Catalina and Martin Mariner flying boats that were ideal for the task.

In the early stages of our operations from Australia before the Allies captured Morotai, and the Yanks the Philippine islands of Tawi-Tawi, Sanga-Sanga and Palawan, all insertions into Borneo were carried out by American submarines, the distances being too far for land based planes. When these bases were captured from the Japanese, parachute drops of personnel and equipment by land-based aircraft such as B24 Liberator bombers or Dakota biscuit bombers - the latter were the army version of the civilian DC3 - became daily events.

As the Americans continued their island hopping strategy and the Australians became involved in Tarakan and Balikpapan, RAAF Catalinas took over most of the work previously done for us by the Americans. Frequently, RAAF PBY Catalinas and our own Flight 200 B24 Liberators used the American bases for refueling when necessary, instead of the long haul necessitated by flying direct from Morotai to Borneo and return non-stop.

Readers need to understand that reliable landing areas protected from the weather and suitable for Catalinas and Martin Mariners were at a premium, as was the case with the Molobong estuary. But, first of all, the enemy had to be eliminated from the area.

Nick was satisfied that the twenty plus Japanese at the Molobong outpost could be satisfactorily handled by his newly trained Malay guerillas after having had the area under daily observation for almost a week. Plans were then set for the wipe out operation.

The one atap hut of the outpost was just large enough to accommodate the Japanese – about 45 feet by 15 feet. It had a door in one end wall leading out to a small narrow verandah with a few steps shaped in an 'L leading to the ground. Inside the hut the Japanese had tiered styled bunks built around the walls and tables in the centre of the hut.

Straws had been drawn by the 'Z' guys as to who would storm the steps of the verandah and rush into the hut during the hours of pre-dawn darkness with a torch strapped to the barrel of a sub machine gun and spray the quarters with fire. Geoff had drawn that short straw and was glad to have done so.

The plan called for the 'Z' boys to cover Geoff's barn storming action. The Malay guerillas were posted around three sides of the building to shoot any surviving Japanese who might tumble out through the atap walls. The unguarded side was the jungle and it was considered highly unlikely that an escape through that wall would be attempted. The unguarded side also minimized the possibility of any of the Malay boys being caught in the cross-fire. There being only one door, it was certain that those within would not head in that direction into Geoff's blazing Austen. If any got out through the walls and headed for the 'hutan' [jungle] our Malay guerillas were bound to get them pronto. At least that was the strategy.

Only late that afternoon, a recce team of Nick, Ma'Aruff and Geoff had satisfied themselves that no changes in the situation had occurred and that the Japanese still suspected nothing.

With that angle covered, the following morning just prior to dawn, the allocated positions around the hut were silently taken up by the Malay guerillas, each armed with a .303 rifle. The night was as black as ink and the approach to the hut area had been reached without incident

On the pre-arranged signal, Geoff headed for the hut in the inky darkness of pre-dawn, up the steps and promptly tripped over a Japanese light machine gun [LMG] on a tripod set up on the verandah, sending it cluttering down the steps.

Realizing that the element of surprise had been lost and that it was useless to back out, Geoff had no alternative other than to race on into the hut cold turkey, spraying the bunks with bullets in one circular sweep.

The torch strapped to the barrel of his Austen gave sufficient illumination and the deadly bullets took their toll. Most of the 'binatangs' died in their cots but a few managed to tumble outwards through the atap walls on to the ground within a few feet of the Malay guerillas..

All outside held abated breaths after hearing the clatter of the Japanese LMG as it tumbled down the steps. None knew the source of the noise or what the follow-up might be.

They however, did not have long to wait. As the first streaks of dawn permeated the darkness of night and Geoff's barking Austen sprang into life, Japanese bodies came tumbling through the atap wall on the side of the hut where predicted.

The collective sound of .303 rifles seemed to Nick Combe and company like a shooting gallery. To their ears the shooting may have sounded like a re-assurance that none of the 'binatangs' [animals] would survive the attack. Although, if any did survive the attack and managed to escape to Langkong, their report would probably support the Japanese belief that the Australians were still actively shooting up Japanese strongholds in the east.

After sun-up Nick could not believe his eyes. Three or four Nipponese were seen to fall out through the atap wall on the Malay side, yet not one Japanese body could be found. Neither could any be found anywhere in the surrounding jungle. .303 bullet holes were everywhere in the ground, some as close as 3 to 4 feet from where the Malay riflemen had been standing when they opened fire. More bullet holes were evident in the walls of the hut but not one 'binatang' was to be found outside. It was almost impossible to believe.

I had been accustomed to working with the Chinese guerillas and they made every bullet count. I was laughingly told later by Nick that the Malays believed the noise killed as effectively as the bullets!

The odds of 36 rifles to 3 or 4 unarmed Japanese without a hit was incredible! However, the truth could not be denied. The few Japanese had escaped, suffering little more than a damned good fright and probably sore bodies when they struck the ground.

The Malay guerillas were of course full of apologies for their failure, offering all sorts of excuses. The truth of the matter was that panic had overtaken them. For most of them, it was their first operation.

We never ever found out whether the surviving Japanese reached Langkong or jungle Malays and Chinese waylaid them. Neither did we learn the exact number of Japanese in the hut before the attack. The number of Japanese bodies on the hut floor and in the bunks totalled 23.

More mystifying was the presence of the LMG on the verandah. Was it merely coincidence or had they half expected an attack? These questions were never answered.

How not one of the 'Z' men or Malay guerillas was a casualty of cross-fire was nothing short of miraculous.

Most others in that situation, realizing that the element of surprize was lost when the Japanese LMG cluttered down the steps, would have cleared their arse out of the hut and planned another attack; one never knows how one might re-act until faced with the situation as Geoff maintained later.

In typical Geoff Watts' style, he immediately sized up the situation and took the initiative; all within seconds. He virtually wiped out the Japanese in the hut single-handed. He showed true guts and determination of the highest order. If my memory serves me correctly, the action earned him a British Empire Medal [BEM].

Unfortunately, Geoff died prematurely in his early thirties a few years after the war as a result of cancer and is survived by his wife Pat and children.

Geoff old son, wherever you are, I again 'lifts me lid to you'.

Chapter 22

ESTABLISHING PITAS HEADQUARTERS

Our sigs and the rest of the overland party including suffering bandy legged Doc May – smiling none the less - arrived in the area shortly after we had settled in and took up residence in the former Coleman home at Pitas Rubber Estate.

One simply had to sympathise with poor old Doc May. He certainly was not cut out for jungle bashing and I think the man who felt Doc's suffering most was Graham Greenwood of earlier orang hutan fame. Graham was a very compassionate type and Gort Chester and myself half expected to see Graham arrive completing the overland bash with Doc May on his back. However, all due credit was Doc's who probably had never walked distances longer or more physically trying than the labour ward of Shanghai's leading maternity hospital where he had been an obstetric specialist pre-war.

The Pitas headquarters provided us with a large padang [field] in front of the house. It was totally covered in lalang (grassed area) that after a day's work put in by the guerrillas in cutting the over-growth with parangs and scythes, proved to be a perfect DZ (drop zone) for the supply by parachute of personnel and supplies.

An atap radio hut (nipa palm leaf thatched building about eight foot square) on 4ft stilts was constructed hastily by the guerrillas on the seaward side of the DZ about 200 yards back from the waters edge. On the immediate arrival of the overland party, aerials and other refinements were completed to Fred Olsens instructions and it was operating as a transmitter station in time for the first drop. Like the early Queensland homes, the radio shack needed to be well clear of the ground as protection against flooding and the necessary clearance provided ventilation to prevent overheating.

Within two days we had a Flight 200 B24 Liberator bomber come over and make a very successful drop of arms and ammunition. The following day a RAAF Dakota biscuit bomber was over head and when satisfied with the ground recognition signals, made a considerable number of 'free drops'. The supply drops comprised mostly food and clothing required for the new guerrilla force in training at the newly established secret training base in the jungle.

The three sigs lived within the Coleman home with the rest of us, and like the Japanese tenants that we had replaced, bed occupancy changed frequently according to the requirements of personnel movements as 'Agas 1' commenced to grow.

Gort had just returned from a rush trip to Melbourne for medical attention to his badly ulcerated elbow and further treatment for bacillary dysentery after discharge from the hospital at Morotai. Skeet was discharged from the same hospital – the 2/5th Australian General Hospital – shortly after Gort left for Melbourne and a week later I was declared free of dysentery and returned to the 'Z' camp at Morotai. The three of us were supposed to return to Borneo on the Australian frigate

'Flight 200' air drop. Chutes landing on D.Z. (drop zone at Lokopas)

HMAS Strahan the following morning.

The night before she sailed, Gort and Skeet were notified that Strahan was sailing early in the morning and to be aboard. I went to the hospital that night and could not be notified. The following morning I was ordered to the orderly room where an infuriated and still slightly intoxicated Flight Lieutenant John North RAAF demanded to know why I was not aboard Strahan. With his thick stale alcoholic breath all over me, I simply explained to him that I was not in the camp that night and had not been notified of the sailing time.

The pompous and short horn rim bespectacled man drew himself to his full height of about 5 feet, puffed out his bantam like chest, mounted his soapbox and began ripping pieces off me, not withstanding the presence of other staff in the room and accused me of disobeying his order. When I repeated that I had not seen anyone from 'Z' the night before, he asked if I was calling him a liar. I politely but firmly replied "take it the way you wish sir" and turned on my heels and walked out despite his angry order to "come back here you chow bastard": I sensed the build-up of a nasty confrontation.

Without wasting any time, I reported what had happened to a senior Army officer adding that I resented being called a 'chow' and I was smilingly told to disregard the incident as the Flight Lieutenant was not a 'well man' and that I was to stand-by to fly out in two days time. I heard nothing more.

On my arrival at Pitas I found that Skeet left the day before with Flight Lieutenant Geoff Ripley and their guerrilla force marching overland for the rescue of Sticpewich, Botterill, Short and Moxham following that group's escape from the Ranau POW camp. Since our departure for operation 'Stallion 4' in May, there had been numerous changes of 'Z' personnel as they were parachuted in or brought in by PBY Catalina or Martin Mariner.

Although I had arrived too late to see him, Geoff Ripley's arrival at Pitas pleased me immensely as I had not seen him since my first course at Frazer Island over a year earlier where he was my Malay language teacher. A police commissioner in Singapore before the war, Geoff spoke fluent Malay and had a sound command also of Cantonese, and we often conversed in one or the other.

When I was in Geoff's class at Frazer Island, my final written Malay examine required me to translate into Malay an English instruction, "tell him to blow down the bridge". The Malay word for bridge is 'Jambatan' and the word for the WC is 'Jamban' and mistakenly, I used the latter.

After marking the papers, Geoff displayed much mirth as he read out the passage in my paper aloud to the rest of the class, adding that I would not be a particularly popular boy with other members of the party if I ordered the Malay to "blow the shit-house down". Needless to say, the remark brought howls of laughter and further ribald remarks from my class mates.

Thereafter, whenever we met on the island, Geoff reminded me by nonchalantly singing "please don't blow, our shit-house down" to the then popular 'Popeye' and 'Olive' tune 'Barnacle Bill the Sailor'. In next to no time everyone on the island was poking fun at me. My paper – the highest in the class – erred in only one word but what a vital word it was. I could see that the word would haunt me.

During the six-week course, the 'Z' men frequently gathered in the mess tent at night on weekends after lectures and other exercises, for at Frazer Commando School, ours was a seven day week.. When sufficient grog had been consumed, someone would break out into song followed by others and a succession of army ditties would bring the house down. My mistake in Malay seldom missed a rendition of -

"Please don't blow our shit-house down,
Please don't blow our shit-house down,
Please don't blow our shit-house down,
Cried the fair young maiden.
Buggar your tits you give me the shits,
Said Barnacle Bill the sailor".

And so on ad infinitum – there were dozens of verses.

As we had only recently captured the Coleman home, the presence of the 'sons of heaven' could almost be felt. Reverting to the young Japanese lieutenant who lost his life in the dunny pit of the servants' quarters, I am certain the reader will feel as I did that morning that his end was a most undignified death. Poor man. In later years I've often wondered whether he was like one of us. God fearing, clean-living and possibly a married man with wife and family, or a young stag with a girl friend in Japan waiting for her hero's return.

In times of peace such an action would be regarded as murder, but, war legitimises murder; not that there is much comfort to be gained by this knowledge. There is little doubt that, considering he was standing in the latrine trench with a cocked 7mm Nambu pistol, it was purely a matter of whether the Japanese 7mm Nambu pistol slug or the 9mm Austen machine gun bullet was first to kill.

Graham often remarked on the bullet holes in his Japanese bed and mattress, but still found the bed far more comfortable and preferable than sleeping in an American jungle hammock slung in the trees at our original 'mud flats' headquarters near Tagahang and the offshore island of Pura-Pura.

We were very mindful of the fact that one found a hammock particularly cosy and comfortable after a night or two getting accustomed to swinging in the trees and being exposed to the weather patterns that varied from night to night. However, the thought of being run down by a wild boar or Orang Hutan was far from comforting. Sleeping in hammocks was at the mercy of the many wild boars that raced through the jungle at night in pursuit of, or fighting over their sows.

There had also been several reports of American soldiers having been cut down in their hammocks while asleep by Japanese infiltrators. It was not a very comforting thought. Bedded down in a comfortable mosquito proof hammock and having one end suspension shroud cut, one could liken it to being a fish trapped inside a mesh net with no where to go and mid tangles, unable to find the exit.

Indeed, former Japanese occupied beds were again better than the rattan [cane] bunks constructed by the Chinese guerrillas of Lokopas. There was no inference of racial discrimination in the choice of beds because Graham was a lover of all mankind, irrespective of colour or creed. In fact, we all grasped the opportunity to sleep – we were generally dog-tired - regardless of the history of the bed. Looking back over the years, we actually had little opportunity to get the head down, our days were so full of activity. In reflection, former Japanese occupied beds were no different to hotel beds. In a pub, no one knows who occupied the bed the night before and no one gives a damn anyway.

However, when it came to 'somewhere to put the head down' or as servicemen and women of world WW 2 fondly referred to it as 'spine bashing', a term never used these days, Graham was no more selective than the rest of us.

"Why do I lay here supine, when I am asked out to wine and dine,
When every inner thought of mine tells me to stay and bash the spine?"

The foregoing two line literary effort – poet unknown - has been taken from an issue of 'Salt', a WW2 servicemen's and servicewomen's regular periodical lent to me by my very good friend, and well-known, highly respected ex digger and businessman of Midland , Western Australia, Mr. Ken Ryan.

On the morning the RAAF biscuit bomber [Dakota] came over the DZ, waggling its wings in greeting and recognition; it flew off to the south so as to avoid attracting undue attention by enemy troops to the area.

About 15 minutes later, it returned at a much lower altitude, and the dispatching crew standing at the open doorway of the aircraft were clearly visible from the ground. On its first run down the DZ, jute wrapped bales of sarongs rained from the sky and landed in the centre of the DZ

A number of similar runs were made – all from about 200 feet or less – free dropping bags of rice, sago, sugar, salt, flour and other urgently needed commodities.

On the final run, it was raining 56 pound bags of rice when we on the ground realised that the aircraft had overshot the release point and that some of the drop would be in the jungle.

A little more alarming was the fact that the radio shack was in the drop path and was in danger of being hit, and most alarming was the fact that Fred was in the shack at the time talking to the aircraft.

When the danger became apparent, about a half dozen voices screamed out in unison, "look out Fred!   Get out of the bloody radio shack". Fred required no further warning. Dropping his hand held mike, he reached the doorway in a single leap and cleared the steps to the ground just as a bag of rice crashed through the atap roof and through the floor. It demolished the chair on which he had been seated only seconds before and finally crashed through the floor of the shack and on to the ground below. Fred was leading a charmed existence.

For that matter, I suppose we were all leading charmed lives, having been behind Japanese lines for some three months or more by that stage and not having lost an 'Agas' operative. We often wondered how long our good fortune would continue. Lady luck had some strange tricks up her sleeve and it was realised by all of us that it was purely a matter of if and when she might deal the wrong card.

Fred was not meant to die. As the Dakota gained height and soared off into the blue, we gathered around a ghostly white and slightly shaken Fred Olsen, thoroughly relieved that the consequences were not more serious and that our communications leader was still with us.

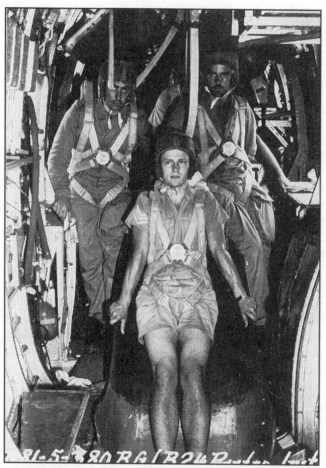

Operative about to slide out of 'Flight 200' B24 Liberator

Chapter 23

CONDOMS GALORE!

The two lovely Chinese nurses we recruited at Lokopas, so enthusiastic about their role as medicos to care for our guerrillas and their families, lost interest overnight. They became morose to the point where Gort decided that unless their attitude changed, we should discharge them from their duties and permit them to resume their former style of living. Their change toward us was as sudden as switching off a light, and left us completely bewildered.

Finally it became my job to find out the reason for their strange and sudden behaviour when Gort said to me "have a good talk to them Jack. They are nearer your age than mine, you speak their lingo and seem to get along pretty well with them. Maybe they will give you a clue but I'm damned certain they just deliberately clam up when I broach the subject with them. If it is obvious that they are not happy in their work: I am prepared to release them to return to their former way of life. We just can't have them going on like this".

When I first brought the matter to their attention, they were reluctant to discuss the matter. They offered piddling bloody explanations that they were not feeling well, the guerrilla families were too demanding in their requests for medical attention, they were working late hours at night and other unrealistic excuses. To me, they were not genuine and I felt certain that the girls were just being evasive.

I waited until another opportune moment presented itself. It came sooner than expected. The next morning I went to their work-room adjoining the medical post below our large atap hut built atop stilts on the side of a prominent hill overlooking Lokopas valley. The Chinese nurses were completing the bandaging of large evil smelling weeping leg yaws on a teen-age daughter of one of the Malay guerrillas. After completing the job they invited me in for morning tea in their usual polite manner "doh sun Wong Sin Sung. Too la!. Yum tong cha, sic Malay beang lah" (good morning Mr. Wong. Sit down and have Chinese tea and Malay biscuits).

I gladly accepted their invitation to join them, and during general conversation and niceties, I explained Gort's concern for their happiness and work satisfaction with us, and his decision that if they were not happy with their work, he was prepared to release them rather than lose their friendship. Their attitude changed immediately and fearing the loss of their jobs, we got through to the truth of the whole matter.

Realising they were now committed to an explanation, or relinquish their jobs as nurses, they hesitatingly rose, blushing very noticeably all the while and invited me to follow them into the packing room. There, they had been checking against delivery documents, supplies removed from storepedos recently dropped in by a Flight 200 B24 Liberator

From one storepedo they removed a four gallon sized kerosene tin fitted with a press seal lid about 9 inches in diameter. The upper half was full of gun cleaning cotton material (4 x 4), and below the material were a number of unlabelled cartons, and to check them against documentation they needed to open at least one.

Chinese nurses working with Dr May and Jack Sue at Lokopas HQ. Ms Cheong Kau Kan (now madam Tan Tek Bak) on the left.

Lokopas Headquarters, "Agas 1" Operatives L to R Maa'ruff bin Said, Jack Sue, Gort Chester, Skeet Hywood, Mohommad.

Hesitatingly and still blushing like crazy, without uttering a word they handed me one of the cartons. They didn't have to say a thing. Their blushing faces almost had written across their horrified looks the words 'please explain'.

On opening the carton I burst into uncontrollable laughter that probably added insult to injury. At last I knew the reason for the girls' strange behaviour over the last few days.

The cartons were full of condoms: if there was one, there had to be 500!!!

The girls had no idea that the material was to be used for cleaning firearms until I explained, but the condoms left them with no doubts. Absolutely staggered, they probably thought many lay-back hours were planned for them with six army men and an airman. In fact, at the time it reminded me of the war-time story of Dumb Dora the blonde bombshell who thought that an endless belt was a week-end with a sailor.

To fully appreciate the situation one has to realise that WW2 Asian girls were very modest and virtuous compared to western girls, and while they are a little more liberally minded these days, I believe they are still behind the eight ball. Their western counter-parts in such matters as sex, sexuality etc. are more liberated.

To me, their unsmiling straight faces only made the situation even more hilarious. Realising that their anxiety needed relief, and quickly, I asked them to follow me upstairs and on to our verandah overlooking the DZ (dropping zone that also served as a vast guerrilla training ground) where we had a large table for our meals.

After sitting them down I went into our sleeping quarters that led off the verandah and where we stored our demolition equipment. A few minutes later I re-joined them and laid out on the table the necessary demolition items to prove to them that the plentiful 'french letters' were a necessary item. I felt I had to prove to them that there was a legitimate reason for the use of the offending items.

The panoramic views of the Celebes Sea behind the DZ, and the newly constructed sig's hut on the intervening hill overlooking the water at the other side of the DZ, were a picture for any artist. The complete valley of Lokopas was a series of gloriously green timbered inner hills, interspersed with fertile gardens, atap huts of the guerrillas and creeks running out of the impenetrable 7,000 feet and even higher ring of outer

Morning tea at Lokopas HQ. *L to R* Maa'ruff Bin Said, Mohommad, Gort Chester, Skeet Hywood, jack Sue. (Note Austin machine gun on table)

213

mountains that protected the valley from the 'binatangs'.

When I reflect today on the beauty of the Lokopas valley and its marvellous variety of wild orchids, birds, butterflies and its exquisite range of animals including the monkeys, it has to be one of the most beautiful places I have ever seen. There were numerous varieties of monkeys including the singing kelowats (gibbons) of the mountains to their proboscis cousins of the mangrove swamps.

In the midst of the beauty described, I sat at the table and demonstrated to them – using a dummy detonator, time pencil, piece of cord in place of cordtex (instantaneous detonating fuse) and a short piece of ignition fuse – the assembling of a PE (plastic explosive) bomb. I explained to them that we used such bombs on Japanese targets. After completing the charge and crimping the dummy time pencil with crimping pliers to the length of fuse, I then waterproofed the time pencil with a condom. I finally explained to them that the condom was necessary for underwater charges or other charges used in areas where dampness was present. I told them also that many pieces of military equipment needed to be water proofed when the need arose, and that condoms were commonly used in clandestine warfare for that purpose.

The almost audible sighs of relief and looks on the girls' faces were understandable. Facial expressions slowly changed from one of concern to wide smiles of humour, and needed to be seen to believe.

When I later related the discussion with the girls to Gort and the rest of the team, uproarious laughter reigned for some minutes. I would not go as far as to say that there were no suggestive remarks made. Clean-living and attractive girls were far and few in BNB during the Japanese occupation.

After the cessation of hostilities, our Chinese guerrilla leader Tan Teck Bak married one of these Chinese nurses, Cheong Kau Kan. He made a pilgrimage to Mecca and because of his high position in the Muslim society, war service, his success in business, he was permitted to have four wives.

Although my 'blood brother' Tan Teck Bak and his number one wife passed away some years ago as citizens in Canada after Australia refused to grant them citizenship, our lovely Chinese nurse is now number one wife and is known as Madam Tan. She lives in Sandakan and has aged gracefully and is as lovely as she was in 1945.

The wives have their own individual homes and they are comfortable luxurious homes even by western standards. There are a total of 17 children of whom a number have been educated in Australian universities in various professions, and all family members are very close.

On the numerous times I have been back to BNB, now Sabah, and during the many occasions we have been together in Perth on their visits and during their university days, I have met most of the families. They refer to me as Uncle Jack; I'm proud of it and love it. I am particularly close to Tan Teck Bak's eldest daughter Bella, her immediate sisters Lucy, Mary and families and I have the greatest admiration for them all.

My eldest son Barry, second daughter Aneeta and fourth son Kim have been to Sabah with me and share my sentiments for the country, its people and in particular the Tan family members of my war-time 'blood brother' Tan Teck Bak. I am proud and privileged to have been associated with such wonderful people.

Chapter 24

RED CROSSES & WHITE CLOTH.

Gort requested another air strike on Sandakan targets including the badly damaged airfield built by the POW who were compelled to do the repairs to the strip, the water-front ship building yards and the rubber estates where, camouflaged by the rubber trees the Japanese had established their camps. Two days later, a US Force of 80 B24 Liberator bombers unleashed from Palawan descended on the ailing township and virtually raised what little was left after their previous raid.

The POW camp was not bombed but given a close scrutiny by the American fighter escort of P38 Lightnings, picking out and strafing Japanese quarters detailed by our 'Agas' agents.

Requests by the senior Australian officers - mostly medical men - for permission to erect or paint red cross signs on POW huts and hospital buildings were met with complete stony silence by the Japanese. Instead, a number of Red Crosses were painted on Japanese buildings effectively protecting them from the strafing American planes. A small number of Australian and British POW were unfortunately killed. Such were the fortunes of war!

At the airfield where the POW toiled filling in bomb craters that pockmarked the airstrip and taxi- ways connecting the revetment areas to the strip itself, another hideous performance was under way. Immediately the 'sons of heaven' were aware of an imminent bombing and strafing run by the American aircraft, POW were herded like sheep and forced to run out on the airstrip waving pieces of white cloth provided by the Japanese. Those who refused to carry out the instruction were mown down by machine gun fire and later bulldozed into the craters on the strip.

The ruse did not work as planned. Whether the strafing Yankee pilots were wised up to the Japanese we shall never now learn. On their first attempt to carry out such a ruse, it backfired on the 'binatangs'. Some thirty or more Japanese were killed for the loss of seven POW.

One Australian who was slightly wounded during the strafing was a Royal Australian Navy seaman by the name of Kelly. This was intriguing information to say the least. We were never aware that Navy personnel were among the ranks of the POW in the Sandakan camp.

The information came from a Chinese man by the name of Joseph Wong Yun Siew - the war-time manager of the agricultural research station bordering the POW camp and a resident at Leila Rd immediately following the war. Wong indicated that 4 or 5 Australian Navy and possibly one USN POW had arrived in the camp during October or November of 1944 from Makassar on the island of Celebes, east of Borneo (now Sulawesi). Wong's information was most valuable as the presence of Australian and American Navy POW was not known at the time.

Pre-war, the eight mile peg on the road to Ranau was a former quarantine staging station before conversion to a POW camp, and was avoided by the locals as it had a reputation of being over run with poisonous snakes and rats.

After the transfer of the POW from Berhala Island off Sandakan harbour – the first camp established after arrival from Changi prison Singapore - to the mile eight area, the rat and snake population was quickly decimated by the POW who trapped and ate them. In quick time both became a rarity.

Because of his ready access to the camps, Wong was the perfect carrier. His information was all the more valuable as he was permitted to enter the POW camp daily, delivering vegetables to the Japanese cook-house, and less frequently, the Australian camp. He was able to conceal among the vegetables in his delivery cart, radio spares and other small pieces of equipment and pistols etc required by Australian Captain Lionel Matthews in the camp. More over, his information was current and accurate.

To the best of my knowledge we never did learn how the contact with Wong was made. It was possible that Wong had been part of an earlier courier service – possibly a backwash from the 'Python' days. The only other way for information to flow regularly was through a dead letter box, but I am reasonably sure the source was never established. It was also possible that he may have been an agent in 'hiding' for Albert Kwok's rebellion of the double tenth and its tragic outcome.

I had the pleasure of meeting Wong through Tan Teck Bak in 1979 and spoke with him on several occasions regarding his experiences in both camps and he was most informative. Sadly, he passed away in 1999, bitterly disappointed that he and his wife – she had preceded him to the grave – had been in-adequately compensated by the Australian Government.

I believe it was through Joseph Wong that we learned that Kempei Tai officers at one stage were living in the home of former American authoress Agnes Keith who wrote 'Land Below the Wind', 'Three Came Home' and other books. Her husband had been the agricultural station's research scientist when the Japanese entered WW2. The postwar award winning Hollywood film 'Three Came Home' was

Japanese pilots taking luncheon at Sandakan Air Strip

based on Agnes Keith's book and starred Ronald Coleman and Claudette Colbert.

Joseph Wong told me shortly before he passed away that a number of locals who were arrested for complicity in anti Japanese activities were beheaded in a coconut grove that led off the same street as the Keith home, and only a stone's throw away from it. He thought it was around about the same time that the radio was discovered in the Australian camp -. He was unsure of the number executed and was unable to state positively whether the Keiths suspected the treachery that finally led to the discovery of the radio at the Australian camp. The last time I visited the restored Keith home – 1998 - it was occupied by Philippino squatters who were expecting to be evicted by the local authorities.

Chapter 25

BONGAWAN RAILWAY STATION

The RAAF PBY Catalina lifted off the Palawan airstrip at 1600 on the 29th May 1945 as I remarked to Sgt. Curly Lang and my buddy Skeet that it was truly an awe inspiring experience to spend time at the 13th U.S. Air Force base at Palawan.

The display of air power there did a power of good to my confidence in the progress of the Pacific war, to say nothing of the quality of meals at the American mess and the clothing issued to their troops, plus conditions under which the Yanks lived. Canned turkey and ice cream plus other foods considered luxuries by the Australians were daily fare at Palawan. It was truly an eye opener and an education to compare their front line conditions with those of our Australian soldiers, sailors and airmen.

Sgt. Curly Lang was one of a two-man 'despatch' team aboard the Catalina and their duty was to get us ashore once the Cat had landed and taxied in to the shallows.

I first met Curly at Frazer Island more than twelve months earlier but had not met his companion whose name I cannot recall. Additionally, a Malay operative by the name of Mandor Bin Ali joined us at Palawan Air Force base who was a stranger to Skeet and myself but was known to Gort our leader. Tall by Malay standards, Ali turned out to be good value in operation 'Stallion 4' as he later proved.

Skeet and I had not anticipated another person joining the three of us and it came as a surprise to say the least. It did seem irregular at first that our team of three who had worked together for many months was to be joined by another and a complete stranger at that.

To this very day I do not know whether Ali came from Morotai in the RAAF Cat or whether he formerly came from BNB or Porta Princessa on Palawan pre-war. I had never seen him until we boarded the Cat and I never met him again after our evacuation on the 9th June. He disappeared as mysteriously as he appeared. However, Gort knew him of old and we had learned by experience that Gort's unerring judgement always proved to be correct.

Our mission was to cross check Dutch intelligence that indicated 7,000 Japanese troops defended Labuan Island and the mainland area 26 miles across the water. These were the areas where the Australian 9th Division intended to land on the morning of the 12th June 1945. As Dutch intelligence had proved very inaccurate and costly in lives at Tarakan, a more accurate update was sought by the Australian High Command.

Additionally, the objective of 'Stallion 4' required us to carry out a reconnaissance of the railway bridge over the Papar River approximately 25 miles north of our insertion point in Kimanis Bay, and if the bridge was still standing, we were to destroy it. It was imperative that the bridge be downed thus preventing the trains from transporting troop reinforcements and essential equipment at night from the northern areas of Jesselton, Langkong and other Japanese defence positions on the Kudat Peninsula to the important railway junction of Beaufort to the south of us.

According to Gort, if destruction of the bridge was not possible, the alternative was to destroy the line in the Kimanis to Bongawan sector before our extraction on the 6th or 7th of June but only if time permitted.

The railway line commencing at Jesselton approximately 40 miles to the north of us followed the coast and terminated at the Beaufort junction. We at Bongawan were about equidistant to Beaufort and Papar. From Beaufort, two branch lines served Weston to the south and Tenom to the south-east. Its nearest approach to the coast was the railway station of Bongawan less than 2 miles inland.

American planes had been regularly bombing the Papar Bridge but were unable to confirm that the bridge was down. Confirmation was one of our tasks and we had the explosives to do the job if the bridge was intact.

Unbeknown to us, as the Catalina lifted off the tarmac at Palawan, a number of planes from the 13th USAAF base were busily bombing and strafing the Japanese in the rubber estates situated on both sides of the railway line adjoining the beach. The idea was to keep the 'binatangs' heads down and give them something to think about while the Cat put down in the sea and transported us ashore before darkness set in.

The Cat arrived over Kimanis Bay on the west coast at 1800 hours and after a thorough inspection of the area, the pilot touched down on the mirror calm surface about 3 miles out to sea and immediately taxied inshore.

When the PBY came to a halt about 100 yards offshore, the despatch team unloaded an inflatable through the blister of the Cat and in a flash inflated it alongside the plane. An outboard motor was then shipped aboard and hurriedly fitted to the transom and all was ready to go.

Stores to last until the 8th June, 84 pounds of plastic explosive and our Boston radio transmitter had been placed aboard the plane at Morotai. These were quickly loaded into the inflatable and when completed the four of us jumped aboard, Curly fired the outboard into life and mid wishes of good luck from the crew of the Cat and the other despatch man, we headed for the shore. The smooth surface of Kimanis Bay resulted in a complete absence of surf off the beach making our insertion a 'piece of cake'.

Immediately the boat hit the sand, the four of us hurriedly unloaded the stores and carried them into the jungle fringing the beach. After wishing us good luck, Curly gunned the outboard and in a few minutes was back at the Cat where the motor was shipped aboard the plane. The boat was then deflated and dragged inboard through the blister of the Cat as it taxied back into the deeper water of Kimanis Bay for take-off. As we melted into the gathering darkness of the jungle, we were reminded that we were entirely on our own by the roar of the Cat's engines as she lifted off the sea on its return to Palawan.

Gort warned us that we could expect no rest until we had crossed the railway line where we would then be in thick jungle and relative safety. Gort, only a few days earlier had made an aerial reconnaissance of the area and knew exactly what to expect.

Laboriously humping the gear between us, we pushed about a mile into the secondary jungle that covered the coastal strip and after finding suitable cover just short of the railway line, exhausted, we settled down for the night.

The next day the 30th May – our first full day in the area – Gort

222

decided that we should make a thorough recce of the area before crossing the railway line. At about 1700 hours we found a suitable spot to cross the Kuala (headland) Sungei Bongawan (Bongawan river) and against a very strong outgoing current, we managed to wade across at chest depth. Just before dark, Gort decided that the heavy parcels of explosives we were carrying, were hampering our progress so a suitable spot under a jungle shrub was found where we concealed the plastic explosive, cordtex, detonators etc, intending to return for them later. Our second night was again spent west of the railway line in secondary jungle.

The following day promised to be very busy. We still had to cross the railway line to gain the protection of heavy jungle. As a safeguard, Gort asked Ali and I to make a recce of the railway line for about a mile or so north and south of where we had spent the night. While Gort and Skeet waited for us under cover, I donned a coolie shirt, a pair of shorts and a pair of latex rubber slippers commonly used by natives in the area and comparable with clothing worn by Ali. We then set off down the railway line checking on both sides of the line for signs of habitation. Finding nothing after walking a mile or so, we reversed direction and checked the line for about the same distance north of where Gort and Skeet were hidden waiting for us to return.

Shortly after passing the spot where Gort and Skeet were holed up, we passed a Malay couple walking south who greeted us as they passed but never spared us a second glance. This pleased me immensely as it proved that my clothing and general appearance created no undue interest. Ali assured me earlier that I had no cause to worry about my clothing but the proof of the pudding was in the eating. Encountering no other signs of human life or signs of habitation, Ali and I returned and reported our findings to Gort.

Because Gort felt that we were losing valuable time, that could prove costly to the operation, instead of waiting for nightfall before crossing the railway line, he decided to take the risk of crossing the railway line in daylight. Accordingly, at 1000 hours we raced across the line and moved east about 500 yards into thick jungle interspersed with fetid swampland.

After Gort selected a suitable spot, we cleared some of the undergrowth and set our hammocks ready for the night. The following morning we were sitting around having a bite of breakfast and a cup of coffee and it was most noticeable that Skeet was strangely quiet. Not normally an uproarious person at any time, on this occasion Skeet was quieter than usual; so much so that Gort eventually asked him if he was feeling well or whether there was something troubling him.

Skeet's reply sunk us all. He was concerned because he could not remember seeing his webbing, the Boston generator handles and the tripod legs come off the Catalina! A quick but thorough search was made of our equipment and in a short space of time, Skeet's worst fears were confirmed.

I expected Gort to break out into his usual expostulation of "A thousand immaculate bastards. Christ Jesus, God Almighty" and was absolutely staggered when he remained mute. I believe now the hopelessness of our situation had taken time to sink in and had left him speechless. I knew how poor old Skeet felt, he being the signaller but blame was not attachable to him. I felt hopelessly dejected myself and no doubt Ali must have felt the same.

To this day I have never learned who was held responsible for the stuff-up. I was however, under the impression – rightly or wrongly – that the radio equipment was newly issued from 'Z' HQ at Morotai and therefore should have been packed aboard the Catalina with the inflatable boat, demolitions and field rations. We were required to take only our personal gear and weapons from Pitas. Unless I miss my guess, the buck would have been passed on and nobody would have been found responsible. However, we were the ones in the gun and would suffer as a result.

There we were behind Japanese lines with at least 7,000 Japanese troops in our immediate beach-head invasion area – according to Dutch intelligence. One might be excused for saying that we were slightly outnumbered, and there we were with a radio that was useless. We were literally stranded. There was no way that we could summon help to get us out of the area and the best we could hope for was to see the war out there, if the Japanese did not get us first. We had supplies for 10 days only, thereafter we would have to survive the best way we could as was the case of the POW. Any intelligence information we could secure was equally useless as there was no way of getting it out

We desperately needed the tripod to mount the generator. That much accomplished, we had to have a pair of handles to wind the generator to produce the current needed by the ATR4 transmitter/radio to enable

Skeet to transmit direct to Fred and Graham at Pitas. They in turn would send our traffic on the powerful Boston transmitter back to our HQ in Morotai and from there it would go to higher commands and possibly the invasion fleet.

The ATR4 was not powerful enough for us to transmit direct to HQ. But how in the name of hell could Skeet get messages to Fred and Graham at Pitas?

Immediately the frightening truth was realised, Skeet in desperation, removed the handles from our American aluminium dixies. He then filed the dixie handle ends to fit the end sockets of the generator – about 5/8 inch square female – and bent the handles to a shape similar to a motor car crank handle.

The handles completed, we still had no tripod on which to mount the generator and some method had to be formulated whereby the head could be firmly held to permit the turning of the handles to generate power.

Skeet like all of us was beside himself with worry! It was fortunate that he had decided to bring a small warding file from Pitas. Although a bit small, it was a case of fourth class ride better than first class walk. After filing and fitting the dixie handles for some hours they were finally ready to test. We attempted to hold the generator head on a log without success. Then a stump about three feet high was found and with some rope from the hammocks, Skeet was able to lash the head down reasonably securely. Then came the big test.

The handles were placed in the sockets of the generator head and the big test got under way. Unfortunately, because the aluminium handles lacked the strength required, after about a dozen revolutions both handles sheared off as a result of metal fatigue. Almost the whole day had been spent unsuccessfully trying to get the generator to work. Skeet laboured tirelessly trying to make other substitutes including bush timber handles that again proved unsuccessful.

On the morning of the 2nd June, Skeet filed up one aluminium dixie handle to the correct width of the generator socket as a pattern. Gort then asked me to don my coolie clothes, take the sample handle and Ali with me, go down the railway line to kampong (village) Bongawan about three miles south of our hide-out. Once there, I was to seek a former pro allied friend of his pre-war by the name of Chin Sung who might be able to put us in touch with a Chinese blacksmith to forge two handles.

After describing Chin Sung, Gort explained that once having located him I would have to establish that he was still pro Allied as Gort had not seen him since the Japanese invaded BNB in 1942. Once satisfied that his allegiance had not changed, I would need to tell him that Tuan Gort Chester from Lokawee Estate out of Jesselton had sent me. Then and not before, was I to expose our identities before explaining the assistance we sought.

We were unsuccessful in our quest to find Chin Sung. Fortunately, we located another young Chinese man by the name of Lee Tong Gwan who told us in Cantonese that Chin Sung was thought to be in the hands of the 'binatangs' on charges of anti Japanese activities. Satisfied that we did not represent a Japanese trap, Lee took us to a pro-Allied Chinese blacksmith who immediately set about forging the handles while we waited.

It was purely a case of 'more arse than Jessie'! A thousand to one chance that came off! A shot in the dark that found its mark! Our contact – a complete stranger – Lee Tong Gwan could so easily have been pro-Japanese and our chips would have been down. If in fact this had been the case Ali and I would have had no alternative other than to liquidate him. Before revealing our identities, I had quickly summed him up and decided that he was an honest good-looking young type and was worth the punt. However, I was extremely careful not to reveal the whereabouts of Gort and Skeet should my judgement prove me wrong. Other than having our 'L' tablets, we were completely unarmed. If we were betrayed and captured, we would take the tablets rather than disclose the whereabouts of Gort and Skeet to the 'sons of heaven'.

There were so many angles to be considered. Lee, if in the employ of the 'binatangs' could have been smart enough to realise that if he played along with us, at the end of the line there was the big fish to fry – Gort Chester. The Japanese had been trying to get their hands on Gort since operation 'Python' back in 1943 and posters still existed in Japanese occupied towns throughout BNB offering huge rewards for 'Gort Chester – dead or alive'

Although the Chinese generally speaking did not collaborate with the Japanese, there were the exceptions. One has to realise that the Japanese hated the local Chinese more than they hated the Malays who they regarded as an inferior race. The Chinese in the eyes of the Japanese were the hated enemies of old and were to be treated harshly at all times. Any excuse to lop a Chinese head was gladly accepted by the 'binatangs'. Our young Chinese contact could have so easily handed us in and probably would have received a handsome reward for his trouble.

Luckily for us, dame fortune had smiled upon us. In the absence of Chin Sung, we were extremely fortunate to find the right contact purely by chance, to whom I reluctantly revealed our identities before he was prepared to take us to his blacksmith friend, who also had to be pro-Allied as he obviously was. It was a chance we had to take.

It was late afternoon before we returned to Gort and Skeet with the finished handles. I felt sure that both were worried about the task we had to do and Gort probably felt that he had consigned us to a certain death, but what else could he have done? If we were unable to get the handles made we were all doomed.

As soon as we arrived, Skeet took the handles and tried them in the generator head only to find them a few thousandths of an inch oversize in the square section. They refused to be coaxed into the sockets. It meant

Jack Sue aged 19 wearing Chinese Coolie clothing. Photo taken in Australia immediately after the war.

that we had to take them back for additional filing the next morning as Skeet's worn file was the worse for wear and had turned up its toes. The other side of the coin revealed the handles while only air hardened, were nevertheless too tough for Skeet's well worn but worn well file.

At some late hour of that night Gort and Skeet were awakened by the train passing up the line from south to north and again some hours later it went through from north to south fully loaded. Desperately tired out mentally and physically, Ali and I slept through it all which was unusual for us. Gort and Skeet told us in the morning that in addition to hearing and seeing the train go through, many Japanese troops had marched down the railway line during the night chattering among themselves as was their practice.

Early the next morning Ali and I set off down the railway line again following small groups of Japanese troops and local natives heading south. Ali and I, mingling with the locals and without engaging in conversation reached Bongawan incident free. The alterations were done to the handles and we returned in due course with them to Gort and Skeet.

The delays involved in making initial contacts and getting the handles made had taken days; days of irretrievable time.

On the 5th June, Gort decided to move our camp about 500 yards deeper into the jungle to lessen the chances of the Boston generator being heard on the railway line. After finding a suitable spot to rig an aerial into the trees and a suitable tree stump on which to re-lash the generator, two of us assisted the rope lashings by physically holding down the generator head while one wound the handles. After a couple of attempts, Skeet finally established radio contact with a much relieved Fred and Graham at Pitas who had given up hope that we were still alive. Our call was days overdue and the boys at Pitas were convinced that we had been killed or captured in the Japanese infested west coast region.

I think all four of us gave a sigh of relief when we realised that our isolation was at an end. Skeet's look of 'Thank Christ for that' spoke volumes. Our first inward message from Fred indicated that D Day had been advanced to the 10th. Whether the 'sons of heaven were aware of the change was anybody's guess. .Fred and Graham told us later that they had conducted a 24 hour vigil on the radio at Pitas HQ waiting hopefully for our call sign to hit the air.

The few days spent going back and forth to Bongawan were not wasted however. Ali and I had eventually made contact with Gort's pre-war friend Chin Sung who did not impress us. He was somewhat evasive about his few days out of town and after learning from Lee Tong Gwan that Chin Sung was a Japanese appointed Chinese district leader, Gort wisely decided to give him the big arse.

We discovered that Ho Ah Lee the Chinese stationmaster at Bongawan was also Japanese appointed and that he was highly regarded by the Japanese hierarchy. As time was not on our side – we only had three days left in which we had to gather the information we needed - Gort decided that we should take the bull by the horns and go direct to Ah Lee the stationmaster of Bongawan. Gort felt certain that Ah Lee would have at his fingertips all the necessary information we sought.

The small station - by Australian standards - of Bongawan was staffed by Ah Lee and four senior Japanese Army railway transport officers plus other ranks, many of whom were camped under trees surrounding the station.

On this occasion Gort suggested that I should go into the station alone while Ali waited for me in the light secondary jungle opposite. Completely unarmed apart from the cold comforting knowledge that I had my 'L' tablets with me, I went on to the station and into the Stationmaster's office where Lee was seated alone at his desk. After briefly greeting Lee, I briefly told him that I needed information regarding the movements of Japanese troops and equipment by rail during the past two months.

The very small man – about 5 feet whose age I estimated at about 35/40 – looked at me quizzically with a half smile on his face and said to me in Chinese "You must be mad. Don't you realise that I only have to call one of these officers and your head will be off?"

I was prepared for his remark and without revealing my identity, countered it by telling him that I was expected back at a certain meeting place by a certain time that day with the information I sought. If I failed to arrive, extremely heavy reprisals would follow and I detailed to him exactly what would happen.

That was June 1945. Ever since that day I have been ashamed of the threats I made to Ah Lee. I have spent many months over years of leading war veterans tours to Sabah unsuccessfully searching for him, to apologise for the dire threats I made to him that fateful day. Reversing the situations briefly, I have no conception as to how I would have handled the situation had the threats been aimed at me.

While I am not a churchgoer since the war years, I am a Christian and uphold Christianity and its principals. I do not accept that one has to regularly attend an elaborate church to be a good Christian and I uphold one of Christ's teachings "where two or more are met in my name, there shall a church be formed"

Additionally, I believe that the Lord hears me when I commune with him in private within the precincts of my home. My threats to Ah Lee troubled my conscience deeply for many, many years.

Those threats I made to Ah Lee that day have never been disclosed to any living soul but Gort Chester, Skeet Hywood and Ali Bin Mandor and I do not elaborate on them here.

Suffice for me to say that the threats had the desired effect. Ah Lee stared at me unbelievingly, then slowly but very positively reached into a filing cabinet, removed a number of files that he placed in a small brief bag and without uttering a word, rose and proceeded to leave the office with me. We left the station and the prying eyes of possible onlookers.

1995 – the 50th anniversary of Victory Pacific and the unconditional surrender of Japan – found me back in Sabah with my 4th son Kim and with a large war veterans' tour group of more than 50 WW2 servicemen, woman and nurses from Australia.

Responding to a hunch, I enquired after the whereabouts of Ah Lee at the Beaufort railway junction and was surprisingly told by the Stationmaster that he as a junior had served his seven years apprenticeship under Ah Lee. He added that Ah Lee had retired two years earlier and was living 'up north' out of Kota Kinabalu (pre war Jesselton) with family members. This was the most helpful clue that I had unearthed since the war.

We were on a very tight schedule and time could not be found to chase clues during that stay in Sabah. I desperately needed to face Ah Lee and tell him how sorry I was on that lamentable day at Bongawan station in June 1945. I have never lost the mental picture of poor Ah Lee's disbelieving stare when I outlined to him exactly what would happen if I was not back at the RV with the information sought by my party leader at a pre-arranged time.

Unfortunately, we had a very full itinerary and could not follow up the information.

In 1998 I was again in Sabah with my son Barry, daughter Aneeta and the film documentary team of Miller/Carlyon of Melbourne shooting the film ' Jack Sue – A Matter of Honour'. The team also included a very helpful Chinese Malaysian lady interpreter Judy Chan who hailed from Kuala Lumpur, spoke perfect English and was fluent in a number of Chinese and Malaysian dialects and into the bargain proved to be a great team mixer.

While in the Beaufort, Membakut, Bongawan area, Terry Carlyon asked Judy to take up the search for Ah Lee from where I had left off in 1995. On our arrival at Kota Kinabalu (formerly Jesselton), Judy checked with police HQ there who enquired further afield, only to learn that Ah Lee had passed away some months before our arrival. I was too late.

With the address of one of the relatives given to us by the police HQ, Terry Carlyon decided to drive out to the family home in the rural area of Kota Kinabalu where we met a number of Ah Lee's sons and daughters gathered there who eagerly awaited our arrival.

Introductions and trivialities over, I apologised to the sons and daughters who surprisingly knew very little of their late father's wartime activities and who accepted the fact that war was war and added that they did not regard my threat as a personal matter. Apparently, their father had never told them of the threats made to him that day at the Bongawan railway station. At long last I felt somewhat relieved. It wasn't exactly as I had wanted, but it was the next best thing.

The sum of the intelligence we gained from Ho Ah Lee and Lee Tong Gwan was staggering to say the least.

The Papar railway bridge was downed by 13th USAAF bombers on the 10th May according to reports received from Chinese rail runners who said that Japanese engineers were attempting to repair it. After the Allied troops landed, the bridge was reportedly sabotaged by Chinese guerrillas and after that the Japanese engineers abandoned all hope of repairing it.

One remaining railway locomotive was still in use running from Jesselton to the Papar River where troops and equipment were unloaded. Troops and equipment were then man-handled across the Papar River by boat, and equipment only was re-loaded on to one of only two locomotives left on the southern bank of the river hauling rolling stock from Papar to Beaufort.

Troops marched down the railway line every night and remained hidden during daylight in rubber plantations or jungle adjoining the railway line. Fires for cooking during the day were banned by the Japanese officers. Trains on the southern side of the river ran only at night and did one run Beaufort to Papar return per night. One loco was still operating on the branch line Beaufort to Tenom.

Between the 18th and 25th May, more than 3,000 'Binatangs' were transported from Jesselton (now Kota Kinabalu) to Beaufort. At the same time an additional 500 troops had marched down the line each night. Well-armed Nipponese troops were permanently camped on both sides of the railway line in the rubber estates from mile 57 to 62 for some weeks and there were approximately 1,000 at Beaufort Estate, 1,500 at Jimpunga and 1,000 at Woodford. The Japanese Commander in Chief and his staff had taken up residence in the manager's house at Sapong Estate and had access to a twin engine plane that regularly flew at night from Keningau to Jesselton – a relatively short flight.

Use of the railway telephone system was prohibited to all railway personnel excepting certain trusted stationmasters including Ah Lee and Japanese railway transport officers.

At 0200 hours on the morning of the 3rd June, two trains travelled south from the town of Papar totally loaded with food supplies. One of the locomotives was badly damaged by American planes at 0900 at Beaufort and rendered it unlikely to run again – that left only one in service. A large number of USAAF B24 Liberators bombed and severely damaged Beaufort and its surrounding rubber and coconut estates but there were very few Japanese casualties.

Japanese intelligence – very much on the ball as ever – were well aware of the proposed landings by the 9th Australian division at Labuan and Brunei and they expected the landings to take place on the morning of the 12th June.

Ah Lee's documentation revealed that Japanese combat troops in BNB numbered 10,000 at Tuaran near Jesselton, 7,000 at Ranau where the death marches ended, 8,000 at Keningau and 5,000 at Beaufort. Most of the troops were battle experienced - ex the Philippines – and had large food reserves.

Nearer to us, the Kuala (headland) Papar was defended on both sides of the river-mouth by a force of 200 'binatangs' guarding the railway bridge that' spanned the Papar River. In addition to a mobile searchlight, they were armed with Bren guns and Thompson machine guns captured from the Americans at the Philippines. 100 more were stationed at Kimanis a short distance up the railway line, 33 at Mandahan estate one mile away from our hideout and 30 at Mempakut the other side of Bongawan railway station. Including the Nipponese in the Bongawan kampong and railway station area, the Japanese were all around us. The Dutch figure was hopelessly underestimated.

Two unidentified serviceable Japanese aircraft were camouflaged 5 chains east of the 5 mile post at Tanjong Aru (today, a fashionable suburb of modern Kota Kinabalu).

Australian Beaufighters flew over the west coast areas on the 4th June and dropped pamphlets over known Japanese camps urging the Japanese to surrender. I managed to secure one pamphlet that I took back to Gort who after reading it said, "that will do as much good as tits on a bull".Skeet having transmitted all the intelligence required of us to Fred and Graham at Pitas, our job was completed.

The unhygienic conditions under which we had existed since leaving the 13th USAAF base had taken its toll. We were short of food, short of sleep, physically and mentally tired out, we had exhausted our supplies of water sterilising tablets and had finally resorted to drinking straight swamp water and as a result three of us had contracted dysentery.

We thought we were pretty tough after three months in the country and all of us as fit as Mallee bulls, but the jungle proved otherwise exactly as it had done to the POW on the Death Marches. With the exception of Ali, whose guts must have been a lot tougher than ours, the three of us were at the stage where we could squirt through the eye of a needle. Nonetheless, Ali like the rest of us could not get out of the place fast enough.

Late into the afternoon of the 5th June, Gort worded a signal requesting a Catalina to extract us from a specified map reference point north west of the Mandahan Estate at dawn on the 7th June and passed it on to Skeet who encoded and transmitted the signal.

The following day the 6th June we received confirmation of our previous day's request to the effect that a US Catalina would extract us at dawn on the 7th at the arranged map reference point as per signal. At 1430 hours Gort decided that we should break camp and head for the coast for the morrow's extraction.

Getting out of the swampy terrain in a different direction presented a host of unexpected problems. It necessitated a considerable amount of waist deep wading through crocodile country. To make matters worse, when passing under a large tree we were attacked by a swarm of wild bees that were particularly attracted to Gort's bald head and he was badly stung.

Realising that it was imperative that we make the coast before dark and that in our weakened condition it was going to be difficult, Gort ordered Skeet to "throw the bloody radio and generator into the swamp". There was no need to hamper our progress with the weight, particularly as the extraction details had been confirmed and we did not wish to miss that plane.

Likewise, the parcel of plastic explosive etc that had been ditched shortly after we landed from the Catalina was a worry and it was to remain that way – just an ongoing worry. Little did I realise at the time that it would develop into a lifetime worry. We just didn't have the time to get there to retrieve it.

If we missed that plane, without the radio there was no way that we could contact HQ to request another, or for that matter, there was no way of contacting anyone on the friendly side of the world. That of course meant that we would have to remain in the Bongawan area and be on the receiving end of the Allied naval bombardment and aerial bombing that was to precede the beach invasion on 'Z' day – 4 days hence. That pounding was intended for the Japanese and there was no way that we wanted any part of it.

After checking that the coast was clear we made a dash across the railway line about 1600 hours and after several stops to relieve our aching legs and anuses, succeeded in making the beach at sunset.

Our map reference point for the next morning's extraction showed nothing else but jungle. However, when we arrived there we were surprised to find a small shed and a salt evaporation pan over a fire. An old Chinese fellow with a goatee beard and two young sons greeted us in Cantonese very cautiously, having noticed that we were well armed.

After speaking with him for a few minutes and assuring him that we intended no harm, he introduced the two boys Ah Fah 13 years of age and Lam Gan 10. A few more minutes of conversation took place during which he announced that he and his boys had just stoked up the fire to burn overnight while they returned to their home for the night. In the late morning they planned to take the treated salt to native tribes in the hills and barter for fruit, vegetables and meat for his wife and family.

Gort then spoke to him in Malay and told him that he and the boys could not go home that night and that we would have to hold them hostage until the morning when we would free them unharmed. Between us we still had a few fruit bars that we, with our painful squirting backsides dared not eat, gladly gave to the old man and his two fine looking young lads who ate them greedily. The boys and the father had no clothes and wore tattered loincloths only. They did not seem unduly concerned that they had to remain with us overnight and prepared to settle down near the warmth of the fire.

We could not allow them to leave the scene until we had left on the Catalina. That night, vigilant as ever, we took it in turn to remain awake should the old man or the boys attempt to leave the scene. However, we experienced no trouble with them.

At 0430 hours on the 7th June, a Yankee Black Widow night fighter arrived overhead and returned our recognition signals before flying off to the south. It never returned and at 0900 hours the Catalina had not arrived. Obviously something had gone wrong. Later at Palawan we were told that the lone Catalina had been shot down.

At the invitation of the old Chinese man, we followed him and the boys to their humble little shanty home not very far from the salt pan where we spent most of the day. We were all very dejected and wondered how the hell we were going to get out of the place with no radio.

At about 1700 that afternoon, we heard the drone of aircraft approaching and recognised the sound of a PBY Catalina. Summoning what little strength we had left, our dysentery wearied bodies hurried down to the beach followed by the old Chinese man and his boys. From the cover of the jungle fringing the beach we saw not one, but two American Catalinas flying low above the sea parallel to the beach and about two miles off shore, while high overhead a number of escorting fighter aircraft circled.

After exchanging recognition signals, they flew south so as not to draw Japanese attention to the area, returning a few minutes later. One immediately alighted on the water and taxied in until it almost beached itself while the other circled above, obviously to protect the first and if necessary, to put down and collect us should an emergency arise. They were hell bent in getting us out!

Hurriedly, the pilot turned the Cat in the light surf until the aircraft was facing out to sea ready for a fast take-off. An inflatable boat with outboard motor left the blister of the Cat and headed to the beach crewed by our ever reliable Nick Combe and George Carter – another 'Z' officer.

Thanking the old Chinese man for his hospitality and at the same time bidding farewell to him and his fine young boys, we dashed across the beach and into the surf where we ditched most of our gear. However, we were thankful to be safe and sound as we clambered aboard the inflatable, gave the old Chinese salt man and his two boys a final wave and in seconds were on the way out to the Cat and ultimate rescue.

Arriving alongside the blister, we were greeted by Datu Mustapha who assisted us aboard as the Cat taxied out into deeper water to get out of gunfire range of the beach should the Nipponese intervene. Once safely out to sea and out of range of shore gunfire, the boat was deflated, dragged inboard through the blister whereupon the pilot gunned the throttles and the Catalina skimmed across the calm waters of Kimanis Bay before lifting off and setting course for Palawan.

On the return journey, the plane's radar operator picked up the blips of Japanese night fighters but they were not sighted. We passed over the 140 ship convoy bearing the Australian 9th Division off Balabac Island in the Balabac Strait that separated the island of Palawan and BNB and what a wonderful sight it was. Stretching from horizon to horizon the convoy was on its way to Labuan Island and Brunei Bay. It was the night of the 7th June and we were only 12 hours late after all our trials and tribulations.

A lone Japanese night fighter from God only knew where, had penetrated the radar screen only a few minutes before our Cat arrived over the American base of Palawan, dropped two bombs and strafed one of the revetment areas before making off at high speed.

Our PBY was on short final approaching the strip when it was ordered by the airstrip control to 'go around' as repair teams were still clearing bomb damage on the strip. Apart from this, our flight had been incident free.

During the one night stopover at Palawan, Skeet and I surprisingly met one of the very popular Malays from Frazer Island, the late Ali Bin Salleh who was waiting for a new parachute to arrive from Tawi-Tawi and an aircraft to take him on some operation.

General Barnes the commanding officer of the 13th USAAF on the following morning – the 8th June – de-briefed Gort who handed the details of Japanese targets to the General. According to Gort, the

American officer had been in touch with the US Submarine Base in Fremantle and was highly praiseworthy of our efforts and assured him that the next day the 9th June, 25 B24 Liberators would be unleashed on Japanese concentrations in the rubber estates. 12 P38 Lightnings would be briefed to locate and destroy the camouflaged Japanese planes at Tanjong Aru and added that 8 Black Widow night fighters would take care of the lone Japanese plane flying nightly between Keningau and Jesselton. In addition, further B24 Liberators would continue to bomb the Papar Bridge to keep it down.

At 0630 on the 9th we departed Palawan on the Catalina bound for Morotai via Zamboanga in the Philippines and arrived there late in the evening where we taken to the A.I.B. camp (Allied Intelligence Bureau) before admission to the 2/5th Australian General Hospital. There, Gort was de-briefed by the big brass of the 9th Australian Division. All of us were quickly worsening severe cases of dysentery. Mine had deteriorated into bacillary dysentery. Skeet was also suffering from a shocking ulcer on an ankle. He was admitted to ward 15 and I to ward 18. Gort was to be flown to Melbourne for further de-briefing and medical attention.

Skeet and I woke on the morning of the 10th June 1945 ('Z' day) in the luxury of comfortable beds, beautiful white linen and lovely nurses taking good care of us. They were luxuries that we had almost forgotten.

As far as I know, Ali Bin Mandor was not admitted to hospital and I'm not even sure whether he returned to Morotai with us. We were too sick to worry about who was aboard the plane. He disappeared out of our lives as mysteriously as he had appeared.

Later that morning we heard from our HQ that the naval bombardment of the invasion areas of Labuan and Brunei was creating havoc among the Japanese defenders and that the invasion was well under way and making fine progress. Perhaps our efforts had been worth while and had contributed to the success of the invasion.

Still concerned about the 84 pounds of plastic explosive (PE), cordtex, detonators and fuses left behind in the Bongawan area, I was told in about 1982 that a girls' college had been planned for an area just north of the Bongawan railway station. I immediately wrote to the Chief Minister of Sabah in the interests of the people in the Bongawan area and told him about the cache of explosive and offered to go back to BNB and endeavour to find it.

I had arranged for my wartime mate the late Lieut..Don Harlem to accompany me, plus a former English Army man from Perth, Alex McGuiness who was an expert at divining all manner of things. He proved his ability by locating a small piece of plastic explosive I had planted in the huge premises at the rear of my Murray St. Perth dive store.

The Chief Minister of Sabah replied to my correspondence expressing his thanks and his cabinet's concern and offered the assistance of Malaysian Army personnel equipped with detection apparatus. Sadly, after an amount of correspondence had floated back and forth over a period of some months, the matter died a natural death following a change of Government in Sabah. The explosives are possibly still there.

In the late sixties or early seventies an Italian bulldozer driver of a Caterpillar D8 was clearing land somewhere west of the Whitfield Ranges out from Cairns, North Queensland. Suddenly there was a mighty explosion and only the density of the Caterpillar shielding the driver saved his life. When eventually helpers arrived, they were confronted by a huge hole in the ground, the Cat was on its side and the deafened Italian operator was still wandering around in a dazed state, his clothing completely blasted from his body. When able to speak, the shocked driver said that the dozer blade had struck something that exploded.

Windows in private homes and commercial buildings for miles around were blasted out including those of 'The House on the Hill' (THOTH) at Kingsford, west of Cairns. THOTH had been the advanced training base of 'Z' during WW2 (Cairns 'Z' Experimental Station) and many famous raids behind Japanese lines emanated from that establishment.

Following the cessation of WW2 and closure of THOTH as a training base, a problem faced the 'Z' hierarchy. What were they to do with the excess PE, Cordtex (both on the top-secret list) and detonators etc held at the house? A decision must have been made at the time to bury it in a safe place way out the back of the Whitfield Ranges. There was no habitation and there was not likely to be any for years to come – so the authorities thought.

Nobody at that time foresaw the expansion that Cairns and areas west of the Whitfield Range would undergo. The explosives lay there undisturbed for a number of years until the Italian bulldozer driver apparently struck a detonator that fired the underground mini mountain of Plastic Explosive (PE).

Well-known Cairns builder and proprietor of THOTH the late Arch James related this incident to me many years ago during one of the frequent stays of my diving groups from Perth while diving the Barrier Reef. The remarkably versatile and amiable Archie and his lovely wife Gloria – they ran the establishment - and other members of the James family, purchased THOTH after the war and converted it to a hotel/motel. The House before the turn of the century was connected with famous Australian aviator Sir Charles Kingsford Smith from where its location at the lower slopes of the Whitfield Range commanded a marvellous panorama of Cairns, the coastal plain and Green Island on the Great Barrier Reef.

The explosion was written up in the media at the time as 'a mysterious explosion' and the theory was expounded by the media that perhaps former 'Z' Force men at THOTH were involved. Although it was never positively solved, the explanation as outlined above cannot be overlooked. No other explanation was ever offered and to this day the explosion remains a mystery.

To the best of my knowledge, the explosives ditched at Bongawan were never recovered and similarly, could at some future date represent a danger as that area, while still sparsely populated is nevertheless expanding.

It possibly would only need a dozer blade, garden shovel or chungkol to detonate the charge. When we ditched the parcel of explosives – sufficient to destroy the steel and concrete railway bridge that spanned the Papar river - it was almost lying on the surface under a shrub and covered only by vegetation. Lack of time prevented us from burying it deeper. I only hope that some poor innocent person never accidentally detonates that cache of PE at Bongawan. The outcome could be far more catastrophic

Chapter 26

YANKEE COMPASSION

Shortly after Doc May parachuted in, one of the Malay guerrilla's small infants picked up a load of diphtheria for which certain life saving drugs were needed and urgently. The Americans were the nearest to us; they had recaptured Porta Princessa on Palawan Island from the Japanese on the other side of the Balabac Strait .

While the beach landing was in progress the American 'Seabees' (Airfield Construction Engineers) had landed with tank support, driven into the jungle at two locations miles apart on the beach front, then turned to meet each other to clear a perimeter.

Simultaneously, other 'Seabees' were already bulldozing and laying a metal mesh landing strip within the perimeter while the tanks and infantry cleared the inner area of the hated 'binatangs' who fought like fanatics. Within 6 hours of the beach landing the 13th USAAF fighters were touching down on the newly laid metal strip, re-fuelling and taking off again to support their land forces.

One had to admire the Yanks. Certainly they made their fair share of mistakes and their initial losses were heavy, but in the end, their strategy was cheaper in terms of men wounded and killed. This was so unlike our Australian landings at Tarakan and Balikpapan where our brave troops went ashore undermanned and became bogged down by enemy fire, to the extent of being lucky not to have been driven back into the ocean.

Around about the same time, the tearful young Malaysian mother whose husband had been slaughtered by the 'binatangs' for suspected involvement with us, came to see us carrying the desperately sick boy

240

of about 5. It was very obvious from the lad's condition that he was near death's door.

A message was sent to Doc who was visiting one of the guerrilla families about a mile away and in short time he was back on the scene of his jungle hospital. Meanwhile, the lad's young mother was assigned a bed in the hospital and allowed to freshen up and given a new sarong, shirt and food.

A little while later, after examining the boy, Doc announced to Fred, Graham and myself that the lad was a very serious case of diphtheria and that unless necessary drugs were flown in urgently, the boy would die.

Fred Olsen our sigs officer, with the help of Graham Greenwood encoded an urgent message of appeal to Porta Princessa requesting an airdrop of the drugs.

Apparently the drug was not available at the American base hospital. However, they apparently got on the blower to the 2/5th Australian General Hospital at Morotai who immediately dispatched the drugs to

Chinese guerrilla leader Tan Tek Bak with Malaysian decorations who became Adu Bakar Tan Tak Bak.
His decorations are the equivalent of our KCMG.

the American Airforce base on that island. They in turn flew it out to Palawan by Catalina flying boat where it was transferred to a waiting P38 Lightning twin engine fighter. Within almost minutes thereafter, the P38 was in our area where it shot up our Lokopas DV two or three times to arouse our attention before free dropping the consignment of drugs.

The carefully packed parcel survived the free drop faultlessly. We unpacked the drugs and raced them down to Doc's little atap and mahogany floored eight bed hospital in the guerrilla lines. Although it was less than 24 hours since the sigs had sent out the SOS and the little parcel had travelled many thousands of miles, it none-the-less arrived too late to save the small boy's life. Doc showed me the shocking state of the little lad's throat as he administered the drug. It was a sad moment for all concerned.

Later that evening we had a wake for the little boy with a bottle of Johnny Walker black label that had arrived with the drugs. Attached to the bottle was a label that simply said "Hi guys! Here's hoping drugs arrive in time. Best of luck. Have a drink on us.

The poor distraught mother who had lost her husband to the Japanese butchers followed then by the sad loss of her son, was happily taken in by one of the guerrilla families and thereafter assisted in various duties for 'Agas'. She was still happily serving there when I finally left Borneo to return to Australia.

On the last occasion that an American aircraft came to our area, it was a Porta Princessa lone Dakota (army version of the civvy DC3). It flew down the airstrip in broad daylight for two runs to be sure that we were about and when satisfied we were on the strip, free dropped a parcel. It went around again and flew back over the strip at hedge-hopping height, wiggled its wings as much as to say "See you later guys" and climbed off into the blue yonder.

We were not expecting any drops on the day so imagine our feelings when we unpacked a box of toys, candies. cookies and kiddies' sarongs for the Chinese and Malay guerrilla children. Wrapped in among all the garments was a giant sized bottle of Johnny Walker black label with a simple note "Something for the kids. Also, have a drink on us. It's been great working with you guys. Goodbye and good luck. Signed 13th USAAF base Porta Princessa".

Frequently we had been extracted by PBY Catalina or Martin Mariner flying boats and flown to Palawan, Tawi-Tawi or Morotai for overnight stopovers in the messes of the 13th and 5th USAAF bases. Despite this, none of us ever had the pleasure of catching up with the Yankee aircrews that dropped the gifts to us. What a wonderful bunch of guys they were. We still owe them a drink and it has proved to be a long way between drinking holes.

The first Australian plane in our skies apart from our own Flight 200 Liberators was a lone Beaufighter that flew overhead on the 27th May 1945. We guessed it had come from Tarakan. Formerly we were accustomed to seeing anywhere up to a hundred aircraft per day fly overhead. The big Yankee Liberators and Fortresses looked like huge flocks of cormorants in formation accompanied by busy bee-like swarms of escorting fighters including Lightnings, Thunderbolts, Mustangs and Kittyhawks.

Occasionally, in addition to the heavies going over daily on their way south towards Tarakan and Balikpapan, we saw squadrons of twin engine aircraft and assumed that they came from aircraft carriers out at sea.

After the American planes moved out, nothing moved in from thereon until the end of hostilities. If we saw a flight of five Australian Kittyhawks twice a week we were lucky. What a disappointment it was! Nevertheless, five Kittiehawks were better than none. We thanked the Lord for small mercies.

Chapter 27

SAGA AT DAMPIRIT

Lieutenant Hugh McMasters was flown in from Morotai during mid July 1945 as officer commanding our Telega base. His main task was to take charge of operatives' movements and the rest of his time was to be spent in training Malay guerillas for a proposed attack on Kudat on the extreme northern most point of BNB, the nearest airfield to Palawan in the Western Philippines.

For some time, Japanese forces in Langkong at the foot of the Kudat Peninsular and Kudat to the north had been a concern to us. Japanese activities to the east of Langkong were almost non existent since the Australian 9th Division landed at Labuan Island, Brunei Bay and Mempakul on the mainland.

Approximately 2,000 third class troops remained in Sandakan. Most of them were camped in the Leila Road and surrounding rubber plantations extending to the Beluran area about 32 miles out on the Death March route; they seemed reluctant to leave Sandakan. I believed that the Japanese were aware that operation 'Kingfisher' had been cancelled and that Australian forces no longer had any intention of landing in force in the Sandakan area. Likewise, that was the express reason why General Baba had concentrated all the troops he could muster on the west coast in the oil rich areas of Brunei and Labuan where he expected Australian forces to land.

And yet, that left a big query as to why he still retained 2,000 troops at Sandakan if there were no POW left to guard.

The fourth death march of 78 Australian POW and 100 Japanese guards left Sandakan for Ranau on the 10th July 1945. None of the POW or Japanese guards arrived at Ranau; it was a complete mystery. Whether blowpipe tribes had wiped them out was anybody's guess. Jock Sutcliffe and Don Harlem had not reported the movements of the fourth marchers on either the Northern or Southern Rentises although they were aware that the fourth march had left Sandakan.

It seemed almost as though the Japanese in Sandakan were still expecting 'Kingfisher' to take place. There was no tactical reason why they should want to hold Sandakan otherwise. The port facilities and the POW built airfield had been completely destroyed by the 13th US Air force and American carrier based planes. 4 Yankee PT boats from Tawi-Tawi entered Sandakan Harbour on the 5th June 1945, and shot up what was left of it. Tied to the damaged wharves, crew members of the 4 boats actually went ashore and made a reconnaissance of the area and were entertained in the homes of some of the leading Chinese of the town. This incursion was an absolute mystery as there was nothing to attract them in the harbour. At the time, we thought that the Americans must have been on an independent fact finding or intelligence mission. There had to be some justification for their visit and yet we knew only too well that the harbour installations were totally destroyed by their own planes.

Approximately the third week in July 1945, communications officer captain Lloyd Woods - who had been with Gort on operation 'Python 1' – and I left Morotai by RAAF Catalina bound for Telaga and Pitas HQ. At Tawi-Tawi we changed to an American Martin Mariner flying boat for the balance of the journey. We were given to understand that the Mariner drew less water than the Catalina and this was an important consideration when landing in the shallow waters of the Telaga estuary.

Despite the caution exercised, the Martin Mariner landed on an outgoing tide and in short time was high and dry much to the concern of the Yankee air-crew. They were forced to remain overnight as guests of Hugh McMasters, Lloyd Woods and myself while the Malay guerillas unloaded our radio equipment and general stores including ammunition from the stranded aircraft.

Fortunately for the Mariner crew, no Japanese aircraft or patrol boats spotted the high and dry sitting duck and they were able to take off with the morning incoming tide for the return flight to Tawi-Tawi none the worse for the experience.

Lloyd Woods remained with us while he and our sigs Fred Olsen and Graham Greenwood set up new communication systems. During the few days Lloyd was with us he witnessed a Flight 200 B24 Liberator drop of supplies and further weapons and ammunition for our planned attack on the Kudat Peninsular.

During the first week of August, I received instructions from Captain Roy McLean to rendezvous with him at Telaga and sail immediately for the western shore of the peninsular. I set about preparing weapons and ammunition for a 52 man Malay guerilla force to attack a Japanese post of 19 men at the base of the Kudat Peninsular and left Pitas within a few hours for the three hour boat journey to Telaga, there being an incoming tide.

On the way downstream, we passed under a canopy of overhanging trees. I was standing in the bow of the leading boat when all of a sudden, the steersman called out loudly "Jaga Tuan" (danger sir). As I instinctively ducked my head, I saw about three feet of beautiful emerald green and black tree viper suspended from a branch; it must have missed me by mere inches. I had no idea what length of viper was invisible in the foliage but I couldn't help but notice the exquisite beauty of the reptile swinging above me. It was beautiful but deadly danger. I thanked the steersman for his vigilance in warning me in the nick of time. It just proved that in Borneo death did not necessarily come from 'the sons of heaven'. It later occurred to me that the beauty and the fragrance of the large white blossoms adorning the emerald leaves of the tree provided a perfect camouflage for the deadly venomous viper.

I timed our arrival at Telaga perfectly. Roy had only arrived half an hour before us after carrying out a recce with a very reliable Chinese Malay named Yusof in the pay of the Japanese camped at Dampirit. By about 2000 hours that evening, our boat force was westward ho on the briny headed across Marudu Bay into a magnificent silky green sunset studded with gold and red wisps of cloud that adorned the sky with a somewhat herring bone effect.

On arrival at Yusof's home about 0200, there was a message for Roy and I from Fred Olsen. Gort had received news from Jock Sutcliffe and Don Harlem to say that both rentises from Beluran to Ranau had been checked at the leading kampongs en-route and there was no news of the 78 POW and their Japanese guards. Roy and I were of the opinion that the guards had murdered the 78 POW and then fallen foul of the blowpipe boys who would have shadowed them after leaving Beluran. It was possibly a case of tit for tat.

The southern route passed through Boto and Tampias and was more frequently used compared to the northern route via Klagan and Lingkabau – recognized as blowpipe country. The southern route, a little shorter in distance passed through many kampongs plus two small towns, whereas the northern rentis passed through fewer kampongs. Additionally, the Japanese regarded the towns of Klagan and Lingkabau as totally unreliable for food supplies.

Our opinion was that had the 'binatangs' (animals) planned the murder of the POW they would have selected the northern route – this being less frequented. Furthermore, the Japanese probably under estimated the deadly danger of the hostile blowpipe natives.

Details of the two routes had been supplied through Samak of Kampong Menunghutan from another 'Z' agent in Beluran. The appropriate map references were then radioed to SRD headquarters by 'Agas 1' during the early days when we were operating out of the 'mudflats'.

The remaining scattered Japanese troops on the east coast of BNB were subsequently ordered back to the west coast by the Japanese high command to bolster defences there.

After the very successful landing on Labuan Island, the Australians re-constructed the airfield from the shattered remains of old Victoria Town and in relatively short time, RAAF planes were supporting activities from the new airstrip.

Leaving some of the 9th Division boys to mop up tough Japanese resistance in an area known as 'the pocket' on Labuan Island, the principal forces landed on the mainland at Mempakul opposite the island. Once the beach-head had been established they drove inland and fanned out towards Beaufort in the south and northwards along the railway line towards the Papar River bridge and Jesselton.

Kudat being one of two airstrips available to the Japanese, the 'binatangs' considered it desirable to hold the Kudat Peninsular and the airstrip at Kudat that had taken a pasting by the American planes from Palawan prior to the Labuan landings. We were aware that General Baba had a well camouflaged 'Helen' twin engine bomber near his HQ at Keningau and that he might decide to flee to the north, although the capture of Palawan in the west Philippines made air escape almost impossible; even with Kudat in his possession.

General Baba's HQ at Sapong, well inland out of shelling range of

Allied warships, was a rail head on a branch line off the coastal railway line. About a month before the Australian landings, 'Agas 1' radioed General Barnes of the 13th US Air Force at Palawan advising him that a 'Dinah' twin engine bomber flew almost every night between Kuching and Keningau. The aircraft was regularly used by Colonel Suga, the cruel commanding officer of all POW camps in Borne'. Unfortunately he was not on the plane the evening an American Black Widow night fighter lay in wait for the aircraft, intercepted it and shot it down.

After our early morning arrival at Yusof's home, we rested up for the day. Roy, Hughie and I discussed plans for the following day's early morning attack.

Yusof advised us that the Japanese were well armed with automatic weapons and rifles plus at least one 3 inch mortar and a fair swag of grenades. They were not short of rice and other food commodities and in short had lived well off the fat of the land. The 'binatangs' were well supplied by local people who had been badly extorted by the 'sons of heaven', and who feared heavy reprisals if they refused to supply vegetables, poultry, pigs and fruit, not to mention the young girls of the district.

A number of young girls had been murdered when they refused to go to the cot with the barbarian Japanese. Understandably, the local Malays, Chinese and other indigenous races despised their masters and longed for an opportunity to equal the score and it was not long in coming.

Our guerillas were well armed for the situation although everything depended upon the element of surprise – the essence of guerila warfare. 16 of our number were equipped with Owen or Austen sub machine guns, the rest were equipped with .303 rifles. Roy, Hughie and I were armed with Bren guns and in addition, the three of us wore a belt of grenades each.

Our greatest fear and one over which we had no control, was the possibility of a leak or betrayal within the ranks of the Malay guerillas as it was known that there were a few unidentified agents employed by the Japanese on the Kudat Peninsular. Roy decided that he and I should make a personal recce of the Dampirit situation while Hugh stayed with the guerillas.

Late that afternoon we were within 100 yards of the Japanese camp and after studying the lay of the land for about an hour during which time we planned an attack strategy, we melted back into the jungle unobserved.

Our withdrawal necessitated crossing a jungle rentis about 4 feet wide and as we approached it we became aware of an armed Japanese guard on the rentis who was not there when we came through earlier. We were crawling gingerly through the thick undergrowth towards the rentis when Roy signalled to me to freeze, having heard a rustle in the undergrowth between himself and the guard who also froze on the spot, he having heard the same noise and was staring in that direction.

We remained on all fours not game to move when suddenly a large python slowly emerged, passed in front of the crouched Roy and headed in my direction. The hairs on Roy's thinning pate stood erect as the beautifully marked creature cleared him. Rooted to the spot with fear and not daring to move my head, I remained motionless when I realized the python was about to pass between my hands and knees. While I could not but admire the beautiful markings of the approximately 9 inch diameter body, my main thought was "how long before the tail appears"? It seemed like a goods train – endless.

After what seemed an eternity and probably was no more than a minute in reality, the tail of the python passed below me and simultaneously, according to Roy later, its head commenced to cross the bridle track. The Nipponese guard watched as it slowly crossed ahead of him before turning and going in the opposite direction. Perhaps the reptile had saved our lives. To this very day I cannot be certain of the python's length. Judging by its diameter and another python of equal size shot in a chook pen by the hotel's kitchen staff on Tioman Island during a diving safari in the 1980s, it had to be at least 15 feet long!   Not quite as exciting as Graham Greenwood's experience with the Orang Hutan but that, I did not want anyway.

During my school days I remember seeing in the Perth museum the combined skeleton of a West Australian carpet python about 7 feet long that had endeavoured to swallow a small kangaroo or wallaby, and fatally choked in the attempt. Since the days of Borneo, I have many times thanked my lucky stars and realized that God cared for me that day.

The following morning at 0515 our guerillas were in position. It was immediately seen that the Japanese were stirring in the hollow where they were camped. Their cooking fires had been alight for some time for an early breakfast so that their fires could be extinguished before the arrival of patrolling Allied planes, not usually airborne before sun up.

The attack commenced with a grenade accurately thrown by Hughie, that drew first blood. The din in the quiet of the jungle hollow was absolutely deafening as all our weapons opened up on three sides. The surprised Japanese – probably still half-asleep – scattered to their tents for their weapons screaming and yelling, and in that way contributed to the bedlam. If noise killed, there was sufficient weaponry on our side to wipe out a company. Only the Mata-Mata (police boys) made their bullets count. Allowing for the fact that most of the other guerillas had not seen a bullet fired in anger, the Malays did reasonably well.

Roy and I had taken up positions on the right flank of the open end that offered the 'sons of heaven' the only escape possible. While it was obvious that those still alive after the initial attack, would escape through the open side, we were unaware that a four foot deep open drain ran through the camp and out the open flank. We only became aware of it after I spotted a head bobbing along on what first looked like level ground in the area that had been cleared of jungle undergrowth. One burst from my Bren put a stop to the bobbing scone.

Taking up positions closer to the drain that allowed us a better view of the 'binatangs' fleeing along the drain, with our Bren guns firing from the hip we picked off four would-be escapees.

After all the fire ceased and the pungent smell of gunpowder and cordite had subsided, the sunlight of the new day filtered through the brilliant green of the jungle canopy, the cacophony of the cicadas and gentle cooing of fruit pigeons continued as though the morning was like any other.

Then the tally began. 12 dead, 4 died of wounds and 3 escaped. The 4 who died of wounds certainly were wounded but did not die as a result of battle wounds. Before we could intervene, the Malays had gleefully decapitated them with their parangs that in fact, were more effective than their .303 rifles. It was probably a blessing in disguise for we had no means of retaining prisoners. It was known as retribution.

Of those killed in the attack three were commissioned officers – two Captains and one first class Lieutenant – plus one Warrant Officer all of whom were members of the dreaded Kempei Tai. One Captain obviously was a doctor whose medical kit contained an obstetrician's kit, the largest instrument being a pair of delivery forceps. The total kit was later passed on to our Doc May as a souvenir of war. Doc May – in the Chinese language actually 'Moy' – cared for the needs of our guerillas and their families and pre-war had been in charge of Shanghai's leading maternity hospital. We finally souvenired the beautiful quality samurai swords they had in their tents.

The other Captain's gear produced some valuable intelligence including information that revealed another Japanese camp 5 miles south of Dampirit so after securing all the Japanese weapons, ammunition and rice supplies that were returned to Yusof's house, the Japanese radio station was destroyed.

An hour or so after the fighting had died down, two young Malays from a kampong not far distant and who had heard the firing came to investigate. They happily told us that of the 3 'binatangs' who had escaped, two were badly wounded and were heading for the 5 mile Japanese camp they referred to as Pituru. They were of the opinion that the three would be fortunate if they made the Pituru camp before marauding Malays waylaid them with parangs and added a further 3 heads to their belts.

Roy, who sensed that we had two enthusiastic supporters, drew the two smiling young Malays aside and discussed with them a plan whereby they were to return to their kampong and spread the rumour that a large Australian force had landed at the southern end of the Kudat Peninsular. Roy convinced them that we were the advance unit of the Australians and that the total Australian force was heading north to capture Kudat after we had wiped out the Japanese forces at Dampirit and Pituru. Both Malays were happy to co-operate and happier still after Roy gave them 5 gold sovereigns each, plus the promise that they would get a further 5 apiece after we captured Kudat.

4 Malay guerillas were posted as lookouts guarding the approach from the southern direction of Pituru and the large Japanese base at Langkong. A further 4 guarded the northern track to Kudat. The two new Malay recruits reported that the Japanese at Pituru possessed a naval type gun although they had not actually seen it.

At approximately 0800 two Japanese officers, presumably from Pituru appeared from around a bend on the southern rentis. The two 'binatangs' spotted the 4 Malay guards and had the audacity to stand in the middle of the rentis that was about 6 feet wide and menacingly brandished samurai swords at the Malays who opened fire with their two Austens and two tripod mounted Brens.

The Japanese were as safe as houses although the range was little more than 20 yards. Two Brens and two Austens against two samurai swords and yet the 'sons of heaven' got away with it!   We were thoroughly disgusted with the Malay effort.

Satisfied there was nothing further of intelligencee value in the camp, the whole Malay force retired to Yusof's home to re-group and plan the next move.

Later that morning we learned that after we left Dampirit a recce patrol of 10 Japanese arrived on the scene, inspected the carnage and returned hurriedly to Pituru. We subsequently learned that the recce patrol had made enquiries at the nearby kampong, where our new recruits lived. When one of the young Malays of the kampong refused to answer questions put by the Japanese Kempei Tai officer in charge, he was led outside and beheaded in full view of other kampong members.

The Japanese were finally told that a large force of Australian commandos was responsible for the attack on Dampirit. The recce patrol apparently then stumbled on the bodies of their two wounded companions that had escaped from Dampirit and were endeavouring to reach Pituru but had been slaughtered by the Malays en-route. The heads – contrary to Malay practice of taking the Japanese heads as trophies – complete with their Japanese Army caps had been mounted on poles on both sides of the rentis. The recce patrol were unimpressed with this display. Apparently the third survivor of Dampirit headed north and made it safely to Kudat where he reported the attack on Dampirit to the Japanese senior officer in charge.

Realizing that the Japanese were now somewhat nervous, Roy decided to seize the initiative and attack as soon as posssible.

He detailed Hughie McMasters and 37 of the Malay guerillas to wipe out the Pituru base after a couple of our Malays carried out a recce of the base and established that the Japanese strength there was no more than 20 to 25 Japanese. Datu Mustapha, who became Chief Minister of Sabah after the war when the Malays won independence from Britain, led the Malay guerillas on the raid.

The following morning Yusof led Hughie McMasters, Datu Mustapha and the Malay guerillas through a rubber plantation in which the Japanese had established an atap hut not far from the main Japanese house at the base of a prominent hill. In the early dawn hours they approached the atap hut in single file and had about a quarter of a mile to go to the main Japanese building when Datu ordered the Malays to halt.

Apparently a particular little bird was heard singing in a rubber tree. The combination of the bird and its call at night was an ill omen to the Malays. Despite all Hughie's cajoling and attempts to dissuade the Malays, they refused to go any further; the guerillas returned to Yusof's home.

The second morning, Datu (a damned brave Malay) claimed that his wife was very bunting (pregnant) and that he should remain at Yusof's home. Hugh finally convinced him that his bini (wife) was in the good medical hands of Doc May so he agreed to lead his Malay guerillas, but according to Hugh, Datu was decidedly nervous.

In the early dawn hours after having arrived at the outskirts of the rubber plantation, lo and behold, they encountered a rubber tree that had fallen across the track on which they were walking. Another bad omen to the Malays! The fallen rubber tree spelled disaster ahead. After a hurried discussion among their leaders, the Malays decided to abandon the attack again and for the second morning in succession, they returned to Yusof's. Hughie understandably was not happy.

At Yusof's house Roy and I had been preparing plans to attack Kudat as soon as Hughie had despatched the small force of Japanese at Pituru. We were astounded when Hugh arrived with his Malay guerillas and his tale of woe.

Roy was none too pleased with the Malays. The three of us realized that the continued delays could only spell disaster for us all. The Japanese only had to send reinforcements from Langkong and our game would be up.

Roy spoke to Datu Mustapha about the need to do something urgently and suggested that the next morning we should all go back to Pituru. Roy pointed out that there were 37 Malay guerillas plus 15 more held in reserve plus we three making in all 55 – a formidable force. Mustapha in turn spoke to the guerillas and finally decided that with the extra numbers, the operation should be a piece of cake.

The next morning at 0430 saw us on the outskirts of the rubber plantation a further time. Yusof our trusty guide led the way followed by Roy, myself, Hughie, Mustapha and finally the Malay guerillas, all in single file. Not a word had been spoken since we entered the plantation.

We reached a point about two hundred yards from the Japanese house when we spotted a small atap hut ahead brightly illuminated by the moonlight that was as bright as daylight. Well before we reached it, we could see that the narrow track we were on also connected the hut to the house and passed in front of, and close to the open doorway of the hut. Roy tapped Yusof on the back and enquired in a whisper as to what the hut was and was told that it was a garden tool shed.

Re-assured that all was well, we proceeded to pass the front doorway of the hut. Yusof and Roy had just passed the open doorway. As I followed, I glanced into the hut where I saw in the darkness a tall solid figure in white singlet and underpants rise from a bed. Reaching out for something, perhaps a rifle or sword, he headed for the doorway.

I hurriedly tapped Roy on the shoulder and he sensed immediately that an emergency had arisen. I whispered to Hugh who was behind me and about to cross the doorway to remain still. Because of the bright moonlight, we pressed our bodies into the atap wall on either side of the doorway so as to minimize ourselves as much as possible. At the same time the whole file of 52 men behind Hugh stopped as one man.

I was 5 foot 9 inches in height and Hugh was more than 6 feet. The half asleep 'son of heaven' stood just inside the doorway for what seemed like ages but in reality was probably only seconds, but long enough for me to realize that the 'binatang' was considerably taller than Hugh and I. Moreover, he was much heavier in build than both of us. It later transpired that he was a Tiger Marine Captain. So much for the tales told of Japanese people being of small stature. .

He eventuslly stepped out from the doorway and in a flash was silently despatched from this earth to the divine winds or wherever Japanese warriors go.

By this time, the Malays had become increasingly nervous so it did not surprise the three of us when a little further along the track towards the Japanese house, one of the guerillas obviously with a nervous trigger finger, accidentally fired off a rifle round.

The next moment all hell broke loose. Complete panic took over among the Malay boys who commenced running in all directions and within seconds, what had been a tranquil rubber plantation scene with the occasional night bird heralding the approach of dawn, transpired into an unruly mass of humanity. Bodies in their mad rush to put as much distance between the house and themselves, crashed into each other in the semi darkness as they stumbled into the low undergrowth between the rubber trees. Fifty two panic stricken men – and their leader Datu Mustapha no exception – made as much noise as a couple of elephants crashing through the jungle.

Worse, the three men who carried our Bren guns behind Datu, found the weight of the weapons no handicap as they raced off leaving the three of us and Yusof with only side arms, commando knives and a few grenades each.

Minutes later, what seemed like a terrific explosion reverberated throughout the plantation as a mortar shell exploded among the Malays, killing two. Fortunately we were well inside the range of the mortar that seemed only yards away from where we were sheltering behind rubber trees.

Mortars are frightening at any time but in the darkness of the jungle and rubber plantation they are more scary than in open terrain during daylight where the missile can often be spotted as it reaches the limit of its upward trajectory, turns and begins its downward path. In the jungle, most times it cannot be seen above the canopy of trees and for the Malays who had never experienced mortar fire, it was simply horrendous.

The four of us had no alternative than to turn back, being careful to remain inside the range of mortar fire as the Japanese gunners increased their range to trap the fleeing Malays.

We had only begun to pick our way back to the full flight Malays when another different and horrendous explosion that obviously was the reported naval gun set at point blank range – more frightening than the mortar fire – shook the plantation area as shot after shot exploded in the plantation. Added to the din of the mortars plus sub machine gun fire and what sounded like the slower chatter of a Japanese 'woodpecker' as the 'sons of heaven' began firing on imaginary targets, the overpowering noise was nerve destroying. I was able to imagine the terror that must have struck at the hearts of the Malays, who prior to the successful ambush at Damparit had never been under hostile fire.

When we eventually arrived at Yusof's house it was obvious that some of the Malays fearing retaliation by the 'sons of heaven', had gone bush and were making it back overland to our Pitas HQ on the eastern side of Marudu Bay. A headcount revealed that three had been killed and four bore minor wounds. Our score was one Japanese officer killed at the open doorway of the gardener's hut. No other Japanese were even seen. The element of surprise was now completely lost.

After some hours of mental recovery, dressing the wounds of the guerillas etc, Roy conducted an analysis of the morning's fiasco.

A pre-war Mata-Mata (police boy) and prominent soccer player in BNB – Ali – claimed to have seen a Japanese soldier hiding behind a rubber tree and fired on him. He was adamant that his shot was not accidental, although we could see no reason why a Japanese soldier should be out in the plantation alone that hour of the morning, particularly as it was known that they did not like the jungle after dark. Furthermore, the 'binatangs' had not anticipated the attack. The situation then just deteriorated into a flat panic

The morale of the Malays now completely destroyed, an alternative plan of attack was required if we still hoped to capture Kudat.

After some deliberation Roy decided to send the Malays back to Pitas immediately and bring a Chinese guerilla team over to do the job.

Meanwhile, one of the Malays killed by the mortar was a highly respected pre-war police boy who was known for his bravery. It was reported that he had received an award for bravery from the British. A group of Malays returned to Pituru to recover his body and eventually returned with it to Yusof's home.

That evening we were all gathered about the garden of Yusof's home - a mass of fragrant frangipanis and gardenias - discussing the day's unfortunate events and with the Malays in an apologetic mood. One of the Malays came around with a half coconut shell that contained tiny portions of cooked meat. Each man including Roy and I had to take a portion and eat it followed by a small swig of Chinese rice wine. I asked Roy what the meat represented as Roy had spent many years in the islands pre-war but he did not have a clue, other than he thought it was some form of ritual and that we were expected to follow the suit of the head Malay, Datu Mustapha.

After swallowing my portion of meat rather than offend Datu, I moved around to Yusof and asked him in Chinese what I had eaten. I almost threw up when I was told that it was a tiny portion of the police boy's heart that had been removed from the body and cooked. The Malay boys believed that by consuming a piece of the brave boy's heart, some of the bravery would be absorbed into all that shared it! For some inexplicable reason, Roy was none too impressed when I passed the information on to him, neither did his stomach feel particularly happy about it!

After the war was over I ran into Don Harlem for the first time at Ted

Carse's funeral at a cemetery in Sydney where Able Seaman Arthur Jones RAN (operation 'Jaywick') and I were pall bearers for Ted. Later at a wake, we were comparing notes and it appeared that Don had experienced the same heart-eating ritual when on the Death March trail.

Ted Carse was the skipper of our famous 'Z' Force ship 'Krait' that transported the 14 men from Potshot Western Australia to attack Singapore Harbour - the successful operation 'Jaywick' (See Lynette Silver's 'Krait – The Fishing Boat That Went To War').

The following morning Hughie and I took the Malays back to Telega where Hugh and some of the guerillas were dropped off and the remainder were returned to Pitas.

A number of the Chinese had gone on a recce to Langkong and were not expected back for a week. There were however, thirteen top class Chinese guerillas and two former Malay police boys at Pitas. All had the genuine heartfelt hatred of the Japanese and longed to have a crack at their hated captors.

The leader of the section Tan Teck Bak of earlier Musa Island fame who had been my comrade in arms on previous sorties, felt confident that despite losing the element of surprise, his section would be able to handle the small number of Japanese involved. However, he felt strongly that the attack should be carried out relatively soon.

If the Japanese from Langkong or Kudat re-inforced the Pituru area, the attack would have to be abandoned. These Chinese were simply itching to get to grips with the Japanese and had to be admired. They and the two Malay police boys were imbued with the hatred for their arch old enemy. The Chinese section remembered well, not only the atrocities perpetrated by the Japanese on the Chinese and other indigenous races during the Albert Kwok uprising at Jesselton, but also former atrocities perpetrated at Shanghai, Nanking and other Chinese mainland cities during the Sino Japanese war leading up to WW2.

By the following day the Chinese guerillas and I were back at Yusof's place where fresh plans were under way for an all out attack on the Pituru Japanese. The following morning, Roy proposed to approach the house, not through the rubber plantation and the well-worn track but from the hill behind the house that the 'binatangs' considered perfect protection, the jungle at the opposite side of the hill from the house was considered impenetrable.

There was no rentis to the rear of the house and the approach involved jungle bashing for a mile or so before scaling the hill behind the house through secondary jungle. The hill, although being short from bottom to top, its gradient was pretty acute.

Roy, cautious like Gort, decided that in view of the botched up efforts of the Malays, a recce was essential before going in, so without delay, he, Yusof and I went across to the Pituru house.

Strangely, the Japanese did not appear to be unduly concerned and apart from one or two who wandered out of the house occasionally, most of the Nipponese remained inside the house. As Roy particularly wanted an accurate head count of Japanese, I volunteered to sneak up to the far end of the hut where there seemed to be little activity from within and peer through the atap wall provided that he and Yusof would cover me from behind. The jungle was strangely silent as the grave.

Squirming through the lalang on my stomach presented no difficulty and in short time I was behind the wall and in a crouching position about to peer through the atap wall, when from behind me I heard a distinct 'click'. There was no mistaking the noise. Quickly glancing behind me, I was astounded to see a Japanese officer standing outside a small dunny hidden in a clump of banana palms that was unseen by all three of us. Clumps of banana palms and paw-paw trees were in profusion around the perimeter of the lalang.

The 'binatang' who must have been in the dunny for a considerable length of time – we had not seen him enter - was dressed in long army khaki trousers and Army shirt and had a triangular shaped leather holster swinging from his shoulder and a 7mm Nambu pistol in his hands. He was facing me with feet firmly planted apart and apparently had intended shooting me in the back. Unfortunately for the short tubby 'binatang', there was a dud round in the Nambu chamber when he pulled the trigger. This was not unusual for Japanese ammunition - hence the audible 'click', and he was desperately trying to eject the faulty round before slamming home the next round from the magazine into the chamber.

With not a second to waste and knowing that Roy and Yusof could not see the officer to assist me, I had no alternative other than to draw my Browning 9mm automatic pistol and drop the Nipponese. Racing over to where he was spreadeagled, I ripped open his shirt pocket, took all his papers and with the Nambu and its holster slung over my shoulder, re-joined Roy and Yusof who were urging me to hurry. The shot had alerted the 'sons of heaven' within the house and mid a hail of rifle bullets all three of us hotfooted for the cover of the jungle. It was my lucky day!

When we left Tuna we all had silenced Austens and a mixture of side arms. In addition to Welrods, from memory Gort, Fred, Skeet and myself carried .45 colts while Jock, Don and Graham had .38 Smith & Wesson revolvers. Our weaponry left a lot to be desired as we all had to carry two calibres of ammunition – 9mm for the Austens plus either .38 or .45 for side arms - that proved very inconvenient. The new weapons – Owen machine guns more reliable and easier to strip, and Browning automatic pistols - took just the one 9 mm calibre and provided convenience, although lacking the stopping power of the .45s.

When we were re-equipped for 'Stallion 4' at Bongawan, we were issued with the 9mm Owen guns and beautiful newly issued 9mm automatic pistols manufactured by Browning for the officers of the Chinese Army. All markings on the pistols were engraved in Chinese characters.

A star-studded sky greeted us as we set out from Yusof's after midnight with trusty Yusof in the lead again. He was worth his weight in gold. The dawn was just breaking when we began scaling the hill. The kelawat gibbons in the ironwood trees were singing their usual tuneful choruses, interspersed by the early hum of cicadas before the sun climbed into the heavens. Nature seemed unperturbed by our intrusion. We hoped upon hope that the Japanese would be as complacent following our incident the day before, and that their number had not been reinforced overnight.

As we topped the hill we noted that lights or lanterns were in evidence within the house, but there appeared to be nobody moving around within the building which seemed odd in view of the aborted Malay attack of only a couple of days earlier and our interrupted recce.

Commencing our descent, one of the Chinese lost his footing and as he fell to the ground, the trigger of his Owen gun came into contact with a shrub and fired off a round. Roy who was on the opposite flank to me called out "Let's go Jack" and with that we all moved in together.

Roy, Teck Bak and I were armed with Bren guns firing from the hip while the remaining twelve guerillas blazed away on their Austens and Owens spreading a wicked screen of lead as we advanced down the hill to the Japanese house. The row of guerillas had instructions to pick off any 'binatangs' who managed to get out of the building and attempted to flee across the lalang, while Teck Bak provided covering fire for Roy and I as we closed within grenade range of the house.

Protected by the numerous ironwood tree trunks that fringed the foot of the hill, we were able to toss two grenades each into the atap walls or roof and the two shuttered windows facing the hillside.

With the exception of the initial unplanned stumble of the Chinese guerilla, the attack went off without a hitch. A number of Japanese still in sleeping attire, tumbled out through the atap walls. With the exception of one who made it across the narrow lalang (grassed clearing) and into the rubber plantation through a wall of banana palms, paw-paws, mango and coffee trees that bordered the lalang, the grenades and machine gun fire accounted for the rest.

After checking the Japanese lying outside the house to be sure that none were up to the Japanese trick of lying 'doggo', the wounded within the building were dragged clear and were eliminated by the guerillas – mostly by parangs – we had no means of holding prisoners. Again we found geisha girls. Two very attractive and very pregnant girls that we agreed were about 16 years of age and more like Javanese than Japanese girls – they lacked that flat pan like facial features of many Japanese girls. – lay very dead in the hut. We judged they were due to drop their pups at any time.

The building was searched thoroughly and a lot of documentation seized for intelligence purposes. Swords, weapons and ammunition were seized and the building was then set on fire with the 22 bodies inside.

The one Japanese Tiger Marine Corporal who had escaped was re-captured in the rubber. Miraculously alive following the deadly attack, he was brought in by the Chinese guerillas and Roy decided that he should be returned under escort to Pitas HQ where Gort and Nick could grill him for intelligence information. Although they usually preferred to die than divulge information, at least they were given the choice between life and death. If they chose the latter, that could be arranged without too much bother.

Two mortars were captured intact. The Navy type gun spoken of by Yusof in fact was similar to the 4.7 inch stern gun on the 'Marina', a Norwegian aircraft octane tanker that my boyhood mate Bruce Inder-Smith and I had served on back in 1943 in African, Near Middle East, Indian and Australian waters. Although I did not know then, Bruce - in the Royal Australian Navy - was serving on HMAS Arunta, a Tribal class destroyer.

We were however, puzzled by the fact that the gun possessed no identification markings either Japanese or American. It may have been captured from an American ship or it may have been Japanese manufactured. It was mounted on a re-inforced concrete and steel platform on a set trajectory facing Marudu Bay and obviously was lowered to fire point blank through the rubber plantation. As we had no use for it, we destroyed it on its mounting.

The Dampirit saga that started out so successfully then fell in tatters at Pituru was over, thanks to the Chinese guerillas. The thirteen Chinese and two Malay guerillas had acquitted themselves marvellously. They had accomplished the most difficult part of the operation where 52 Malay guerillas had failed on three occasions. Tan Teck Bak and the rest of the team had reason to be proud of their performance.

Only one thing remained to be done. Get our arses out of the joint pronto just in case Japanese reinforcements were on the way, a possibility that could not be discounted.

Chapter 28

UNCLE SAM MOVES ON

Without doubt, the Americans were proving their mastery of land, air and sea. Although we had no opportunity to see their land forces in action – we being in former British territory – we had seen their submarines at work taking a very heavy toll of Japan's merchant and naval fleet. After the war, we learned that their submarines representing 2.5% of the US Navy had accounted for 55% of the Japanese combined Navy and merchant fleet. Their mastery of the air however, was before our very eyes almost every day.

At no set times, their aircraft appeared from nowhere. They had bombed Sandakan since October 1944 and most of the seafront capital was destroyed completely; only the catholic school, a Chinese theatre and an odd building or two remained intact.

Still defying the American bombers, and then finally the RAAF who dealt the final blow to the town in 1945, the catholic school stood tall and proud amid all the ruins like an immune monument. Post-war, to the older residents of the town, it was regarded as an unofficial monument to the Australian and British POW numbering approximately 2500 shipped to Borneo 1942-1943.

Following their arrival from Singapore's notorious Changi gaol aboard the hell ships Ubi Maru, de Klerk and others, 'B' force - the first of the POW to arrive in Sandakan - spent their first night in the catholic church and its surrounding grounds. The next day they marched out to the camp site formerly a quarantine area prior to WW2, off the road to Ranau at the 8 mile peg – Labuk Road - where they began preparing the area for the next shipment of POW to arrive from Singapore, 'E' force.

For the Japanese, their advance forces had come to a grinding halt and reversals were showing in the crystal ball following severe defeats in the Owen Stanley Ranges of New Guinea and the battle of the Coral Sea.

1944-1945 saw the Allies hitting back hard. The American Navy and their other forces re-captured the Philippines including Palawan, with the assistance of the small but hard hitting contribution of the Australian and Dutch Navies, and were well on their westward advance across the Pacific, pursuing MacArthur's island hopping plan towards Japan, the ultimate goal. The occupation of Iwo Jima, Saipan and Okinawa were yet to follow.

The limited supply lines from Japan to Singapore, Borneo, Celebes (now Sulawesi) Dutch East Indies (now Indonesia), Rabaul and New Guinea were effectively cut with the re-capture of the Philippines, rendering completely ineffective large numbers of the 'sons of heaven'; for the Japanese the 'rising sun' was fast setting. Among the many thousands of Japanese troops stranded in the wake of the American advance were 37,000 in Borneo.

The Japanese supply lines were perilously extended. The situation in New Guinea had deteriorated to the point where their troops were reliant on night runs by MTBs, barges and any surface craft they could press into service to supply their troops. When Allied night planes strangled that supply line, the 'binatangs' resorted to submarines supplying their troops using torpedoes filled with supplies minus the explosive head and fired into Japanese occupied beaches.

Around about that stage of the Pacific campaign, Germany surrendered unconditionally. With the writing on the wall, Japan began to cover all tracks and clues leading to the shockingly barbarian atrocities carried out by her forces wherever and whenever their hated flags, the 'rising sun' and the 'poached egg' appeared. The 'binatangs' had plenty to answer to as the end of WW2 approached.

And according to Gort with whom I spent most of my time – I cannot speak for Nick because I do not remember discussing the subject of the progress of the Pacific war with him – the POW were the only meaningful thing worth fighting for in BNB. He contended that the oil wells, rubber and other wealthy commodities of that little known prosperous land would automatically flow on from the inevitable defeat of Japan, so why sacrifice good young Australian lives fighting for it?

News had come through the jungle vine that on the west coast, more and more isolated groups of Australian and British POW were appearing in all manner of localities. All were being used as a carrier force humping rice and other commodities between Ranau, Tambunan, Keningau and the coastal areas from Papar to Mempakul opposite Labuan. Along the railway line and particularly after the bridge over the Papar River had been badly damaged on the 10th of May 1945 by Yankee B24 Liberators, small numbers of Australian POW were regularly reported there.

Reports came from agents in Sandakan – friends of 'Sandshoe Willie', one of Gort's most active agents during operation 'Python' – that the local population on the west coast had verified seeing small numbers of POW rice carriers in Papar, Kimanis and Bongawan. All were starved, beaten and driven, by their 'binatang' masters until they dropped. Similar reports also came from Jock Sutcliffe and Don Harlem in Death March country.

Because of the daylight attacks on the railway line by American aircraft from Palawan and Tawi-Tawi, the three remaining railway engines ran between Jesselton, Keningau and Beaufort only at night.

To reinforce the southern areas of Brunei, Beaufort, Labuan, Mempakul Bongawan and Kimanis, hundreds of Japanese troops and rice carrying parties were compelled to march down the railway line at night. It simply was not safe to march along the line during the day, therefore their troops rested up in the plantations that lined the rail route. The POW and Javanese labourers - they being regarded by the Japanese as dispensable - were compelled to carry on at gunpoint during daylight hours, thereby facing the risk of strafing American aircraft. No doubt, low flying strafing American aircraft unknowingly gunned down some of the POW.

Separate information sources including Jock and Don – their reports were always reliable – revealed that of the 500 Australian and British POW sent out on the first march from Sandakan to Ranau, only 183 had survived; more dead than alive after their month long ordeal. They were set to work building huts for themselves, there being no accommodation awaiting them. During March and April their numbers were reduced further by the introduction of rice carrying parties. By the end of April the number of survivors were variously reported as having been reduced to 120.

Because of the damp and cold conditions, the Ranau valley 7000 feet above sea level where the camp was situated, cold nights, recurring malaria, beri-beri and malnutrition took its heavy daily toll on the survivors. The sick survivors barely had sufficient strength to drag their dead comrades up to the piece of land allotted by their cruel masters for the burials of the Australian and British POW.

When the first marches left the POW camp site, they believed they were headed for the Sandakan dock side to board a ship that was to take them to a new destination; where, nobody knew. However, when the leading POW reached the junction of the camp exit road and the main road - the 8 mile peg -heading west towards Mt. Kinabalu, instead of turning left towards Sandakan and the ocean 8 miles away, they were turned right towards the mountains. It was then that they were told their destination was Ranau, 165 miles west; a wonderful agricultural area that promised 'plenty makan, lekas, lekas' (plenty to eat, hurry, hurry).

It was probably one of the very few occasions that the Japanese had spoken the truth. Ranau's rich volcanic soil was – and indeed is still today – an area of plenty under normal circumstances. However, the Japanese commandeered all produce to feed their troops at the expense of local families. Most of the population moved into remote surrounding jungle areas and grew only sufficient for their own needs and a little that was bartered with coastal Malays and Chinese for fish, salt and other commodities.

When the POW and their Japanese escorts arrived from Sandakan, Mother Hubbard's cupboard was completely bare and as expected, the POW suffered the worst. Deprived of food supplies in the Ranau valley, the Japanese were compelled to turn to other areas for supplies at the expense of the local population, hence the hastily formed 'binatang' POW rice carrying parties that spelled the death sentence of many an Australian POW.

The Japanese regarded these parties a legitimate way of killing off the POW, short of outright murder.

The daily meagre ration of rice issued per man was again reduced to barely half a cup of rice per man per day, the prisoners were then almost totally reliant on the jungle to provide their needs. Obi kayu (wild tapioca) that soured the stomach, kangkong (swamp spinach), rats, snakes, caterpillars became regular fare. Like the Sandakan POW camp, rats and snakes – plentiful when the POW first arrived on the scene – quickly became a rarity.

In the 70's I re-call interviewing and recording for television news, Private Nelson Short AIF of Ashfield, New South Wales (now deceased) a survivor of the third march. Nelson said that he had seen men in the Ranau camp who regularly ate rat, develop a strange scaly skin and die. He repeated this statement in 1980 to host interviewer Ian Leslie and camera crew of '60 Minutes' when Nelson and I went to Sabah with Ian to make the first documentary on the Borneo Death Marches 'Return To Sandakan'. It was Nelson's first visit to Sabah since the POW days, his epic escape from Ranau and eventual rescue by Malay Bariga and an 'Agas' team.

During the late 40's or early 50's an army investigation team retraced the Death March route led by Major Harry Jackson and Warrant Officer Bill Sticpewich AIF. Sticpewich, also a survivor, escaped from Ranau, only to meet his death post-war in an automotive accident in Melbourne. These two men led an Army Graves Recovery Unit accompanied by an Australian Broadcasting Commission team (Colin Simpson) and were among the first to re-trace the Death March route after the war (see ABC documentary 'Six From Borneo').

This group retraced only the southern route; they were not aware of the northern route, or if they were, they ignored it. Therefore, it is safe to assume that of the large number of missing POW, some still lie somewhere out in the jungle along the former northern route, although it is highly unlikely that the original rentis could now be re-located, the jungle certain to have reclaimed it. Unless rentises were regularly used, they became completely overgrown within weeks.

In view of the Australian Government's reluctance to do anything constructive regarding our missing WW2 warship HMAS Sydney, there is little hope that the recovery of POW lying in the jungle will ever be undertaken.

Is it little wonder that the surviving operatives of 'Agas 1' inserted by American submarine to locate the POW and report on their welfare, were never called upon to give evidence during the relevant war crimes trials after the war?

Our officers debriefed after the war, strangely, were never called on to testify against the Japanese at the war crimes trials. In the early 1950s when Prime Minister Sir Robert Menzies discharged hundreds of Japanese war criminals, he proved beyond doubt that it was by design, in favour of trade. Maybe our men knew too much of the truth – the truth the Australian Government wanted to cover up. However, Don Harlem told me in no uncertain terms that his reports on war crimes never were submitted during the trials, and despite his briefing descriptions of Japanese atrocities, nothing was done.

Likewise, following the end of the war and return to Australia and New Zealand of 'Agas 1' operatives, (mostly ORs – other ranks from staff Sergeants down) – none were interviewed for war crimes trials. None were invited to testify at the trials of Japanese Major Hoshijima and Captain Takakuwa who succeeded 'Hosi', or for that matter, any other Japanese war criminal.

Additionally, there were many of our guerrillas who were eye witnesses to atrocities – particularly Don Harlem's group – after he and Jock split and operated separate guerrilla groups. Don, during one of our last telephone conversations before his sad passing, assured me that he was holding a list of witnesses – names and addresses – that he would send to me along with his script for our proposed jointly written book. Unfortunately, his script was never found and even if the list was located today, it is far too late; officialdom couldn't care a damn.

Now at 75 years of age, I have a better understanding of life and the appreciation that " war is like business on a giant scale where currency used is not money but men's lives" . I cannot but help feel that our presence in BNB was meaningless, and our efforts were just a waste of human lives, time and cost. Regardless of all the good work done by the 'Agas' parties, our efforts were lost to the top brass, many of whom didn't care a hoot about the fighting men or POW lives.

The Commonwealth War Cemetery panels at Labuan list hundreds of Australian and British POW missing, most of whom today lie out in the jungle on the Death March routes. Additionally, there are at least 200 to 300 POW and possibly more Javanese labourers who were bulldozed into trenches on the Sandakan airstrip and never recovered.

About 1983 I led another war veterans' tour to Sabah including former Australian POW officers who had worked on the strip under Captain Hoshijima and were later transferred to Kuching POW camp after the Australian camp radio was discovered by the 'sons of heaven'.

While workers were busy on the new Sandakan International airstrip – under construction - I interviewed on video, an American engineer Henry Ford , who was in charge of a team of men constructing the new airstrip. Malaysian Airline System (MAS) planned to introduce Boeing

737s to replace F27 Fokker Friendships.

The new airstrip resumed portion of the original built by the POW, and according to Ford, the resumed portion gave the project engineers a real headache. They experienced extreme difficulty in compacting the surface of the strip to the required standard, despite the amount of fill used. The new foundation laid over the POW built section continued to sink, finally resulting in a piece of heavy machinery falling through the newly compacted surface where it became hopelessly bogged for days. Henry Ford was interested to learn from me, that a number of POW and Javanese labourers were reported buried in a bomb crater on the strip during WW2 by the Japanese. He thought there might possibly be a connection between the problem of sinking foundations and the buried men.

Asked if any human bones had been recovered during the construction of the new airstrip, Henry Ford was understandably evasive. He probably reasoned that the project – already running behind schedule as a result of the sinking section - would never end should an official enquiry be conducted into the discovery of human bones.

My first post war visit to Sandakan was in 1979 specifically to find Tan Teck Bak – reported to me in Perth as having been dead for a number of years - who had more recently been reported as being well alive and living in Sandakan. I was searching for him in Kudat. After my arrival in Sandakan and finally locating some family members, I was very disappointed to discover that he and his number one wife were in Hong Kong on business.

Later, by arrangement with Teck Bak and the kind co-operation of Malaysian Airline System (MAS), I returned to Sabah, taking Don Harlem who was on his first post-war visit to his old stamping grounds – determined to show him the wartime POW campsite. Not withstanding, the fact that our '60 Minutes' team had located Bertha the boiler a year or so earlier, it was completely overgrown again and was just as difficult to re-locate.

The superstitious local Malays and Chinese inhabitants stayed clear of the POW camp area. They maintain to this very day, that on certain hot still tropical nights, the ghosts of the Australian POW can be heard singing in the jungle " She'll be comin' round the mountain when she comes" or " A tisket a tasket, the little yellow baskets". Sung in unison by their work parties as they marched out to, or back from the airstrip work site in darkness under the watchful eyes of their guards, who not understanding the meaning behind the latter song, joined heartily in the singing, much to the mirth of the POW.

In the search for the campsite, we eventually stumbled across the old boiler more by luck than good judgement. We happened to look upwards at the precise moment and place, and spotted the dark brown rusting top of the smoke stack peeping above the secondary jungle. The boiler unit itself was completely overgrown with lantana vine and other jungle growth that took us fully thirty minutes to reach, despite the fact that the boiler was only slightly further than 20ft away and that we were slashing our way through with parangs. The secondary growth was unbelievably dense.

Having established the position of 'Bertha the donkey' (the boiler so named by the POW) and the old water hole nearby, we were able to determine roughly the location of the pre-war Agricultural Research Station. However, the area was unrecognisable because of the secondary growth on the lower approaches to the higher ground of the Research Station. We did however, locate the foundations of the manager's house (Mr. Wong) and what appeared to be a concrete water trough of some type.

The water hole that supplied most of the water for the camp, and where one POW accidentally drowned, had changed very little over the intervening years.

In our efforts to circumnavigate the high ground, we heard before we sighted, heavy earth clearing machinery preparing an area for the establishment of a Government sponsored kampong providing 300 small low cost homes suitable for native families. From memory, the new area was to be named Kampong Sungei Kayu (river tree village).

We then found between the kampong site and the Agricultural Research Station area, a bulldozer clearing ground for a soccer field for the proposed kampong residents. As a result of the closeness of the wet season, the bulldozer was only working spasmodically – a day or two a week. However, walking over ground turned up by the dozer, we found empty bullet casings both Japanese 7mm and Australian 9mm which fact posed a number of queries, the most important being:-

1. Did they belong to the Japanese or the Australians?
2. In which compound were we?
3. What were the prospects of delaying the bulldozing while we

rushed a team from Australia of former 'Z' men and Special Air Services (SAS) regiment personnel?   Before leaving Perth, SAS support in principle had been assured to assist in establishing the perimeters of the campsite. There were no longer any visible remains of buildings; the sum total had been burned to the ground by the 'sons of heaven' as the third Death March left for Ranau.

Former Australian POW Officer Tony White AIF, of New South Wales, transferred to Kuching POW camp when the Japanese found the radio in the camp, went to Sandakan a little more than a year earlier than

According to Tony, because 'the big tree' that identified the WW2 parade ground of the camp from the ground and air no longer existed, – a prominent feature – identifying land-marks were difficult to pin point.

Until he eventually found the 'donkey', Tony experienced problems establishing perimeters. He was the first Australian - that I am aware of - to locate the 'donkey' post-war. When I first met him at an annual dinner conducted by the 'Old Sandakians' Association' in Sydney where I was invited as guest speaker, he gave me a rough idea as to its position.

When 'Kingfisher' was in the' pipe-line,' the beautiful wartime aerial photos taken by American reconnaissance aircraft, clearly featured the huge tree that was visible from almost everywhere, and was used as a navigation mark by aircrews.

Teck Bak, Don Harlem and myself were unable to answer the first two questions at the time. On the matter of the third question, Teck Bak felt that a request to the Malaysian authorities for a stay in bulldozing activities would be unsuccessful. The SAS were very anxious to send a team from Campbell Barracks Swanbourne to establish and map the former camp-site, and do an organised search for historical souvenirs, but the Malaysians at the time were not interested. They were to regret this decision in 1995, the 50th anniversary of the end of WW2, when their celebrations were noticeably marred by the lack of WW2 history of their own country.

The wheel has since made a complete turn, and I believe the Malaysian historians – now still desperately short of WW2 material – are regretting that which has been lost. Since 1995 (the 50th anniversary of WW2 celebrated in no mean fashion by the Sabah Government) to mark the 1995 celebrations, the archives in Kota Kinabalu have since published a history of Sabah and its earlier days as the colony of BNB.

Invited as a participant of the 50th anniversary of Victory Pacific

(VP), I led a tour group from Perth of 56 ex-servicemen/women and civilians including 2 junior lads – one being my 14 years old son Kim – organised by tour company 'New Horizons' of Perth. Because of the size of the tour, I was assisted by one of the company's directors, Tony Brbich.

In July 1997 – I was fortunate enough to receive from the Sabah archives a copy of their book and an accompanying letter requesting additional WW2 material.

After the early re-discoveries of the campsite by Tony White, myself and '60 Minutes', 'Z' Special Unit International Inc (Perth) believed that an appropriate live memorial to all the Australian and British POW who lost their lives, was preferable to a piece of stone or similar. We decided there and then that the former POW Camp-site would make a fine recreational reserve cum botanical garden cum kiddie's play-ground cum historical museum for the benefit of the new Kampong Sungei Kayu inhabitants.

Our unit intended raising funds with the assistance of The Special Air Services Regiment (SAS), Australian and British POW, our London Special Forces Club, the Sabah Ex-Services Association and other overseas members to build it. And that motivated our discussion (Sir Reginald Barnewall, Datuk Abar Bakar Tan Teck Bak – and yours truly) with the Sandakan District Officer.

The exact same method was used by the late New Zealand 'Z' man Major Toby Carter (Operation 'Semut') Sarawak, shortly after WW2, when he organised and built the beautiful scenic Kundasang Rose Memorial Garden near Ranau to commemorate the POW who perished in the Death Marches of 1945.

In due course we received advice from the Sandakan District Officer acknowledging receipt of our letter from Perth and that it had been forwarded with his recommendation to the Chief Minister (equivalent of our Prime Minister).

No reply was ever received despite numerous letters to the Chief Minister requesting the reasons for the delay. It was respectfully pointed out that our association had recently completed a restoration project - 'The Heroes Grave' - in the graveyard of the prestigious St. Joseph's Church Kuching, the capital city of Sarawak. It made no difference.

Jimmy Choo, Chairman of Directors of Sarawak Travel Agencies was a young man in Kuching when Lionel Matthews was executed.

Years earlier, he drove me to Setapok outside Kuching and indicated the spot where Matthews and the civilians from Sandakan were executed. For the courage he displayed in his leadership of the clandestine movement within the POW camp, Matthews MC (Military Cross) was further decorated with the George Cross (posthumous).

Captain Lionel Matthews – plus all suspects arrested – was tried in the Japanese Military Court situated within today's Saint Teresa's College Kuching. The eight civilians led by Alexander Funk were found guilty of complicity and sabotage and were sentenced to death. Five of their number, however, died in the Jalan Jawa gaol, from torture and ill treatment before they could be executed.

The eight civilians plus Matthews were exhumed from the execution ground at Setapok after the war. Captain Lionel Matthews was taken to Labuan Island and re-interred at the Australian Commonwealth War Cemetery; he is the highest decorated serviceman there.

The eight civilians were re-interred with the five Kuching heroes in a vault at St. Joseph's Church and promptly forgotten following a scrub fire that went through the area, burning down the surrounding timber posts and damaging the vault.

Organisers of 'The Heroes' Memorial Fund, 'Z' Special Unit International (Inc).organised funds Australia wide. Supporting us, the

'Z' Operatives at 'Z' Intelligence School, Mount Matha Agriculture Research Station, Victoria

272

Kuching 'Holiday Inne' (Manager Peter Mueller) and the Recreational Sporting Club of that hotel along with Sarawak Travel Agencies (Jimmy Choo) provided additional finance for the project. Kuching's Malaysian Army 3rd Garrison Battalion (Commanding Officer Colonel George Ghui) came to the party and provided all the 'know how', labour and transport required.

All in all, a magnificent result was achieved. Today, completely restored, 'The Heroes' Grave' is the focal point of St Josephs Church cemetery and is a popular venue for tourists and particularly Australian tour groups interested in the history of WW2.

'The Heroes' Grave' draws attention by virtue of its unusual design that characterises the men whose memory it immortalises. They were truly upstanding, tough, resilient and unusual men - brave to the tragic end.

Reverting to our proposal on the Sandakan Memorial Park, stymied by the silence and lack of communication from the Chief Minister in Kota Kinabalu, we were hand-tied and there the matter died. Meanwhile, other wheels were turning, over which 'Z' had no control.

Seeking some enlightenment from Sabah, our association was finally advised by an independent source whose identity must remain nameless, that the National Returned Services League (RSL) in the Eastern States of Australia had become involved in our proposed project and that we could expect to be displaced. Again, Western Australia had become the 'Cinderella' State.

Following my next war veterans' tour to Sabah approximately 12 months later – including Sandakan – I was surprised to discover that most of the secondary jungle between the camp site and the roadway had been cut down and the lalang surrounding the camp water hole had been mowed. It was obvious that the mowing had been done for some time as the growth of the lalang was back to about two feet high.

I was even more surprised, bordering on alarm when I discovered many Nama Jalan (street names) hammered into the lalang, to indicate footpaths or roads to be constructed, proving at that stage, the Sabah Government intended to build roads across the former POW campsite. I photographed these signs and today both correspondence and photographs, in still and video, are in my possession.

During the clearing, the secondary jungle surrendered more of its long hidden secrets when the foundation bed of what had once been the power house generator and a sizeable – for those days – piece of road construction machinery was exposed. This I later learned from POW Lieutenant Clive Boundy AIF, a surveying engineer in the Sandakan campsite, was used by the POW to build roads around the campsite.

Unable to gain any enlightenment in Sandakan on these new developments and having insufficient time to spend in Kota Kinabalu to visit the Chief Minister's office, our group returned to Perth where our 'Z' Association again wrote to the Chief Minister seeking an explanation. Our letter was completely ignored.

Our next visit to Sabah and the Sandakan POW campsite yielded a newly constructed memorial adjacent to the 'donkey'. It is still there today.

'Z' Special Unit International (Inc) were disappointed that there was no mention on the monument, of the roles operations 'Agas' and 'Python' played behind Japanese lines in the saga of the Borneo Death Marches. The association did not feel soured by the fact that another party, the National body of the RSL, had been authorised to build the memorial park; we just felt that we had been 'left out in the cold'.

Although we were not in favour of what we considered was purely a piece of stone – we having suggested a botanical garden incorporating a children's play-ground for the benefit of the new kampong residents – we were pleased that at least something was being achieved to consecrate the POW site. However, the fact that the Sabah Government had ignored all our correspondence did hurt, particularly in view of the fine job that we felt we had achieved in restoring 'The Heroes' Grave' at Kuching.

The hurt of course was further aggravated by the National body of the RSL who made no attempt to contact us, and who must have been aware of our earlier attempts to establish the memorial garden at the POW campsite. 'It's no good crying over spilled milk' as the saying goes, but nonetheless, we were hurt. Australians will at least know now, that we in the western hemisphere of Australia, were the first to attempt dedication of the former POW campsite to the memory of the 2,500 Australian and British POW in a worthwhile manner; something that had been lacking for many years.

It is sad to reflect that politics had poked its unwelcome nose into the delicate matter of memorials to Australia's brave dead.

At this juncture, it may be of interest to the reader to learn that the first memorial created at the end of the Death March trail – Ranau - was the result of a project commenced by 'Z' man the late Major Toby Carter of New Zealand.

Former WW2 operative Major Toby Carter of operation 'Semut' whose operational area was Sarawak, returned to his pre-war occupation of geologist with the Shell Oil Company following his discharge from the British Army when 'Z' was wound up. He remained virtually until his retirement, finally returning to New Zealand where he saw out his final days.

The kind and compassionate 'Semut 2' party leader like Gort Chester, was idolised by the local inhabitants. Toby became interested in the Borneo Death March routes post war, even though those routes were in the 'Agas' territory of his pre-war friend Major Gort Chester. Toby Carter contacted former 'Z' men world wide who with other organisations, raised funds to build a memorial in the foothills of towering Mt. Kinabalu near Ranau. The memorial park was to preserve for posterity, the memory of the POW who had perished on the Death March routes.

Funds came from the Special Forces Club in London and 'Z' Associations in Australia based at Perth and Sydney. They came from Commando Associations, many of whom included former members of 'Z' Special Unit ('Z' Force), Services Reconnaissance Department (SRD.), 'M' Special Unit ('M' Force), Allied Intelligence Bureau (AIB.), Force 136, Far Eastern Liason Office (FELO.), MI5, Flight 200 and other similar units. These special units were involved in clandestine activities against the Axis Forces of Germany, occupied France, Italy and Japan. They all subscribed to the Toby Carter fund. The former British Colonial Office, the future Sabah Government, sympathetic individuals and trade houses etc, responded to the call.

With the finance thus raised, Toby Carter set about the task of building the high granite walled memorial garden. Like a lone sentinel on guard, it stands today in the hills behind the small town of Kundasang at the foot of South East-Asia's highest monolith, Mt. Kinabalu, and should be visited by every Australian and Englishman in the course of a lifetime.

The large impressive granite enclosed area is divided into separate rose and other flower gardens, each of which is named after the nationalities of the services represented among the officers and ranks of the POW who perished at Sandakan, on the Death Marches or Ranau and other parts of BNB. Surrounding the stone walls are the trees of the jungle, like duty bound sentries jealously guarding the POW, whose memories the hillside granite garden perpetuates.

A separate enclosed and roofed area within the memorial comprises a long lily pond with fountain fronting a large brass wall mounted memorial plaque detailing the march route and brief history of the men who perished. The soothing sound of running water emanates from a small waterfall that exists at one end of the lily and hyacinth pond and creates an appropriate feeling of rest and tranquillity.

I was extremely moved – almost rendered to tears – by this section when I first visited there in 1979. Standing there by the plaque and looking along the placid surface of the water lily and water hyacinth clad surface of the indoor Pool of Remembrance, I reminisced the inhumane suffering inflicted on the POW during the marches and elsewhere in BNB. This, plus my soul wrenching knowledge that the last 32 POW alive in the Ranau camp – including hopelessly sick doctors still caring for their ailing mates – were cruelly slaughtered by their Japanese captors after the cessation of hostilities.

During the closing stages of 1945, these details were known only to 'Agas' members and were never leaked to the media, even though the top echelon of our defence forces were familiar with the facts. The 'Z' men had done their duty by reporting the details of atrocities to superiors further up the long line of command.

Unfortunately, the good work of the wartime clandestine parties was overlooked after the war; the atrocities were conveniently forgotten by the Prime Minister of Australia, Sir Robert Menzies who preferred the huge trade anticipated between Australia and her former enemy Japan, rather than punish her war criminals. More than 200 Japanese war criminals awaiting trial were discharged in the early fifties in favour of the dollars – or pounds as the currency was then – to come from the build-up of trade between the two nations. Forget the war crimes???

It should never have been forgotten that the bestial and cruel Captain Takakua who succeeded Hoshijima at Sandakan received orders from his superiors to eliminate all POW before the end of hostilities. Nor should it have been forgotten that the last POW slaughtered occurred after the cease-fire was announced on the 15th August 1945.

In the first week of July, 'Agas' agents learned that four Australian POW had escaped from Ranau assisted by a friendly Japanese Christian guard, who provided food for them. He told the escapees 'all men go now. All men soon mati (die)'.

He then returned to his quarters where he took a 7mm Nambu pistol from its holster, searched for and found Captain Takakua and Lieut. Suzuki in Takakua's quarters. He shot both men killing Suzuki and wounding Takakua. Three soldiers who came to the aid of their officers were also killed or wounded. The friendly Japanese then turned the Nambu on himself and suicided.

He had been embarrassed by both officers earlier in Sandakan and had promised himself to get even with them sooner of later.

Six POW actually escaped from Ranau in two parties during July 1945. The first consisted of Lance Corporal Bill Moxham and Privates Keith Botterill, Nelson Short and Andy Anderson. The second party comprised Warrant Officer Bill Sticpewich and Private Ritchie Reither – the latter a very sick man.

Reither died in the jungle and Andy Anderson who had been the personal mate of Nelson Short back in the Singapore days, died in a hut hurriedly constructed for them by a Malay Orang Tua (Kampong headman) 'Bariga' who found them. This brave man, later awarded the British Empire Medal (BEM), risked his all for the Aussie POW. Both Reither and Anderson died a few days short of rescue as Bariga led Moxham, Botterill on stretchers and Short – still on his legs– back to an 'Agas' rescue party in the jungle. Sticpewich when rescued by the 'Agas 3' men, surprisingly came in mounted on a horse.

My commiserations were interrupted by the arrival of a number of wing whirring jungle fruit pigeons perching on the exterior wall. Their distinctive, gentle soul soothing cooing, and the forever present clicking of thousands of cicadas in the jungle tree-tops mingled with the continuous sound of cascading water in the Pool of Remembrance, were like a sad reminder of bygone days. Occasionally, monkeys interrupted by calling from the lower limbs of the secondary vegetation.

As I stood there musing over the tragedy of the marches and the marches, the elapsed time of some thirty or more years dwindled to what seemed like 'only yesterday'.

The jungle sounds and the sighing of the wind through the foothills of Mt. Kinabalu were reminiscent of a soft and sad requiem to those souls who perished on that tragic death trail to the feet of towering 'Chinese Mother' - Mt Kinabalu, South East Asia's highest monolith

13,450 feet. 'Kina' was the early Malay word for China and 'Balu' mother - 'Chinese Mother'.

The war was moving ahead at an incredible speed. The Americans were ready to further their push towards the Japanese mainland where the fighting was expected to develop into a fanatical stand by the Japanese who could be relied upon to defend every inch of their home islands by whatever means they had at their disposal.

These would undoubtedly include Kamakazi piloted aircraft, human manned torpedoes, Kaitan underwater suicide craft and many other forms of 'war bastardry' that the 'sons of heaven' were dreaming up. Anything was possible as they had proved so frequently in their former heyday when they walked through Asia and most of the South West Pacific area.

With absolute disdain they had belittled both Britain with the Singapore catastrophe and America with Pearl Harbour, and both goals accomplished with what could only be described as consummate ease.

But, the boot was now on the other foot and Japan's immense land forces were effectively bottled up in numerous of its occupied territories. To worsen matters – if that was remotely possible – there was little likelihood of Japanese forces fighting an effective rear-guard action back to their home islands. The 'sons of heaven' had been deprived of their formerly effective Navy and merchant fleet, most of both in Davey Jones Locker and their Air Force shot out of the skies.

More information filtered through from our covert agents in the Sandakan area towards the end of April. The main Japanese forces had evacuated the town area and were concentrated in the many rubber estates, particularly in Leila and Labuk Rds, the latter leading to Beluran and Ranau. Their only occupancy of Sandakan was effectively at the Chinese school.

Gort, very dejected at that stage having realised that operation 'Kingfisher' was never to be, requested another strike on Sandakan's badly damaged airfield built by the POW and who were compelled to do the repairs to the strip. Air strikes were also ordered on the waterfront ship building yards and the rubber estates where the Japanese had established their camps. Two days later, a US Force of 80 B24 Liberator bombers unleashed from Palawan, descended on the ailing township and virtually raised what little was left after their previous raid.

All this information had come via our dear friend Samak of

Kampong Menunghutan who said that Joseph Wong had also indicated that 4 or 5 Australian Navy and one American Navy POW had arrived in the camp during October or November of 1944. They were reported as having been transferred from Makassar on the island of Celebes east of Borneo to Semporna and thence to Sandakan. Why they were transferred to Sandakan we had no clue. Wong's only reward from the Australian Government for what he had done was a creased up letter of commendation that he produced from his wallet and showed with pride to interested people. Joseph – he spoke perfect English - told me that he had applied unsuccessfully to the Australian Government for citizenship. He humbly added that unfortunately the letter did not assist him in any way to provide food for his wife or himself in their final years of retirement. Mrs Wong died three years before Joseph, who said when I spoke to him in 1995 that there were many like himself in Sabah who felt they had been inadequately rewarded by the British and Australian Governments.

My daughter Aneeta, eldest family member Barry and I last spoke to Wong in 1998 when we were in Sabah with documentary cameramen Terry Carlyon and Keith Platt of Carlyon/Miller during the shooting of 'Jack Sue – A Matter of Honour' for SBS Australia. Joseph Wong Yun Siew appeared in a number of shots in that documentary and sadly, passed away shortly after our return to Australia, a lonely and a forgotten man.

The handful of Navy men in Sandakan were possibly survivors of HMAS Perth the Australian six inch cruiser that together with the eight inch American cruiser USS Houston and some destroyers were sunk in the Sunda Strait. Both ships at night, while trying to escape from the Java Sea into the Indian Ocean and   then to Fremantle Western Australia, met a vastly superior invasion fleet of nineteen Japanese ships.

Hopelessly outnumbered by the Japanese armada, the Allied ships succumbed to the uneven match, still firing as they slid below the waves. Perth's ammunition expended, she was down to firing star shells as the waters of the Sunda Strait closed over the proud ship that had served with distinction against both superior Italian forces in the Mediterranean and Japanese in the Java Sea.

Chapter 29

TWO DOWN AND ONE TO GO

The stage was set and everything pointed to success, provided lady luck dealt the right cards. A full suit of 'twos' would be almost a full hand. We would need every bit of luck on our side as our latest intelligence reports indicated that there were at least 300 Japanese occupying Kudat. Kudat was our trump card; if we could drag it off. The odds were approximately 300 to 20.

Our recently recruited Malay 'rumour team' from Dampirit started the jungle vine humming. The rumours were gathering momentum from kampong to kampong between Kudat, our goal in the north, and our Chinese guerrillas near Dampirit. The rumour was that a large force of Australian commandos had landed at the base of the Kudat Peninsular and were about to advance overland to the west coast thereby cutting off Japanese escape from Kudat

The surviving 'binatangs' from our attacks on Dampirit and Pituru arrived at Langkong and Kudat where they reinforced the rumours spread by the Malays - their long suit – that Australian commandos in large numbers had landed at the southern end of the Kudat Peninsular. Not in a very happy frame of mind, their reports of our successful attacks were certain to alarm their superior officers.

According to Nick Combe who had spent many years prior to WW2 as district officer in BNB and understood the Malays from A to Z, always said that if a rumour was to be spread successfully, give it to a Malay and he never taught us a better lesson. Nick's advice had been put to the test on many occasions since our insertion into Borneo.

After a night of rejoicing at Yusof's home where many scotches and local concoctions were consumed and tales were told reliving the attack on Pituru over and over again as mountains of barbecued venison were consumed late into the night, a day of rest was announced.

The Chinese and Malay girls who were our hostesses for the evening's celebrations were dressed in their beautiful national cheong sams and sarongs that were buried after the Japanese occupation along with table cloths, crockery and other treasured family possessions. On that night of nights, it was abundantly evident that these treasures had been brought in from their jungle hiding places and displayed for the benefit of their men folk and the two Tuans, Captain Roy McLean and Captain Wong.

The Japanese plundered anything of value they laid their eyes upon. To protect their treasured possessions the indigenous women woke up to the fact that everything had to be buried in the jungle.

I noticed that since my return to Borneo from hospitalisation at Morotai following the 'Stallion 4' operation at Bongawan, the Chinese and Malay guerrillas were addressing me as Captain which surprised me. Roy did not question the new address. Admittedly, at the time, Skeet Hywood and myself were unaware that Gort had recommended us for decorations and promotions.

Field Service for Japanese killed during skirmish with us. Each plaque and jar of ashes represents a serviceman,and were returned by Japanese commanding officer to relatives in japan.
Photograph taken from a coconut tree in the plantation.

One of the Chinese nurses, Cheong, confided in me later that Major Nick Combe told her that we were due for decorations and promotions. The decorations for Gort, Skeet and myself did eventuate; the promotions did not, which was expected. The end of WW2 was fast approaching and recommended promotions were on the back burner. At best, Skeet and I could only expect to be promoted to Warrant Officers – the top rung of the ladder for non commissioned officers - or perhaps Skeet to Lieutenant and myself to Pilot Officer – the bottom rung of the ladder for commissioned officers.

Sadly, I was never able to learn whether local Malay Mandor Bin Ali who joined us solely for the Bongawan operation, was ever decorated or rewarded; I did not see him before or after that horrendous ten days operation.

When I arrived back at Pitas HQ, Fred Olsen told me that Skeet had left the day before as radio operator with Flight Lieutenant Geoff Ripley and a party of Malay guerrillas heading overland for the Ranau area. Part of 'Agas 3', they were attempting to intercept 8 Australian prisoners ex Sandakan reported by our Malay contacts as having escaped from the POW camp at Ranau.

Apparently, the Japanese also were feverishly searching for the POW. Japanese General Baba had ordered that all surviving POW had to be killed so that none would live to testify against the 'sons of heaven'. Gort was hopeful that Geoff and Skeet would be able to locate the POW before the Japanese did, or before the thick jungle foothills surrounding Mt. Kinabalu claimed their lives. To survive, they would be forced to live off the land if they were fit enough to capture anything that moved such as pelandok (mouse deer), snakes, jungle rats, animals, grass-hoppers etc; this was extremely doubtful.

Two days after our party, Roy, myself, Tan Teck Bak and the rest of the Chinese plus 2 Malay guerrillas ex the Pituru attack, set off along the main road to Kudat, approximately thirty miles. After having taken Dampirit and Pituru it was a case of two down and one to go.

We were well aware that the war was fast drawing to a close and victory was certain for the Allies. Both Gort and Nick had told us so, but none expected the end when it came. Thankfully, the dropping of the atom bomb saved thousands of lives both Japanese and Allied.

Party leader Geoff Ripley, a high-ranking police officer in Singapore pre-war, spoke very good Malay and had a working knowledge of

Cantonese as well. Like most of the officers of 'Agas', Geoff was a very likable man, he was my Malay language instructor at Frazer Island before he joined 'Agas' and was inserted into Borneo where he touched base with us at Pitas for the final weeks of the war.

Following our hospitalisation at Morotai, I never saw Skeet again until 1950 when I visited him, his wife Violet and young family in Adelaide. We remained close friends and only lost close contact after my wife Pam was fatally injured in a car accident in 1974.

The progress towards Kudat took us through a number of kampongs where it was perfectly evident that our two Dampirit recruits had done their work admirably. At the last kampong only about four miles from Kudat proper, the young men told us that during the last few days the Japanese had set mines on both sides of the road into town to slow our progress. Little did the Japanese know that the villagers would show us the exact locations of the mines that commenced about a mile north of their kampong.

Roy and I were amazed when we reached the site of the first mine buried approximately a yard off the edge of the road, where the dirt road terminated and the bitumen surface began. We were even more amazed after we gently dug and exposed an aerial bomb of about 250 pounds. Having had no experience in de-lousing mines or aerial bombs, Roy suggested that I should move clear of the area while he de-loused it. I needed no second urging. Roy had de-loused many aerial bombs while fighting against Rommel's crack German troops in the North-African campaign, and rendered the bomb safe in short time.

From memory, I think there were about ten similar bombs spread over about a half mile of road. We later learned that the Japanese were expecting the Australian troops to head north to Kudat in Bren gun carriers, light tanks or armoured cars which would have detonated the aerial bombs. Our Malay rumour spreaders had done us proudly. However, the only transport we possessed was shanks pony and even shanks were becoming a little tired.

We reached a point about a mile from the town when we saw a small group of men approaching. As they drew nearer we noticed that one was a solid built Chinese and the other five or six were smaller Chinese and Malays.

The solid built Chinese man who spoke perfect English proved to be the spokesman for the group and introduced himself as Padre Chong. He was noticeably cheery in countenance and proceeded to introduce his companions. It was obvious that they were all wildly excited and confirmed their feelings as they tearfully embraced both of us. Padre Chong said that it was wonderful to see white men back in BNB.

What was it about this BNB that produced such happily countenanced people as this man confronting us? Gort Chester, Nick Combe, Tan Teck Bak, and the majority of the people that became our leaders and guerrillas and others we met were of the same calibre. They all simply radiated friendliness, happiness within themselves, despite the shocking ordeals they had experienced over the three years of Japanese occupation. They were all so genuinely lovable. One could only admire them.

The introductions and friendly chat over and normality regained, Padre Chong said that the Japanese had destroyed most of the better buildings within the town including the power station and had commenced to burn their own go-downs (warehouses and quarter-master's stores) as Chong and his companions left to greet us.

He also said that the Japanese had immobilised all the vehicles they left behind by removing batteries and distributors. As he spoke, we could see dense black smoke rising from the direction of the town and airstrip which was a fairly sure sign that fuel or similar volatile liquids had been ignited.

Chong asked where the rest of the Australian forces were and was

Some of those contained in the jars of former photograph.

staggered when we explained to him that we were that sum total force – all 17 of us including only two Australians, Roy an AIF Captain and yours truly a RAAF Sergeant.

Padre Chong then in turn staggered us. He informed us that the whole Japanese force was at that very moment destroying everything possible and intended to evacuate Kudat in a road convoy within the hour because they feared the arrival of a large force of Australians. Before the Australians had sufficient time to cut off their proposed escape route, the 'sons of heaven' planned to escape to the western coast of the Kudat peninsular through the town of Sikuati, then down the coastal road to Kota Belud and on to Jesselton

Padre Chong next informed us that the Chinese mechanics employed at the Japanese motor transport division workshops had over a period of time, stolen from the Japanese a good stock of spare parts, batteries and fuel, and buried the loot in the jungle for such an eventuality. Before leaving town, he instructed the mechanics to recover the parts and fuel as soon as the last of the Japanese had left.

On arrival at Kudat proper, we were mobbed by excited people. Mostly women and elderly men, they sensed liberation from their cruel murdering Japanese masters of the past three years. The moment was full of emotion as copious quantities of tears bordering on uncontrolled weeping of the women both old and young - many accompanied by children. Roy and I were overcome by the moment but we were happy to admit later that we also shed a tear or two. We had never seen anything like it before; it was rare to see Asian women so openly emotional.

The only men evident were the old folk; the young men were out in the jungle busily locating and digging up automotive parts and fuel.

The complete town was covered in smoke from the burning fuel dumps and buildings. There was no justification for our feelings of uncertainty as there was not one 'son of heaven' in sight and the locals assured us that the 'binatangs' had gone.

The women told us that American planes from Palawan regularly bombed and strafed the town or flew over the town almost daily on missions to the southern areas of Labuan and Keningau and the railway line. They added that the rubber estates in the Beaufort area – Woodford, Jimpunga, Beaufort and others - where the Japanese forces were concentrated, had been heavily hammered by American and Australian aircraft since the Labuan and Brunei landings.

285

The locals told us that the last Japanese staff cars, trucks and motor cycles left the town headed west for Sikuati about an hour before our arrival.

The young men of the town started arriving with wheel barrows and hand carts loaded with batteries and parts and in a short space of time, had prepared a 30cwt Maple Leaf truck – probably captured during the battle of the Philippines. With our guerrillas on the tray of the truck waving their weapons gleefully, we passed cheering Chinese, Malays and Indians gesticulating wildly and giving the 'V' for victory sign; we gave chase.

There was little hope that we would overtake the tail-enders of the fleeing Japanese, but we figured that we might possibly catch up with a broken down truck or staff car and take some prisoners for intelligence purposes.

After driving ten miles through hilly country with numerous bends requiring constant braking, Roy who was driving, complained that the brakes were beginning to bind and before another mile had gone by, they were smoking badly and we were forced to abandon the chase.

We gently nursed the smoking vehicle back to Kudat where with Padre Chong as our guide, we surveyed our trickery-gotten gains of the town. The numerous fires had to be extinguished and the local population had to be assured that the Japanese were gone for good. More 'Z' men would have to be organised immediately to occupy Kudat. Likewise, more guerrillas would need to be stationed there, to discourage the 'binatangs' from returning once realising they had been duped. Meanwhile Australian troops on the mainland were fighting their way north along the coastal railway and over the Papar River, then on to Jesselton and further north to Kudat to finally relieve the 'Z' men.

Once Jesselton was captured, organised Japanese resistance would virtually cease. Enemy troops in outposts like Langkong, fearing encirclement, were expected to fall back towards the Keningau area where Baba and his main forces were concentrated for a final stand if and when the Australian troops decided to fight their way inland.

Logistically, such a move was unlikely once the Australians captured the railway line and the west coast towns and ports. Japanese dispositions well noted, it was purely a matter of starvation by isolation of the main Japanese forces in similar manner to what was happening to thousands of ineffective cut-off enemy troops in the Philippines, the Halmaheras, Celebes and most islands in The Dutch East Indies chain of islands.

MacArthur's brilliant concept of island hopping and policy of starvation by isolation, was saving thousands of men's lives, both Allied and Japanese and the same policy should have been applied to Tarakan and Balikpapan. The atom bomb freed Burma, Singapore and other areas without having to fire a shot. The same strategy would have applied equally with the two Dutch Borneo oil centres.

More than 300 Japanese fled Kudat that day. 17 had defeated 300 without having to fire a shot. The booty we captured included 23 trucks, Japanese and American. The Japanese trucks had six cylinder engines almost exactly the same as Chevrolet and Maple Leaf, as did the 3 staff cars captured on the day. Additional booty included 2 Japanese light tanks, 2 Harley Davidson 750cc motorcycles, a mobile searchlight and a damaged truck.

Other captured stores included small items such as hundreds of Japanese army shirts, trousers, single toed jungle boots, heaps of 'binatang' caps and smaller clothing items, all of which were later given to the local people who had been deprived of clothing and footwear for years.

Three completely intact Japanese stores were captured on that auspicious day. The first when broken into revealed aerial bombs including 450x100 pound, 235x50 pound, 80x25 pound, 10 cases of grenades, 15x7mm rifles, 10 Thompson sub machine guns and 42 cases of ammunition of all calibres.

The second store was packed with new aircraft parts. The third store contained radio and radar equipment. Another smaller shed contained 250 bags of rice, all of which were distributed to the locals.

Finally, we went out to the airfield only to find complete devastation everywhere. The strip itself was just a mass of huge water-filled bomb craters, aircraft revetment areas rendered useless by bombing and strafing, and burnt out stores, buildings, hangars and fuel tanks; a legacy of the American saturation bombing by mostly B24 Liberators and strafing P38 Lightnings from Tawi-Tawi and Palawan. The scene of complete destruction was reminiscent of Sandakan's airfield.

Near a distant destroyed revetment sat a lone Zeke fighter, obviously caught by a strafing Lightning as it was emerging from the protection of the mud revetments in a vain attempt to taxi out to the airstrip and get airborne to give fight to the American flyers.

After a considerable walk across the airfield, picking our way through the maze of water-filled bomb craters, we arrived at the bullet-ridden Zeke and immediately noticed that the 'son of heaven' pilot was still in the seat with his head slumped back and the cockpit glasshouse closed. On closer inspection, it was apparent that the pilot had been there for some length of time as his head and neck was dried out and screwed up like a dried out apricot. A throat microphone – normally a neat fit around the throat - was still attached and appeared in death to be many times too big for the dehydrated neck.

Amazingly, when we slid the cockpit glasshouse cover back and allowed air to enter the cockpit, we could scarcely believe that there was little offensive odour. The Borneo sun had done a good job; the Zeke glasshouse had amplified the sun's heat and completed the sun drying process; he was completely mummified. I later enquired from the locals as to how long ago the Zeke was shot up but none knew and none wanted to venture anywhere near the fighter and its pilot anyway. The Chinese in particular did not care to be anywhere near a live 'binatang' and even less where a dead one was concerned. This was evident by the watch still hanging loosely on the pilot's wrist and fountain pens clipped to the pocket of his shirt.

There was nothing on the side of the aircraft's cockpit to indicate how many kills the pilot had made, if indeed the Japanese observed the custom of most fighter pilots, irrespective of nationality.

I souvenired the engraved watch from the wrist of sun-dried skin and bone. His fur lined flying helmet was still hanging on a hook behind his head. His fountain pen engraved with Japanese characters that I presumed was the pilot's name, was in his tunic pocket and is now part of a display of interesting 'Z' artefacts in the Rockingham Historical Museum, Western Australia. Time did not permit us to explore more of the airfield that day, we had to return to Kudat.

The only other acquisition was one of personal interest. I was thrilled to find an old American Cable player piano with candle holders – shockingly out of tune – that Padre Chong said possibly came from the Philippines and was used by the Japanese in a Kudat house they used as an officers' club.

To me, it was a refreshing sight. I immediately sat down at the keyboard and hammered out a rendition of 'It Had To Be You' that sounded like Winifred Attwell's honky tonk piano, if not Winifred's playing style. Roy and the guerrillas simply loved the number – despite the piano being out of tune.

I played piano and banjolin from the age of nine until classical music ceased to interest me and modern piano replaced the banjolin. While still at school, I played banjolin Saturday nights with Patrick O'Hagan's Old Time dance band at The Railway Institute Perth for approximately one year for the princely sum of ten shillings ($1) per night (4 hours). At the same time I met Bob Seery, a 6.5 feet drummer now retired living at North Yunderup south of Perth through Frank Haycock's Music Store in Perth. With rythmn almost oozing out of every bone in his body, Bob and I formed 'Jackie Sue's White Coats', a three bit dance band with Jack Martin a 16 year old clerk and an alto sax player. Bob was 16 and I was still at Perth Boys' School so must have been 13/14.

At the time, our music left a lot to be desired and I am certain we were appreciated only because the war was in progress and class musicians had enlisted in the services. That was probably the only reason the dancing public tolerated our amateurish musical efforts; but 'fourth class ride better than first class walk' as the Chinese say. In any case, one had to start somewhere. Our interest in music cemented a friendship with Bob I have treasured since. Only distance and my inability to drive after I suffered the stroke, preclude me from seeing him more frequently.

Bob joined the Australian Military forces less than two years later and Jack Martin enlisted with the RAAF. Finally I enlisted in the Norwegian merchant marine with another lifetime pal, Bruce Inder-Smith. We were just over 16, both of us were employed as junior clerks at Attwood Motors, West Australian distributors for Oldsmobile, Vauxhall Bedford etc.

The war over and back in civvy street again, Bob Seery and I teamed up again during 1947 in the dance band game and continued together with many various musicians until we settled down with Alan D'Arcy, a Sydney alto sax player. About 1984 we disbanded after more than thirty happy years of professional dance band work ranging from regular 7 piece band -'Music for Dancing by Jackie Sue' - engagements, down to 3 bit gigs.

Padre Chong suggested that I take the iron frame Cable piano back to our Pitas headquarters. I was sure that while I was no piano tuner, I could improve on its then condition. The only problem was transportation, but I felt sure that Gort would be able to organise with the Americans at Tawi-Tawi for a PT boat to pick it up for me the next time one was in Kudat.

While in Kudat, Gort or Nick sent Hughie McMasters and 47 Malay guerrillas back to Pituru after reports came in that a recce patrol of 8 Japanese had arrived there. Unfortunately for Hugh, the 8 Japanese at Pituru were reinforced overnight by 18 more 'binatangs' from Matungong, a small neighbouring kampong. They had with them a 3" mortar, a 37mm anti aircraft gun and a 'woodpecker' machine gun. All were equipped with rifles, so it was obvious that the Japanese high command intended to hold Pituru, come what may.

A report was also received that Datu Mustapha's brother imprisoned in Jesselton on charges of suspected anti Japanese activities had died of torture, starvation and dysentery. We later learned that he died as a result of the 'water treatment' torture.

As Hugh felt that he needed additional support, Roy, Tan Teck Bak, two Malay police boys and myself went down to join him.

That afternoon, a Malay youth arrived at Yusof's house where the guerrillas were spending the night prior to attacking the following morning. The young man had a mailbag from the 'binatang' CO (commanding officer) at Langkong for personal delivery to the Japanese officer at Pituru. Using a duplicate key, he gladly unlocked it so that we were able to scrutinise the contents and documents, then re-locked it and went on his way as though nothing had happened.

Ah Mun our Chinese guide who was leading Hugh's group on this attack, translated the Japanese documents warning the new Japanese arrivals at Pituru to keep a wary eye on the area as it was known that the Australians were about. Hughie couldn't help but have a little chuckle inwardly; he was the only Australian there before we arrived. It was apparent that the Japanese at Langkong had re-established Pituru as a forward observation post. But why the anti aircraft gun?

Dualog was another small Kampong in the area. It was also there that Ah Mun's parents and younger brothers lived. Roy, Tan Teck Bak, myself and the Malay police boys had only been there a short length of time when Ah Mun's parents and brothers were brought in – the parents on hastily made stretchers. The Japanese had arrested the whole family and questioned them about Ah Mun's activities. When they failed to give the desired answers, they were all mercilessly whipped. My heart bled for the aged parents. The Japanese had no peers when it came to bestiality.

After bathing and dressing their wounds they were put down to rest and a couple of the local women were instructed in the care of the family while we were away.

At 0330 the following morning we departed for Pituru led by Ah Mun but once again ran into problems regarding traditional superstitions. The Malays were still nervous after the last attack on Pituru, despite the good work that Hughie had put in since then, convincing them that they had the ability to do the job with their superior numbers and firepower. One had to admire Hughie's patience – he was like a mother hen with her chicks.

To me, the Malays were a peace loving people and apart from the Dyaks and other exceptions, did not generally appeal to me as fighters. Unfortunately, my experiences with them under fire left a lot to be desired. The exceptions – pre-war police boys - again proved the rule and those exceptional Malays were fantastic.

Once again the Malays numbering 43 failed us and on the third attempt, broke ranks and ran in all directions leaving Roy, Hughie, Tan Teck Bak, police boys Sergeant Yusop, Corporal Eshak, Constable Abdulla, Datuk Mustapha and myself. We were compelled to move out and immediately found ourselves between Japanese fire lines from behind and live fire ahead from the Malays who had fled and were firing at anything that moved including their own men and us. Once again, I thanked the Lord that the Malays couldn't shoot straight and frankly, I think Datuk felt the same way.

Roy wasted no time in sending for the remaining Chinese guerrillas at Kudat who came down and for the second time within days, we wiped out the Japanese defenders.

On our return to Dualog, I found that Ah Mun's parents and brothers were responding well to the treatment prescribed. I also found a QSQ message from Gort who was in Labuan for planning conferences. My instructions from Gort were to return to Pitas post haste and organise with Fred and Graham to get a message off to Morotai requesting the bombing and strafing of Pituru, Dualog, Matungong and Dampirit to prevent the Japanese from attempting re-occupation of Kudat and the peninsular.

Gort added that he had taken care of Kota Belud and RAAF fighters from Labuan had strafed it. Unfortunately there were no heavy bombers operating out of Labuan; they had to come from Morotai.

Apparently orders were issued from the Australian top brass shiny bums that we were not to seek further help from the Yanks just across the Balabac Strait that separated Kudat from Porta Princessa in Palawan – 30

291

minutes away compared to hours of flying from Morotai. Maybe politics were at work again.

On the 9th August 1945 at about 1400 hours Fred and Graham transmitted a QSQ message to our HQ at Morotai requesting the bombing. We had no response to our urgent request for the rest of that day or the following day the 10th. The entry in my diary for that day finished off with the remark, "typical SRD bungling".

On the morning of the 11th at 0800 hours a PBY Catalina circled our HQ at Pitas as was the usual practice before landing at Telega, Hugh's HQ. Although we had not been advised that the aircraft was coming - not unusual for SRD HQ - I immediately left by boat for Telega just in case the Cat stayed at anchor or took off and returned. Nearing Telega we met another of our small boats from Telega returning to Pitas with stores and a written message from Nick who was on the Cat.

Nick's message was the greatest. It simply read "The war is over. Japan has agreed to a non-conditional cease-fire. Am taking off immediately to pick up Roy and Hughie" but not a word about Gort's request for the bombing of the peninsular kampongs which seemed strange.

I discovered later at Morotai that Nick – the only 'Agas' officer on the island and who had gone there for conferences re 'Agas 2' activities - knew nothing of Gort's request and yet Nick had been there when the QSQ message arrived. SRD's right hand had no idea what the left was doing. That we were winning the war was certainly not due to any of their efforts.

By the time I arrived at Telaga – about 1030 - the Cat had taken off and it did not return. I immediately headed back to Pitas arriving there at 1230 to await Morotai's reply to Gort's QSQ message, but nothing had arrived. Fred and Graham were thoroughly disgusted to think that Roy, Hughie and all the guerrillas were out in the field trying to stay alive and depending on air support, and Morotai HQ couldn't care a damn.

The date was still the 11th. August 1945. At 1400 a QSQ message from Morotai was received and when Fred and Graham deciphered the five letter groups of the message it read "expect Catalina Telaga 0800 on the 11th. Stop" and was signed "Flight Lieutenant North"; six hours after the Cat had landed, unloaded stores and taken off on its return journey. To put it mildly, Fred, Graham and I could scarcely believe our eyes. Obviously HQ were whooping it up at Morotai while we poor bastards in the field were left to fend for ourselves.

Fred, almost in disbelief encoded another QSQ message with Graham which was immediately transmitted and it read "Have received report from natives that armistice with Japan has taken place stop if it is true please repeat please confirm same". No reply was ever received. Obviously the sarcasm of our signal was not appreciated by the shiny bums who had more to do - filling their guts with grog - than worry about guys still out in the field.

The day after we had been advised that Japan had accepted the cease-fire – 12th. August - the Japanese fatally shot one of Hughie's Malay police boys near Pituru. Gort's immediate re-action was contained in an order to all 'Agas' parties "Unless it is obvious that enemy is surrendering, shoot to kill. Beware of trickery". It seemed that the Japanese were unaware of the cease-fire or were disregarding it and intended to continue fighting. We were advised by the local natives a few days later that the 'sons of heaven' in the areas of Pituru, Dualog, Matungong, Dampirit had no radio communication and intended to continue fighting.

On the 13th August 45 at 0900, I received an instruction from Roy to return to Pituru to bring him up to date regarding the cease-fire. Nick had not landed off Pituru as originally planned, but had flown over Dualog and dropped a message that said "The war is over". I rounded up our boat crew and sailed immediately for the Kudat Peninsular again.

The following morning we arrived at Dualog around about 0100 hours after a long tiring trip across Marudu Bay during which we almost ran into a Japanese night patrol craft and were saved by the timely intervention of a Sumatra (tropical rain squall).

Roy, Hughie, Datu Mustapha and the Malay guerrillas had gone in and attacked Pituru the day before my arrival, after learning that more Japanese had arrived there but they were badly repulsed by the 'binatangs' resulting in the loss of a Malay police boy. Four other guerrillas suffered minor wounds. Datu Mustapha, Malay police Sergeant Yusop and eight other Malays returned to Telaga.

It was the last straw for Roy. He and Hughie rounded up Tan Teck Bak and the Chinese guerrillas and we immediately returned to the hoodoo Pituru area. After a short sharp but furious exchange of gunfire – 7 Bren guns, 11 sub-machine guns - cleaned out the area without loss to our forces. The Japanese never returned and pleased us all the more by withdrawing the last of their troops from the Kudat Peninsular, much to the rejoicing of the local population. Gratifyingly, we had avenged the little Malay police boy's death.

Within a day or two of the Japanese withdrawal, the whole atmosphere of the peninsular kampongs changed. Malay men, women and children were seen sporting gaudy bajus (shirts), sarongs and sandals. A number of Chinese women both old and young - a little more formal – were arrayed in cheong sams and black cheong foo (long trousers) that obviously were getting their first airing after being buried in the ground for yonks. Household comforts began to appear almost out of thin air.

One Chinese girl I spoke to made it perfectly clear that for the first time since the Japanese had invaded her country, she felt no impending danger of rape and degradation when she ventured from her own home. She added that it was great to welcome Australians. It felt just like the good old days under British rule.

I watched the scenario of the men as the tension of living for years under a despot nation seemed to visibly drain from their faces. The laughter and chatter of the lovely young children brought tears to my eyes as memories of my own five younger brothers and sisters back in Australia flashed across my mind.

Mothers and mothers to be were about, herding their children hither and thither like a mother duck escorts her ducklings across a busy street. Without one was conscious of the war damaged homes etc, it was difficult to appreciate that a war was on and that one of their number had died the day after the cease-fire was announced and only a few miles away. The 'passing parade' was an interesting one. Would any more of us lose our lives in the same manner as that of our brave little police boy?

I even felt a pang of sympathy for our 'sons of heaven' and wondered whether the average Japanese serviceman wanted to conquer the world or were they like us?   Were they like Gort, Nick, Roy, Hughie and the younger of us: Fred, Graham, Skeet and myself – I was the baby of our team. None of us wanted to be killers.

How did the Japanese mind function?   They had two arms, two legs; an anatomy like ours. Why shouldn't their minds be the same? Maybe the announcement of a cease-fire had softened me, and that, was unthinkable. One brief unguarded moment could be fatal. However the feeling did not persist and in a flash I was back to reality.

A small Malay boy aged about three, timidly approached and asked me in Malay for a chocolate. His dear little face was a picture. I did not carry chocolate because the tropic heat quickly converted it into a thorough mess unless one was in a folboat where it could be stored free of the body. Instead, I reached into the pocket of my jungle overalls and handed him a fruit bar. He cautiously tasted it, his eyes never leaving my face, and when he found that it was to his liking, he smiled, thanked me and ran back to where his mother was standing. The experience was like a breath of fresh air.

With the Japanese gone from Kudat and 'all quiet on the western front', Roy, Hughie and I decided to check out the hospital at the mile 4 but it was a pointless exercise. There was nothing left to check; American bombers from Tawi-Tawi and Palawan had seen to that.

From there we went to the airfield for a more leisurely inspection and en-route checked out a damaged radio installation where we salvaged a quantity of Japanese radio parts and a couple of small transmitter units complete in almost new condition for Fred and Graham at Pitas.

The airfield yielded little of value. Apart from the 'Zeke' fighter that we had previously examined, there were two 'Bettys' (big bellied Betty, so named because of its bulbous fuselage). The twin engine Betty was Japan's most successful bomber of WW2. Nearby, there was a 'Kate' torpedo bomber, two 'Sonya' fighters and another 'Zeke; all damaged beyond repair. They were all single engine aircraft and all were bullet ridden.

The only other items of interest worth inspecting were two Japanese ships that had been torpedoed. With Padre Chong as our guide, we did not have to travel very far along the north beach of the peninsular before encountering both beached vessels that obviously had been run onto the shore while under attack.

One was a Navy survey vessel of about 1500 tons that had been badly damaged by aerial bombing and the other was a crude-oil tanker of approximately 20,000 tons maximum that displayed a huge hole in the starboard side, the result of a direct torpedo hit.

We boarded both vessels and salvaged small items of souvenir interest. On board the Navy survey ship, under a heap of rubbish in the officers' mess, I found a white porcelain plate complete with the Japanese blue star (bintang in Malay) the symbol that appeared on Japanese Army caps, badges of rank and other insignia. Completely undamaged, it only required washing to restore it to its former new state.

Today, this Japanese Navy bowl is one of my treasured souvenirs.

Chapter 30

SUBMARINES OUT – AIRCRAFT IN

The speed with which American forces advanced through the south west
Pacific in their leap-frogging was almost frightening. They virtually
cake walked from Guadalcanal to Palawan and were almost on the
threshold of Japan's home islands. The loss of American troops while
alarming was considerably fewer than the losses of the enemy. Japanese
dead could only be described as horrendous.

And yet, worse was to come for both sides as the US forces captured
Saipan, Okinawa, Iwo Jima and other islands closer to Japan.

In many ways, our Australian Navy and Air Force gave very worthy
support to the Americans. The small but efficient Royal Australian Navy
(RAN) threw its might into beach bombardments with the US Navy
(USN) 'heavies' while the Royal Australian Air Force (RAAF) flew
many sorties against Japanese positions as the 'sons of heaven' steadily
fell back from whence they had come in 1942.

As a result of Allied advances, air distances from home bases to
enemy targets shortened. This in turn brought aircraft in range of 'Agas'
operations in BNB, and submarine activity in our area faded out as US
submarines ranged far and wide in their relentless hunt for Nipponese
shipping. Japanese home waters such as the Sea of Japan were no longer
safe to their own ships.

'Z' then looked to inserting parties behind Japanese lines by
parachute from RAAF planes on a larger scale than before.

As a result, an air arm was developed within the organisation of 'Z'
under the banner of Flight 200 led by RAAF Squadron Leader Graham
Pockley DFC & Bar. Pockley had won the Distinguished Flying Cross

for sinking a German U boat in the Bay of Biscay while flying Short Sunderland Flying Boats during his tour with the Royal Air Force. He then won it a second time - hence the bar - for services in the Mediterranean.

During the last six months of WW2, the RAAF had a surplus of aircrew and ground crew fully trained on 'heavies' (B24 Liberator 4 engine bombers) at Tocumwal New South Wales. These crews like the fighter pilots, were anxious to get into the fray before the war ended. Meanwhile, the pool surplus was building up and all feared that they would still be pool-bound when hostilities ceased.

There was excitement among the aircrews one day when notices were posted in the respective messes calling for Liberator crews to volunteer for special missions. Needless to say the notices brought forward a host of applications and so Flight 200 was born.

After training of the selected crews had been completed at the top secret training base of Flight 200 Leyburn Queensland, six specially converted B24 Liberators and crews were dispatched to the operational areas of Darwin and Morotai in the Halmaheras – the latter being General Macarthur's advanced HQ. All six had been specially fitted to take storepedos instead of bombs in the bomb bays plus chute slides in the tails for dropping parachuting 'Z' agents. The special conversions

'Flight 200' B24 Liberator, burning after a drop for 'Agas 2' at Melobong, British North Borneo, May 1945 13 killed.
Note two 'Z' Force operatives on left and tail fin of smoking wreck.

were designed and tested by our popular 'Z' Captain Sam Carey before the aircraft were declared operational.

The B24 Liberators were stripped of excess armour plating to reduce weight so that more fuel could be carried to enable them to make the return journey to operational parties in the field of which 'Agas' in BNB (British North Borneo) was the most distant.

Flights of this nature generally required taking off from the home airfield early in the evening to enable them to arrive over the target areas of 'Agas' (Sandfly) or 'Semut' (ant)) in Sarawak. At dawn, they made their drops of personnel and storepedos before hauling their arses out to begin the long flight home - usually in daylight - as enemy dawn patrols hit the skies. The prodigiously long journeys were very trying on aircraft and crews, who accepted that these long lone vigils were of necessity undertaken in darkness and were completely without fighter escort because the distances to targets and return were beyond the range of fighters.

The Flight 200 crews were all very dedicated to their work and many a 'Z' operative alive today owes his very existence to these men including Jack Wong Sue. I was always proud of my association with Flight 200 and still hold those flying men in my highest admiration. All the tea in china would not tempt me to swap for their lot. Being depth charged at 150' or more in submarines or being shot out of the skies was not Mrs. Sue's little boy's kettle of fish.

Flight 200 also possessed an Anson twin engined army co-op plane for the maintainance of lines of communication within Australia.

Within 5 weeks of the commencement of operations, 50% of Flight 200 had been lost.

The commanding officer's plane with Graham Pockley in the left hand seat disappeared off Sarawak's capital city of Kuching after making a successful supply drop to the 'Semut' party in Sarawak. His and another Flight 200 Liberator commanded by Flight Lieutenant Frank Ball headed out into the bay off Kuching where they encountered a Japanese gun-ship approaching the Kuching River. Pockley, who was known to be a dare-devil-come-what-may, decided to shoot up the ship; both aircraft went in at low level and strafed the Nipponese gun-ship.

Having carried out the first strafing pass, the second B24 broke off the engagement and the last they saw of Pockley's B24 was going in again to attack the gun-ship after which he and his crew were never seen or heard from again.

Tail-gunner Sergeant Colin Hawkins who with his wife Edna live in Albany Western Australia today, related the story to me many years ago and he obviously would have had the last glimpse of Pockley's aircraft as it went in for the second strafing run. From Colin's description of the action, Frank Ball put the nose of the Liberator down and dived towards the ship to strafe it from end to end, while Pockley came in from the side.

Colin complained to his skipper on the intercom that "Pockley's tracers are dangerously close to us skipper" whereupon Frank Ball pulled out of the action adding as he did, "Let's get out of here and leave the glory hunting to Pockley".

On that particular mission, Frank Ball had as his first officer Flight Lieutenant Charlie Cox - in the right hand seat who later was skipper of the third Liberator loss - plus another pilot the late Flight Lieutenant Ray Storer, both of whom were 'learning the ropes'. Additionally, they carried another observer the late Major John Ellis AIF, originally from Merredin in Western Australia.

Frank Ball's aircraft carried on to the mainland and as they approached Kuching's Lintang Oval they noticed that the oval was jam-packed with Japanese forces on parade at what appeared to be a funeral service - indicated by a coffin clearly visible from the air. Not believing their luck at finding a huge concentration of undefended 'sons of heaven' at their mercy, the B24 went into a steep turn and came back on the strafing run-track spreading Browning .5 machine gun fire in all directions.

Colin told me that they had a real turkey shoot on the day and that if the ceremonial occasion was indeed a funeral service, the Japanese would be having many a longer observance for their dead as there were Japanese bodies lying everywhere after their first strafing run.

Japanese were running like a horde of ants to get off the parade ground as the big B24 Liberator climbed out of the joint. Colin added he was fairly sure that the shoot-up took place on the same day that Pockley disappeared but "40 years is a long time to re-call exact details". He remembered that they itched to have stayed on a while longer but they had a long way to go home and fuel was limited.

However, they were ordered to Mindoro in the Philippines where they re-fuelled, then remained for a few days while they went out daily, searching for Pockley's aircraft and crew without success.

The Japanese never laid claim to having shot Pockley's Liberator down in Kuching waters or any where else, but a large patch of oil was seen some distance off Jesselton –now Kota Kinabalu, the capital of Sabah. Other than that, no wreckage was ever located; he and crew just disappeared into thin air.

Graham Pockley the submarine hunter of some distinction and his brave Flight 200 crew had disappeared off the face of the earth.

During one of my many post-war visits to Sabah, I spoke with a native of the Dusan race who had just left the area of Sepulot in the heavy jungle interior south east of Kota Kinabalu. According to his report, a four engine bomber had crashed in the Sepulot area during WW2 and although access to the crash site was limited to four wheel drive vehicles, by exercising care and patience, it was still possible to reach the wreck-site in dry weather. According to his story a considerable amount of the aircraft was still visible.

Sensing that this could be the wreckage of Graham Pockley's B24, I decided to do something about it.

On a later tour to Sabah during the mid eighties, I called on the curator of the Sabah National Museum at Kota Kinabalu who I understood had a particular interest in WW2 planes posted as 'still missing' in BNB and explained my mission. Unfortunately, I cannot recall his surname but his Christian name was David, a very co-operative, cheery, tubby little Scott or English gentleman of about 30/40 years of age. He was married to a very beautiful local native lady and he did have a great interest in WW2 events and in particular, aircraft wrecks.

Many letters flowed back and forth between Western Australia and Sabah, and eventually some months later, a letter arrived advising that he had pin-pointed the wreckage and was putting together a four wheel drive expedition to inspect the site and identify the aircraft. I was invited to join him.

Unfortunately, due to family commitments I was unable to go along at the last moment. Getting to the wreck site alongside a roaring mountain water course in the thick rain forest presented great difficulty to the experienced museum party. There they found an engine and portion of an undercarriage that were positively identified as being B24 Liberator. A large swathe through the huge timber of the area indicated the plane's final moments. The wing was found standing on end in the huge trees of the thick rain forest and the identification was as clear as a bell – the Yankee star on the tip of the main-plane.

I subsequently received from curator David a complete set of photographs of the wreckage and a full account of the expedition. It was disappointing that it was not Pockley's aircraft but it was still an important discovery. Pockley's disappearance remained a mystery.

Shortly after the discovery, David returned to England to visit his parents and sadly, was killed in a car accident. For some years later, his beautiful wife was the proprietor of the coffee shop at the interesting and fascinating Kota Kinabalu Museum before I lost contact with her.

Following her husband's unfortunate death, I sent a set of photos and covering letter to the White House in Washington outlining my minor connection with the late curator and the expedition plus the curator's fabulous work in locating the wreckage.

Eventually, I received a letter of thanks from an American War Graves Recovery Unit in Hawaii saying they had sent a recovery team to Sepulot, located the wreck and brought back the remains of eight of the crew from the wreckage and in the surrounding jungle. The unit had also written to the curator's widow and commended her on her late husband's efforts. The War Graves Recovery Unit added that they would notify the next-of-kin of the aircrew that the plane had been recovered. For some thirty years the bomber and its crew had been posted 'missing in action, believed killed'.

To this day, Flight 200's original Commanding Officer Graham Pockley's aircraft and crew are still officially 'missing – presumed killed in action'.

Chapter 31

THE UNCERTAIN YET CERTAIN END.

How long would it be before the Japanese units - scattered throughout Borneo - received official orders from their Emperor to lay down their arms? Bearing in mind that many of the smaller outposts – and there were plenty of them – were without radio communication and would have to rely on eye to eye contact with their own Japanese before accepting the fact that Japan had surrendered unconditionally; it was an uncertain situation.

It was certain that the 'sons of heaven' would never regard information received from the locals as gospel truth; never in a million years. The local co-operation that had been so unreliable during the Japanese occupation, plus the hatred of the locals for the 'binatangs' had brought about an irreparable rift between the indigenous people and the Japanese. It was an example of the ruled and the ruler, the oppressed and the oppressor, the tortured and the torturer. The Japanese would rue the day and yet, they had only themselves to blame.

With just a little management and kindness, the Japanese could have had the coloured races of the South West Pacific areas and South East Asian territories they had over run, eating out of their hands. Instead of using such a simple strategy, they chose to embitter the people they had conquered.

The Nipponese despised the foes who surrendered. That may have been the reason why the Japanese had little or no respect for the Malays but that reasoning could not have applied to the Chinese who hated the guts of the Japanese from way back. Since time immemorial, the Japanese warrior had been indoctrinated with the Samurai or Bushido belief that it was preferable to die in battle than surrender to the enemy. They had lived by that belief and demonstrated their determination to die in that belief as they proved at Sydney Harbour in 1942. Their midget submarines penetrated Australia's defenses in their quest to sink the big American warship USS Chicago, and on land, at almost every battle ground they had contested throughout the Pacific campaign.

Their Kamikazi planes, human torpedoes, Kaiten midget submarines were just a few examples of their suicidal policy, and even their soldiers preferred to die by holding a grenade against their chests in preference to surrendering, demonstrating their desire to die for the Emperor and take the enemy with them. Was it too much to expect that they would all surrender now, even with the Emperor's orders?

Requested by our HQ then in Labuan, Gort approached me with the news that HQ was asking for volunteers to take radios into the Japanese. It was the only way that their troops would hear the broadcasts by their Emperor, ordering his troops in all theatres to lay down their arms and surrender to the nearest allied forces.

With his next breath, Gort added that he did not expect that I would be interested in volunteering my services, or for that matter, any other man of our 'Agas' organisation. Gort was able to read my mind perfectly. It was hardly necessary for me to reply. The quizzical look on my face would have been sufficient to convince.

Three of the six death march survivors photographed at an 'Agas 3' Kampong House. *Left to Right* Short, Botterill, Moham.

As far as Japanese troops were concerned, the war was still on. They were still firing real live bullets and had already killed one of our guerrillas after the cease-fire. After the hard time we had given them over the past six months, I guessed that they really hated our guts. They would not have hesitated to shoot any one of us who dared to walk into their outposts waving a white handkerchief in one hand and a radio in the other. No way did I want any part of such a foolhardy plan!

I suggested to Gort that the shiny bums from Labuan should come out themselves and do their own bloody dirty work. Gort's reply was short and to the point. "They should send Paul Bartram or John North out to approach the Japanese unarmed, holding a radio receiver in one hand and waving a white handkerchief in the other. North would never get here on time and Paul would come with some hair-brained scheme of his own".

I don't re-call ever having refused to do anything for Gort before – I would have given my life to protect him and of that I'm sure he was well aware. Furthermore, I knew the feeling was mutual after what we had been through together.

However, in this case I had no qualms about my decision and I could tell by Gort's look and further remarks that he concurred with me but had been ordered to find volunteers for the task.

It was simple enough on the part of 'Z' HQ to come up with their hair brained ideas like their QSQ message transmitted to us at a very delicate period "Can you build airstrip suitable for Vultee Vengeance dive bombers ex number of feet long and ditto wide? Stop signed Flt. Lt. Paul Bartram". That was the craziest and most unbelievable 'urgent' traffic transmitted during the history of the 'Agas' operation, and   particularly, as it happened shortly after our insertion by the American submarine Tuna when security was on for young and old and an order for radio silence was in force.

Needless to say, nobody in 'Agas' took a radio in to our 'sons of heaven'. From what I have gleaned since the end of the war, there were no takers in 'Semut' in Sarawak or any other 'Z' party in Borneo and finally, radio sets were dropped in by air to the 'binatangs'. This should have been done in the first instance.

While all this was going on, Gort told me to go back to our Pitas HQ and prepare to return to Australia while he secured the necessary releases and other security requirements for me now that the war was over.

We had on many occasions discussed my desire to go back to Perth after the war was over to do first year medicine, provided my little brain could handle the difficulties of the situation after years away from study. Gort's advice was that I should get back to Perth as soon as the war was over because there would be thousands of servicemen and women with the same goal in mind. The desire to do medicine was a far cry from taxidermy or entomology (butterflies in particular). That had always been my boyhood dream.

Meanwhile the war was in an uncertain situation despite the fact that the official cease-fire was announced as 1200 hours 15th August 1945. The limbo existed in all theatres where the Japanese were entrenched. Reports continued to come in to the effect that civilians suspected of anti-Japanese activities were still being tortured to death. The worst affected areas in BNB were the hinterland bounded by the northern and southern Death March routes where our parties were involved and Jesselton. It seemed that the Japanese were hell-bent in exterminating those already imprisoned who could testify against them later.

Our HQ at Pitas became a hive of activity for Army watercraft overnight. Gort arrived from Labuan at 0900 16th August aboard AM1499 with sub Lieut. Mick Miller and two petty officers.

Captain Roy McLean and I said our farewells at 1000 the following day, the 17th. August 1945 as he departed on AM1499 for Kudat. He went aboard after wringing my hand off to the elbow, smiled and assured me that he would give my thanks and regards to Padre Chong as well as an affectionate pat to the Cable piano at the former Japanese officers' mess that obviously would not now go to Pitas. Roy liked music and had a leaning towards modern music bordering on jazz; it was right up my alley. He was going to miss the old goanna as much as I. He had been a wonderful officer and companion in many a tight spot and I enjoyed every moment I served under him.

At 1800 the same day, I said another sad farewell to Major Nick Combe and Sergeant Curly Lang who left Pitas aboard one of the snake flotilla, HMAS 'Black Snake' bound for Kota Belud. The Snake Class were small ships specially designed for covert operations. They looked like native sailing fishing prahus but were motorized and had a mighty turn of speed belying their humble appearance, and they were armed to the gunwales for their type of operations. The flotilla leader was HMAS 'Krait' of Singapore fame.

As a result of their great work behind enemy lines, Gort was promoted to Lieut. Colonel, and Nick to Major. I never did learn whether Roy finished up as a Major or Hughie a three pipper (Captain). If not, they should have been promoted. I know that Jock Sutcliffe finished up as he started with 'Z'- a Captain and Don Harlem a Lieut. Don particularly had done a meritorious job and deserved promotion over and over again.

As much as we all disliked Jock, nonetheless I still feel that Roy, Hughie, Jock and Don were never adequately rewarded for their outstanding work and courage. And of course the same applied to our sigs of 'Agas' 1 and 2 - Lieut. Fred Olsen, Staff Sergeant Graham Greenwood, Sergeants Skeet Hywood and Geoff Watts – all of whom I feel were left out in the cold.

Skeet and Geoff Watts were fortunate in that they were often on special field jobs in their roles as 'sparkies', but Fred and Graham never got away from their sets. The final few weeks found them glued to their transmitters and Boston generator almost 24 hours per day as the traffic was so heavy. I think it would have driven me mad. Obviously, the old adage of "one man's meat is another man's poison" was not so silly after all.

I did not serve with later arrivals of 'Agas', and as a result am not conversant with their achievements but of one thing I am certain. They were all volunteers and wonderful men, even to have been selected to join 'Z' in the first place. Secondly, they served with one of the finest operations of 'Z' when they were inserted behind Japanese lines as members of 'Agas' and I humbly 'lifts me lid' in proud salute to them all.

Shortly after Gort's arrival from Labuan, he told us that he had sent a message to Geoff Ripley instructing him to discontinue activities as he feared that the lives of the POW were in jeopardy while there were continued activities against the Nipponese. This seemed strange to me as Geoff, Skeet and guerrillas had been sent into the Lansat area for the specific task of attempting to rescue the POW. How would they handle the situation now with Gort's restriction in place?

Geoff and Skeet's guerrillas had barely established themselves in their new surroundings when further activity took place. A native Orang Tua (Head man) by the name of Bariga arrived bearing a note from three POW who had escaped from Ranau with one other who died in the jungle. Bariga was given food and medical supplies to take back to the jungle hide-away that he had built for the POW while he contacted 'Agas 3'.

Gort also told us that shortly after the rescue of the 3 POW who had escaped from Ranau, a couple of Malays led a POW into Geoff's HQ riding a horse. In comparison with Dick Braithwaite and Owen Campbell who had escaped separately from the Death Marches and when rescued by our agents, were clad in loin cloths and bare footed; the POW on the horse was well dressed.

When interrogated by Geoff he said he was Warrant Officer William Sticpewich. Again, when compared to Braithwaite and Campbell who were virtually walking skeletons, Sticpewich was in good physical condition and good health.

In a later discussion with Gort I reminded him that our first agent Samak of Kampong Menunghutan had mentioned to us that there was one Australian officer in the Sandakan camp who was very unpopular with his fellow Australians. He often had meals with the cruel and arrogant CO of the notorious camp, Captain – later Major – Susumu Hoshijima, and it was further reported that Sticpewich had been on fishing and hunting trips with Hoshijima. Samak said that the Australian officer was referred to as 'Jepun Puti' - 'the white Jap' by the Australians in the camp. It was later established that Sticpewich was that man.

While Gort was with us at Pitas, a message came through from Geoff that a Flight 200 aircraft had made a successful drop at Lansat on the 18th. The drop consisted of supplies – "sufficient to feed a battalion for a month" according to Geoff Ripley. A 7 man team led by Captain Henry Nicholls and a doctor, Major Forster were then parachuted in to reinforce Geoff's 'Agas 3' party. The other 5 men were Sergeant Jack McNeale, Corporals Eric Gore, Les Grinham, Privates Lofty Hodges and Norm Wallace.

The three escapees found by Bariga were Bombadier Bill Moxham, Privates Keith Botterill and Nelson Short. The fourth member was Short's pal, gunner Andy Anderson who died before he could be rescued. Lofty Hodges and his recce party searching for Bariga finally intercepted him and his stretcher bearers who had been delayed while bringing in the three POW.

Note: For a full chronological account of the rescue of Braithwaite, Campbell, Moxham, Botterill, Short and Sticpewich, refer Lynette Ramsay Silver's 'Sandakan – A Conspiracy Of Silence'.

Following the departure from Pitas of Nick, Curly, Roy and company on their respective ways, the rest of us were relaxing with Gort over an enjoyable drink or two and reminiscing about the events since our arrival in Borneo when Hughie arrived from Telaga by native prahu to join us.

My last night with the boys at Pitas was full of emotion and happiness. Gort and I were packed ready to leave by Martin Mariner the following morning for Morotai.

The morning of the 18th August dawned and I rose early after a disturbed night during which I lay in my bed tossing and turning and thinking about Geoff Ripley and Skeet Hywood and wondering whether they had contacted any more escaped POW.

My thoughts were further interrupted by the realisation that I was leaving these wonderful men behind me and possibly for good. Was I doing the right thing by forsaking the companionship of the men I had faced death with, laughed, joked and cried with? It troubled me to think that I might wake up in a few days time regretting my decision.

I'd been fighting a war since the age of sixteen and never experienced the fun and excitement of the adolescent years enjoyed by civilian lads who had not had their lives interrupted by a war. However, there was some comfort in the knowledge that there were many others in the same boat – I was not a lone sailor. However, the uncertainty of going back to civilian life was weighing heavily on my shoulders.

The sun was beginning to filter through the treetops as the singing of Kelawat monkeys and the ceaseless clicking of the cicadas in the trees put an end to my fitful dozing. I slowly stirred myself to a beautiful August morning that only BNB could turn on. A few dwarf bats flitted here and there, seeking the last morsel of food on the wing before retiring to their refuge for the day. At the same time a colony of large fruit bats or flying foxes as we prefer to call them in northern Australia, squealing incessantly, arrived overhead and gradually settled in to the huge mango trees before hanging upside-down to sleep for the daylight hours.

Birds of every description were tunefully chirping everywhere, interspersed by the gentle cooing of jungle fruit pigeons and the raucous calls of a common jungle bird, not unlike the Australian raven. As kids holidaying at the YMCA camp Rottnest Island off the coast of Western Australia's capital city of Perth, the identical bird was known to us then as the Australian Crow, but today it has been promoted to Australian Raven.

Over breakfast, further discussions continued concerning Geoff, Skeet, their guerrillas and carriers who had penetrated deep into the jungle areas at the foothills of Mt. Kinabalu, hopeful of intercepting escaped POW should any be successful in fleeing the Ranau camp sites. None of us were very optimistic about further rescues as we were aware that Japanese

General Baba had issued orders to the effect that all POW were to be massacred before the war ended.

While the Japanese had no communications with the outside world or their own headquarters, they could plead ignorance on the one hand while they systematically knocked off all POW with the other. And who could blame them? After all said and done they were not honourable warriors. Instead, they had proved themselves unworthy of even being called animals.

They had tortured, murdered the aged and the young. Many a baby had been tossed in the air and caught on the end of a bayonet, and there were many reported incidents of pregnant women being sliced open; the unborn child and the mother left to perish. All this carried out in ghoulish fun, often with other 'binatangs' looking on and obviously enjoying the spectacle.

Rapes, merciless whippings and unspeakable forms of torture made the Nazis appear as learners, but all these atrocities were part of the sport for the day to the Nipponese 'sons of heaven'. There were numerous incidents of cannibalism in New Guinea, the Philippines, Borneo, Okinawa, Iwo Jima and if the truth be known, in many other theatres. During the final weeks of WW2, approval of cannibalism was officially sanctioned by the Japanese High Command but the eating of their own dead was taboo. Yes, the Japanese had conducted the most animalistic of wars that would still be discussed a hundred years hence.

Breakfast completed, I made the rounds of farewell to all the boys, drank in my last fond look at the beautiful surroundings of our Pitas HQ gardens and fringing jungle. I appreciated fully as I gazed, how the Coleman house must have been like a divine dwelling in the heavens to the former tenants, 'the binatangs'.

It had been a veritable Eldorado to us compared to the 'mudflats' and I can still picture the rooms with the mother-of-pearl wall friezes, the sitting room sized toilet with bookshelves alongside the pedestal and pictures adorning the walls.

I viewed for the last time the cuckoo chiming clock on the wall still ticking away merrily after having had its inner self freed of dwarf bats by Graham. I again admired the beautiful Borneo timbered wall of the same verandah cum dining room where Chinese 'Cookie' served up our delicious venison steaks and where the wild jungle bees behind the mahogany wall were building up their stocks of honey again. The same strain of bees had been responsible for chasing Gort, Skeet and myself in the jungle near Bongawan during those tough ten days of 'Stallion 4', finally concentrating their attention on Gort's bald head, much to his discomfort and disgust.

Strange it was that the unpleasant experiences of the same Coleman home - and there were plenty of them – had been forgotten, and in their place, the happy moments reigned supreme.

Gort and I boarded the Army Motor Launch AM1499 tied up at the homestead jetty. To the accompaniment of good wishes and singing by a crowd of Chinese and Malay guerrillas, wives and families led by my dear blood brother Tan Teck Bak, Cheong our nurse, and a number of Chinese guerrillas from the days of Lokapas, AM1499 cast off and headed downstream for Telaga. I unashamedly wiped away a tear or two as the wishes of 'Farewell' in both Chinese (ho hung) and Malay (jumpa lagi) were still ringing in my ears as we rounded the bend of the river near the homestead jetty.

On our arrival at Telaga, Gort and I went aboard an American Martin Mariner as our faithful Malay boat crew bade us farewell with "jumpa lagi tuan" (see you again sir). This was before the days of 'see you later alligator'.

At 0100 hours we taxied out to the take-off path and after final warming up, the Mariner developed full power with a mighty defiant roar and hurtled across the estuary. Lifting off the smooth waters it banked and made a last circle of our Pitas HQ. We gave the guerrillas a final wave before setting course for Mandahan Estate in Kimanis Bay, our extraction point at the conclusion of 'Stallion 4' to make an airdrop to the Chinese salt maker and his two lovely boys.

Only a short flight down the west coast found us over Kimanis Bay and headed in for the beach near Bongawan where the saltpan was situated. The pilot lined up the humble dwelling that was the home of the old Chinese fellow and at about hedge hopping height zoomed over the saltpan and home to attract the attention of the family. After another couple of passes we noticed father and sons emerge from the light jungle between the house and the beach, intently studying the aircraft to make sure that it did not carry the 'poached egg' identification of the hated Japanese.

Convinced that we were friendly, they raced down to the beach just in time to intercept the next pass of the Mariner as it flew along the beach. At the appropriate moment, a large parcel of sarongs and assorted clothing with white cloth streaming from it as a marker, was free-dropped from the aircraft and retrieved by the father and sons team. The second time around, an even larger parcel containing a bag of rice and other assorted foods plus fruit bars and chocolates was free-dropped and seen to land undamaged near the party. Both parcels had the names of the father and his two sons scrawled on the outside and a short note written in Malay within, from the four of us in 'Stallion 4' thanking them for their hospitality.

As we went round for the final pass, the father and sons team on the beach recognised Gort and myself waving to them and they waved back excitedly. The pilot climbed out for the blue yonder and set a course for Pulau (island) Kaniogan just south of Pura-Pura where we were first inserted by the American submarine Tuna.

The Mariner arrived there about three hours later, touched down on the glassy smooth surface, taxied in and anchored so that Gort and I could go ashore briefly before we took off again for Tawi-Tawi.

Kaniogan was in the territory of Captain Rex Blow who was inserted at nearby Pulau Libaran by American PT boat and was the party leader of 'Agas 4'. Unfortunately, I never had the opportunity to meet Rex and his party but had heard a lot from Don Harlem post-war about one of Rex's party, Corporal W.A.C. (Waca) Russell. Waca played a big part in identifying Japanese war criminals and in the search for POW bodies with the Australian War Graves Unit involved in retracing the southern Death March rentis.

Rex was one of a group of the first escapees from the newly established Sandakan POW compound who succeeded in eluding the Japanese search parties and making the crossing from the mainland to the pre-war quarantine station of Pulau Berhala off Sandakan Harbour in June 1943. This took place before Gort Chester's ill-fated first insertion into Borneo, operation 'Python 1'.

Commandeering native Prahus on the island they finally reached Tawi-Tawi and joined Philippino guerrilla leader Colonel Suarez. The Philippino and his force harassed the Japanese like hounds snapping at the heels of a mule. Rex Blow, Jock McLaren and the other Australians spent many months with the Philippinos before eventually being extracted by American submarine to Australia.

By about 1400 hours on the 18th August the Martin Mariner was on the water again at Tawi-Tawi. We were ferried from the aircraft across to the American hospital ship 'USS Hokamote' where we spent the night with the US 62nd portable surgical unit. This great outfit had initially taken care of gunner Owen Campbell after Owen's amazing escape from the clutches of Hoshijima and his murdering gang, and to eventual rescue by 'Agas' agents.

Today, Owen Campbell is the sole surviving escaped POW from the Sandakan Ranau Death Marches; the infamous Borneo Death Marches of 1945.

He and bombardier Dick Braithwaite were the only two POW who escaped from the actual Death Marches and survived the end of the war. The other four surviving POW escaped from Ranau POW camp.

Aboard 'Hokamote' we ran into 'Z' personnel Captain Paddy O'Keefe who was an old pre-war mate of Gort Chester and was involved in a support role for Gort's 'Python' groups. Paddy was with Lieutenant Alan Pearman, both of whom I had met at our Melbourne HQ 'Harbury', opposite the Botanical Gardens in Toorak. They had with them a Corporal Lampshire who I had not previously met.

During what was a pleasant evening spent in the ship's mess with delightful food, scotch, bourbon, the company of delightful American nurses and other hospital staff, a comfortable bed with clean white sheets; it was not difficult to take.

A radio message came through from Fred back at Pitas during the course of the night, the contents of which changed Gort's plans to fly with me to Morotai. The following morning the 19th. he and Paddy O'Keefe left the 'Hokamote' at 1100 hours by PT boat bound for Pulau Libaran.

It was a difficult moment for both of us when it came to parting. I felt that I was saying goodbye to someone dear for keeps; just like saying farewell to one's arm or leg for good. Gort, looking gaunt was obviously not well. The usual eye sparkle that had been his winner and had won him many a fair heart at the Morotai 2/5th Australian General Hospital was lack lustre. I stood there at the rail waving to Gort and Paddy as the PT boat sped them out of sight, experiencing a feeling of empty vastness that I could not then or even now, adequately explain. I think now that I must have had an inner feeling then that we would not see each other again.

Gort Chester was going back to an uncertain war and myself to an uncertain way of life in civilian life.

The bacillary dysentery that had knocked the hell out of us both - and in my case was followed by my first malaria attack while recuperating in the Morotai 2/5th Australian General Hospital - caught up with Gort twice more before Christmas. He then suffered another relapse that developed into black water fever, finally claiming his life in February 1946 at the relatively young age of 46.

The next time I was in his presence was 1980 when I first caught up with my 'blood brother' Tan Teck Bak at Kota Kinabalu – wartime Jesselton cum new capital of Sabah after Malaya won independence and became Malaysia and the Malays became Malaysians. Teck Bak drove me to the European cemetery where we located Gort's grave on the far side of Signal Hill. We observed a two minutes silence as our minds went back 34 to 35 years. The wartime pioneer of British North Borneo had fought and lost his last battle against the deadly black water fever.

Had it not been my heartfelt desire to do medicine, I probably would have remained in BNB with Gort, Nick and Roy. Gort had mentioned that there was room for me with the newly formed British Borneo Civil Administration Unit (BBCAU) should I have a change of mind.

The change of arrangements meant that I had the 20th August at Tawi-Tawi. Early am the following morning we were airborne aboard an American Catalina and arrived at Morotai about noon.of the 21st.

At the 'Z' camp Morotai I surrendered my trusty personal Owen gun, and other odds and ends. De-briefing, security checks and a few matters that I had to handle for Gort and Roy took 3 days to finalise.

After bidding farewell to the nurses I had befriended at the 2/5th Australian General Hospital where I sat in as pianist with a three piece dance band frequently, I finally departed Morotai. Aboard one of our Flight 200 B24 Liberator bombers, we took off at 1300 hours on the 24th for Biak, New Guinea where we were to overnight. On arrival there, the B24 was directed into a special bay and a guard placed around it after refuelling and no unauthorised person was permitted anywhere near the kite, which pleased me immensely.

My kit bags were bursting at the seams with weapons, personal souvenirs, Japanese swords etc, all of which would have been confiscated by the Australian Military Police who were checking air transports, troopships, troop trains and truck convoys for souvenirs and documents of intelligence value. Because of the tight security thrown around Flight 200 crews and their B24s, they remained immune to normal security searches and checks. The aircrew and 'Z' personnel merely took from the plane, personal gear sufficient for the overnight stop, and all other gear remained in the aircraft under wraps. I breathed a sigh of relief.

Following a very early breakfast, we took off on the final leg to Australia at 0500 hours on the 25th. After an uneventful flight, landed at Charleville North Queensland for refuelling before resuming the flight to Leyburn, Flight 200's own strip and HQ where we touched down at 1730 hours after a long tedious hop of over 12 hours. I was back in Australia!

I had nothing to complain about, but back in Borneo the curtain was about to come down on the final act of the 'Borneo Death Marches 1945'.

Our Malay and Chinese agents learned that some 32 POW were still alive in the Ranau area at the end of July, but only just alive. In the first week of August it was reported that the 'binatangs' had culled out 17 POW suffering from beri-beri, dysentery and malaria considered too ill to work. These unfortunates were regarded as unproductive and a liability to the Japanese.

They were forced to walk up the hill to the camp cemetery – many with insufficient strength to make the last few yards, resorted to crawling – and there they were compelled at gun point to dig their own graves. Their pitiful efforts provided much amusement to the Japanese guards standing by smoking and laughing.

Once completed they were made to kneel while the guards shot each man through the back of the head. Those who did not die immediately were bludgeoned to death.

Don Harlem told me that on the 17th August – the day I left Pitas - the remaining 15 Australian prisoners were taken out a few miles along the Tambunan rentis. The Japanese guards told them that they were to build a Pondok (small hut) for the 'sons of heaven'.

At a pre-arranged spot they were led off the rentis to a prepared clearing and murdered in the same manner as those at the cemetery. One by one they fell like a pack of cards. Those who failed to die after the shot to the head were bludgeoned to death. Yet the war was supposed to be over? What a shocking finale!

And so the curtain closed on the uncertain future of 'B' and 'E' force Australian and British POW shipped from Singapore in 1943, not knowing where they were headed. The tear-jerking end of the last 32 was a complete reversal. They knew the outcome. Theirs was undeniably certain. 6 survived out of 1800 - purported to have gone on the Sandakan to Ranau Death Marches - and only one of those is alive today. Please God, grant Owen Campbell good health and happiness.

Airborne again, our next stop was Sydney where some of the men left the aircraft and other 'Z' men joined it for Melbourne. By that time, I was the last of those that had boarded the aircraft at Morotai including the crew. The long air journey and the increasingly cold weather, getting colder the further south we flew, took its toll on me and by the time the aircraft landed at Melbourne I was feeling none too well.

While stretching my legs to restore circulation and gain some body heat, I was approached on the tarmac by the ATO (Air Transport Officer). He advised me that there had been a change of arrangements and that the same aircraft was flying directly through to Perth and if I wished to avoid a transit delay that could amount to hours or days, I should continue the flight. Anxious to get home and realising that all my gear would have to be unloaded and possibly security checked, I took advantage of the offer.

After a hurried meal and the aircraft re-fuelled, we again became airborne on the long final hop to Perth, my home and family. The unpressurised B24 Liberator bomber flying at 10,000 feet was like a refrigerator in the southern climes of the Great Australian Bight, and by the time we landed at Dunreath Airfield (now Perth Airport) I had little feeling other than that of an icicle. My tropical clothes provided little warmth.

Again, the 'Z' aircraft was directed into a special bay and the aircraft was fenced off for security. Apparently, special top secret equipment had been on-loaded at Melbourne for destination unknown. My last flight as a 'Z' man had been as secretive as my first. From the time I boarded the B24 at Morotai until finally leaving the kite at Perth, my papers were not checked once. Yet, at every check point or stopover it was evident that my name was on a manifest somewhere by the personal treatment handed out from the transport authorities and the Flight 200 aircrews.

Finally, about to leave the aircraft at Dunreath, I was flabbergasted when an army jeep with a security officer arrived, introduced himself and asked for my baggage. My uneasiness was hastily dispelled when unexpectedly, he packed all my gear into the jeep, handed me a leave pass for 60 days and drove me to the city where he transferred me to a civilian taxi and paid for me to be taken home. My transfer from a battle zone to my parent's front door in West Perth had been very efficiently handled for which I felt very grateful. My last impressions of 'Z' and Flight 200 were great.

A few days later, I was admitted to Hollywood Hospital suffering from a severe attack of malaria as a result of the long and towards the end, bitterly cold flight, but I was home.

Chapter 32

KUCHING AFTERMATH

In the mid 1980s I led a group of 'Z' men on a tour of BNB to attend the official unveiling of the newly restored 'Hero's Grave' at St. Joseph's Catholic Church Kuching in Sarawak.

During that tour, we visited Labuan Island where I was able to take my 'Z' Force tail-gunner mate Col Hawkins of Flight 200 - now resident of Albany - to the waterfront where the wartime City Padang (square) was situated. There I showed him the footpath memorial erected to the memory of the high ranking and extremely popular Japanese officer, who during the Japanese occupation of the island was appointed as Governor. Immediately after his death – killed when his aircraft was claimed shot down by a Yankee P38 fighter - the island of Labuan was renamed Maeda in memory of the man, and it retained that name until Japan's capitulation when it reverted to Labuan.

This was the man for whose memory the funeral service at the Kuching Lintang oval was in progress when Frank Ball and his Flight 200 Liberator and crew appeared out of nowhere and converted the solemn service into a veritable turkey shoot. I was happy to identify the day and place for Colin as we had received reports on Maeda's funeral service through Samak, and Chinese guerrilla leaders Tan Teck Bak and Datu Mustapha.

From all post war accounts submitted by the wartime residents of Labuan Island, Colonel Maeda was not only idolised by his own troops, but was one of the very few popular Japanese rulers. He was highly respected by the indigenous people, and his loss was mourned by all.

Our group of 'Z' men then visited the Lintang Barracks, the former

316

wartime site where the Australian and British officers who were transferred from Sandakan were imprisoned after the discovery of the radio in the Australian camp.

The civilian internees had been placed in a separate compound alongside the Lintang POW compound. It was in this compound where famous authoress Agnes Keith, her husband and their son were incarcerated. Agnes Keith wrote her award-winning book 'Three Came Home' while there under sufferance of the Japanese beast, Colonel Suga (Officer Commanding POW Borneo). In addition to the award winning book, the film of the same title starred Ronald Coleman and Claudette Colbert also won awards as a best seller in Hollywood. The black and white film is still available today in video stores throughout Australia.

Following Japan's unconditional surrender, the cruel Colonel Suga committed suicide in a Labuan cell while awaiting trial as a war criminal.

Prominent businessman Jimmy Choo, retired as proprietor of Sarawak Travel Agencies in favour of his sons who continued the business, took us in his coach to the chapel on top of the hill at Lintang barracks. The area overlooked the oval where he showed us the original site outside the chapel where Maeda's body was interred following the turkey shoot. Maeda's remains were exhumed and removed to Japan after the war.

Over the burial spot, the Lintang College students had erected a marker in the form of a wrought iron bantam atop a wishing well like structure in memory of the popular ruler of wartime Kuching. It is still

Haunted Japanese goal and torture house in Jawa Road, Kuching, Sarawak where some of the 13 heros died

there today, although regrettably for WW2 history, there is no plate to indicate the significance of the wrought iron bantam.

The loss of Pockley's aircraft out from Kuching signalled the commencement of a very dark period of Flight 200's early history. Not long after the commanding officer's aircraft and crew were posted 'missing', the second Flight 200 B24 Liberator was lost on 'Agas 1' territory at Molobong - one of our guerrilla training areas - on the 21st May 1945

Skippered by Flight Lieutenant Keith Emmett, the aircraft crashed with the loss of all hands –11 aircrew plus two 'Z' men, Captain Tom Eltham AIF and a signaller who I had not previously met. I was subsequently told that he was Lieutenant I.A. McLaren AIF. Both had come from New Guinea where they were involved fighting the 'binatangs'.

According to my diary entry, I rose at 0430 and with Tan Teck Bak and a few other Chinese guerrillas, went out to our Lokopas DZ (dropping zone) and lit a pre-arranged pattern of fires. The aircraft was to do the first supply drop at Molobong on the other side of the impenetrable mountain range that separated our Lokopas HQ and Molobong, then come over and drop supplies to us before returning to the Philippines.

At 0530 the Liberator arrived overhead, spotted our fires and our ground signals and flashed his wing-tip lights in recognition. It then flew over the range to Molobong not more than a minute or two away as the crow flies, where Captain Nick Combe, Sergeant Geoff Watts, Captain Roy McLean and our newly arrived Captain medico 'gynaecologist' Doc May were awaiting the drop with their guerrillas.

Only minutes later we heard a loud report from the direction of Molobong that we identified later as the aircraft crashing into the mountain. We were aware that something untoward had occurred when the aircraft failed to return and drop our supplies. We noted as we extinguished the signal fires that the weather was fine and warm with very little wind movement.

Subsequently, we learned from Nick that the aircraft had acknowledged their ground signals, then contrary to the usual practice of dropping the two 'Z' men first, went in and dropped the storepedos, intending to do a 'go-around' to drop the 'Z' operatives next. Apparently, with insufficient airspeed to climb out of the valley and over the mountain range top, the heavily loaded Liberator stalled and slammed into the side of the mountain.

The wreckage was still smoking two days later. Only one had escaped from the blazing fuselage. Although injured, he managed to drag himself free of the inferno but must have lost consciousness and was finally consumed by the flames, and like all the others, burned beyond recognition. When recovered, the body had a stainless steel meat tag (ID) with just the figures 5312 or similar that we assumed was a RAAF identification.

The third B24 lost was that of Flight Lieutenant Charlie Cox and crew that I understand was lost over Timor with all hands, but I am not conversant with the exact details of the tragic loss. I was told that the plane was shot down by a Japanese machine gun on top of a hill after the Liberator had completed a successful drop to a 'Z' party.

Charlie Cox was second dickie (co-pilot) on Frank Ball's aircraft the day Graham Pockley's B24 Liberator mysteriously disappeared after the two aircraft attacked the Japanese gunship out from Kuching.

Back in Australia at Togumwal RAAF base, as the frightening news of the sudden loss of half the squadron of Flight 200 aircraft in the short space of three weeks filtered through, the enthusiasm of RAAF Liberator crews waned. Many were still anxious to get into the fray and have a 'crack at Tojo' before the war ended, but none wanted to lose their lives in a 'special duties' squadron during those last few months, and after all, who could blame them?

In the short space of weeks only, three Liberators, thirty-three highly experienced airmen, four 'Z' operatives plus stores had been lost. Tocamore air crews started asking the obvious question, "What sort of bloody hoodoo outfit is this special missions squadron?" At that late stage of the war, because of the tight security thrown around its activities, even the name of Flight 200 was still strictly 'hush-hush' and remained so for some twenty years after the war.

The three aircraft and aircrews were replaced and no further losses were experienced for the remainder of the war. Meanwhile, they set up an admirable record of hours and distances flown on those lonely unescorted flights behind enemy lines. One day a Flight 200 airman will write a book and it will prove to be a top seller.

When Graham Pockley and his crew perished, the very experienced and popular Squadron Leader Frank Ball – a future pilot check and

319

training Captain for Trans Australia Airlines (TAA) - was appointed Officer Commanding Flight 200. Wing Commander Eric Read of Queensland was then appointed Commanding Officer of the unit.

After the losses, they continued to fly missions into 'Agas' territory including Jambongan, Lokopas, Molobong, to Jock Sutcliffe and Don Harlem in the Death March country, Kudat and many other dropping zones. In addition to 'Agas' parties, they dropped agents and supplies right throughout the Japanese occupied territories of the South West Pacific and South East Asian theatres.

Few - if any - Flight 200 members received the due recognition for their incredible work and even today, they remain the least known arm of our 'Z' Special Unit, or as it is more popularly referred to by the Australian community, 'Z' Force. Operatives like myself, whose very existence depended on their lone nocturnal flights to the deepest pockets of Japanese occupied territory, will never forget them.

Even worse, because they were regarded as non-entities of the RAAF once in with 'Z' Special, the RAAF could scarcely have cared a damn about them. Provided they did not 'create a ripple' they were forgotten men in the eyes of the RAAF, as were many other 'Z'men like myself, during the latter stages of the war and subsequent Government ministers and departments post war; in particular, the Department of Veteran Affairs.

Many brave 'Z' operatives had difficulties following the war, and even as I write these words, some are currently unable to secure pensions

One of the water torture tanks in the yard of the Jawa Road goal and torture house.
(Photo courtesy of Jack Bickford)

and other benefits to which they are entitled. Many of us do not receive service pensions because of the 'means test', or are hamstrung because of assets exceeding the allowable maximum figure, assets that we obviously can not eat. Many of us are strapped for ready cash as we have no income. And why should we be forced to dispose of hard-earned assets over a lifetime's savings just to stay alive, after having risked our lives to defend our country? Unlike others who chose to squander their money or 'piddle it up against the wall', some, a little more astute, now pay the price for their astuteness.

These 'Z' men very often came from professions and trades that provided them with incomes well beyond the maximum allowable assets figure to retain the right to a pension. However, this unfair 'means test' set by our Australian Government, was never taken into consideration when we were asked to volunteer our services for missions behind enemy lines. Our Government couldn't have cared a tinker's cuss, and as I have endeavoured to illustrate in this chapter, still doesn't.

Content to sit in their comfortable parliamentary positions receiving regular salary increases while the aged veterans wait forlornly, they have additionally disregarded the fact that those veterans on pensions, have suffered erosions to their meagre handouts when they most need

The Heroes Grave. Saint Josephs Church cemetery. Kuching.

321

the money to guarantee themselves a reasonable standard of living in their retirement years.

In 1914 during WW1, legislation was passed to guarantee ex-servicemen a pension of not less than 100% of the male Basic Wage. During the mid-thirties, the percentage actually increased to a figure approaching 130% or more; today that figure has eroded to 44% of the present Male Average Total weekly earnings (MATWE). Confirmation of these figures can be found in Hansard.

Our big-hearted Government – unlike their salary increases – proposes a pension increase to 75% over three years, applicable to special pensions only. While our politicians continue to procrastinate over this matter, they are smart enough to realise that in three years hence, many more veterans will have fallen off the perch and will cause no further problems. I am one of the youngest surviving operational 'Z' men and I turn 76 in September this year - 2001.

Sadly, our National RSL – the veteran's supposed supporter – sworn to fight for veterans' entitlements, could not be less interested. Like our 'pollies' in their armchairs, Generals. Air Marshals and Admirals take the attitude of 'to hell with you mate, I'm alright'.

My reader may think that I am a bitter veteran, and for this I humbly apologise, but yes – I am bitter for not me alone, but for all ex-servicemen, women, war widows and their children who have all been deprived of their lawful entitlements.

By virtue of our oriental appearance, combined with our ability to speak the necessary languages that enabled us to act in a clandestine capacity, and masquerade as 'locals' in Far Eastern countries, we were guaranteed rewards by our Australian Government 'if we survived the ordeal'. A number of Australian born orientals plus the loveable Malay Pearl divers, and those in professions from the Far East, did not survive. Captured by the Japanese, they were tortured to death while others survived torture, only to lose heads later to Japanese Samurai swordsmen. However, a few did survive the war. All had one thing in common.

When Japan entered the war, we were interviewed individually by a British Intelligence Officer whose name cannot be divulged - yet. All were promised a home after the war. Not one received one. It is little wonder we feel cheated? A few of the Malay boys have since died almost poverty stricken, some unable to secure a pension. As I type this passage I am reminded that only weeks ago, the Department of Veteran Affairs refused my request to have my cardio vascular condition (stroke 1997) accepted. However, a few years after WW2, they accepted my conditions of neurosthinia (war nerves), rhinitis and hypertension as war related. Double standards?

A few months earlier, I received a flowery two-page letter from the Minister of Veterans' Affairs in which he praised my efforts during WW2, adding words to the effect, that in the eyes of the Australian community I was great. Sadly however, no, the Department of Veterans' Affairs refused to re-instate my service pension that was revoked in 1997 while flat on my back in Royal Perth Hospital's Shenton Park Annexe.

My total right side was paralysed and I was unable to speak. I was told I would never walk again then treated in the barometric chamber (diver's de-compression chamber) for an air embolism that apparently occurred during heart surgery. I remained in hospital for 11 months, despite having been told – pre-surgery – that because of my physical fitness, a non-smoker and current diver, I could expect to leave hospital within 10 days. 11 months later, I was wheel chaired out and taken home by my family.

To further 'heap coals of fire', I am confined to a wheel chair at home where I mostly live alone and depend on the hospitality of my many friends and carers, or my family members – the nearest being some 30 miles away – for outings. Since the department's refusal to re-instate my service pension, I applied to DVA for a recreational transport allowance. Again I was refused. Is it any wonder that I feel the Minister and his Department are conducting a vendetta against me? Maybe the fault is all mine and I expect too much!

Because we undertook special missions into enemy held territory and, or operated out of American bases where there were no Australian RAPs (regimental aid posts) or hospitals, consequently, no official records of our activities and medical problems were found, due to the ultra strict secrecy under which we operated.

Is it simply a matter of 'no records, no proof, no benefits'? If so, this is not good enough. Men who fought for their country and prepared to pay the supreme sacrifice, should not be subjected to 'penny pinching tests' or unfairly treated. Once again, America leaves us for dead. In the US one rarely hears of a poorly treated returned veteran.

Having finally alighted from my soap-box and freed myself of my bitch, I will finalise the story of Kuching and its WW2 aftermath.

As Flight 200 and the RAAF moved in, the American forward bases with their aircraft plus the Yankee submarines, moved out and headed towards Japan's home islands.

The American submarines in the early days of operations 'Python' and 'Agas' proved to be our only saviours. As well, they were our only means of back-up supplies and transport into former British North Borneo which ironically, we were endeavouring to recover, not for the Americans or Australia, but for the British. The Yanks were certainly great ambassadors in the respect that the territory, while not being theirs, they were still prepared to take the war to; in fact, wherever the hated 'sons of heaven' existed. What a contrast to Tom Blamey's attitude! Blimey!

Tuna was the last submarine we saw in our area, and the last few American aircraft we were to see in our skies left us with lasting and beautiful memories.

Chapter 33

WE KNOW NOTHING?

Seeking a grant to jointly write a book on the Sandakan saga under the AWM Research Grants Scheme, Don Harlem and myself approached the Australian War Memorial Canberra in the early 1980s after Don's first visit to Borneo since WW2; we were welcomed with open arms.

AWM readily admitted they knew little or nothing about the Borneo Death Marches other than information volunteered from escapees of the POW camp when it was originally on Berhala Island before the camp was transferred to Sandakan. These men escaped via Tawi-Tawi in the Philippines and were picked up by an American submarine and returned to Australia. The famous six who escaped after Sandakan had been established – Braithwaite and Cambell escaped during the marches and Sticpewich, Moxham, Botterill, Short from the Ranau camp - had been effectively gagged. Even the Australian Government was still tight-lipped about the Sandakan tragedy.

As the AWM were desperately short of material relevant to the Sandakan story, we donated some of the first clear aerial shots of the campsite before and after its burning down by the Japanese and photographed by American reconnaissance planes. We also donated some small artifacts that we had retrieved from the campsite as a Malaysian bulldozer contractor leveled part of the hilly ground. Don and I were following in the wake of the dozer as it chewed through lalang and secondary jungle, exposing all manner of artifacts that we were not permitted to remove, and in any case, were too large to consider bringing back to Australia.

In the hope that we might be able to save some of the larger artifacts, we placed what we could in a chosen spot in secondary jungle with the idea of getting them home to Australia somehow, some day. Twelve months later when next there, I discovered that the location where we had concealed the artifacts had also been leveled and the artifacts probably re-buried by the dozer blade.

Included in the smaller artifacts recovered were Lewis and Vickers Machine Gun ammunition belts, clips and empty shells by the dozens. Confined to a small circular area, Don suggested that they were probably from captured guns taken in Malaya, Singapore or the Philippines and mounted in the former Japanese machine gun pit. The bulldozer was cutting a swathe some 10/15 feet deep into the hill, so the high position would have been an excellent spot for an anti- aircraft gun to be positioned. Today, that hill is a soccer ground. The camp boiler (Bertha) had also originated from the Philippines as the nameplate still indicated.

The most interesting personal item I recovered was a bottle opener that when cleaned of the caked clay upon it, clearly revealed the brand 'Tooheys' on one face. I could not help wondering how many owners had possessed it. How much wine, women and song had it witnessed? Who owned it last? What atrocities had it witnessed? How had it finished up where I found it? Was the last owner still alive? However, regarding the last mentioned query, there was little hope of that, whether a Japanese soldier of Sandakan or an Aussie POW. Most of them are dead.

Don and I reflected on all the possibilities for several nights over several cold beers at Teck Bak Tan's recently opened Hotel 'Tsiang Gardens' in Sandakan. To our way of thinking, it was worth more than money could buy – just a simple Toohey's bottle opener. But if it could only speak, what stories it could tell. It had been buried for more than 40 years!

On our next appearance at Canberra AWM, we showed them the artifacts including the bottle opener which they photographed for posterity, giving Don and myself a copy each.

Looking at the surviving six men out of 2,500, one was Queensland gunner Owen Colin Campbell who was rescued by native guerrillas acting on orders of the late West Australian Lieutenant Jock Hollingsworth AIF from 'Agas 4' HQ. Campbell was the sole survivor of five who made a dash for freedom when aircraft ordered by Gort Chester - RAAF P40 Kitty Hawks, the first Australian planes seen by the marching POW - strafed the Death March route east of Boto.

Braithwaite was also an escapee from the Death March route but west of Beluran, who made the coast and was rescued by an American PT boat summoned by an 'Agas' party radio.

The remaining four, Botterill, Short, Moxham and Sticpewich were all picked up by a 'Z' rescue party led by Private 'Lofty' Hodges of New South Wales who had parachuted into the area for just that purpose. With the exception of Sticpewich, the other three – nearer dead than alive - were found in the jungle a few miles west of Kundasangby the late Malay Orang Tua (headman) Bariga BEM (British Empire Medal – Civilian Award) of today's Kampong Kipas. Bariga built a shelter and provided food for the three, while he went off to contact 'Lofty' Hodges and others of the 'Agas' parties who ultimately rescued Bariga's three POW.

Sticpewich had a companion with him when he escaped from the Ranau camp and came in riding a horse escorted by two Malays; his companion Ritchie Reithaer died in the jungle after the two escaped together from the Ranau camp.

The long and short of the situation amounted to the undeniable fact that when I was last there in June 1998, although 5 of the 6 survivors were brought out by our 'Agas' parties, we did not rate a mention on the memorial plaque at the Sandakan Memorial Park.

With my son Barry, daughter Aneeta and the Miller/Carlyon/Platt Film documentary team, we were there for the shooting of 'Jack Sue – A Matter of Honour' which, at the time of publishing this book has been screened on SBS Australia on several occasions.

Several former authors who have written on the marches have also passed 'Agas' by, or but very briefly made mention of our efforts.

During the clearing performed by the local Sandakan contractors to construct roads and establish street names – Nama Jalan - the secondary jungle had surrendered more of its long hidden secrets. The clearing revealed the foundation bed of what had once been the powerhouse generator and a sizeable - for those days - piece of road construction machinery. I later learned that the machine had been nick-named 'Annahoriki' by the late West Australian POW engineer Lieutenant Clive Boundy, who by virtue of his profession worked closely to Hoshijima, also an Army Engineer. 'Annahoriki' was used by the prisoners in building roads around the prison compound (see chapter on Clive Boundy).

In short time, a memorial appeared on the hill of the former POW compound, which under the circumstances was not surprising. What was surprising however, was the descriptive wording of the history of the site, march routes and POW personnel, yet not one mention of 'Z' Special Force or operations 'Python and 'Agas'.

'Agas' operatives had spent up to seven very successful months in the Sandakan and Death March route areas, particularly Jock Sutcliffe and Don Harlem. Similarly, no mention was given to Gort Chester's earlier operation 'Python' sent in to the Lahad Datu area to gather intelligence as to the whereabouts of the POW, believed to have been shipped from Singapore to Borneo. A costly operation, 'Python' involved two parties that were finally extracted by the skin of their teeth and at great risk by the US Submarine Harder. 'Python' lost three men in the process; Bill Brandis, Don 'Macka' McKenzie and A.J. Rudwick who were captured and executed. Yet 'Python', 'Agas' and 'Z' rated no mention? . Hopefully this omission has since been rectified.

To refresh my memory on these events, last night (2nd March 1998) I had a long telephone conversation with well known Queensland business man Sir Reginald Barnewall and his wife Maureen of Tamborine Mountain Queensland.

I have been closely associated with Reg and Maureen since about 1974 after a weekend re-union of 'Z' men and ex commandos organised by President the late Jack Guyder and the members of the Queensland Commando Association. The re-union at McKenzies Landing on the west coast of Frazer Island Queensland took the form of a long week-end camp in the open, in bitterly cold nights with a monster fire burning all night to provide warmth and to keep the many howling dingoes at bay. The site was our former training ground after we were first formed as SRD (Services Reconnaissance Dept) around about 1943.

Reg sent his private plane down to the island's 'Happy Valley' airstrip to collect my close 'Z' mate the late Keith Scarff and myself – we were the only West Australians at the re-union – so that we could have additional time with our hosts, the Barnewalls.

Reg and Maureen pioneered Frazer Island as a commercial holiday resort when they established the new and luxurious Orchid Beach Resort at the northern end of the island, shortly before our re-union team of about 60/70 men were hosted by them for a night and a day. The highlight of our visit occurred the following day when our truck convoy, returning from a 'round the island' tour was suddenly subjected to a mock ambush a few miles south of the resort by our hosts, Reg and Maureen.

They had cunningly selected a spot in the rain forest on the east coast of the island to conceal themselves. All of a sudden, as our trucks approached their position, they appeared from nowhere complete in camouflage and mock weapons and we found ourselves ambushed. We were done like a dinner.

Reg was a campaigner of earlier days and was an instructor in commando tactics, as he and Maureen had so effectively demonstrated.

Reg went to Borneo on one of my tours and distinctly recalled having attended the initial interview we had with the Chief Minister's representative in Sandakan. During a phone conversation with him early this year – 2000 - he vividly remembered me handing over a letter seeking the permission and approval in principle from the Chief Minister and outlining 'Z' Special Unit (International) Inc plans for the development of the present Memorial Park, then light jungle. He also reminded me that it was only through the influence of Haji Abu Bakar Tan (Tan Teck Bak, our leader of the Chinese guerrillas in 'Agas 1') that the District Officer agreed to a discussion with the three of us at short notice.

Reg pointed out that we discussed with the DO the beautification of a triangular piece of land encompassing the boiler (Bertha) as the focal point, plus the land to the road and stretching back over the hilltop where the present Memorial is situated. He also recalled that the DO appeared enthusiastic and agreed in principle with our plans to establish recreational facilities for the low cost housing project under construction nearby, now known as Kampong Sungei Kayu.

The DO added that he knew of no existing plans for the beautification of the area, other than the clearing of the secondary jungle and proposed roads and names on the former POW campsite. Is it possible that the low cost housing area was to extend into the former POW campsite? The DO assured us that our proposal would be relayed to the Chief Minister's office in Kota Kinabalu and that we could expect a reply in due course from that office.

The reply never eventuated.

Chapter 34

CLIVE BOUNDY'S 'ANNAHOROKI'

In 1990, on behalf of Perth based tour company 'New Horizons' (Tony Brbich), I led a war veteran group to Sabah. On that occasion I was accompanied and assisted by my eldest son Barry, a former pilot with 'Air Niugini' (Papua New Guinea's National Airline) and later with various air-charter companies flying corporate jets. Included in the group was a man and real gentleman, former Sandakan POW AIF Lieutenant Clive Boundy and his wife Verna who lived in Applecross, a suburb of Perth Western Australia.

On the first day in Sandakan, the group visited the former POW campsite just off the mile 8 peg on Labuk road leading from Sandakan to Ranau. As soon as Clive set eyes on the piece of road machinery, his eyes immediately lit up and his first remark was "My dear old Annahoriki - I never thought I would ever see it again".

In 1980, Nelson Short, Ian Leslie and I with the '60 Minutes' team went to Sabah to make the documentary film 'Return to Sandakan'. We located the camp boiler (Bertha) by the tall chimney pipe, the tIp of which was poking just over the top of the dense secondary jungle. We never suspected that there would be other pieces in the nearby jungle that eventually transpired. Who discovered them I had no idea, but one of the preserved pieces was a portion of the old powerhouse generator and the other was Clive Boundy's piece of road machinery, 'Annahoriki'.

Incarcerated in the POW camp as an engineer/surveyor, Clive worked very close to Japanese camp commandant Captain – later Major - Susumu Hoshijima (Hoshi), often spelt Hosijima, who himself was an engineer. It naturally followed that both men had a common language in their mutual qualifications and in the course of their work, got to know each other fairly well. This unfortunately counted against Clive Boundy in the eyes of his fellow Australian officers who probably regarded him as a 'suck-hole' to Hoshijima. He told Barry, Tony and I that he believed - even 50 years after the events of those haunting POW experiences – he was still regarded as an outcaste in the eyes of the Old Sandakians Association based in Sydney.

In many private conversations with Clive Boundy in Borneo, and later in his Applecross home (a suburb of Perth), Barry and myself found him to be most pleasant, an immense source of knowledge, co-operative, genuine and down to earth. He was the least embittered towards his former fellow Australian POW companions. He was forthright and "I have nothing to hide" said Clive.

"Hosi was a scoundrel and a bastard, but a bastard of a special type. In the course of his work, he was a brilliant engineer and gentleman, and no different to you Jack, Barry or myself. However, when the mood struck him or perhaps because of demands made upon him by his superiors, he became the uncontrollable arrogant Japanese officer bastard. He was the real Dr. Jekyll and Mr. Hyde - perfectly educated Japanese engineer cum arrogant, cruel bastard, cruel beyond belief".

As soon as Clive Boundy set eyes on the road grader - or whatever he said it was - he told us that he and his POW work mates used the machine many, many times adding with tongue in cheek "that's when the bastard was running". It was nicknamed 'Annahoriki' by himself and the POW road gang who regularly sabotaged the machine by adding sugar stolen from the Japanese kitchens into 'Annahoriki's' fuel tank, rendering it unusable for unrealistic lengths of time, much to the frustration of Hoshijima.

On such occasions, Hosi's junior officer frequently felt the wrath of his bad temper in the form of a slap across the face or a punch on the nose. From there, the junior officer inflicted the same punishment to the next junior officer, and so on progressively down the line of seniority to the final Nipponese private screaming orders to the Australian POW working on the airstrip.

Clive said "we Australians while not daring to smile, had many a laugh inwardly at the strange antics of the bloody Nips and particularly so when a hated Nip officer or soldier was bashed by one of his own superiors. We learned to make ourselves scarce as quickly as possible, and enjoy the spectacle from afar. However, if a prisoner was handy at that particular moment, the Jap bastard would take it out on the prisoner and from that point it degenerated further to a rifle butt slam, a kick in the cods or similar treatment " said Boundy, puffing away at his pipe.

Very often the punishment took the form of the 'aeroplane treatment' for a number of hours. The POW was made to stand facing the blazing hot Borneo sun holding a stick overhead with both hands and then on each end of the stick, the Jap guard hung a shovel. They were cruel bastards".

Some years earlier when Nelson Short, myself and Ian Leslie went back to Borneo with '60 Minutes', while posing in a 'mock-up' of the 'aeroplane treatment for filming by '60 Minutes' on the Sandakan airstrip, Nelson said "Christ help the POW who faltered during this punishment"!

Among Clive Boundy's many admirable characteristics was his penchant to speak his mind after considerable consideration of the point under discussion. He could always be relied upon to be straight to the point. No dilly-dallying, no exaggeration, he impressed his listeners who could not but feel that Clive always engaged his brain before his mouth.

Later when in his eighties and living alone after his wife Verna passed away, his mind was still very agile and he had a good recollection of his POW incarceration days.

He spent one complete day with my son Barry at the former POW campsite searching for artefacts. What impressed us all the most, was his ability to recognise the topographical features of the campsite as though he had been there only a day or two ago; instead it had been almost fifty years. He had not been there since the day all the Australian and British officers of the camp plus all those arrested on espionage counts were moved to Kuching for questioning by the Kempei Tai.

In contrast, all former inmates of the POW camp who had been back to Sandakan in the numerous tour groups I had taken there since 1979, had to spend quite some time re-orientating themselves to the surroundings.

Without exception, all had expected to see the 'big tree' and because of the missing 'big tree' found it difficult to determine the former location of the main guard house, main gate, original road out to Labuk

Road – the road to Ranau - even though Bertha the boiler was readily visible. No doubt with the whole area overgrown with jungle, it was little wonder.

Because of its enormous height, the huge tree pinpointed the camp parade ground for miles around and from the air. Unfortunately, it had either been felled or had died over the intervening years since the war. Without 'the big tree', and unable to position 'Bertha' the camp 'donkey' (boiler), most former inmates had difficulty in deciding where the two camps – the British and the Australian - had been situated.

As indicated elsewhere in this book, the 'donkey' was first discovered by Tony White of Sydney, a former AIF officer POW about a year before our discovery. With my 'war-time' Chinese guerrilla leader Tan Teck Bak of operation 'Agas 1' and a current resident of Sandakan , we were the second to locate it. The TV documentary team '60 Minutes' (Ian Leslie) was the third. Between each discovery, the jungle had reclaimed the boiler.

For reference purposes, on my first visit to the former POW camp, I took a number of USAF enlarged aerial reconnaissance photos of the campsite before and after the concentrated bombings of the airstrip by the Americans commenced in October 1944. I had further reference photos of the Sandakan airstrip after the bombings when the Japanese declared it 'beyond repair', and more photos of the burning campsite taken 29th May 1945 when the last big Death March commenced. In all photos, the 'big tree' was prominent and was used as a reference point by USAF pilots when bombing, strafing or aerial photographic runs were conducted.

Don and I donated copies of these aerial shots to the Australian War Museum who claimed they were unaware of their existence.

With the 'big tree' missing, the jungle growth having taken over completely, plus the lapse of fifty years, it collectively presented a 'guess where' problem for all.

Not Clive Boundy! From the camp water hole, he was able to pinpoint the 'donkey', the cemeteries, the main gate of the camp and as overgrown as they were, the main tracks throughout the area. These included those that led to the Japanese camp, pig pens, Hoshijima's house, sentry towers, the home of the former agricultural research station manager Joseph Wong and almost any feature I cared to nominate. All his recognised spots could be confirmed from the wartime aerial photos taken by the American pilots, copies of which have been in my possession since 1945.

Barry and I agreed later that Clive Boundy's incredible memory of the POW campsite had to be attributed to his professional vocation of surveyor cum engineer despite the jungle growth that had resumed the area during the elapsed 50 years. Clive's intimate knowledge of the area defied explanation. He simply amazed us.

His quiet unassuming mannerism was completely misleading. I could not help but notice at one stage while he was sitting on a tree stump, stoking up his pipe and taking a long draw through it, that he was

a wonderful study for an artist or photographer.

The former Sandakan POW engineer/surveyor , Lieutenant Clive Boundy AIF has since passed on.

During my last telephone conversation with him, he said that he hoped the lack of recognition of the fine work done by 'Z' operatives behind Japanese lines would be rectified in due course. In his unassuming but firm manner, he said that most of the POW officers – Australian and British - in the camp at mile 8 before the radio was discovered, were aware that clandestine forces – hopefully Australian – were operating outside the wire. Even Hoshijima had hinted to Clive that other anti Japanese forces were actively working against him, but he never enlarged on the matter.

In reflection, he was probably referring to Gort Chester's operation 'Python' that was finally driven out of Borneo in 1944.

Giving credit where credit is due, although I have yet to see the museum since established in the Memorial Park – I have not been back to Sandakan since 1998 - from all reports, those responsible for the development of the museum are to be congratulated on a fine job done.

Chapter 35

PADDY FUNK

Poor Paddy Funk! Our hearts bled for him. He stood idly by, watching as we diligently cleared mosses, lichens and rock ferns growing atop the historic vault head stone. Almost fifty years of weather, bushfires and the ravages of wear had completely hidden the names of those eight famous Sandakan men executed, plus five additional men from the area of Kuching who, like the eight, dared to oppose the Japanese by assisting the Australian POW.

Paddy Funk had not seen his brother Alex since their pre-trial imprisonment in Kuching. He was aware of his execution however, but had no idea where Alex had been buried other than 'somewhere in Kuching'. Paddy had been to Kuching many times since the war but was unable to find where Alex and the other heroes were buried.

Our tour group, determined to assist Paddy in finding the grave during our stay in Kuching, investigated numerous cemeteries without success. We finally went to St Joseph's and were cordially received by a priest of Dutch parentage who said he had served in Kuching for 17 years.

When he learned of our mission, he immediately replied "I can tell you boys that no such grave exists in my churchyard. However, you are welcome to leave the ladies here for a cold drink while you all search the yard; I'm afraid its far too hot for the ladies and myself to accompany you".

After locating the vault, I invited the priest and our ladies to brave the heat and inspect it; he expressed surprise and was almost speechless. With the assistance of the ladies, it took considerable time to clean the engraved stone face sufficiently so that a photo could be taken, showing all the names of the Sandakan locals who had been executed or died in prison.

To make matters even worse for Paddy, the heroic men including his brother Alex were not only forgotten men but as Paddy said in Malay to me later "buried like forgotten dogs" and left to the ravages of bushfire, weather and neglect.

It was little wonder that in short time, Paddy was reduced to tears.

For poor Paddy Funk, the realisation that Australia and the local Kuching and Sandakan people thought so little of his brave brother Alexander and the other heroes in the grave, was heart breaking. More disappointing was the knowledge that Australia couldn't care a damn, even though the men had sacrificed their lives in the interests of the Aussie prisoners

It was particularly hurtful to Paddy. He was granted citizenship in Australia post war for the part he and brothers Alex and Johnny played in their efforts to sustain the lives of the Australian POW at the Sandakan camp.

Later that evening, while our group was enjoying a lovely cold beer or two at the 'Holiday Inn', and Paddy was out of earshot, it was resolved that we, 'Z' Special Unit International (Inc) would seek the support of the local people to restore the grave to the decency it deserved

The five Kuching men were confined at the Batu Lintang barracks before eventual transfer to the notorious Kempei Tai headquarters in Jalan Jawa to join Captain Matthews and the Sandakan eight who earlier, had been imprisoned there. Matthews was tortured mercilessly, as only the Japanese Kempei Tai knew how. The Nipponese made certain that there were no witnesses to testify against them in what was obviously a war crime. There are relatively few cases where the Japanese actually admitted to a beheading.

The five new prisoners were then put to the same torture including the 'total water treatment' where the victim was immersed and the head forcefully held underwater. Then dragged out of the trough just short of losing consciousness, he was beaten and re-immersed repeatedly until he confessed, or the answers sought by the Japanese were forced out of the victim. This treatment was repeated over and over again. Barbaric Kempei Tai methods seldom failed to produce the desired result.

Like the eight locals, further indescribable tortures followed before

Matthews – tight lipped to the very end - was taken out for execution. The Kuching five were tortured to death in Jalan Jawa and the eight Sandakan men died by the sword at Setapok. The thirteen men of all races paid the supreme sacrifice in their efforts to help their fellow men, the Australian POW. Captain Lionel Matthews MC (Military Cross) died the heroic death of a martyr. For his services in the Sandakan POW Camp, he was later awarded the George Cross (posthumous).

However, there appears to be considerable doubt regarding Lionel Matthew's execution. Even his close officer companions are divided in their opinions. Early reports claimed he was crucified before execution, but there was never confirmation of this. For that matter, there was no official confirmation as to what his end was, and the Japanese are not saying. And even if they do, there is no guarantee of truth in what they say.

There were other fanciful descriptions that Lionel Matthews had faced a firing squad of 7mm rifles mounted on tripods point blank range, but this seems so un-Japanese like and scarcely deserves a second thought. If a prisoner was to be shot, more often than not, they resorted to shooting the victim in the head from behind.

Our reports indicated a be-heading, and we had no reason to doubt the authenticity of those reports. Beheadings occurred somewhere in

L to R Johnny Funk, Warrent Officer Bill Sticpwich, unknown, Patty Funk Taken in Sandaken about 1947.

Borneo almost as often as the sun rose. One does not need to be a mathematician to realise that taking into consideration the huge areas and the population of the Pacific and Asian areas occupied by the Japanese, beheadings were commonplace. If POW were beheaded – and we know that they were - God help the local population, regarded as cheaply as chickens or beasts of burden at best.

At this juncture I must state that since 1979, I have led a number of veteran tour groups back to Borneo including former POW in Sandakan who were transferred to Kuching after the discovery of the camp radio by the Japanese.

The puzzling point is whether Matthews was shot or beheaded. Nobody has been able to state definitely. In one of my tour groups in the 80s, former Sandakan POW AIF officers Russell Ewen, John Doswell, Ken Moscher or possibly it was Frazer – a Ford agent in Proserpine Queensland – were members of the group. All were closely associated with Lionel Matthews and his underground movement behind barbed wire in the Sandakan POW camp. Russell Ewen and Ken Moscher/Frazer claimed to have been pallbearers at Lionel Matthew's burial.

Disregarding my inability to recall the correct surname for which I humbly apologise, Ken – since deceased – was emphatic that "judging from the amount of blood pouring out of the bottom of the crude casket, Matthews must have been beheaded. The Japanese never afforded firing squads, preferring to shoot a man in the head from behind like an animal. There was no way that the issuing quantity of blood could possibly have come from a single bullet wound".

Russell Ewen on the other hand seemed unsure. John Doswell was well aware of both opinions and kept an open mind on the point.

Ken and his very attractive wife were the ideal couple that every tour leader welcomes. Always the life of the party and possessing a keen sense of humour, I particularly recall him relating among many others, an incident that occurred at the Sandakan POW Camp.

Australian prisoner cooks apparently were employed in the Nipponese kitchen and were required to carry the cauldrons of soup etc to the Japanese Officers' mess. En route, they necessarily passed through the Australian Officers' lines and according to Ken's story, every Aussie within coo-ee, hawked, spat into the cauldrons and others, ready for the occasion, urinated in as it passed by. The good Australian cooks, mindful of the welfare of their Japanese Officers, made sure that the food, POW added urine and disease infected 'oysters' (phlegm) in the cauldrons, received that necessary, final professional brisk stir before delivering to the tables of their hated Nipponese Officers!!!.

One thing is painfully obvious. There were no Australian or British witnesses to Matthew's execution. In reflection – 55 years later down the track - I am reminded that almost all 'Z' men captured by the Japanese and deemed guilty of clandestine activities were executed by samurai sword. Why should Lionel Matthews be an exception?

The most published photo of a wartime beheading was that of 'M' Special Force (Coastwatchers), - a sister unit to 'Z' Special Unit - member Hugh Sifleet. Shown wearing a blindfold in the kneeling position alongside a prepared hole in the ground to receive his tumbling headless body, his hands were tied behind the back. His executioner – a Japanese serviceman - was pictured with Samurai sword raised high above his head ready to deliver the blow.

The photo, published worldwide, had the unfortunate effect of branding all Japanese as war criminals. We know of course that this is not the case. There are good and bad in all races. As I write, I am reminded that the crime rate within Australia right now is none too flash.

And the most remarkable feature of the grizzly picture was the large number of onlookers, both Japanese servicemen and civilians alike. Obviously, a beheading was an occasion not to be missed, much in the same manner as public hangings of men and women in early London.

Getting back to the matter of the weathered and burned tombstone, not even the Australian Government had seen fit to restore the historical stone. Captain Lionel Matthews was exhumed and re-buried in a specially marked grave in the beautiful Commonwealth War Cemetery Labuan Island.

Beautifully cared for by former school teacher Joseph Lim and his wife for many years – both since retired – they doted over the cemetery and its occupants, a large percentage of whom were 'nameless, known only to God'. Today, like all Australian Commonwealth War Cemeteries, Labuan is well cared for by the new caretaker and remains as always, sacred ground totally free of vandalism.

Her Majesty Queen Elizabeth during her tour of Sabah some years ago, visited the cemetery and particularly selected Lionel Matthews' grave; it being the focal point. It is uncertain whether she was aware of the grave of the thirteen indigenous men who had sacrificed their lives so that Australian and British POW might live.

To make matters even worse, the heroic men were forgotten men; men buried and left to the ravages of bushfire, weather and neglect. They deserved better.

Despite the bushfire and moss cover, after cleaning it ready to photograph, their names on the stone slab were still legible.

Our Australian community, known world wide for its unstinted support of the under-dog, would regard this sad matter of affairs as discriminatory. It was little wonder that in short time, Paddy was reduced to tears. The name of our Australian hero Lionel Matthews, immortalised for posterity; the 13 heroes representing a number of races of the indigenous people of BNB, forgotten and unfortunately, remained forgotten. They sacrificed their lives in assisting the POW behind barbed wire: now gone and totally forgotten. The tomb was just an eyesore

The Malaysian media ran the story after the grave had been located and Kuching was abuzz with discussions as to how the wrong should be righted.

Shortly after our party's return to Australia, the Perth Sunday Times ran a story of our discovery in Kuching, the Funk brothers' involvement in the Sandakan clandestine movement and a picture of the grave as discovered, before cleaning by our tour group.

Some years before Paddy arrived from Queensland to live in Perth, I met Paddy's sister Violet, and according to her, their father was a judge in Beaufort BNB pre-war. He then moved to Sandakan.

Later, the POW were transferred from Berhala Island - temporary incarceration after arrival from Changi Gaol Singapore - to the mainland camp at Mile 8 Labuk Road. It was then the Funk brothers became involved in assisting the Australian POW through the Sandakan underground movement formed by Australian civilian Doctor JamesTaylor who was permitted to continue his practice after the Japanese occupied Sandakan. The Japanese were desperately short of medicos and tradesmen.

Taylor was in constant contact with Captain Lionel Matthews who formed the underground movement in the camp. They agreed to leave secret notes in pre-arranged places (dead letter boxes) in the jungle surrounding the airstrip workings. To hide their identities they used cover names; the doctor signed his secret notes 'Geebung' and Matthews' used the cover name of 'Roslyn' - thought to be his wife's name.

The Funk brothers were part of Doctor Taylor's underground movement. Alex played a major role that cost him his life. Paddy played a lesser part that earned him a prison sentence at Outram Road gaol Singapore where he was finally released after the Japanese surrendered. Johnny, who did a lot of the courier duties transporting the secret notes between 'Geebung' and 'Roslyn', to and from the dead letter boxes at the airstrip, was fortunate not to be arrested by the Kempei Tai when the organisation was betrayed and the secret radio built by Lieut. Rod Wells and other radio technicians in the camp was located by the 'binatangs'.

It was rumoured after the war that Judge Funk had been a staunch supporter of Albert Kwok and the 'double tenth rebellion'. Alex Funk was a member of the incensed and disgusted Volunteer Defence Group ordered by British Prime Minister Winston Churchill to lay down its arms and offer no resistance to the Japanese.

Many friends and close contacts of the Funk family lost their lives fighting with the Albert Kwok patriots against the Japanese. When the inevitable defeat of Albert Kwok and his rebels occurred, many more subsequently were executed for their involvement who today rest among the 171 slaughtered civilians in the mass grave of the Petagas Memorial Garden, now a busy suburb of Kota Kinabalu.

Consequently, it required little encouragement for the three brothers Alex, Paddy and Johnny to become involved further in the Sandakan underground movement. After the 'binatangs' surrendered and Alex was executed as one of the ringleaders, Alex was regarded as an undisputed hero the length and breadth of BNB for some of the brazen feats he carried out in his efforts to assist the Aussie POW and Lionel Matthews' group in particular.

Organisers of 'The Heroes' Memorial Fund, 'Z' Special Unit International (Inc).organised funds Australia wide. Supporting us, the Kuching 'Holiday Inne' (Manager Peter Mueller) and the Recreational Sporting Club of that hotel, along with Sarawak Travel Agencies (Jimmy Choo), provided additional finance for the project. Kuching's Malaysian Army 3rd Garrison Battalion (Commanding Officer Colonel George Ghui) came to the party and provided all the 'know how', labour and transport required.

341

All in all, a magnificent result was achieved. Today, completely restored, 'The Heroes' Grave' is the focal point of St Josephs Church cemetery and is a popular venue for tourists and particularly Australian tour groups interested in the history of WW2 and our POW.

'The Heroes' Grave' draws attention by virtue of its unusual design that characterises the men whose memory it immortalises. They were truly upstanding, tough, resilient and unusual men - brave to the tragic end.

Paddy, lhis wife and family lived in Medina, a suburb of Perth Western Australia where he passed away in the 1970s. Paddy's young brother Johnny and his family, lived in Queensland, where he passed away in 1996.

The day following the Sunday Times' story, I received a phone call from a Mrs. Rita Fisher of Rivervale, a Perth suburb, who said she had seen and read the article. She had taken particular notice of the accompanying picture of the grave and fancied that she could see the name of 'Felix Azcona' – her father - on the tombstone. Rita then explained that if this in fact was the case, she was looking at the grave of her father for the first time. She did not think she had seen the grave as a small girl while living in Borneo.

Before I finally lost contact with their family, Rita and husband Hal attended a 'Z' memorial service or two in Perth. I have on several occasions unsuccessfully attempted to contact Rita to ask her to elaborate on her childhood experiences when visiting her father at the prison. Unfortunately, she is no longer listed in the Perth telephone directory under her previous listing of 'Fisher H.A.L', these being her husband's initials. Hal was an oil industry employee back in Borneo and it is highly likely that they are now overseas.

Rita's mother related how her father had been involved in the Sandakan movement, and how he and his companions along with their leader Alexander Funk, was found guilty of espionage and other charges by the Japanese Kempei Tai, imprisoned and eventually executed or died in prison.

While in prison at Jalan Jawa, her mother regularly visited her husband, taking food and other comforts to him. On several occasions, she was raped or molested by Japanese guards until she could bear the humiliation no longer; fearing finally for her safety and life.

At that point, Rita Fisher's mother was told that the Japanese while uncouth and animalistic towards women, they would not harm children. With this in mind she then sent daughter Rita to the gaol bearing parcels of food etc for her father Felix, and according to Rita Fisher, "I was never molested by the Japanese guards'.

The know-how for the Hero's Grave project was provided by Kuching's Malaysian Army 3rd. Garrison Battalion (Commanding Officer Colonel George Ghui). The Heroes' Grave was beautifully restored and it was re-consecrated at a special service conducted at St. Joseph's Catholic Church during a special tour for that specific purpose in June 1982.

All in all, a magnificent result was achieved. Kuching's major hotels now distribute literature describing 'The Heroes' Grave', its history and location and its unusual design. Unique in St. Joseph's Church Cemetery, it is a popular tourist venue, particularly Australians and English folk.

In 1982 during another tour to Sabah, my personal and scuba diving friend Mr. Jack Bickford, a farmer from Yericoin in Western Australia, now retired at Jurien, was a tour member. A former veteran of the 2/5th Australian Commando Squadron and a highly respected member of 'Z' Special Force International (Inc), Jack's squadron landed on the beaches of Tarakan on the east coast of Sabah and south of Sandakan. There the Japanese fought fiercely in an unsuccessful attempt to dislodge and drive the Australians back into the sea.

On an afternoon set aside as free, Jack accompanied me to the then existing Jalan Jawa former HQ of the Kempei Tai where we were extremely fortunate to meet the caretakers of the building – a retired Chinese school principal and his wife – who made us very welcome.

We were shown around the building and its precincts. The concrete water torture troughs – one on each side of the building - were still in a very good state of preservation. The dismal cells in the basement of the building, lacked daylight, were tiny and it required little imagination to realise the plight of those unfortunates cooped up in the confined cells. There certainly was insufficient room to swing the proverbial cat. There was no evidence of ablution areas and it could only be described as a hell- hole, as was the case with any Japanese place of torture.

Twelve months later during my next tour group there, I discovered that the notorious building had been demolished by the Kuching city planning group or a similar body, hoping the prestigious piece of real estate could be sold through one of the wealthy Chinese or Malaysian finance groups. Little did they realise that the haunted property would be avoided by Malaysian and Chinese buyers, all of whom have a dreaded fear of 'hantus' [Malay for ghosts] and 'gway' [Chinese].

The Chinese caretakers had told us that there were odd ghostly happenings within the building. Strange repetitious noises and voices were heard, doors opened and slammed, and sensations of strong wind currents occurred within the building, even though no windy conditions were evident outside. Frequently, they experienced the strange sensation of another being in close proximity or someone brushing by.

I could see that Jack was highly amused by the descriptions and gesticulations of the caretaker and his wife. The high point was reached when they described how at certain times a straw broom, that normally rested against one of the living room walls, mysteriously began sweeping the room in a furious manner. If however, the caretaker or his wife happened to be using the broom at the time, a very strong invisible force snatched the broom from the user's hands. The force was such that it was impossible to retain the broom when the unseen force wanted it.

The caretaker and his wife had their own home not too distant, and made it perfectly clear that there was no way they wished to be associated with the building and its 'Nippon Gway' during the night. They were adamant that the house was not haunted before the Japanese took over the building and murders commenced. The previous tenant to the Japanese agreed that he was unaware of any strange activity within the building.

Today, Jalan Jawa the wartime notorious HQ of the Japanese Kempei Tai in Kuching – Sarawak's capital city – is no more. It has been demolished to make way for the city's expansion.

Purely imagination the reader might say. Back in the mid 1950s, I had a similar experience. Appointed as a 'stringer' cameraman in Western Australia for TV Station Channel 9 Melbourne, my first assignment was a story at Boyup Brook in the dairy country of the south west. The station's chief cameraman Mr. Les Platt of Beau Maris, Melbourne – he also owned a panel beating and spray painting business – flew to Perth to check my suitability for the position and to educate me in TV news camera techniques.

The story surrounded the 10 year old son of a well-known and reputable dairying couple and an active poltergeist on their property. Unfortunately, space does not permit me to elaborate on the many queer happenings: all verified by neighbours and the staff of the local police station.

Among the very strange more recent happenings on the property of the cow cocky, the milking shed was regularly patronised by friend poltergeist. Often, a straw broom left the spot where it normally stood against a wall and furiously swept the floor unsupported. If someone was already sweeping the floor, the broom was forcefully taken out of the user's hands and it continued to sweep the floor.

During my time as a 'stringer' – 3years GTV9 Melbourne, 4 years ATN7 Sydney – it was one of the strangest stories I covered, and equalled the haunted wreck of the WW2 American Liberty ship 'Alkimos'. Rotting away since wrecked in 1963, she sits on a reef 30 miles north of Perth and has featured in a number of documentaries during those years.

Is it a case of people of orthodox wisdom not wanting to accept the unusual, or is it possible that these strange occurrences only manifest themselves on certain people?

Jack Bickford and I have often discussed the strange incidents of Jalan Jawa Kuching where resistance fighters were tortured to death and POW murdered by the WW2 Japanese. Like the Japanese Rafter Ghosts at Musa Island and the 'Alkimos', there appears to be no answers.

Jimmy Choo my Kuching friend from 1979 and whose business was Sarawak Travel Agencies, was a sponsor of 'The Heroes' Grave'. He visited me in my dive store at Midland, an eastern suburb of Perth in 1996 during a business trip to Australia. I was fascinated to learn that the Jalan Jawa real estate had not yet been sold and that the Kuching authorities had changed their tack and were looking overseas for prospective buyers in the European market who hopefully, were less superstitious.

Chapter 36

THE MUDDY WATER CLEARS

In view of the apparent approval of the Malaysian Government and the flattering publicity of the leading newspapers in Sarawak, Sabah and mainland Malaysia re the unveiling of the restored 'Hero's Grave', we were completely staggered by the silence and lack of communication from the Chief Minister in Kota Kinabalu. Our proposal to establish the Memorial Park at the former POW campsite off the Mile 8 peg on the road to Ranau appeared to have stagnated. Meanwhile other wheels were turning, over which 'Z' had no control.

Seeking some enlightenment from Sabah, our association 'Z' Special Unit International (Inc) was finally informed by an independent source within the Chief Minister's office - whose identity must remain un-named - that the National Returned Services League (RSL) in the Eastern States of Australia had become involved in the project. Furthermore, it was possible that our proposal might be rejected and another from the RSL accepted in its place.

Why all the secrecy? While we accepted that the RSL was much larger than our tiny unit association, we were disgusted that we were not advised of the change of plan by the Chief Minister's office or the National RSL of Australia. The lack of the courtesy of a reply from Sabah and some communication from the RSL could not be overlooked. Had we been approached, we would have co-operated to the best of our ability.

The RSL official magazine 'Listening Post' summer 1997 page 28 published a story headed 'Sandakan Story Preserved For Future Generations' and I quote from the article:-

"We want to preserve and present the story of Sandakan and honour the memory of the allied POW who suffered and died in the Sandakan/Ranau experience" said Director of the Australian War Graves [OAWG], Air Vice Marshall Alan Heggen.

"The development will inform visitors through a visitors' centre, restored wartime relics, walking trails and information panels identifying the location of significant elements of the wartime POW camp".

The project which includes measures to arrest the decaying wartime relics, including the remains of the boiler and dynamo will be managed by OAWG.

Air Vice Marshall Heggen said the veteran community, especially the ex-POW association will be consulted and invited to provide artefacts and other material for the museum and displays.

The Malaysian State and Local Government authorities will also be involved in planning and development of the memorial park.

In 1995 a memorandum of understanding between the Australian Government, the Returned Services League [RSL], the Government of Sabah and the Sandakan municipal council was signed, agreeing on arrangements whereby existing facilities will be maintained with funding to be provided by the Commonwealth and the RSL.

"This project will build on those arrangements to enhance and preserve existing facilities and to add a museum and information centre displays to enable visitors to better appreciate the history and commem-orative significance of the site ", Air Vice Marshall Heggen said.

He said that Sandakan municipal council has begun negotiations with prospective contractors for the ongoing maintenance of the memorial park and that work on preserving the relics and planning the museum will begin later this year.

In the 1996 budget, the Federal Government promised $250,000 to begin the further development of the site of this former POW camp which with its infamous death marches, is described by the Australian War Memorial as Australia's worst war atrocity". End of quote.

That's fine and I congratulate all those involved but let's tell the whole story, exactly as it should be told. Let's not forget those involved in the efforts to locate the POW [Operation 'Python'], proposed rescue of the POW [Operation 'Kingfisher] and eventual rescue [Operation 'Agas').

It was clear from the Air Vice Marshall's statement that 'Z' had not been approached on the matter of the Memorial Park plans at the time of signing of the memorandum of understanding 1995. Neither had we been approached to make suggestions re the development of the park, or to contribute artefacts found in the campsite as early as 1979/80 by Nelson Short, the '60 Minutes' documentary team (Ian Leslie) and myself. In our possession are maps, photographs, personal letters and other documentation that would have been invaluable in the Memorial Park Museum collection.

We were left out in the cold, and this was strange when one remembers that we had discussed our proposals with the District Officer of Sandakan nearly ten years before the memorandum was signed.

Had we been aware or officially advised of the National body of the RSL's involvement, we would have set up correspondence with them offering assistance in the project

Is it any wonder we felt as though we have been left out in the cold and unwanted?

Not for one moment do I think that the members of operations 'Python' and 'Agas' were the 'see all' and 'be all' of the sad Sandakan saga, but by the same token the contribution made by both operations seems to have been overlooked and possibly lost to history. When I was last at the Memorial Park in June 1998 there was still nothing on the Memorial to indicate that 'Z' men had been involved in the matter of intelligence sought by Operation 'Python' or the three men captured and beheaded by the Japanese in seeking that information.

Equally forgotten were the efforts made by Operation 'Agas' to observe and report on the Death Marches to Ranau and the eventual rescue of five of the six survivors. I have not been back to Sandakan since July 1998 and now that the museum has been established in the Memorial Park, I trust for the sake of military history and the fighting men of our nation that this oversight has been rectified.

Much has been said about Operation 'Kingfisher' – the operation that never made the starting post because of General Blamey's personal differences with the US Supreme Commander Douglas MacArthur. Our unit SRD [later re-named 'Z' Special Unit] including personnel of 'Python' and 'Agas' were lost in the 'hoo-ha' created by Blamey. In the interests of the accurate history of Australia's worst military atrocity, it is high time the situation was rectified.

Despite Blamey's accusations that MacArthur was responsible for the loss of the 2,500 POW because MacArthur refused to make Dakota aircraft and landing barges available and that the American leader was interested only in former US territories, the truth was different.

According to Gort Chester, the Yanks were never ever short of Dakotas and landing barges. Allegedly, they were not interested in former English held territories – according to the press releases from Blamey's office – and yet, strangely enough, the Americans supported the 9th Australian Division at the Labuan and Brunei Bay landings with aircraft, landing barges and other naval units. They did the same at Tarakan and Balikpapan where US Navy ships joined Australian and Dutch naval units in the softening up of Japanese shore positions. The only planes that bombed BNB and Sandakan airstrip during the incarceration of the POW were American. There is not one report of a British or Australian plane having been seen over the camp.

This then posed another question. Why did Australian General Blamey differ with the opinion of MacArthur and commit Australian troops to Borneo? Perhaps the American Supreme Commander did not favour fighting over territories captured by the Japanese south of the West Philippines – former British and Dutch.

MacArthur maintained that Japanese forces in the areas including Singapore, Celebes, Borneo, Dutch East Indies etc, were effectively bottled up and could not withdraw from them. Therefore they could take no further active part in the war and represented no threat to the Allies. Japanese land forces were completely land-locked and rendered ineffective after the defeat of their Navy, Air force and heavy loss of commercial shipping. It was purely a matter of leaving them to their own resources, or the lack of them.

Had the Japanese not surrendered after the dropping of the atom bomb, who knows how many more good Australian lives would have been lost fighting over the pre-war territories of the Dutch and British and to what purpose? While the fighting in these territories contributed minimally to the end of WW2, the defeat of the Japanese in these areas was a foregone conclusion for the 'sons of heaven' had become a spent force long before the beach invasions of our Australian troops at Tarakan, Balikpapan and Labuan.

Japan, deprived of her Navy and Air Force, was unable to maintain the long lines of communication established in South East Asia and across to the South West Pacific Islands. The reader need not be an Einstein or a military expert to appreciate that the many thousands of Japanese troops isolated in the hundreds of islands from Guadalcanal and New Guinea in the east to Burma in the west were in a hopeless position. Without food, any hope of urgently needed military supplies and no hope of evacuation, their effectiveness as a fighting force was neutralised.

The atom bombs dropped by the Americans on Japanese home soil and the resulting tremendous loss of life virtually ended WW2 overnight. The combined effectiveness of all the island fighting spread over thousands of miles of ocean compared with the immediate results of the atom bombs is like comparing a pimple to a pumpkin.

It should be borne in mind also that following the fall of Singapore in early 1942, the Allies were on the defensive. The cream of Australia's fighting force was bottled up in the Middle East or as POW of the Germans and Japanese. As the worm slowly turned, America and Australia were jointly involved in a contained land war in New Guinea and New Britain. Only the Americans had the capability of carrying the war into Japanese occupied territories; a fact so frequently lost on our war historians.

Yankee submarines roamed the seas as far north as the China coast, including the waters of former English and Dutch territories. In their patrols, the submarines representing only 2.5% of the total US Navy, accounted for 55% of Japanese Naval and commercial shipping, and in so doing, sunk a huge tonnage of enemy shipping in South East Asian waters. They fought in areas where they were sorely needed.

'Diggers at war' - an Australian publication distributed to the fighting forces – pages 38 and 39 vividly describes the landings that pictured MacArthur and Australian General Morshead going ashore at Labuan from an American LST [landing ship troop and tanks]. There they inspected the infamous 'pocket' area that had cost so many lives, both Australian and Japanese. And yet the Americans were not interested in fighting for former British territories? What a load of rubbish!

It is little wonder that MacArthur went ashore with Blamey's 'fill-in' General Morshead. Blamey was probably too ashamed to show up, and furthermore, – unlike MacArthur and Morshead,- was regarded by his own frontline Australian troops as having a distinct dislike for action areas, and as a result, not welcomed by his own troops. Australia's top General is well remembered for his address to Australian Militia Forces (the chocos) in New Guinea after their decisive defeat of Japanese land forces on the Kokoda Trail across the Owen Stanley Ranges. This was the first outright defeat inflicted on Japanese land forces in the South West Pacific area. His words did not go down well with the battle wearied Aussie Diggers when he said 'only the rabbits that run get shot'.

With this remark in mind, and his well known attitude towards Lieutenant General Gordon Bennett when that great fighting leader escaped from the debacle of Malaya and Singapore – Britains worst defeat ever - one wonders about his attitude towards the POW of Sandakan.

Was he genuinely interested in Operation 'Kingfisher' and getting the POW out of Sandakan.? Is it possible he envied the American Supreme Commander's deserved reputation as a fighting leader and that he (Blamey) was not prepared to play second fiddle?

Perhaps we don't have to wonder why the Borneo Death Marches and Operation 'Kingfisher' were hidden from next-of-kin and the Australian community for so long.

I have to thank Mr. Ben Hart of Wooroloo – a rural area near Perth who was one of my 1996 Borneo tour members - for access to 'Diggers at War' which features in a fine album of his 1996 memoirs. Ben was a member of the 9th. Division Cavalry Commando Regiment and fought in 'the Labuan pocket' with another mutual friend and Ben's best mate, Ron Simmons formerly of Beverley, and later Rockingham Western Australia.

Because of the feud between the two leaders, many young lives were un-necessarily lost in Borneo. Had the feud never occurred, it is so painfully obvious these days that the majority of the POW in Sandakan would have been saved by Operation 'Kingfisher'. Meanwhile, the 'Kingfisher' force was languishing on the Atherton Tableland itching to go.

The same can be said of 'Z' men Don McKenzie, Bill Brandis and A.J. Rudwick of Operation 'Python' captured by the enemy and beheaded after 'Python's insertion into the country to gather intelligence for Operation 'Kingfisher'. These men plus many other 'Z' men – not necessarily operations 'Python' and 'Agas' - lost their lives needlessly. I wonder how their families feel about this lot.

Had 'Kingfisher' eventuated, the whole course of the Borneo campaign might have been different and many lives saved in addition to those of the POW.

What of Sergeant Ma'Aruff bin Said, former indentured Malay pearl diver from Broome Western Australia pre-war, cum operative/agent parachuted in with Major Nick Combe 'Agas 2' party and was shot or captured and beheaded after transfer to operation 'Platypus 7'? Like a lot of mystery surrounding missing 'Z' men behind Japanese lines, there appears to be no certainty as to how happy-go lucky gold toothed Ma'Aruff met his end. My parents, brothers and sisters were very grieved when Ma'Aruff - one of the most popular of the Malays in 'Z' – was posted missing after the war.

Consider the cost of the Flight 200 Liberator flown by Flight Lieutenant Keith Emmett and his crew of ten, plus the 'Z' men, Captain Tom Eltham and signaller Lieut I. A. McLaren, when that aircraft stalled during a drop and plunged into 'Agas 2' territory, killing all on board. All were indirectly involved in locating and rescuing POW. And there were many more 'Z' men lost in operations behind Japanese lines who were lost to no purpose.

All these brave young men sacrificed for nought. All men long forgotten heroes of the Sandakan POW saga and its tragic marches. All volunteered to go in behind Japanese lines in some form or another in the quest to rescue the suffering POW of Sandakan and Ranau. Will we ever learn the truth from our Australian Government.?

And what of the men in 'The Heroes Grave', their families and relatives, many of them now fine Australians? And there are approximately 171 Malays, Chinese, Eurasians and Indians in the mass grave at Petagas Kota Kinabalu who indirectly played a part in the tragic story of Australian POW in BNB. The heart breaking tragedy of those indigenous people of Borneo 'the land below the wind' who sacrificed their lives so that Australian and British POW might live, is yet another story.

Note: For the full account of the Double Tenth Rebellion of 1943 and Lieut. Albert Kwok US Army see 'Kinabalu Guerrillas' by Maxwell Hall - available in Malaysia only.

Had Blamey been less obstinate, it is even possible the battles of Tarakan, Labuan, Brunei, Balikpapan may never have occurred. Certainly MacArthur did not want to go that way. The total number of lives lost in those campaigns plus the maimed and wounded represents a frightening thought. Add to this figure the lives of those lost in the Sandakan purge and the Borneo Death Marches and one wonders if our Australian Field Marshall, Police Commissioner and brothel owner Sir Thomas Blamey ever possessed a conscience. I repeat myself by asking, will we ever learn the truth?

A YOUNG SISTER'S RECOLLECTIONS

I am Jack's sister Gladys. I feel that a tribute should be paid to our mother Mary, a young woman and mother of six children whose oldest boy Jack went off to war at the tender age of sixteen in a very dangerous service – the Norwegian Merchant Navy on the aircraft octane tanker "MT Marina".

When Jack came back to Fremantle, he broke his hand and was unable to re-join his ship. He then became of enlistment age and initially signed on briefly with the Royal Australian Air Force Air Sea Rescue before signing on with the secret service, Services Reconnaissance Department (later 'Z' Force).

He came and went and we had no idea of what he was doing.

We weren't aware of his leaving Fremantle in the USS submarine "Tuna" until three months later when three taxis with several submariners came to our house and said that when they last saw Jack, he was well and ready to take on the Nips.

Of course they did not say where or when they said their last farewells to Jack and his little group, but they did say that Mum should be proud of her son who was very brave to be doing what he was doing. They even bought Mum a bouquet of flowers.

During the time Jack was away, we couldn't communicate with him – the only message we had was from the Army Office every three months saying briefly –

"Sgt. J.W. Sue was reported to be well as at this date"

I often thought Mum must have had many sleepless nights wondering where and what her little boy was doing. She was only young herself, being in her thirties.

We were thankful to see him return after the war was over, safe but very nervy and he spent some weeks in Hollywood Repatriation Hospital with a malaria attack.

At home he slept on the front verandah as lots of us did those days, and he even attacked our poor milkman who delivered our milk early in the morning (everybody used to leave the money and billy adjacent to the front door for the milkman and he would ladle out the ordered amount from a large milk container). Apparently somebody had been stealing the money and Jack was determined to get him. In the darkness of approaching dawn one morning, Jack was awakened by the rattling of money in the billy, peered over the top of his bed blankets and spotted a capped figure stooping over the billy

.It seemed that Jack pounced out of bed, seized the dim figure by the throat, threw him violently to the ground, sat astride him and commenced bashing his head on the concrete verandah and in time with Jack's raised voice:-

"I'll... teach... you... you... so and so... to... steal... bloody... money"

With every emphasised word, the unfortunate man's head struck the concrete with renewed vigour. Suddenly, fate fortunately intervened when another voice joined in:-.

"Let him go Jack, let him go. It's the bloody milkman"!

It was the voice of my Uncle Joe who slept in the bed behind Jack and it was he and my cousin Charlie – also sleeping on the front verandah - who told us of the near disaster later in the morning. Howls of laughter ensued from our family after the incident was related but it could so easily have had tragic consequences. One could never have found a more placid and harmless creature than poor Mr. Massey. and to think that Jack had killed men for far less!.

Uncle Joe Clements was a 2/3rd Machine Gunner AIF (Australian Imperial Forces) captured in Java by the Japanese and imprisoned in Changi before detailed with other Australian POW to the horrors of the Burma Railway.

Cousin Charlie Wong AMF (Australian Militia Forces) was a Motor Transport Driver at Corunna Downs, a very large bomber airfield in the north of Western Australia. Both had arrived at our home within weeks of each other, slept behind Jack and were witnesses to the milkman incident.

A YOUNG SISTERS RECOLLECTIONS

Towards the close of that afternoon, my mother answered a knock at the door to discover that it was our poor milkman Mr.Massey of Osborne Park, a suburb of Perth..

"I've been serving you with milk for many years Mrs. Sue but I feel you must look for another supplier after this morning's experience. That war maddened son of yours nearly killed me. My head's still aching and feels as though it is detached; I'm really sorry to have to say this".

However, Mum calmed him down, sympathised with him and in the end managed to assure him that it would never happen again.

Jack was very unsettled for a long time when he came home, having made so many important decisions while away and was not keen to work for a boss. Eventually, he went into his own business, W.A. Skin Divers.

Jack was always a very adventurous child and used to get into all sorts of naughty behaviour; like pushing Dad's pot plants off the window-sill, lighting fires under the house etc. He must have been a worry to Mum and Dad and was always on the receiving end of many smacks.

At the age of about ten years, he would take his butterfly net and ride his bike out into the bush catching butterflies to put in his own home museum in which he had all sorts of natural history, snakes in bottles, dead scorpions, centipedes, sea shells, stuffed birds etc. He was a real nature boy. On arriving home from Borneo, he placed a Japanese skull prominently in his museum. Thereafter, my father – being Chinese and therefore highly superstitious – refused to enter Jack's museum.

I've scarcely mentioned Dad (Jack) yet, but he was a fairly quiet reserved man, close to Jackie and a good father to us kids. He must have worried a lot during Jack's war exploits but said very little. He was a Chinese herbalist and was never keen for us to visit a western doctor and he always managed to keep us all well.

I have often been asked what sort of child was Jack, but it would take another book to describe this daring, venturesome lad.

Gladys E. Whyte,
Wembley Downs   Western Australia
28th October 2001

355

AUTHOR'S FINALE - ANIMALS V STARS

The record of the Japanese occupation of British North Borneo during WW2 was one that Japan could never feel proud of in a million years, despite her attempts to hide the truth!

Given that there are good and bad among all nationalities, notwith-standing, the former category was indeed rare among the WW2 Japanese servicemen.

Admittedly, one very kind humane Japanese soldier made it possible for the escape of the only 4 POW from Ranau - Sticpewich, Botterill, Short and Moxham. In addition to these 4, Braithwaite and Campbell escaped during the marches; making a total of six survivors – all Australians.

The six survivors were assisted to freedom by 'Z' men of Operation 'Agas'. Today, of the 'Six from Borneo', only Owen Campbell of Queensland is still with us; the rest have succumbed to the ravages of life and time.

Utilising the old adage that 'the exception proves the rule', until 1979, I hated the Japanese people with a vengeance more than words can adequately describe.

The exceptions included Qantas national sales representative for Western Australia Goro Miyata – later promoted and transferred to Tokyo – and Japan's leading underwater photographer of the day by the name of Tatashi whose first name eludes me. He was visiting Australia at the time with an attractive Japanese diving model. When I had the pleasure of meeting and diving with them, they were well aware of my war record.

However, I was careful not to breach the subject of WW2, bearing in mind the advice of my long departed parents 'never judge a book by its cover' and 'all that glitters is not gold'. Neither Goro Miyata nor Tatashi was old enough to have taken part in WW2 and both had been extremely courteous towards me. And more importantly, I realised that my life was still engaged in a learning curve and I needed to keep an open mind on many aspects.

Perhaps at this early stage of my summing up, I should point out that my personal hatred for the Japanese was confined to the 'binatangs' (Malay for animals) of the war years, who in their own peculiar way. regarded themselves as 'bintangs' (Malay for stars). Additionally, I imagine also that my surviving mates of the original teams of 'Agas 1' and 'Agas 2' – they can be counted on the fingers of one hand - feel exactly as I do.

Concerning the notorious 165mile Borneo Death Marches, I do not condone the brutality, murders and shortages of food, medical supplies etc. However, in hindsight, while there is no excuse for the Sons of Heaven who were hoping to justify their actions, I reluctantly see the viewpoint of the Japanese top brass in their submissions to the War Crimes Trial Courts after Japan's surrender.

When their intelligence learned of the Australian 9th Division's plans for a major invasion of the west coast of Borneo, in order to reinforce

Interpreter and Japanese Commander General Baba 37th Japanese Army. *Photographed in Catalina after the surrender. Later hanged for war crimes.*

their defenses there, the Japanese sorely needed to shift thousands of their troops from the east coast of Borneo to the west coast. With no Air Force, Navy or Merchant shipping left, the Japanese High Command were left with no alternative other than to march their troops along the jungle bridle tracks across Borneo - there being no constructed roads.

As early as August 1944, marches comprising more than 500 medically tested and well equipped Japanese troops commenced the mammoth trek. They did not march from Sandakan to Ranau but from areas south of Sandakan between Lahad Datu and Tambisan. Again, these troops did not terminate their marches at Ranau, but continued through to Jesselton on the west coast. One group marched to Kota Belud north of Jesselton, a total distance of approximately 480miles through some of the thickest jungle and mountainous terrain anywhere in the world. It was a real challenge. A hard march in anyone's language and is positive proof of the toughness of the Japanese jungle fighters of WW2!

My late uncle, Private Joe Clements 2/3rd Machine Gunners AIF – a survivor POW of the infamous Burma Railway – was captured by the Japanese in Java. During his training at rural Northam Military Camp outside Perth and just prior to embarking on the Queen Mary for the Middle East, purely as an exercise, the unit was marched from Northam to Perth, a distance of 60 miles. Only a very small percentage of them made the full distance; most fell out as a result of exhaustion and foot soreness.

Although no exact figures are known, it was rumoured the Japanese

Japanese soldiers arrive at Ranua Airstrip to surrender to 'Agas 3' operatives September 1945.

group that marched to Kota Belud suffered 90% fatality rate and these were all medically tested men!!!

What chance of survival did the poor starved, diseased and sick, barefooted, loin-clothed, more-dead than alive POW have? Prior to the commencement of the march, these poor wretches had been imprisoned for three years before the march and had suffered starvation, cruelty, torture and every indignity that could be handed out by their animalistic captors. They were simply marched until they died in their tracks or were murdered.

It has also been established that after the surrender, a force of 900 medically fit and armed Japanese soldiers were ordered to march from Pensiangan near the Kalimantan border to the Australian surrender point at Beaufort in British North Borneo, an approximate distance of 250 miles. 180 very sick and sorry troops finally dragged themselves into the surrender point and gladly gave themselves up to the Australians. The remainder had perished en route; the majority picked off by pygmies equipped with blowpipes who were anxious to level the score a little. Apparently the little jungle dwellers had a ball.

If the Japanese thought their marches constituted an open license to force-march POW overland, they were sadly mistaken.

The appeals for clemency submitted by the Japanese High Command deservedly fell on the deaf ears of the War Crimes Courts.

I have never, and to my dying day, I will never forgive the old

Three Japanese surrender and submit to body search by 'Z' Force 'Agas 3' operative,

359

Japanese 'binatangs' for their inhumanity to their fellow creatures, be they Prisoners of War or the indigenous civilian people.

Young and old of both sexes commanded no respect from the Sons of Heaven in their relentless attempt to conquer the Far Eastern and Pacific Nations of WW2.

Frequently, I have discussed this point with Australian WW2 veterans who fought and defeated the Japanese at their own specialised game – jungle warfare.

These veterans and POW of the islands and South East Asian campaigns have an entirely different hatred to mine. One needs to consider the following explanation to fully appreciate the sentiments of the situation in which 'Agas' men found themselves after being inserted behind Japanese lines.

For regular soldiers who survived - victims of unspeakable atrocities and jungle warfare at its worst - there is little wonder that so many have become opposed to anything Japanese, be they Japanese cars, house-hold goods or the people themselves.

But, with this knowledge firmly embedded in mind, I ask readers to consider the hatred held by 'Z' men for the enemy, particularly those who served behind Japanese lines in a clandestine capacity and within close proximity to the bestial Japanese.

Although many 'Z' men were horribly butchered and beheaded for clandestine activities, those that survived were witnesses of an entirely different scenario to that of jungle combat fighters or infantry.

Our operation 'Agas 1' (Malay for sandfly), involved 7 operatives clandestinely inserted by the American submarine 'Tuna' behind Japanese lines into the midst of 7,000 combat Sons of Heaven for 9 months, 24 hours of each day. During that time, we witnessed brutalities and plain cases of murder carried out against POW. Worse, we were eye witnesses to the unmentionable crimes that constituted murder of non-combatant Chinese, Malay, Eurasian, Indian and Javanese. Even elderly men, women and babies were slaughtered, and young women horribly raped and savaged!

Technically, we were free men witnessing previously unrecorded horrors and perpetrated crimes committed by an unbelievably cruel adversary. Because of our role, we were unable to avoid seeing these horrors, yet, we were unable to lift a finger to assist in any manner for fear of unreasonably severe, inhumane reprisals that the Japanese imposed on the POW and civilian indigenous folk.

In order to discourage insurrection, for every Japanese killed, the reprisals in the Sandakan POW Camp usually numbered 10 and in civvy street, anywhere between 10 and 20 depending upon the severity of the charges. On the other hand, the sons of heaven – from the lowest private to top commissioned officer - remained immune from charges of beastly crimes committed against POW and civilians alike.

Stopping just short of murder, the cruel Japanese preferred to watch POW offenders slowly die; to them gradual death was more gratifying: bordering on sadistic pleasure The three 'cages' in the Sandakan Camp bore evidence of slow horrific deaths.

Civilian men, in addition to undergoing torture including the 'water treatment', the 'log treatment', thumb hanging, finger and toe-nail pulling and total water trough immersion, frequently underwent the burning of male prisoners' bodies including their genitals.

Neither were civilian women prisoners spared. If considered justified, they were subjected to the forms of torture referred to above plus, very often and particularly where young attractive, shapely women were involved, had their breasts sliced off. In the latter, Japanese sadism dictated such atrocities without reason, other than the woman being attractive or the satisfaction of the sadistic warrior ego.

Regardless of the torture used, the victims, after torture were thrown into cells to die of starvation, illness or disease; whichever came first.

THERE WERE MOMENTS WHEN ONE ITCHED TO PULL THE TRIGGER AND TO HELL WITH THE RULES OF WARFARE. SOME 'Z' MEN SUCCUMBED TO THE TEMPTATION AND GOT RID OF THE OFFENDING 'ANIMALS'. TO SAY THAT OUR FRUSTRATION WAS WORSE THAN WATCHING THE MASSACRE OR INHUMANITY DISPLAYED BY THE 'BINATANGS' IS A GROSS UNDERSTATEMENT. THESE WERE THE ANIMALS WHO HAD THE AUDACITY TO REGARD THEMSELVES AS 'BINTANGS' (STARS),

I take this opportunity to point out or remind readers that the advance of the Japanese Imperial hordes through China, South East Asia, the Dutch East Indies and finally New Guinea, was brought to a halt by troops of the Australian Military Force – the 'chocos' (conscripts) - on the Kokoda track. The 'binatangs' were defeated by sheer guts and determination of young Australian soldiers conscripted to defend Australia. It heralded the first defeat of the Japanese in WW2. The Japanese - regarded as the invincible masters of jungle warfare - as they had so conclusively proved in Malaya, Singapore, Borneo and elsewhere in South East Asia..

Furthermore, this victory was achieved without the assistance of British Forces of any description and at only minimal assistance from the Americans.

The Japanese lightning advance was halted in the Owen Stanley Ranges within sight of Port Moresby, the Japanese objective. Advanced scouts of the Japanese had been detected in the area where the Bomana War Cemetery is situated today, within ten miles of the New Guinea

Some of Jack Sue's war souvenirs. Perth 1946. Note Japanese Nambu 7mm pistol and holster to right of Samurai sword

362

Capital. Had Moresby fallen, we would have had an entirely different world today. The Coral Sea battle possibly would have been a non-event. The defeat of the Japanese at the Owen Stanley Ranges saved Australia from Japanese, old boxer type 'binatang' rule and the yen.

Furthermore, we would have had little left to defend ourselves other than the remnant American and Australian forces within Australia against the thousands of 'binatangs' about to engulf our nation.

US Army Air Force plus Navy planes and ships had been evacuated from Pearl Harbour after the debacle of December 7th 1941 to Brisbane, Perth and Albany in Australia, and were still reeling from that attack but, were to bounce back later with a vengeance.

Darwin, Broome, Exmouth, Sydney Harbour, Woolloomooloo, Glebe Point, Newcastle, all suffered hostile action; the first time the Australian mainland had been attacked by a hostile nation. Enemy planes bearing the 'poached egg' insignia conducted reconnaissance flights at will over every Australian capital city plus many in New Zealand. Ships around the Australian coastline were being sunk every day or two by Japanese and German submarines.

Meanwhile, children and hospital cases were evacuated to safe country centres, and Australian men were considering liquidating their wives and daughters, rather than allow them to fall into Japanese hands or the 'yellow peril' as the Australian media described it!

Judging from the plight of the 4,000 Javanese 'comfort' girls imported into Borneo during the Japanese occupation of that country, our beautiful Australian girls and women would have been subjected to unimaginable physical suffering and degradation of the lowest possible order.

The opening chapter of this book described the discovery of a crucified Australian POW supposedly protected by the rules of warfare. From that watered-down description, it requires little imagination to visualise the atrocities our fair sex in Australia would have suffered at the hands of the Japanese had they conquered 'down under'.

The foregoing is not imaginary, and if the reader is too young to remember WW2, he or she is indeed lucky, but I urge that reader to please believe these words.

We Australians as a nation are too complacent. We are regarded as a 'soft touch' by other nationalities. There are many nations out there today that have their covert eyes focussed on Australia. Should another world war break out, maybe we won't be as lucky again. I hope this message is read and heeded by every Australian citizen who possesses a breath of patriotism in his or her body for one of the finest countries in the world – Australia.

"Breathes there a man with soul so dead, who never to himself hath said, this is my own my native land".

Many of the sons and daughters of our deceased 'Z Special Unit' comrades, and those of our kindred units, 'M Special', AIB, Coast Watchers, SRD, Force 136, Flight 200, FELO and their European equivalents, march under our flags on Anzac Days. In Perth, we have the white, red and black 'Z'flag of 'Z' International and a composite black flag for 'Z' Western Australia.

Today, those sons and daughters march, proudly wearing their father's medals on the right chest although   most are unaware of the roles their fathers played in their respective units. Worse, sons and daughters of the few surviving operatives who served behind enemy lines will never know, despite their pleas, attempts to persuade, cadge. The lesson "can't divulge' - taught at Queensland's Frazer Island Commando School and the research station at The House on the Hill Cairns, Mt. Martha Research Station Victoria, Garden Island Western Australia and many too numerous to enumerate here but deserving of mention - still holds.

And yet, despite the dismal foregoing, for me a light penetrated the gloom.

After attending the 1979 World Boat Show at Genoa Italy with a group of Australian water sports specialists, including my Eastern States diving counterpart and friend of some 50 years - Jim Agar of Airdive Equipment Melbourne - I left Italy with the Australian Water Sports Trade Mission headed for home. On our plane's arrival in Singapore, a message awaited me requesting me to do some promotional work at Tioman Island in the South China Sea for the Malaysian Airline System.

At the same time, I was asked by my Japanese friend Goro Miyata – previously in Perth - who had been promoted to Qantas Tokyo, to go to Japan to present the Nikon Japanese Underwater Photographer of the Year trophy. I accepted the invitation with mixed feelings.

After approximately two weeks there, on one of my final evenings with Goro, his lovely wife and children, I boarded an underground train after midnight for the Hotel in which I was staying, some eight miles out of the city.

To this very day, I do not know what induced my chain of thought during that journey.

Suddenly, I became aware of the fact that I was sitting in a spotlessly clean and long carriage. It struck me with equal awareness that there were no coin scratched windows and graffiti clad walls, no vandalised carriage fittings, my fellow passengers – at a guess between the ages of 18 and 30 - were neat and clean in appearance and extremely well behaved. There were no beer cans rolling around the floor. There was no obscene language. No drunken male miscreants annoyed passengers with beer sodden and belching breath or with hand thrust down the blouse or up the skirt of a girl. There were no ladies tightly clutching handbags for fear of losing them to bag snatches, or being otherwise assaulted. It was readily obvious that the youth of Asian countries held a profound respect for themselves and their elders.

It immediately occurred to me that the youth in my carriage could teach our youth back home in Australia a thing or two. What was different about the youth of Singapore, mainland Malaysia, Borneo, Sulawesi, Indonesia, Hong Kong, mainland China and Japan that made

The Rabaul gallows where Japanese war criminal including Major Hoshijima and Captain Takakuwa were executed. The site is now a police training academy.

them differ from our own youth in Australia – right then embroiled in a crime and graffiti wave that we had not seen the equal to or since?

With their Asian pattern of courteous behaviour and obvious civic pride, plus their respect for their elders, how could one hold these lovely looking young Japanese people responsible for the shocking wartime crimes of their warmongering traditional Bushido and Samurai forefathers of the WW2 era?

Mentally, I reversed the situation and was unable to accept that my own lovely 5 sons and 2 daughters back in Perth could be blamed for atrocities that I may or did commit during that same WW2

I have never forgotten the lesson I learned on that underground railway that night; nor have I ever regretted it.

Since then, I have taken numerous diving and war veterans tours to Tioman Island, Langkawi, Maldives, Sabah, Kalimantan, Sulawesi, Singapore, mainland Malaysia, Java, Ambon, Ternate, Morotai plus the islands of the Pacific. In all these venues, I have never been treated with anything but respect or been faced with graffiti. Again, the exception proves the rule and that exception is Bali, often frequented by our Australian youth.

I make this observation knowing full well that I stand to be roundly criticised, but sorry readers, it is an undeniable fact of life. No one regrets more than I, that such an admission is appropriate.

In my tours – particularly those that are of interest to war veterans – I have encountered many tour groups of Japanese WW2 'binatangs' from Japan, and I have to admit that I am as bitter towards them as ever and I know I will never change.

And yet, as I said earlier in this book and again in this finale, "there are good and bad among all nations".

In September 1983, retired Yericoin farmer Jack Bickford - now living with his charming wife Nancy in Jurien Bay north of Perth - accompanied me on one of my tours to Ternate, a small volcanic island between Celebes (now Sulawesi) and Morotai in the Halmaheras to the east. The hub of the spice island trade during the 14th and 15th centuries and now part of the Indonesian Empire, Ternate was recently visited by the tiny West Australian Maritime Museum built 'Duyfken', a replica of the first Dutch ship to land on Australian soil in 1607.

During the week we spent on the island, we stayed at its only hotel the Nirwana - small in size but big in hospitality and service – that literally was situated in the tiny town nestled at the foot of the volcano. Our task was to search for the graves of Japanese soldiers killed by 'Z' operatives of Operation 'Opossum' April 1945.

Eight 'Opossum' operatives boarded an American PT boat at Morotai and were inserted into Ternate waters. There, they fought their way ashore and into the British appointed Sultan's castle where they extracted the Sultan with his four wives and 17 children to the waiting PT boat, and finally to safety back on Morotai. The Sultan and his family were then evacuated to Australia for the duration of WW2. During 'Opossum', 11 Japanese were killed for the loss of 2 'Z' men, one being West Australian party leader Lieut. George Bosworth.. The bodies of both 'Z' men were recovered.

While forced to rule under Japanese direction, the Sultan had been a veritable source of political embarrassment to the British Government and therefore, had to be rescued.

On Ternate, we were hosted by the current Sultan, the eldest son of the 17 WW2 children who were all delighted to learn that 'Z' men were back on the island – the first since the success of 'Opossum'.

Staying at the hotel was a former Japanese WW2 Navy Gunnery Officer, a consulting advisor in the Pacific area for the Tokyo cosmetics manufacturer Kao Corporation. His name was Kanzo Sugita, a very pleasant, fine, upstanding and handsome Japanese man, and like most Asians, looked much younger than his actual years.

Drinking alone and looking lonely, our small group befriended him after Jack Bickford made the initial approach; a move that I admired, knowing full well that Jack had fought the Sons of Heaven in New Guinea and generally, shared my sentiments regarding WW2 Japanese servicemen, as do most Allied veterans. The former Japanese Navy Lieutenant thanked Jack for the invitation and gladly joined us.

Like the licensees of the Nirwana Hotel (Mr & Mrs Polar), the Japanese Navy gunnery officer spoke flawless English. Because Malay, Indonesian and Chinese were the principal languages spoken on Ternate, we looked forward to having a chat and a cold beer or two with him each evening.

During one such discussion he laughingly told us that during WW2 he served on Japanese destroyers and seemed somewhat amused by the fact that he had two destroyers shot away from under him. He said the first was sunk by an Australian destroyer in the Biak area, and the second, by an American submarine in the Lombok Strait; that treacherous swift flowing narrow piece of water that separates Bali and Lombok islands. For some unknown reason, the Yankee submariners nicknamed the Japanese destroyers guarding the Lombok Strait 'The Bali Professors'. Finally, Japan with no more destroyers for him to join, he was sent to a coastal anti aircraft gun battery on Ambon where he remained until the Sons of Heaven capitulated on the 15th August 1945.

To Kanzo Sugita's credit, it would be impossible to find a more likeable and pleasant former adversary and we felt all the richer for the experience. I repeat "there is good and bad within all of us".

In conclusion, as a loyal Australian, I urge you the reader to remember that 2,400 Australian POW were shipped from Changi Gaol Singapore to Sandakan, British North Borneo to build an airfield for the Japanese Emperor during WW2. Of this number, more than 1800 were marched to their deaths. There were only 'Six Survivors from Borneo'. Today there is only one – Owen Colin Campbell of Queensland.

I thank you for your forbearance, and I hope you have enjoyed reading 'Blood on Borneo'.

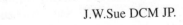

(Kindly excuse left handed signature)

J.W.Sue DCM JP.